D1685655

TER

Fight
back

MANCHESTER
1824

Manchester University Press

KA 0432069 7

Fight back

Punk, politics and resistance

EDITED BY

THE SUBCULTURES NETWORK

UNIVERSITY OF WINCHESTER
LIBRARY

Manchester University Press

Copyright © Manchester University Press 2014

While copyright in the volume as a whole is vested in Manchester University Press, copyright in individual chapters belongs to their respective authors, and no chapter may be reproduced wholly or in part without the express permission in writing of both author and publisher.

Published by Manchester University Press
Altrincham Street, Manchester M1 7JA, UK
www.manchesteruniversitypress.co.uk

British Library Cataloguing-in-Publication Data is available

ISBN 978 1 5261 1879 0   paperback

First published by Manchester University Press in hardback 2014

This edition first published 2017

The publisher has no responsibility for the persistence or accuracy of URLs for any external or third-party internet websites referred to in this book, and does not guarantee that any content on such websites is, or will remain, accurate or appropriate.

Printed by CPI Group (UK) Ltd, Croydon CR0 4YY

UNIVERSITY OF WINCHESTER

But after the gig ...

Contents

III When the punks go marching in:
punk, communication and production

Contributors

Giacomo Bottà is a docent in urban studies at the University of Helsinki. He received his PhD in comparative studies from the IULM University (Milan, Italy). His main interests are urban cultures, popular music, urban branding, interculturalism, creative cities, cultural planning and temporary uses.

Jonathyne Briggs is an associate professor of history at Indiana University Northwest. He received his PhD in history from Emory University and has written extensively on the history of French popular music in the post-war period.

Ivan Gololobov is a research fellow at the department of sociology, University of Warwick. He studied at Kuban State University (Krasnodar, Russia), the Moscow School of Social and Economic Sciences, and the University of Essex. He has previously worked as a research fellow at the Norwegian Institute of Foreign Affairs, the Institute of International Law of Peace and Armed Conflicts (University of Bochum, Germany), and has taught at the University of the West of England. He is currently working on an AHRC-funded project on post-socialist punk.

Matt Grimes is a senior lecturer in music industries and radio at Birmingham City University. He is a member of the Birmingham Centre for Media and Cultural Research where he is currently undertaking PhD research into British anarchopunk, the punk canon, fandom and popular/cultural memory. Other research interests include radio and marginalised communities and the use of radio as a tool for change.

Martin Heřmanský is a socio-cultural anthropologist working as an assistant professor in the faculty of humanities, Charles University in Prague. His research interests, besides youth and youth subcultures, include body modifications and Native American cultures. Since 2008 he has participated in long-term ethnographic fieldwork relating to the Slovak post-rural community. His PhD dissertation addressed questions of transgression, liminality and agency of body-piercing among Czech youth. He also serves as a member of the executive committee of Czech Association for Social Anthropology.

Michelle Liptrot is a part-time lecturer in social sciences at the University of Bolton. Her extensive doctoral research investigates the longevity of the DIY punk subcultural movement in Britain. Michelle's interest in the subject stems from her lengthy involvement with this subcultural movement, during which time she ran a DIY 'distro' and played bass in punk bands. Since conducting her research Michelle has ceased to play an active role in DIY punk, though she maintains an interest in both DIY culture and music cultures.

Hedvika Novotná is a social anthropologist and head of department for social studies in the faculty of humanities, Charles University in Prague. Her PhD focused on the construction of individual and collective memory within the Jewish minority in Czechoslovakia after the Second World War. Her other interests include the post-rural Slovak community and issues of urban anthropology (urban tribes, continuity and discontinuity of city space, etc.). She is the editor-in-chief of the English edition of the scholarly journal *Urban People*.

Bill Osgerby is professor of media, culture and communications at London Metropolitan University. His research focuses on twentieth-century British and American cultural history, and his books include *Youth in Britain Since 1945* (1997); *Playboys in Paradise: Youth, Masculinity and Leisure-Style in Modern America* (2001); and *Youth Media* (2004).

John Parham teaches media and cultural studies at the University of Worcester. He has published ecocritical essays on British and Australian punk, looking respectively at X-Ray Spex/The Jam and The Saints. He is currently writing a book entitled *Green Media and Popular Culture*, as well as being co-editor of the journal *Green Letters: Studies in Ecocriticism*.

Hilary Pilkington is professor of sociology at the University of Manchester. She has researched and published widely on late and post-Soviet Russian youth practices, including *Russia's Youth and its Culture* (1994); *Looking West? Cultural Globalisation and Russian Youth Cultures* (with E. Omel'chenko, M. Flynn and E. Starkova, 2002); and *Russia's Skinheads: Exploring and Rethinking Subcultural Lives* (with E. Omel'chenko and A. Garifzianova, 2010). She is currently coordinating an EC-funded FP7 'MYPLACE' project on youth and civic engagement.

Herbert Pimlott is an associate professor of communication studies at Wilfrid Laurier University (Ontario, Canada) whose research and teaching interests include radical journalism, alternative media, political communication and social movement campaigns. Having published articles in journals such as *Journalism Practice, Socialist Studies* and *Media, Culture & Society*, his first book, *Wars of Position: Marxism Today, Cultural Politics and the Remaking of the Left Press, 1979–90*, will be published in 2015. Three decades after experiencing the 'structure of feeling' of 1976–83, his 'career opportunities' have kept him 'out the dock' (so far).

Melani Schröter is a lecturer in German at the University of Reading. Her research interests focus on the communicative phenomenon of silence as well as absences in discourses (*Silence and Concealment in Political Discourse* (2013)), Critical Discourse Analysis of German public/political discourse and, more recently, (defiant) discourses within subcultures, especially punk.

Aimar Ventsel is a senior research fellow at the Department of Ethnology, University of Tartu, Estonia. He has conducted fieldwork in Siberia, Kazakhstan and East Germany on underground and mainstream cultures and was associated with the ARHC-funded project 'Post-socialist Punk: Beyond the Double Irony of

Self-abasement' (University of Warwick). His publications may be found in the *Journal of Legal Pluralism*, the *Electronic Journal of Folklore*, and *Punk & Post Punk*.

Tim Wall is professor of radio and popular music studies in the Birmingham Centre for Media and Cultural Research at Birmingham City University. He leads the Interactive Cultures research team who explore the relationship between culture, technology and the media. His published research includes studies of music radio, internet radio, online fandom, and popular music history. He works with the music and radio industries on solutions to the challenge of new online environments. The second edition of his *Studying Popular Music Culture* was published in 2013.

Laura Way is currently completing a part-time PhD on the topic of older women punks. She teaches sociology in the post-compulsory sector.

Peter Webb is a researcher and lecturer in sociology at the University of Cambridge. His main areas of interest are popular music, globalisation, new technology, cultural theory and the links between popular music and outsider politics. He is an author, writer and commentator mainly in the field of the sociology of popular music. He is also a published musician and has worked in the music industry and with theatre and film companies.

Matthew Worley is professor of modern history at the University of Reading. He has written widely on twentieth-century British politics and is currently researching a project on the link between youth culture and politics in Britain during the late 1970s and early 1980s. He is a co-editor of *Twentieth Century Communism* and member of the Subcultures Network steering committee.

The Subcultures Network

The Subcultures Network formed as the Interdisciplinary Network for the Study of Subcultures, Popular Music and Social Change in 2011. Its inaugural conference was held that year at London Metropolitan University, and since then the Network has organised various panels, seminars and workshops around the UK, in Europe and the United States. In 2013, the Network received an Arts and Humanities Research Council (AHRC) grant to develop its activities, which are shaped around five key aims: to promote and facilitate research exploring the ways in which subcultures and popular music serve as mediums for social change; to encourage interdisciplinary and multidisciplinary approaches to the study of subcultures, popular music and social change; to initiate and sustain a dialogue between scholars whose work focuses on subjects relating to subcultures, popular music and social change by way of regular workshops, symposia and conferences; to provide support and opportunities for peer-review towards funding proposals related to the study of subcultures, popular music and social change; to instigate and amass a significant body of scholarly work examining the relationship between subcultures, popular music and social change.

The Network is open to all and directed by a steering committee that in 2011–13 comprised:

Jon Garland (University of Surrey)
Keith Gildart (University of Wolverhampton)
Anna Gough-Yates (University of West London)
Paul Hodkinson (University of Surrey)
Sian Lincoln (Liverpool John Moores University)
Bill Osgerby (London Metropolitan University)
Lucy Robinson (University of Sussex)
John Street (University of East Anglia)
Peter Webb (Cambridge University)
Matthew Worley (University of Reading)

Information about the Network can be found at:
www.reading.ac.uk/history/research/subcultures
www.facebook.com/groups/17543791954
Contact: m.worley@reading.ac.uk

Foreword

Steve Ignorant

If you were in it, you didn't just wear it, you were it. A catchy name created by a journalist tried to describe it, but how could it? Punk was never a London radical chic, it was and is an attitude that stirred the hearts and minds of like-minded misfits to question, question, question; to no longer blindly accept; to push the boundaries.

From all over came a tidal wave of bands, making their own music, shouting their own words of discontent – no more dippy dreamy pop slush, this was real, this was life – battle cries screaming for a light in the darkness of the tyrannical government's nightmare. And not only bands: poets, artists, playwrights and film-makers also made their marks; in yer face images and statements describing the anger and despair of disillusioned people, a glorious twos-up to anything and everything that had gone before. Racism got a good kicking, sexism a good confronting, the class system a good hammering; from the meat industry to the arms trade, it all came under scrutiny and came up short; it was all a load of old flannel and it wasn't wanted any more.

Over the years many people have tried to write the definitive article on punk. It'll never be done, it's too myriad and diverse: from the terrace-born chants of the Cockney Rejects to the anti-political rages of Crass; from the feminist melodies of the Posion Girls to the surrealism of the Cravats (to name but a few) – all with a different take on what punk was but all eventually saying the same thing: we want change and we ain't asking, we're telling.

Journos tried to soften it, the music biz tried to absorb it, the fashion industry pur-loined it, the establishment tried to crush it. Yet punk survived the onslaught, battered and with a few casualties, and remains to this day a thorn in the side of society, rude, crude and full of attitude. It'll never die, the contributions in this book prove it; it's no longer a lonely scream from a grotty back-room of a pub, it's global, it's massive and it's here to stay. We're proud to be punk and don't you forget it, because we never will.

Acknowledgements

Our thanks go to the contributors and all who attended the inaugural conference of the Interdisciplinary Network for the Study of Subcultures, Popular Music and Social Change (London Metropolitan University, 2011). Thanks, too, to Jon Savage for agreeing to be interviewed for the afterword and to Steve Ignorant for the foreword. Throughout, the support offered by Manchester University Press has been exemplary. The activities of the Subcultures Network have also been made possible by funding from the Arts and Humanities Research Council. Finally, thanks to our sister/brother network of punk scholars for their encouragement and to those readers from outside the Subcultures Network steering committee for their insightful comments on the chapters herein.

Introduction: from protest to resistance

MATTHEW WORLEY, KEITH GILDART, ANNA
GOUGH-YATES, SIAN LINCOLN, BILL OSGERBY,
LUCY ROBINSON, JOHN STREET, PETER WEBB

Rumours of punk's death have long been exaggerated. The earliest known record of its passing was Monday 20 September 1976, the first of a two-day 'Punk Special' held at London's 100 Club featuring the Sex Pistols, The Clash and a handful of other bands converging towards a distinctive scene based on stripped-down rock 'n' roll and a confrontational aesthetic at odds with mainstream pop culture and the last residues of 1960s hippie-dom. The witness was Vic Godard, whose band (Subway Sect) were that night making their debut performance. According to Godard, both the Pistols and The Clash had already 'reached their peaks' by the end of 1976's hot summer. Thereafter, he insisted, 'all the energy had gone', leaving him to ruminate on how best to move his own band forward via songs reminiscent of Jane Birkin's 'Je T'aime' or calypso beats attractive to a disco audience.[1] With the British music press still debating just how the Sex Pistols related to an analogous scene already forged in New York, and before any UK record deals had been signed or moral panics instigated within the mainstream media, so Godard claimed to have spotted the first signs of punk rigor mortis. No sooner had punk been named than it was deemed to have passed away.

Over thirty-five years later, of course, and punk continues to assert a cultural presence. In 2012, as the contributors to this book were working on their chapters, the Russian band Pussy Riot provided yet another example of punk's ability to articulate discontent and, in certain circumstances, realise what Vivienne Westwood insisted was its *raison d'être*: to 'threaten the status quo'.[2] In this case, Pussy Riot's protest led to the arrest of three band members on charges of blasphemy as a result of their entering Moscow's Cathedral of Christ the Saviour to perform a 'Punk Prayer' in opposition to the Russian president Vladimir Putin. All were convicted and sentenced to two years in a penal colony, provoking controversy worldwide as images of the all-female group dressed in Dayglo balaclavas became a staple of the Western media.[3] In their wake, moreover, newspaper columnists followed Pussy Riot's lead to 'uncover' burgeoning punk scenes in places such as Burma and Indonesia.[4] Far from having died, punk appeared to have survived and reproduced itself as a politicised form of cultural protest that cut across continental boundaries.

More importantly, perhaps, the controversy surrounding Pussy Riot made clear what most with a passing interest in punk already knew: that it was about more than just the music. Indeed, the objective of this book is to explore some of the different ways in which punk has been understood, adopted and utilised since it first established itself in the cultural consciousness from the mid-1970s. Though punk's roots were embedded in rock 'n' roll, and though popular music provided the principal medium through which punk found expression, it comprised a confrontational attitude, approach and aesthetic that resonated beyond the aural. Even then, any definition of 'punk', either in a cultural or a political sense, will forever be contentious. From the outset it appeared to contain inherent points of tension: avant gardism and popularism; creativity and negation; artificiality and realism; conflicting political symbolism; individualism and collectivism. And yet, there runs through the various manifestations of punk emergent into the twenty-first century at least four defining points of connection. First, punk has tended to situate itself in opposition to any dominant culture or perceived status quo. Second, it exudes an irreverent disregard for symbols of authority and pre-established hierarchies. Third, punk typically purports to provide a voice or means of expression for the disenfranchised, marginalised and disaffected. Finally, punk has consistently demonstrated a commitment to some form of self-sufficiency or autonomy: do-it-yourself, be yourself. Thus, from the bohemian enclaves of New York's Bowery district through the backstreets and suburbs of Britain's inner cities into the battered squats of Amsterdam, Berlin and elsewhere, punk has long provided a cultural process of critical engagement. In different ways and in different contexts, punk has offered a means to reflect, reject, critique, expose, engage and explore – to say 'no' and to fight back.

Punk inn'it ...

This book seeks to break from most existing studies of punk in a number of ways. As noted above, it interprets punk as being far more than a brief moment in popular music history or sartorial style.[5] It does not contain a reassertion of the Sex Pistols' undoubted importance, nor does it seek to analyse the diverse routes into punk provided by the New York Dolls, Patti Smith, The Ramones, Suicide, *et al.* If Jon Savage's *England's Dreaming* (1991) remains the definitive account of punk's initial burst, then it is supplemented by numerous useful studies of particular bands, oral testimonies and academic interpretations of variable hue.[6] Indeed, the current collection seeks to eschew concentration on any particular band or country at a fixed moment in time. As this suggests, *Fight Back* is not a book about popular culture in the 1970s. Rather, it includes chapters that combine to present punk as an ongoing, evolving cultural form that continued to exist, transform and develop long after the mainstream media turned its attention elsewhere.

Second, and linked to this, the transmission and development of punk scenes beyond the UK and USA provides a core component of this collection. For reasons of space and coherency, there is a Euro-centric bias in place. However, the objective is to begin a debate as to the ways and means by which punk's protest, aesthetic and style found expression in different national, cultural, socio-economic and political contexts. Given that a number of nation-centric (and regional-centric) studies of punk now exist, the time is surely right to move towards a comparative analysis.[7] It is hoped, therefore, that the chapters gathered here will provide clues as to punk's continuities and divergences, thereby prompting researchers to forge collaborative projects and engage in broader debates relating to punk in Europe, the USA and beyond.[8]

Third, *Fight Back* is more concerned with punk as a culture than it is with punk rock as a musical form. Attention is therefore focused on the various ways in which punk has been expressed, understood and adapted over the past thirty-odd years. Of course, music and groups remain integral to this. But the emphasis is typically redirected toward punk's serving to construct a politicised (sub)culture (particularly in relation to conceptions of anarchy and autonomy) or as a means to shape and reflect personal and collective identities. So, while certain sub-genres of punk are engaged with (anarcho-punk, immigrant punk, Oi!, etc.), the authors tend to concentrate their analysis on aspects of cultural production or politicised expression: that is, on conscious attempts to challenge or circumnavigate the prevailing structures of the culture industry; on the locales and spaces claimed by punk(s); on the language, presentation and samizdat tradition that gave punk substance. In so doing, *Fight Back* hopes to build on recent attempts to understand punk in its broadest cultural sense, be it via aesthetics, empowerment or personal identity.[9] If punk pushed at the parameters of post-war (youth) culture, then just what did it mean to those involved and what were they trying to achieve/say/resist/negate?

Fourth, as should be clear, punk is here presented – and recognised – as a contested cultural form. Though seen to assume a meaning beyond the ephemeral, punk's 'politics' are nevertheless read as diverse and often conflict-ing. Not surprisingly, perhaps, there have been numerous attempts to claim punk as reflective of a particular political perspective.[10] Punk, particularly in its British incarnation, appeared to contain explicit political content; in the USA, fanzines such as *Maximum Rock 'n' Roll* sought to imbue punk with a relatively distinct political philosophy.[11] Certainly, many drawn to and involved in punk have endeavoured to filter or apply political ideas through its cultural medium. Others have espoused an anti-politics position that nevertheless retains an implicit political meaning in its rejection of prevailing polity. Here, then, the political purpose recognised in punk is not interpreted in a way that validates or invalidates one reading of punk against another. To state the obvious, punk meant and means different things to different people; the range and variety of its expression reflects this.

Fifth, *Fight Back* draws from a number of academic disciplines. In so doing, it hopes to open up a dialogue across designated research areas and provide a conduit for interdisciplinary study into both punk and youth cultures more generally. In particular, it seeks to provide a historical dimension to the study of popular music, youth and subculture, subjects that very few historians have deigned to engage with previously.[12] Indeed, academic interest in youth culture has tended to be concentrated in the social sciences, primarily criminology, cultural studies, politics and sociology. For the historians involved in the Subcultures Network that compiled *Fight Back*, therefore, the book forms part of a wider objective to, first, claim such an area for serious historical research and, second, to learn from and contribute to the ongoing debates elsewhere.[13]

Finally, this collection is NOT designed to intervene in the ongoing debate surrounding subcultural theory. As is well known, the stimulus for youth cul-tural study was in large part provided by the Birmingham University Centre for Contemporary Cultural Studies (CCCS) established by Richard Hoggart in 1964. From the late 1960s into the early 1980s, the centre generated a series of pioneering papers, books and articles that suggested aspects of youth culture be read as sites of 'resistance' to prevailing socio-economic structures, class relations and cultural hegemony.[14] In other words, the CCCS infused youth subcultures with a political sub-text: they argued that such cultures reflected and revealed the shifting contours of class relations, socio-economic and cultural change. With regard to punk, Dick Hebdige's account – *Subculture: The Meaning of Style* (1979) – remains the most renowned of the CCCS 'tradition', in which a semiotic analysis is applied to reveal a musical, stylistic and aesthetic response to the economic downturn and accompanying rhetoric of crisis that informed the political and media climate of the time.[15]

Not surprisingly, perhaps, such an approach has proven contentious and given rise to numerous critiques pointing either to the overly theorised analysis of the CCCS or its authors' tendency to prioritise certain socio-economic, racial, gendered, spatial or 'spectacular' expressions of youth culture at the expense of others.[16] More recently, therefore, youth cultures and subcultures have tended to be viewed through the prism of postmodernism to reveal their mutability, temporality and subjectivity. Though still accorded a cultural (maybe even a political) relevance, the class basis of the CCCS has been eclipsed by studies more likely to draw from Bourdieu than Gramsci.[17] As a result, debate over the meaning and relevance of youth/subculture remains vibrant in the social sciences, with new vistas opening up as cultural forms and spaces continue to develop, transform and appear. The focus here, however, is directed beyond such debate and towards the activities and expression of those associated – or self-identified – with punk culture.

Of course, punk also remains the preserve of ageing pop journalists and documentary makers. Rarely a year goes by without a production company rerunning the stock archive of punk footage from 1977; rarely a month goes by without a magazine retrospective of that band or this band's tales from the punk wars of yesteryear. Clearly too, as the reformation of bands to play at showcase festivals such as Blackpool's Rebellion demonstrates, punk continues to mean something for people of *a certain age*. We would argue, however, that punk's cultural importance extends further than a box of battered 7 inch singles and a musical narrative time-trapped by taste-setters from the *NME*. Punk's histories are multiple and its meaning diverse; punk provided a critical space that has resonated across time and space. Just as punk's spirit of volition has been diagnosed in a range of historical and cultural precedents, so it will no doubt continue to spread and mutate through generations to come.[18]

It's time to see who's who

The Subcultures Network is a cross-disciplinary research network for scholars and students interested in the relationship between subcultures (in all their forms) and wider processes of social, cultural and political change.[19] Bringing together theoretical analyses, empirical studies and methodological discussions, the network is designed to explore the relationships between sub-cultures and their historical context, the place of subcultures within patterns of cultural and political change, and their meaning for participants, confederates and opponents.[20] *Fight Back* is very much a product of the Network's brief and emerged, in large part, from the inaugural symposium held at London Metropolitan University in September 2011 that brought together a wide variety of studies, insights and methodological approaches to what is a vibrant, interdisciplinary field.

The book is divided into three Parts, each with a broadly defined theme. The first of these relates to punk and identity, particularly with regard to gender, class, age and race. So, for example, Hilary Pilkington's chapter explores the contemporary punk scene in Russia, concentrating on the nexus between violence, masculinity and subcultural affinity, while Matthew Worley looks back at British Oi! to locate its meaning in class terms rather than the racial connotations too often drawn from its links to the skinhead subculture. Questions of age and gender are brought to the fore in Laura Way's chapter, with an emphasis on constructing and retaining a punk identity amongst 'older women punks'. Ivan Gololobov, meanwhile, examines the transgressive concept of 'immigrant punk' to present bands such as Kultur Shock as both reflecting and resisting the processes of postmodernity. Finally, Pete Webb assesses the extent to which Crass helped forge a politically active 'milieu' that cut across class, gender and prevailing political positions. In each, punk is seen to have provided a cultural space or a cultural form through which individual and collective identities were forged or given substance. In providing a forum for expression, punk paved the way for multiple and divergent interpretations of Johnny Rotten's insistence that 'I wanna be me'.

The second Part looks at punk's relationship to locality and space. In particular, the authors are concerned with two overlapping processes. First, the ways in which punk's transmission allowed for diverse interpretation and utilisation of the cultural form beyond local, regional and national boundaries. Second, the extent to which punk's aesthetic and expression was shaped by, inspired and reflected the environments in which its protagonists lived. Thus, John Parham frames the poetry of John Cooper Clarke within the urban setting of Salford, suggesting that locality provided both a source of punk's alienation and a central component of its commitment to engage with the world 'as it is'. Beyond the UK, Jonathyne Briggs, Giacomo Bottà, Aimar Ventsel, Hedvika Novotná and Martin Heřmanský examine punk in France, Italy, Germany and the Czech Republic respectively. In each case, punk's meaning and its possibilities were manifestly read and communicated in different ways. This, as Briggs argues was the case in 1970s France, could sometimes give rise to tensions between indigenous and endogenous conceptions of punk's point or purpose. Alternately, punk's politics and aesthetics were adopted and adapted to relate to particular socio-economic, cultural and political environments. The outcome or expression of this could, again, vary. But punk evidently provided a cultural protest that resonated and proved able to adapt itself across time and space. If the political activism of Torino's Collettivo Punx Anarchici was cast in the shadow of the city's Fiat production line, so the punk (and skinhead) identities of (East) Germany and the Czech Republic have filtered through the historic upheavals of the past thirty years. Simply put, punk's oppositional position looks very different in both countries when viewed either side of communism's collapse in 1989–91.

The third and final Part concentrates on communication and reception. Bill Osgerby examines the representation of punk in film, exploring the diverse forms of 'punk cinema' forged since the 1970s. By contrast, Herbert Pimlott draws on Raymond Williams's concept of the 'structure of feeling' to explain just why punk – not to mention reggae, 2-tone and other 'crisis music' – resonated in the context of late 1970s and early 1980s Britain. From within the culture, the *language* of punk is brought under discursive analysis by Melani Schröter, who looks at the critiques of 'normality' contained within the lyrics of German punk bands from the late 1970s through to the present day. Not dissimilarly, Matt Grimes and Tim Wall examine punk fanzines, comparing the print originals with the digitised variants of the twenty-first century. In so doing, they complement Michelle Liptrot's reaffirmation of punk's do-it-yourself ethos, all of which combines to make a case for punk's protest being shaped far more by its practice and content than by the semiotic or stylistic signifiers emphasised in previous studies. Punk's claims to challenge, oppose and resist were not merely symbolic or tokenistic; they were an inherent part of its cultural practice.

Of course, no edited collection is definitive; and *Fight Back* makes no claim to be. The chapters collected here are, instead, designed to highlight just a few current areas of research interest and, it is hoped, point towards further avenues of enquiry. No doubt, myriad other themes or foci could have been covered and explored – some of which are touched upon in the concluding interview with Jon Savage. No doubt, too, punk's irreverent, humorous, commercial and nihilistic impulses deserve equivalent analysis. In the meantime, it is hoped that the chapters included here serve to extend academic and non-academic interest in the politics of a cultural form that continues to reverberate across the world.

Notes

1 D. McCullough, 'The Northern Soul of Vic Godard', *Sounds* (2 December 1978), 16–17.

2 *Anarchy in the UK*, 1 (London: 1976), p. 8.

3 The three band members arrested were Mariya Alyokhina, Yekaterina Samutsevich and Nadezhda Tolokonnikova. Samutsevich's sentence was later reduced on appeal to two years' probation.

4 See, for example, J. Harris, 'Punk Rock: Alive and Kicking in a Repressive State Near You', *The Guardian* (17 March 2012), pp. 36–7.

5 P. Strongman, *Pretty Vacant: A History of Punk* (London: Orion Books, 2007); S. Colegrave and C. Sullivan, *Punk: A Life Apart* (London: Cassell, 2001).

6 S. Frith and H. Horne, *Art into Pop* (London: Methuen, 1987); C. Heylin, *From the Velvets to the Voidoids: The Birth of American Punk* (London: Penguin, 1993); and *Babylon's Burning: From Punk to Grunge* (London: Viking, 2007); J. Savage, *England's Dreaming: The Sex Pistols and Punk Rock* (London: Faber & Faber, 1991); L. McNeil and G. McCain, *Please Kill Me: The Uncensored Oral History of Punk* (London: Abacus, 1997); G. Marcus, *Lipstick Traces: A Secret History of the Twentieth Century* (London: Faber & Faber, 1989); S. Reynolds, *Rip it Up and Start Again: Post-Punk, 1978–84* (London: Faber & Faber, 2005); J. Robb, *Punk Rock: An Oral History* (London: Ebury Press, 2006). For academic studies, see T. Henry, *Breaking All Rules: Punk Rock and the Making of a Style* (Ann Arbor, MI: UMI Research Press, 1989); D. Laing, *One Chord Wonders: Power and Meaning in Punk Rock* (Milton Keynes: Open University, 1985); N. Nehring, *Flowers in the Dustbin: Culture, Anarchy, and Postwar England* (Ann Arbor, MI: University of Michigan Press, 1993). See also the journal, launched in 2012, *Punk and Post-Punk*.

7 Most obviously, histories of punk's development in the USA are now legion. For an important contextual analysis, see R. Moore, *Sells Like Teen Spirit: Music, Youth Culture and Social Crisis* (New York: New York University Press, 2010). For various scenes, see M. Anderson, *Dance of Days: Two Decades of Punk in the Nation's Capital* (Brooklyn: Akashic Books, 2003); S. Blush, *American Hardcore: A Tribal History* (London: Feral House, 2010 edition); J. Boulware and S. Tudor, *Gimme Something Better: The Profound, Progressive, and Occasionally Pointless History of Bay Area Punk from Dead Kennedys to Green Day* (London: Penguin, 2010); R. Haenfler, *Straight Edge: Hardcore Punk, Clean-living Youth, and Social Change* (New Brunswick: Rutgers University Press, 2006); S. Marcus, *Girls To The Front: The True Story of the Riot Grrrl Revolution* (London: Harper, 2010); M. Masters and R. Young, *No Wave* (London: Black Dog, 2007); T. Rettman, *Why Be Something That You're Not: Detroit Hardcore, 1979–85* (Huntingdon Beach: Revelation, 2010); M. Spitz and B. Mullen, *We Got the Neutron Bomb: The Untold Story of L.A. Punk* (New York: Three Rivers Press, 2001). See also S. Sutherland, *Perfect Youth: The Birth of Canadian Punk* (Toronto: ECW Press, 2012). Just a few examples of European studies would include H. Schreiber, *Network of Friends: Hardcore-Punk der 80er Jahre in Europa* (Duisburg,

Germany: Salon Alter Hammer, 2011); (Czechoslovakia) F. Fuchs, *Kytary a řev aneb co bylo za zdí: Punk rock a hardcore v Československu před rokem 1989* (Brno: self-published, 2002); (France) P. Herr Sang, *Vivre pas survivre* (Paris: Editions du Yunnan, 2007); (Germany) I. G. Dreck auf Papier (ed.), *Keine Zukunft war gestern. Punk in Deutschland* (Berlin: Archiv der Jugendkulturen, 2008); F. A. Schneider: *Als die Welt noch unterging. Von Punk zu NDW* (Mainz: Ventil-Verlag, 2nd edn 2008); H. Skai: *Punk: Versuch der künstlerischen Realisierung einer neuen Lebenshaltung.* (Berlin: Archiv der Jugendkulturen, 2008); M. Boehlke and H. Gericke (eds), *Too Much Future: Punk in der DDR* (Berlin: Verbrecher Verlag, 2007); (Netherlands) J. Goossens and J. Vedder, *Gejuich Was Massaal: geschiedenis van punk in Nederland 1976–82* (Amsterdam: Jan Mets, 1996); (Serbia and former Yugoslavia) Dragan Pavlov and Dejan Šunjka, *Punk u Jugoslaviji* (Yugoslavia: IGP Dedalus, 1991); S. Savic and I. Todorovic, *Novosadska Punk Verzija 1978–2005* (Novi Sad: Studentski Kulturni Centar, 2006); (Sweden) P. Jandreus, *The Encyclopedia of Swedish Punk 1977–1987* (Stockholm: Premium Publishing, 2008); (Turkey) S. Boynik and T. Güldalli, *An Interrupted History of Punk and Underground Resources in Turkey 1978–99* (Athens: BAS, 2007).

8 For a non-Western focus, see E. Baulch, *Making Scenes: Reggae, Punk and Death Metal in 1990s Bali* (London: Duke University Press, 2007); J. Matsue, *Making Music in Japan's Underground: The Tokyo Hardcore Scene* (London: Routledge, 2009); A. O'Connor, 'Punk Subculture in Mexico and the Anti-globalisation Movement: A Report from the Front', *New Political Science*, 25:1 (2003), 43–53. Also, *Beijing Bubbles: Punk and Rock in China's Capital* (directed by George Lindt and Susanne Messmer, 2005).

9 R. Bestley and A. Ogg, *The Art of Punk* (London: Omnibus, 2012); P. Dale, *Anyone Can Do It: Empowerment, Tradition and the Punk Underground* (Farnham: Ashgate, 2012); S. Duncombe and M. Tremblay (eds), *White Riot: Punk Rock and the Politics of Race* (London: Verso, 2011); J. Kugelberg and J. Savage, *Punk: An Aesthetic* (New York: Rizzoli, 2012); L. Leblanc, *Pretty in Punk: Girls' Gender Resistance in a Boys' Subculture* (New Brunswick, NJ: Rutgers University Press, 1999); M. Raha, *Cinderella's Big Score: Women of the Punk and Indie Underground* (Emeryville, CA: Seal Press, 2004); H. Reddington, *The Lost Women of Rock Music: Female Musicians of the Punk Era* (Aldershot: Ashgate, 2007); R. Sabin (ed.), *Punk Rock: So What? The Cultural Legacy of Punk* (London: Routledge, 1999).

10 M. Worley, 'Shot By Both Sides: Punk, Politics and the End of "Consensus"', *Contemporary British History*, 26:3 (2012), 333–54; J. Street, *Rebel Rock: The Politics of Popular Music* (Oxford: Blackwell, 1986).

11 See also C. O'Hara, *Philosophy of Punk: More Than Noise!* (San Francisco: AK Press, 1999). Overtly anarchist bands, too, have tended to frame punk within recognisable political paradigms, as in Crass, *A Series of Shock Slogans and Mindless Tantrums* (London: Exitstencil Press, 1982).

12 For a few exceptions, see the work of Arthur Marwick, especially his *British Society Since 1945* (London: Penguin, 1982) and 'Youth in Britain, 1920–60', *Journal of*

Contemporary History, 5:1 (1970), 37–51; also D. Fowler, *Youth Culture in Modern Britain, c. 1920–c. 1970* (Basingstoke: Palgrave, 2008); A. Horn, *Juke Box Britain: Americanisation and Youth Culture, 1945–60* (Manchester: Manchester University Press, 2009); B. Osgerby, *Youth Culture in Britain Since 1945* (London: Routledge, 1998).

13 See, for example, Interdisciplinary Network for the Study of Subcultures, Popular Music and Social Change, 'Youth Culture, Popular Music and the End of "Consensus" in Post-War Britain', special issue of *Contemporary British History*, 26:3 (2012), 265–425.

14 Such an argument was best expressed in J. Clarke, S. Hall, T. Jefferson and B. Roberts, 'Subcultures, Cultures and Class: A Theoretical Overview', in S. Hall and T. Jefferson (eds), *Resistance Through Rituals: Youth Subcultures in Post-War Britain* (London: Hutchinson & Co., 1976), pp. 9–74; see also P. Cohen, 'Subcultural Conflict and Working Class Community', *Working Class Papers in Cultural Studies*, 2 (1972), 4–51.

15 D. Hebdige, *Subculture: The Meaning of Style* (London: Routledge, 2006 edn), p. 87. See also Laing, *One Chord Wonders*; I. Chambers, *Urban Rhythms: Pop Music and Popular Culture* (New York: St. Martin's Press, 1985).

16 For a good overview of the debate, see P. Hodkinson, 'Youth Cultures: A Critical Outline of Key Debates', in P. Hodkinson and W. Deicke (eds), *Youth Cultures: Scenes, Subcultures and Tribes* (London: Routledge, 2007), pp. 1–22.

17 The best overtly punk-related study of the post-CCCS era is D. Muggleton, *Inside Subculture: The Postmodern Meaning of Style* (Oxford: Berg, 2000).

18 For books exploring punk's cultural precedents and continued mutations, see Dale, *Anyone Can Do It*; S. Home, *Cranked Up Really High: Genre Theory and Punk Rock* (Hove: Codex, 1995); and *The Assault on Culture: Utopian Currents from Lettrisme to Class War* (AK Press, Sterling, 1991); G. McKay, *Senseless Acts of Beauty: Cultures of Resistance since the Sixties* (London: Verso, 1996); Marcus, *Lipstick Traces*.

19 The original steering committee that founded the Network comprised: Jon Garland, Keith Gildart, Anna Gough-Yates, Paul Hodkinson, Sian Lincoln, Bill Osgerby, Lucy Robinson, John Street, Pete Webb and Matthew Worley.

20 For information on the Networks and news of its activities, see www.reading.ac.uk/history/research/hist-subcultures.aspx. A Facebook page is also available under the name 'Subcultures, popular music and social change'.

I wanna be me: punk and identity

'If you want to live, you better know how to fight': fighting masculinity on the Russian punk scene

-HILARY PILKINGTON-

The discussion of masculinity and femininity on punk scenes is a relatively recent phenomenon.[1] The emphasis in published work to date has been on reclaiming young women's experience and practice; driven, in part, by their increasing visibility thanks to the emergence of the Riot Grrrl scene in the 1990s. The broad consensus reached might be encapsulated in LeBlanc's conclusion that 'gender is problematic for punk girls in a way that it is not for punk guys, because punk girls must accommodate female gender within subcultural identities that are deliberately coded as male'.[2] LeBlanc substantiated the claim with ethnographic research that shows how, through punk, young women enact 'strategies of resistance to both mainstream and subcultural norms of femininity' but also how the subjectivities they forge remain circumscribed by male punks' creation and maintenance of the masculinity of the punk subculture.[3]

Leblanc argues that this closing down of space is a product of the replacement of spontaneous, diverse and gender-transgressive style and body practices on early punk scenes by the masculinist stylistic uniformity of North American hardcore.[4] However, testimonies from the early UK scene suggest that although punk created a space where women 'felt free to express difference', female punk musicians were often attacked physically and abused from the floor for their appearance.[5] Thus, O'Brien suggests, 'contrary to the myth, punk was not necessarily woman-friendly' and 'while there were men wrestling with questions of masculinity and feminism, there were just as many content to leave it unreconstructed'.[6] Arguably, the 'myth' that punk scenes were the site of anti-sexist practices and alternative masculinities has inhibited the discussion of masculinity in punk. Recent studies of hardcore scenes, however, suggest dancefloor – including fighting – practices are central to constructing and maintaining a 'masculine sense of community and collectivity'.[7] Hardcore slamming or thrashing is interpreted as 'a dance of male hardcore solidarity' constituting symbolic rather than genuine fighting.[8] Simon's study of slam dancing,[9] however, suggests a fine line between order and chaos in 'the pit'; while scene participants do not seek violence, it is always a potential outcome.[10] Haenfler's study of the straight edge movement within hardcore confirms incompetent dancing to be a common cause of violence; in a typical scenario someone new to the scene pushes or runs into someone else and the act is interpreted by regular scene members as deliberate.[11] However, he suggests, violence could also result from internal divisions within the movement – specifically between 'militant' and 'positive' elements[12] – making fighting, at some events, ritualised rather than incidental.[13] The role of fighting among diverse elements within the straight edge movement illustrates the 'contradictory' expressions of masculinity as members aligned themselves with anti-sexist and anti-homophobic sensibilities but also engaged in practices that tacitly support hegemonic masculinities.[14] This suggests, contrary to LeBlanc's assertion, that gender may be a problem for male punks too.[15]

Violence and ritual fighting has been considered within the literature on subcultural studies primarily in relation to 'deviant' rather than 'spectacular' subcultures. This violence, it is argued, is rooted in a sense of territoriality 'deeply ingrained in most working-class parent cultures' albeit mediated through institutions such as the local pub, shops, political, religious or cultural associations or, in the case of young people, the 'gang'.[16] The exception is the study of skinhead culture, in which fighting is understood to be central to group solidarity and identity; 'A skinhead cannot claim to be a "skin" if he does not fight'.[17] Fighting provides the public opportunity to demonstrate loyalty to the group and to further one's reputation and is directly linked to the expression of masculinity since 'never backing down, no matter what the odds are', is central to proving one's 'hardness'.[18] This understanding of fighting as strongly ritualised is a core element of critical deviancy approaches, which suggest that what is often interpreted from the outside as 'violence' and 'disorder' in youth spheres (on the terraces, in classrooms) is narrated from the inside as strongly rule-bound suggesting 'an order in their actions that is their own'.[19]

More recently, this kind of violence has been categorised as 'audience-oriented' or 'staged' fighting.[20] Despite its usual association with gangs and football hooliganism, Collins suggests that audience-oriented fighting is most frequently encountered at entertainment venues, bars and parties.[21] This is helpful for thinking about the kind of fighting that has been a consistent, if under-researched, element of 'spectacular' subcultural practices. Fighting between punks and Ted gangs, for example, was a characteristic of the early UK punk scene[22] and New York City straight edge scenes in the 1980s were 'legendary for their brutality'.[23] Indeed American punk and hardcore scenes of the 1980s were often intersected with skinhead scenes, which wavered between being 'united' and fighting each other,[24] while punk gigs in the UK in the late 1970s and early 1980s regularly attracted skinheads in search of a fight.[25] Even later anarchist scenes that adopted a pacifist stance as part of a wider struggle against institutionalised militarism, saw members abandon the pacifist commitment after experiencing violence from police and skinheads.[26]

Gigs, clubs and other leisure spaces, it follows, might be seen (like football 'Ends') as sites of territorialism where groups protect 'their' space against invasion by incompetents or 'others'. However, punks manage those spaces differently to football hooligans and this varies also over time and space. Thus, thrashing constitutes a rule-bound arena in which violence breaks out when rules are not known or conventions broken,[27] while straight edge scenes may have internal factions between which fighting could be anticipated.[28] Moreover, other forms of punk aggression may be less rule-bound. Tsitsos differentiates between slamdancing (characterised by apparent chaos and rejection of order in the pit yet evoking a certain 'unity' among dancers) and moshing (as developed by straight edgers), which places greater emphasis on individual dancers' control of the pit.[29] This, he argues, reflects an ideology among straight edgers of rebellion against rules not in order to eliminate them, but to impose their rules on others.[30] Collins's focus on the situational and interactional nature of violence is helpful here since it shifts attention from macro-level social factors in explaining violence to the micro dimension and interaction taking place in violence-threatening encounters.[31] This more personal and situational approach facilitates the understanding of violence within the punk scene, which may be categorised as 'audience-oriented violence' but is not necessarily perpetrated for the purposes of initiation or ritual.

This article compares practices of fighting on punk scenes in two cities in Russia: St Petersburg and Vorkuta. This was not among the original aims of the research but arose in the course of ethnographic fieldwork as fighting emerged as an important aspect of punk practice and narrative (especially among male respondents). In both cases, the scenes were predominantly male and governed by dominant gender norms, notwithstanding the active participation of a small number of women. However, the positioning of punk in relation to other youth cultural scenes in the cities, as well as the very different socio-economic, cultural and territorial contexts of those scenes, revealed significant variation in the kinds of violence encountered as well as the meanings attached to them. Three characteristics of punk fighting are explored here. The first is the interactional nature of violence indicated by the dominant narrative of fighting on both scenes as a 'response' to attack (from 'local thugs', from 'skinheads'). This discussion highlights the similarities with skinhead fighting – its rule-bound nature, territorial solidarity and readiness to defend the home district or other 'own' space – but also the differences, not least the fact that participation in fighting is not essential to the more individualistically oriented punk scene. Secondly, the relationship between fighting and ideology is discussed through examples of solidarities with both anti-fascist and racist skinhead groups that reflect the traditionally ambiguous political positioning of punk. Thirdly, the frequently chaotic and opportunistic nature of punk violence is considered. This mode of fighting is articulated not only as intensely pleasurable but through a peculiar narrativisation of punk fighting as tales of 'heroic incompetence' that constitute an important resource for ironic story-telling. The discussion aims to contribute to understanding the meanings attached to fighting as well as the ambiguities over masculinity within, and around, punk culture.

Research context and method

This chapter draws on ethnographic research conducted in Vorkuta and St Petersburg under the auspices of the project 'Post-socialist punk: Beyond the double irony of self-abasement' (2009–13).[32] These two case studies are indicative of the wide spectrum of punk scenes in contemporary Russia. Vorkuta is an isolated, deindustrialising and depopulating city in Russia's Arctic North. It was founded in 1932 as part of the Gulag system as prisoners opened up the Vorkuta mines to exploit the northern reaches of the Pechora coal basin. Following the closure of the camp in 1962, people came voluntarily to the city, attracted by higher wages and early pension rights. Vorkuta's population peaked in 1991 at 180,000 but thereafter the city experienced rapid deindustrialisation and out-migration leaving its population standing at less than half that size and widespread speculation that the city is in its death throes. Vorkuta has a small alternative music scene in which punks and others (skinheads, emos and hard rock fans) overlap. The first punk band – Mazut – was formed in 1988 and continues to perform alongside a handful of younger punk bands. The constant 'drain' of musicians through out-migration from the city, as well as the difficulty bands face in finding rehearsal and performance venues, makes the scene highly intersected and mutually supportive.

In contrast, St Petersburg, founded in 1703, is the second largest city in Russia with a population of just under 5 million. It straddles forty-seven islands of the Neva delta and this physical location, together with its historical role as the country's former capital, lends the city the basis for its claim to be the 'Venice of the North'. Today St Petersburg is an economically dynamic city and a popular destination for migrants from other parts of Russia and the Commonwealth of Independent States (CIS). It is a hub of alternative music and culture and, arguably, the birthplace of Russian punk.[33] From 1991, the scene became more susceptible to western genres with both US hardcore (in the early 1990s) and pop-punk (in the late 1990s) developing significant followings.[34] Today the St Petersburg punk scene is vibrant and differentiated, including relatively autonomous pop-punk, hardcore and ethnopunk subscenes, and intersects with various political movements including DIY, anti-fascist and anarchist scenes.

The research in Vorkuta was conducted with a total of twenty-six respondents recruited from existing contacts with punk musicians; acquaintances made at gigs; local 'chats' and forums; and contacts from existing respondents. Respondents were aged from 17 to 43 years; twenty-three were men and three were women. Approximately one-third of respondents were working – usually employed at the mines or on the railroad, on construction sites and in garages – and around one-third were still in education. Only one respondent had higher education; the modal educational status was having, or studying for, vocational education (PTU or *tekhnikum*). In St Petersburg research was conducted with a total of thirty-four respondents from a range of subscenes in the city (pop-punk, hardcore, ethno-punk, radical art) with little or no organic connection with one another. Respondents were aged from 17 to 49 and nine were female. In contrast to Vorkuta, the majority of St Petersburg informants had, or were studying for, higher educational degrees and about half earned their living from the scene; earning money as freelance photographers, sessional musicians, producers, and club managers or directly from their music or art. Those employed outside the scene were mainly working in management, the entertainment industry, and informational technologies.

This article draws on thirty-three recorded interviews (eighteen in Vorkuta, fifteen in St Petersburg); field diaries recording events and informal communication; still photos; video footage made by researchers and respondents; social networking site (*vkontakte*) communication; art work; and song lyrics. Respondents are referred to throughout using pseudonyms[35] (given in brackets after their quoted interviews or reported views), although, following explicit requests from interviewees, band names are retained in the original. The city in which cited respondents were resident is indicated in the text; in Vorkuta interviews were conducted in October 2009, in St Petersburg, interviews were conducted in March and April 2010. Interviews and other materials were coded using NVivo 8 based on a coding scheme generated from the data themselves and standardised across the project's three Russian case studies through a process of merging, refining and recoding.

'If you want to live, you better know how to fight': punks as victims

Fighting on punk scenes was largely interactional, taking place when defending oneself against attacks that usually occurred when individuals were readily identifiable as 'punks' (for example before or after concerts). The scenes differed, however, in both the prevalence of reactive fights and in the identification of the most common aggressors.

Fighting the 'grey mass': territorial violence in Vorkuta

Fights were mentioned twice as often by Vorkuta than St Petersburg respondents. Attacks were attributed to local thugs (*gopniki*)[36] or 'gangsters' (*bandity*) who, in a practice carried over from the Soviet era, targeted youth with alternative appearance. Vitya describes a classic situation when 'you're just walking down the street and they are coming towards you, they say something, make a comment or something and a fight starts'. Discussing what made punks a target of *gopnik* violence, members of the band Marazm cite their non-conformity to gang culture:

> Interviewer: Why do the *gopota*[37] attack you?
> Grisha: Well they think Vorkuta is just one big prison camp.
> Yaroslav: They live by its lore [*po poniatiiam*] and there's no way we fit their way of thinking.
> Grisha: Yeah. It's like, how can a normal, proper lad pierce his ears, or like shave something into his head … It's just not what lads do basically.

These encounters are often accompanied by complaints that the '*gopota*' attack when they have numerical superiority. In the following excerpt from a longer narrative, Kostya recounts such a scenario after a gig the band (Mazut) had played at a local club:

Kostya: They waited until the end of the concert when only me and Savva were left and … and a crowd went outside … and yelled until a great big moose, twice as big as me, came out … This great big ape came out and it was like, let's have a punch up … So, basically, I go, 'Come on then, let's thrash 'em,' while the ones at the end threw bottles, bits of metal …

Interviewer: At you?

Kostya: Yeah, at my head. I turn round – something has hit [names friend] in the eye, he had to have an operation, and then basically Savva hurtles in … just as the iron pipes start whistling past my head. And I get myself out of the crowd and me and Savva begin to lash out … We didn't care about the blood, and then basically the great hulk starts shooting rubber bullets at us from a pistol. It wasn't enough that it was eight against two, he had to start shooting as well …

Interviewer: Didn't Savva get hurt?

Kostya: Yeah, Savva [broke] his finger, I was cut on the head. But we gave them a hiding too – if we had just had a couple more strong lads, we would have beaten the whole crowd …

But not all punks had the same resilience; Gleb explained how the punk crowd in a mining settlement outside the main city had collapsed as people gradually dropped out after becoming fed up with being the object of *gopnik* aggression.

St Petersburg respondents mentioned attacks by *gopniki* much less frequently; one exception was a story recounted by a female punk (Tina) whose friend had been beaten up, on her way back from a heavy drinking session, by three thugs who had called her 'a piece of shit' and a 'scarecrow'. In contrast St Petersburg punks positioned themselves as the victims of aggression by the police or local security guards (at music venues). Recounting the police brutality she had witnessed as punks were evicted from a squat in the city, Tina reflects more widely on police tactics:

Our police are really brutal. We have a department for fighting extremism … [and they] just fuck you over, trying to get any information from you, to get you to 'cooperate', so you turn in your friends. If you don't give anyone up, you just get a fucking beating. All the pigs [police] have martial arts training … They beat you in a way that leaves no traces. Everything hurts but you can't go to A&E or photograph the beating, because you have no marks.

The aggressive attitude of the police in St Petersburg was confirmed by Vorkuta respondents (such as Kirill) who complained that they had got 'fucked' by the police in St Petersburg for what would have been considered something and nothing in Vorkuta.

An explanation of the differences between the two punk scenes lies less in the individual actors than in the interactions they have. While territorial gang culture no longer dominates the youth cultural scene in cosmopolitan St Petersburg,[38] in Vorkuta the *gopniki* still 'think of themselves as leaders … that everyone else is shit' (Kirill). This creates many more random encounters in which violence is threatened or actual and to which punks have to respond as Kirill recounts:

> Once, we were walking down the street and they just jumped out of a car and started to beat us up. Once we snapped. There were three of us walking along and four of them jumped out of a car and started to beat the shit out of us. We turn round and start giving some back. And in the end they got back in the car and drove off.

In the Vorkuta context, therefore, masculine pride and authority becomes attached to the ability to respond to aggression successfully. Kirill expresses his respect for older punks in the city for not letting themselves 'be walked all over' and notes that not only do he and his group do the same, but 'sometimes we seek out *gopniki* ourselves, because they get in our way'. As this statement makes clear, punk violence is not always wholly reactive. In fact, Demid reported dressing as a skinhead in order to provoke the *gopniki* into picking a fight with him (Field diary). Demid's story indicates another important contextual factor; not only were *gopniki* still active and hostile to alternative youth groups, but youth cultural trajectories were also deeply interwoven. He had found it hard to get the fight he craved with the *gopniki* because his brother had been 'a *gopnik* authority' and thus he had a kind of 'protected' status. This proximity to the *gopniki* was not unusual; Savva was described by Kostya as 'an old *gopnik*' and Savva confirmed this:

> We gathered and fought gang against gang, sometimes with fists, sometimes with iron bars, with stones. They were serious wars[39] … I think that in all cities people fought street against street. Maybe in Vorkuta it was more organised.

Respondents agreed that the current situation with *gopnik* gangs was 'significantly calmer' than it had been at the end of the 1980s but practices of yard against yard and district against district fighting that had characterised the youth cultural environment of the late Soviet period, remained largely intact and were crucial to how youth cultural trajectories were forged today. Punk respondents had spent their early teenage years in precisely these kinds of territorially based groups with the attendant norms of 'prison camp' loyalty, authority and masculinity. It is through what Fine and Kleinman call these 'communication interlocks'[40] that common cultural reference points and practices, such as fighting, are developed.

Defending 'our' space: internal and external 'others'

The proactive territorialism of punk violence is also evident in punk aggression towards those who appeared to invade their space. This was most frequently expressed in relation to emos who shared many public spaces (such as live music venues) with punks but whose younger age and predisposition to emotionality made them easy targets of aggression. Members of the band Marazm described the Biker club[41] as having been 'occupied' by emos and the latter featured as figures of hate in numerous songs and artwork of the band.

In contrast, on St Petersburg's much more diverse scene, territories were defended by factions within the punk scene. Thus, Tina complains that hardcore punks set themselves apart from other punks, thinking they were 'cooler'. Yet, when confronted by aggressive sailors (at an event), she says, it was these 'huge hardcore blokes' that were the first to run away, while 'we drunken alcopunks' stood our ground (Tina). The alternative perspective is provided by hardcore respondents, who describe how those drunken punks unskilled in hardcore dancing might be treated with aggression:

> Here there are certain, specific dances like. But when some drunken shit
> appears and starts colliding with everyone. Well, I think it's acceptable to get
> him in the head with your swinging arm. That's really lush. So that the guy
> understands like, 'Look mate, you can't just come here and be in front of
> lads who have been going to concerts together their whole life, who dance
> together, who really know this stuff. And you are some drunken freak who is at
> this kind of gig virtually the first time. You haven't a clue what mayhem you're
> starting. (Pasha)

This appears to confirm that the major cause of violence within scenes is failure to conform to established conventions, which disrupts the release of aggression in a physical but non-violent way that established scene members enjoy from an 'ordered' pit.[42] However, the complaint that the drunken punks were unleashing 'mayhem' also reflects the 'volatile play between order and chaos' in slam dancing[43] as well as a wider tension within the punk scene between traditional punk values of individuality and non-conformity and the desire among hardcore crowds to impose order on 'their' space. The issue here is not only one of hardcore versus other forms of punk, but also of context.

Resistance to rules is highest where a demand for conformity to externally imposed order is greatest. In a city like Vorkuta, where street life remains domi-nated by the lore of territorial gangs, punk becomes a strategy for differentiation from the 'grey mass' of *gopniki* with their 'single, collective brain' (Polad). At the same time, pressure to conform is aggressively pursued and, whatever your philosophy, lifestyle or pretension to alternative masculinity might be in other circumstances, Demid concludes, 'if you want to live, you better know how to fight' (Field diary). Moreover, the fact that Vorkuta punks shared the yard and district backgrounds of their aggressors, often having 'run with' such gangs in their early teenage years means that they can call on the shared cultural prac-tices (fighting skills) and values (loyalty, not allowing oneself to be 'walked over') required to respond to frequent violence-threatening encounters.

Fighting with a purpose: ideological solidarities and antagonisms

Punk has been positioned ideologically in an ambiguous way. This is iconi-cally evident in the punk use of the swastika and other fascist/Nazi symbols, readings of which range from its employment for shock value only, through being a conscious attempt to subvert its meaning,[44] to the suggestion that the aim was precisely 'to wear the swastika with complete ambivalence … to get people wondering "What the fuck is happening here?"'.[45] Thus, while in the public mind, punk has been associated primarily with the anti-fascist cause (as part of a wider left-wing tradition of dissent), academic research has suggested that punk's engagement with anti-racism has been exaggerated and the movement's political ambiguity, and elements of overt racism, could be exploited by the extreme right.[46] Contextualising punk within the wider political landscape of the UK in the late 1970s and early 1980s, Worley charts the struggle by both left (primarily the Socialist Workers' Party through the Rock against Racism campaign and the Anti-Nazi League) and right (par-ticularly the National Front's Rock against Communism campaign and the British Movement) to harness punk to their particular ideological struggle.[47] The left, Worley suggests, saw music as a medium for protest against the inequi-ties of capitalism, while the right focused on gaining footholds in venues and localities, and control over particular bands, and thus often overlapped more traditional subcultural, football or territorial tensions and hostilities.[48] Thus punk in the UK – as a musical form and a wider youth culture – was never incorporated fully into either left or right-wing ideological frameworks but remained a contested site of political engagement, which often took a very physical form as punk gigs were disrupted by competing political factions.⁴⁹

Outside of the UK, where punk often emerged later and shared scenes with the skinhead movement or, alternatively, was embedded within wider anarchist, pacifist, feminist, vegan and/or animal rights movements, there were myriad local constellations of stylistic, cultural, musical and political allegiances, further problematising the attribution of a definitive ideological positioning to punk. The two punk scenes under discussion in this article epitomise the unfixed relationship between punk and ideology. In St Petersburg, where the punk scene is diverse and fragmented, reference to ideology or politics was made primarily by younger hardcore respondents who also participated in anti-fascist direct action. In contrast, in Vorkuta, the majority of younger punks on the scene shared friendship groups, values and attitudes with members of the (racist) skinhead movement in the city and some had participated in xenophobic violence.

St Petersburg: trophy-hunting and its consequences

In St Petersburg, hardcore respondents such as Andrei recounted participation in a trophy-hunting practice; having identified individuals sporting 'fascist' symbols – boots, caps, scarves, badges – they relieved their wearers of them. These incidents often involved violence and are remembered and recounted as deeply pleasurable. Thus, while Pasha had given up the more political elements of his anti-fascist engagement, a fight on a Saturday night remained attractive:

> I count myself as an anti-fascist … I have been on actions and been arrested many times … But the stuff I did before – various actions, signing up, all kinds of meetings … I don't do that any more. I only go for a beer. Well, I do love to fight, I'm not denying it. It only needed a Saturday for us to end up in a scrap. It was fun.

He goes on to talk about now seeing this type of action as pointless; only getting involved in politics 'seriously' could be effective. Contrasting current activists with founding members of the movement, he complained that today there was 'no real movement'; for current activists, 'being an anti-fascist is associated with drinking, clothes, concerts, they don't do anything else … it's not a movement, it's complete crap … just another excuse to fight'.

Another group of respondents – active on the punk music scene in a number of bands – shared anti-fascist principles and an anti-xenophobic stance but did not involve themselves in direct action or include such themes in their lyrics. As WhiteofFf explains, since, personally, he was not prepared to engage in violence, he chose to keep his politics to himself:

> Nationalism and xenophobia are stupid – that goes without saying. But if you make a stance against it then you are obliged to either beat others up or get it in the head yourself. Of course I would be prepared to take it in the face myself, but I don't see my calling as to go around beating up others for this cause … I am on the same front, on the left, like and, if something affects me directly, I will offer support, but otherwise …

Just why WhiteofFf is 'not prepared' to articulate his views explicitly becomes clear from respondents' discussion of the potential consequences of so doing. Pasha recounted how his address had been 'outed' and, as a result, he had received 'visits' from 'boneheads'[50] three times, forcing him to move out temporarily. He was lucky, he went on, to be in St Petersburg, since 'in Moscow they would have just shot me straight away'. Tina also discusses the constant fear she experiences of being 'fucked over by *gopniki*, police or bone-heads'. In the context of the infamous murder of a young anti-fascist activist in 2008, she concludes, all punks and anti-fascists have to 'live everyday as if it were their last'.

Vorkuta: skinhead solidarities

The anti-fascist scene in Vorkuta was virtually non-existent and, in sharp con-trast to St Petersburg, the punk and skinhead scenes were closely intersected. While this is not unusual, especially on American, provincial hardcore scenes, it was not common music tastes but shared origins that shaped the solidari-ties in Vorkuta. Younger punks (those aged 17–22 years) had been in their early teens at the peak of the skinhead movement in Vorkuta. At this point (2002–03) classic territorial gangs (*gopniki*) were reinvented as skinhead 'bri-gades' taking on, partially at least, a function of routine protection. 'Almost every other person was a skin' (Petya) and this teenage immersion in the same neighbourhoods, schools and gangs left a legacy of friends and acquaintances with those who had remained active on the skinhead scene (Field diary). This is a classic illustration of Fine and Kleinman's recognition that members of 'subcultures' may participate in several groups simultaneously and maintain acquaintance relationships outside the major groups with which they commu-nicate.[51] In this case, several Vorkuta punks had gone to school with prominent members of skinhead groups (Stas, Kirill), participated in their activities in their early teens (Petya, Tofik), or made friends with skinheads more recently

(Sonya). Two respondents (Boris, Kirill) trained at the same basement gym used by a group of authoritative skinheads and participated in social events (drinking nights) with them there. A skinhead, who had participated in earlier research,[52] reported that he had been approached by two young punks (Petya and Grisha) wanting him to reinvigorate the movement. Thus, many younger punk respondents viewed skin and punk as effectively 'one movement' that only subsequently 'parted and went their separate ways' (Boris).

These common acquaintances and friendship groups translate into much common ground in terms of political views and identities. Demid described himself as 'a punk with a skinhead world view' (Field diary). Kirill claimed that 'the majority of Vorkuta punks are nationalists' and declared all three members of his own band to be 'Nazi punks'; a label he also ascribed to three other members of the Vorkuta punk scene. It is perhaps Sonya who best epitomises the ideological ambiguity of punk discussed above; having been deeply conflicted trying to combine her own 'Nazist' proclivities with her affinity to punk (believing that punks were inherently 'anti-Nazi'), her identity crisis had been resolved by her discovery of the concept of 'Nazi punks'.

Shared views across punk and skin scenes were evident in everyday xenophobic statements made by respondents (Field diary) and their song lyrics. The chorus of Mezhdu Prochim's 'Zoo city'[53] speaks for itself: 'Zoo city, zoo city/ Clean your homeland without sparing fists/ Zoo city, zoo city/ Clean your homeland, you know yourself how.'

And the third verse implies the need to combine forces with skinheads to achieve this 'purification' of the city: 'With your shared idea you won't go wrong/ Unite with your friend and brother/ Together we will cleanse our city/ We'll cleanse the country and our race …'

Personal participation in violent skinhead actions was reported by a number of respondents (Field diary), often justified by claims of a two-tier justice system; attacks by members of ethnic minorities on Russians were ignored by the police, while if one of 'them' is attacked it is treated as xenophobic extremism (Demid). In other cases, however, xenophobia appeared to be simply a product of intolerance to difference (Field diary). Even older punk scene members, whose views generally are better described as 'patriotic' than xenophobic or 'racist', recounted how they had physically 'sorted' an incident with ethnic minority traders at the city market; a fighting tale that was prefaced by a complaint that the market was 'full of Azeris' who showed no respect for Russian women (Kostya). Perhaps the overwhelming power of context is best illustrated by the case of Roman. He was the only person in the city of African heritage and had himself experienced racial abuse and 'constant fights' that had forced him to move schools a number of times. Nonetheless, he was acquainted with the skinhead community and recounted his own participation in a skinhead 'action' against '*khachi*'[54] whom he saw as legitimate targets of violence if they 'don't behave themselves right'.

Dissenting voices can also be heard within the Vorkuta scene. Valera dismissed skinhead ideology as no more than 'beating blacks' while Grisha had a hatred of skinheads ascribed to having witnessed his father being beaten up by them when he was eight years old. Artur and Kristina naturally aligned themselves with the anti-fascist rather than skinhead movement; Artur had participated in an 'Anti-fa' movement but had left after six months because they had only ever managed to beat up one skinhead and the group's activities consisted of meeting and drinking. Among the older generation of punks, there was also more talk of conflictual situations arising between punks and skins (especially at concerts). Indeed, according to Savva, it was during these encounters – where skinheads learned that 'we are not little boys ... if something kicks off, we can stand up for ourselves' – that the mutual physical respect between punks and skins, on which the 'good relations' with the local skinheads was based, was forged. The importance of this masculine fighting identity to punk and skinhead solidarity is summed up by Kirill's characterisation of the commonalities between punks and skins as 'some of our views on life are similar ... Freedom and a kind of struggle. Skinheads are fighting lads themselves.'

Although common acquaintances, common pasts and common xenophobic views draw punks in Vorkuta into skinhead-related violence, there remain fundamental differences between skinhead and punk fighting. Firstly fighting was not integral to punk scenes – unlike Moore's Australian skinheads,[55] Russian punks *could* claim to be punks if they did not fight. Secondly, while the employment of violence to resolve relationships and other power issues certainly conformed to the dominant regime of masculinity, punk fighting bent those rules. Thus while skinhead fighting was central to proving one's 'hardness', where hardness was predicated on winning one's fights and 'never backing down, no matter what the odds are', punks can, and do, avoid fights.[56] Moreover when fights do occur, they are often accidental or opportunistic, conducted in inebriated conditions, characterised by being abandoned by one's mates and frequently lost in a spectacular display of heroic incompetence.

Heroic incompetence and fighting masculinity

Narratives of punk fighting often suggest it is an unplanned but routine part of a 'good night out'. Members of the Vorkuta band Marazm recounted how the night they played their first ever live set at the Biker club ended:

> Yeah. So we like played our set, everybody liked it. Then we, basically, of course everyone got their heads kicked in back then. Well, not everyone, me and ... to be precise, because of some stupid thing. Nothing to do with the group or the music – someone pushed somebody or looked at someone funny. That kind of thing. And we had to fight. (Polad)

Indeed Boris (Vorkuta) saw a good fight as cathartic; fighting, like slamming, he said, 'lets out all the tension and that's it, everything's calm'. The routine and pleasurable nature of fights was articulated clearly by Demid (Vorkuta) who called fighting his 'hobby'. After recounting how he had sustained his bleeding hand and bruised face during a fight with local punks in the neighbouring city of Inta while at a concert, he concluded there was nothing better on a night out than the combination of good music, good beer and a good fight (Field diary).

While audience-oriented violence frequently takes place at entertainment venues, bars, and parties,[57] a striking characteristic of punk fights is that, after 'beating the shit out of one another', the protagonists 'become best friends (Valera, Vorkuta). This is how members of the Vorkuta band Mezhdu Prochim narrated the origins of their friendship with Demid (now the group's bass guitarist):

> Demid: We made friends because of a fight basically ...
> Interviewer: How do you mean because of a fight? Were you all fighting on the same side?
> All three: No!
> Demid: I had a fight with him [looks at Kirill] basically ... We were in the park. At the start, we were arguing about these white bootlaces, then about principles (*poniatiia*), this and that, then we fought, and then, with another bloke, they gave me a bit of a kicking.
> Stas: We went to get booze. When we got back, there was a fight kicking off ...
> Interviewer: And what was the thing with the white laces all about?
> Demid: I had one green lace, the other was painted ...
> Kirill: No – one was black and the other was white ...
> Interviewer: [to Stas and Kirill] and you didn't like that ...
> Demid: Basically we resolved the issue of not liking it, but then we had our own issue ...

Stas: I don't know what started the fight.

Demid: He said 'I don't like you.' I went, 'So what? What d'you want to do
about it?'. He goes, 'I want to hit you.' I go, 'Okay'. He hits me. Then, it was,
'I want another go.' 'Okay, fine.' And it kicked off …

This excerpt from a much longer story is included here as an indication
of how fighting for punks constitutes a rich resource for ironic story-telling.
These narratives play on the drunken state of the combatants, the hopeless
prospects of victory (due to inferior numbers, physical strength or inebriation)
and the frequent meaninglessness of the action (with whom or why a fight had
occurred was often forgotten). Such tales of heroic incompetence, I suggest,
are what distinguishes punk from other subcultural fighting. A classic illustration of this is Petya's ironic narration of how he had ended up fighting 'eight
khachi-gopniki' at Vorkuta's Black Moon club after treading on one of them
accidentally on the dancefloor (Field diary). Kirill also recounts how what
should have been an easy put-down of an emo resulted in having to take on
a car-load of local Vorkuta gangsters whom the emo called up to defend him.

In these stories, the failure of other punks to help out is part of the joke
rather than a treacherous act. Members of the Vorkuta band Mezhdu Prochim
laughed about how one of them had a kind of sixth sense that 'always senses a
drinking session, in which case he appears, or a fight, and then he immediately
disappears … ' (Demid). This is a clear indication that punk masculinities
are not secured necessarily through street positioning as 'fighters'. Indeed,
Valera, who was widely considered one of the most authentic punks on the
Vorkuta scene, only got involved in fights when 'dragged into it' by others. Artur
(Vorkuta) said he had not been involved in a fight for three years and Natella
(Vorkuta) said she did not tolerate cruelty or violence. Even Kostya and Kirill
(Vorkuta), both of whom participated in fights relatively frequently, said it was
often wiser to try to talk one's way out of situations. Equally, punk femininities
did not necessarily exclude fighting. One female punk on the St Petersburg
scene was admired for her ability 'to break men' including 'boneheads' (Pasha).
Tina also got a buzz from the fights in which her group of friends participated
and was an active participant herself in hardcore dance practices that often left
dancers battered and bruised (Field diary, St Petersburg). Sonya's narrative of
her drunken fighting experience at the Evropa club in Vorkuta, moreover, displays similar style and content to the tales of heroic incompetence recounted by
male punks. Here a short extract is reproduced from a much longer narration
of events sparked by an initial altercation with some local *gopniki* after they
objected to Sonya entering the club with a drink in her hand:

Sonya: They apparently had decided it was their club, their territory and they would introduce their rules. But I told them to fuck off ... At the beginning we jostled a bit, then basically we went out to 'talk'.

Interviewer: You and this girl?

Sonya: Yes

Interviewer: You went out to fight?

Sonya: Sometimes you have to. And the fortified wine got broken ... by then I was already quite drunk ... . I drank more beer, drank just about anything. Then, when I was already pretty out of it, this *gopnik* started having a go at me. I was already mad because ... at any concert, if I feel like climbing onto the stage ... I climb onto the stage and I don't see why anybody should stop me ... . But here this great brute starts pushing me off the stage ... I was so mad with him. And every time I climbed up, he pushed me off again ... I was having great fun, I was so mad. And then again some *gopnik* started giving me grief and I smashed the fortified wine against his head. I was already out of it. And then a third time, I failed to get the fortified wine through. So I drank it in one – I was completely wasted by then. I got this idea about getting in from the inside, where the musicians hang out. I haven't a clue how I got there. But I got to the stage and fell asleep [laughs].

Interviewer: So do you often get involved in scuffles, in fights?

Sonya: Not often but it happens.

Interviewer: And you can stand up for yourself?

Sonya: Of course. I learned to do that quite a long time ago. Because you can't get by without being able to here.

This research was not designed to explore specifically the relationship between violence, gender and punk and the conclusions that can be drawn from it are limited. That fighting is narrated by both male and female punks and often as tales of heroic incompetence, however, suggests that, at the very least, there is nothing straightforward about the relationship between fighting and masculinity on contemporary punk scenes.

Conclusion

Punk, like many other 'spectacular' subcultures, has been dominated numerically by men and, despite the gender transgressive aspects of early punk scenes and later scenes' allegiances with anti-sexist, anti-homophobic and pacifist movements, punk has failed to significantly disrupt hegemonic gender regimes. While there is an emergent scholarly interest in gender identity and punk, it is difficult to conclude anything more than that masculinities on punk scenes are ambiguous and contradictory. Drawing on data from ethnographic research, this chapter has attempted to contribute to the understanding of this relationship through a particular exploration of the role of fighting and violence on punk scenes.

The evidence from these scenes suggests that punk violence and fighting shares some commonalities with that found in other subcultures (skinheads, football fans) in terms of its audience-oriented and rule-governed character. The ritualised nature of punk violence, and its generation of loyalty and authority is most apparent in traditional clashes with 'subcultural' or ideological 'others' (*gopniki* and emos in Vorkuta, 'boneheads' and 'drunk punks' in St Petersburg). However, it has been suggested here, most violence and fighting on punk scenes is neither ordered nor rule-bound but opportunistic, chaotic and incompetent. Collins argues that the tension that dominates emotion in the course of violent confrontations, makes the performance of violent acts almost always 'inaccurate and incompetent'.[58] While this may be so, what is argued here is that it is the narration of fighting not as an expression of hard masculinity, loyalty and bravery but as heroic incompetence, that makes punk fighting distinctive. This may, indeed, mirror Russian punk aesthetics more widely in which 'the value of the fight lies not in victory, but in the ability to engage wholeheartedly in the losing side. Status is gained through being beaten to pulp by an overpowering opposition … '[59] Thus, punk fighting might be seen as 'audience-oriented' but functions less as a mechanism of initiation or ritual than as a source of material for ironic reflection and story-telling.

Through a comparison of fighting within punk cultures on two different scenes in contemporary Russia, this chapter has sought to demonstrate also the importance of socio-cultural context and inter-group communication in shaping cultural practices and strategies. While violence, it has been suggested, is predominantly situational or interactional (as opposed to being attributable to particular socio-economic or socio-cultural factors of either individuals or micro-environments), the prevalence and nature of violence-threatening encounters differs significantly across the two research sites. These differences, it has been argued, reflect different constellations of social connections and communicative interlocks,[60] most notably the continued significance of territorially organised youth groups (*gopniki*) in the city of Vorkuta and the fusion of these groups with (racist) skinhead culture at a particular point in time that was important in shaping individual youth cultural trajectories. This, it has been argued, explains not only the highly intersected nature of punk and racist skinhead scenes in the city, but also the diffusion of communicative practices (including xenophobic and racist talk) and everyday behaviours and values (such as fighting and the valorisation of 'standing up for oneself') that are absent from the St Petersburg punk scene. Punk lives are deeply embedded in everyday lives and, in Vorkuta, punk or not, if you want to live, you better know how to fight.

Notes

1 For an early, and notable, exception, see L. Roman, 'Intimacy, Labor, and Class: Ideologies of Feminine Sexuality in the Punk Slam Dance', in L. Roman and L. Christian-Smith (eds), *Becoming Feminine: The Politics of Popular Culture* (London: The Falmer Press, 1988), pp. 143–85.

2 L. Leblanc, *Pretty in Punk: Girls' Gender Resistance in a Boys' Subculture* (New Brunswick, NJ: Rutgers University Press, 2006), p. 8.

3 *Ibid.*

4 *Ibid.*, pp. 51–2.

5 L. O'Brien, 'The Woman Punk Made Me', in R. Sabin (ed.), *Punk Rock: So What? The Cultural Legacy of Punk* (London: Routledge, 1999), pp. 191–3.

6 *Ibid.*, p. 194.

7 S. Thompson, *Punk Productions: Unfinished Business* (Albany, NY: State University of New York Press, 2004), p. 38.

8 Leblanc, *Pretty in Punk*, p. 51.

9 'Slamdancing' emerged on American punk scenes in the late 1970s and early 1980s as a modification of the pogo. 'Moshing', a variation of the slam dance, appeared in the mid-1980s. The terms are often used interchangeably although, as discussed below, some argue that there are significant distinctions between them.

10 B. S. Simon, 'Entering the Pit: Slam-dancing and Modernity', *Journal of Popular Culture*, 31:1 (1997), 164–5.

11 R. Haenfler, *Straight Edge: Hardcore Punk, Clean-living Youth, and Social Change* (New Brunswick, NJ: Rutgers University Press, 2006), pp. 29–30.

12 In broad terms 'positive' straight edgers saw the movement as looser and were relatively tolerant of individual interpretation of straight edge. They were also less inclined towards hypermasculinity and aggressive dancing. In contrast 'militants' were more dedicated to the movement and more vociferous about it, less tolerant of lapses in straight-edge behaviour. They were also more likely to be homophobic and more hypermasculine and participatory in hard dancing.

13 Haenfler, *Straight Edge*, p. 82.

14 *Ibid.*, p. 103.

15 Leblanc, *Pretty in Punk*, p. 8.

16 D. Robins and P. Cohen, *Knuckle Sandwich: Growing Up in the Working-class City* (Harmondsworth: Penguin, 1978), p. 74.

17 D. Moore, *The Lads in Action: Social Process in an Urban Youth Subculture* (Aldershot: Ashgate, 1994), p. 66.

18 *Ibid.*, pp. 65–7.

19 P. Marsh, E. Rosser and R. Harre, *The Rules of Disorder* (London: Routledge & Kegan Paul, 1978), p. 2.

20 R. Collins, 'Micro and Macro Causes of Violence', *International Journal of Conflict and Violence*, 3:1 (2009), 12.

21 *Ibid.*, p. 13.

22 Robins and Cohen, *Knuckle Sandwich*, p. 171.

23 W. Tsitsos, 'Rules of Rebellion: Slamdancing, Moshing, and the American Alternative scene', *Popular Music*, 18:3 (1999), 410.

24 J. Ward, '"This is Germany! It's 1933!": Appropriations and Constructions of "Fascism" in New York Punk/Hardcore in the 1980s', *Journal of Popular Culture*, 30: 3 (1996), 164.

25 S. Reynolds, *Rip it Up and Start Again: Postpunk 1978–1984* (London: Faber & Faber, 2005), p. 112.

26 C. O'Hara, *The Philosophy of Punk: More than Noise* (London: Cherry Red Books, 1992), pp. 87–9.

27 Simon, 'Entering the Pit', pp. 164–5.

28 Haenfler, *Straight Edge*, p. 82.

29 Tsitsos, 'Rules of Rebellion', 413.

30 *Ibid.*

31 Collins, 'Micro and Macro Causes of Violence', 10.

32 The project was funded by the Arts and Humanities Research Council (AHRC) and involved a team of six researchers working on case studies in the Russian Federation (Hilary Pilkington and Ivan Gololobov), Croatia (Benjamin Perasović and Ivana Mijić), eastern Germany (Aimar Ventsel) and the Netherlands (Kirsty Lohman). The empirical research drawn on in this chapter was conducted in Vorkuta by Hilary Pilkington assisted by Al'bina Garifzianova and in St Petersburg by Ivan Gololobov assisted by Hilary Pilkington and Yngvar Steinholt. Financial support of the AHRC (ref: AH/G011966/) is gratefully acknowledged. The opinions expressed in this chapter, however, are those of its author.

33 Both bands that are variously accredited with being the first Russian 'punk' band – Zoopark (formed 1980) and Avtomaticheskie udovletvoriteli (formed 1979) – were from St Petersburg (Leningrad). See Y. Steinholt, *Rock in the Reservation: Songs from the Leningrad Rock Club 1981–86* (Bergen, Norway: The Mass Media Music Scholars' Press, 2005), pp. 69–70.

34 Y. Steinholt, 'Punk is Punk but By No Means Punk: Definition, Genre Dodging and the Quest for an Authentic Voice in Contemporary Russia', *Punk and Post-Punk*, 1:3 (2012), 264–84.

35 There is one exception to this rule where the respondent's explicit request to be referred to by his nickname has been followed.

36 *Gopniki* is a term used popularly and by subcultural youth to refer to territorially based groups (gangs) hostile, and often physically aggressive, towards alternative youth cultural groups (punks, metalheads, emos etc).

37 This is a colloquial collective noun for '*gopnik*'.

38 The exception to the rule here is the description by young hardcore respondents of the solidarity in their district which meant that, regardless of subcultural affiliation, if anybody from the district came under attack, thirty or so people would come out to support them within minutes (Pasha, Andrei, Venia).

39 He goes on to say that some of these fights had resulted in fatal injuries.

40 G. Fine and S. Kleinman, 'Rethinking Subculture: An Interactionist Analysis', *American Journal of Sociology*, 85:1 (1979), 7.

41 This is the only alternative music venue in the city, rehearsal space and 'HQ' of the long-standing punk band Mazut.

42 Simon, 'Entering the Pit', 161; Tsitsos, 'Rules of Rebellion', 407–10.

43 Simon, 'Entering the Pit', 161.

44 See, for example: G. Marcus, *Lipstick Traces: A Secret History of the Twentieth Century* (London: Faber and Faber, 1989), p. 118; M. Sinker, 'Concrete, so as to Self-destruct: The Etiquette of Punk, its Habits, Rules, Values and Dilemmas', in Sabin (ed.), *Punk Rock: So What?* p. 124; Thompson, *Punk Productions*, p. 29.

45 J. Savage, *England's Dreaming: Sex Pistols and punk rock* (London: Faber and Faber, 1991), pp. 241–2.

46 R. Sabin, "'I Won't Let that Dago By": Rethinking Punk and Racism', in Sabin (ed), *Punk Rock: So What?*, p. 199.

47 M. Worley, 'Shot By Both Sides: Punk, Politics and the End of "Consensus"', *Contemporary British History*, 26:3 (2012), 333–54.

48 *Ibid.*, 342.

49 *Ibid.*, 334.

50 'Boneheads' (*bonkhedy*) is a term used widely in St Petersburg to refer to neo-Nazi or racist skinheads.

51 Fine and Kleinman, 'Rethinking Subculture', 10.

52 See H. Pilkington, E. Omel'chenko and A. Garifzianova, *Russia's Skinheads: Exploring and Rethinking Subcultural Lives* (London and New York: Routledge, 2010).

53 From an unreleased recording; lyrics reproduced with kind permission of Mezhdu Prochim.

54 A pejorative term used to refer to ethnic minority groups primarily from the Caucasus region.

55 Moore, *The Lads in Action*, p. 66.

56 *Ibid.*

57 Collins, 'Micro and Macro Causes of Violence', 13.

58 *Ibid.*, 10.

59 Y. Steinholt, 'Siberian Punk Shall Emerge Here: Egor Letov and Grazhdanskaia Oborona', *Popular Music*, 31:3 (2012), 411.

60 Fine and Kleinman, 'Rethinking Subculture'.

2

Oi! Oi! Oi!: Class, locality and British punk

[What is punk?]: That's an open question. It always was. You can't put it into words. It's a feeling. It's basically a lot of hooligans doing it the way they want and getting what they want.[1]

Writing in late 1981, the punk poet Garry Johnson described Oi! as being 'about real life, the concrete jungle, [hating] the Old Bill, being on the dole, and about fighting back and having pride in your class and background'.[2] For Garry Bushell, who adopted the term in late 1980 as the title for a compilation LP designed to reassert punk as a form of 'working-class protest', Oi! comprised 'a loose alliance of volatile young talents, skins, punks, tearaways, hooligans, rebels with or without causes united by their class, their spirit, their honesty and their love of furious rock 'n' roll'. In the context of a Britain racked by mass unemployment and simmering social tensions, bands such as the 4-Skins, Blitz, The Business, The Exploited, Infa Riot and the Last Resort were presented as a 'teenage warning' to the 'smug politicians and greedy bosses' who had 'destroyed whole communities and thrown an entire generation on the scrapheap'.[3] Oi!, Bushell surmised, was 'anti-pose, anti-privilege and solidly pro-working class'; a 'reaffirmation of punk values' divorced from the art school influences and music industry machinations he deemed to have neutered punk's original spirit of rebellion.[4]

No sooner had Oi! been defined as a street-level expression of revolt, however, than it was embroiled in controversy. On 3 July 1981, a gig at the Hambrough Tavern in Southall involving three bands aligned to Oi! was attacked by local Asian youths objecting to the arrival of a large skinhead presence in an area with a recent history of racial conflict.[5] Come 10p.m., and the pub was ablaze beneath a hail of petrol bombs; the next day, newspaper front pages were dominated by images of cowering police officers, burnt-out vehicles and stories of a 'race riot'.[6] By extension, therefore, Oi! was presented as the musical expression of racist, neo-Nazi skinheads. From the *Daily Mail* to the *NME* and on to sections of the far left, Oi! was accused of flirting with the language and imagery of National Socialism to provide a conduit for 'violent-racist-sexist-fascist' attitudes to feed their way into popular music.[7]

In terms of cultural and political history, it is this second interpretation of Oi! that has tended to hold sway. If mentioned at all, Oi! is typically dismissed either as a lumpen by-product of punk's death throes or a cog in the wheel of the transnational 'white noise' movement initiated from within the National Front (NF) over the 1980s.[8] As a result, shorthand reference to Oi!'s being 'right-wing', 'Nazi' or 'racist' now pepper more general accounts of pop, punk and late twentieth-century British culture.[9]

This chapter seeks to present a more nuanced reading of Oi! To be sure, Oi! contained elements that contributed to its demonisation. The media association of skinheads with racial violence was crudely superficial and often exaggerated, but it harboured a kernel of truth.[10] Similarly, Oi!'s combination of social resentment and patriotism provided a potential pathway to and from the far right. But Oi! also comprised a class awareness and a cultural heritage that suggested it was a rather more complex phenomenon; one that reflected tensions inherent within the socio-economic and political realities of late 1970s and early 1980s Britain. Like the punk culture from which it emerged, Oi! provided a contested site of critical engagement that allowed voices rarely heard in public debate to articulate a protest that cut across existing notions of 'left', 'right' and formal political organisation. More specifically, it revealed and articulated processes of political and socio-cultural realignment directly relevant to the advent of Thatcherism and collapse of the so-called 'consensus' that informed British politics from 1945.

Such a study takes its cue from the basic Centre for Contemporary Cultural Studies (CCCS) thesis that aspects of youth culture may be read as sites of 'resistance' to prevailing socio-economic structures, class relations and cultural hegemony.[11] In so doing, it does not thereby assume that such cultures were (or are) coherent, homogenous or wholly self-contained. Nor does it subscribe to a particular methodology proposed from within the CCCS. These, after all, were varied, though tended to assume that subcultures enacted a stylistic response to shifting socio-economic, cultural and political relations in society.[12] The CCCS arguments remain contentious and have given rise to numerous critiques pointing to their overly theorised approach and tendency to prioritise certain socio-economic, racial, gendered, spatial or 'spectacular' expressions of youth culture at the expense of others.[13] Nevertheless, the underlying premise of the CCCS remains relevant to the current chapter for three principal reasons. Firstly, because it was developed at a particular historical juncture during which youth cultural styles and class divisions in British society were thrown into sharp relief.[14] Not only did the CCCS form part of the political and cultural history of the post-war period, but its reading of youth culture helped shape the contemporary responses to the subject discussed below. Secondly, the basic premise of youth culture harbouring implicit and explicit political meaning has an obvious relevance to punk, which emerged replete with political signifiers and positioned itself as a confrontational form of cultural expression. Thirdly, the relative lack of an empirical basis on which to place to the CCCS' thesis provides opportunity for the historian to test it against the intended meanings and motivations of those participating within the culture. In this instance, to what extent did the political meanings projected onto Oi! reflect the views held by those involved in or associated with it?

For the historian, moreover, this chapter proposes that youth cultures and popular music provide a portal into the formative thoughts, aspirations and concerns of a not insubstantial (and often overlooked) section of the population. With regard to Oi!, an analysis of its bands, audience and ephemera reveals much about class identity in the late 1970s and early 1980s, offering a snapshot of working-class youth in a period of significant socio-economic change. Notably, too, the debates that surrounded Oi! were informed by realignments ongoing within British politics, both in terms of youthful disengagement from the political mainstream and the 'cultural turn' generated by a growing emphasis on 'new' spheres of struggle (race, gender, sexuality, youth, culture, language, consumption).[15] Put bluntly, the politics of class were being overtaken by what some on the left called a 'consciousness of oppression' located in personal identity.[16] This, in turn, shifted attention from the socio-economic to the cultural and, in the process, served to scramble some of the class and racial certainties that had once underpinned the politics of left and right. As the left became associated with students and 'minority groups' that made headway on questions of race and identity, so sections of the far right set out to ensure that the 'grass-roots movement of workers and leadership of the working class does not rest with the communists and left but with the right'.[17]

In amidst all this, Oi! was caught in the crossfire: a medium for working-class protest interpreted as a recruiting ground for fascism.

The objective, therefore, is to reassess, contextualise and explain the contentious nature of Oi! in order to recover a marginalised voice that offers insight into aspects of broader socio-economic, political and cultural change. In particular, emphasis will be placed on Oi!'s class rhetoric and use of locality as key components of class-cultural identity.[18] Implicit, too, is recognition of Oi!'s overt masculinity. Though women formed an integral part of the wider social milieu from which Oi! emerged, its bands and core audience were primarily male: the focus of the article reflects this.[19] In terms of structure, the chapter is divided into three sections. Oi! will first be located within the broader trajectory of British punk. Competing interpretations of Oi! will then be discussed with regard to wider debate on the politics of youth culture that emerged over the 1970s. Finally, Oi!'s predominant motifs will be outlined in relation to the working-class milieu from which it emerged. If Oi! offered a view from the dead end of the street, as Garry Johnson insisted, then this chapter hopes to historicise its vision of a blighted early 1980s Britain.

'Here comes the new punk': Oi! and British punk, 1976–84

Oi! presented itself within a particular narrative of British punk. Most obviously, it drew from the class rhetoric and inner-city iconography that first helped define the emergence of bands such as the Sex Pistols and The Clash in 1976. Early coverage of the Pistols made much of their coming from 'the wrong end of various London roads', with tales of petty crime, violence, vandalism and remand centres serving to present an image of 'deprived London street kids' from 'working-class ghettoes' who stood in marked contrast to the wealthy rock 'aristocracy' of the 1960s generation and the 'middle class, affluent or university academics' of 1970s progressive rock.[20] Oi!, in many ways, provided a continuation of Tony Parsons' view of punk as 'amphetamine-stimulated high energy seventies street music, gut-level dole queue rock 'n' roll, fast flash, vicious music played by kids for kids'.[21] It picked up on the social reportage of bands such as The Clash and The Jam, whose songs were seen to offer 'a mirror reflection of the kind of 1977 white working-class experiences that only seem like a cliché to those people who haven't had to live through them'.[22] And if, as Julie Burchill insisted, punk was 'reality rock 'n' roll', then Oi! sought to authenticate her description of early punk gigs as 'like being on the terraces'

...ices comprised of 'working-class kids with the guts to say "No" to being office, factory and dole fodder'.[23]

Of course, punk's genesis was far more complex than it first appeared.[24] Not only were many of its early protagonists from distinctly suburban or middle-class backgrounds, not least Joe Strummer (The Clash) and the core of the 'Bromley Contingent' that formed the Sex Pistols' early audience, but the politics, strategies and designs that Malcolm McLaren, Vivienne Westwood and Jamie Reid used to cultivate punk's image revealed long-standing art school and counter-cultural pedigrees.[25] From this perspective, punk's adoption of working-class signifiers was part of a broader arsenal of symbols designed to 'threaten the status quo'.[26] Working-class revolt – be it represented through delinquency, rock 'n' roll or even militant trade unionism – was aligned with emblems of political 'extremism' (anarchy, swastikas, Marx), explicit sexuality, inverted religious symbols and criminality as a challenge to the bastions of the British establishment.[27]

As this suggests, punk married social commentary with stylistic innovation to forge a populist but subversive cultural force that dramatised, reflected and commented on the wider socio-economic and political climate of its time. Not surprisingly, it soon fractured beneath the weight of its own inner tensions; a split often portrayed as dividing those who saw punk as a medium for cultural and musical experimentation (the 'arties') from those who held fast to its claim to represent 'the kids' on the 'football terraces' and 'living in boring council estates' (the 'social realists').[28] In truth, punk's trashing of pop's past led to a range of sometimes overlapping musical styles and subcultural forms emerging from the debris.[29] But even amongst those who remained avowedly *punk*, there existed by the turn of the decade a mesh of mutating sub-scenes: the anarchist bands inspired by Crass; the proto-gothic tribes gathered around Siouxsie and the Banshees and the early Adam and the Ants; the hardening punk thrash pioneered by Discharge; the guttersnipe ruck 'n' roll of the Cockney Rejects; not to mention the numerous provincial scenes concentrated on local venues, record labels, squats, fanzines and shops.

Oi!, then, was rooted in a post-Pistols lineage that stretched from bands such as Cock Sparrer, Menace and Sham 69 through the Angelic Upstarts and Cockney Rejects. Each played aggressive stripped-down (punk) rock; each brought punk's class rhetoric to the fore; and each claimed to engage with aspects of young working-class life from authentic experience. Theirs were songs of youth cultural antagonisms, work (or the lack of it), football violence, petty crime, police harassment and a suspicion of authority in all its forms.[30] They rejected punk's supposed elitism – its art school heritage and the *haute couture* of McLaren and Westwood – in favour of its rhetorical populism, drawing from a wider sense of working-class youth culture to which punk was but a part or a continuation. 'We wanted a band that could reach other people like us', Cock Sparrer's Garrie Lammin argued, 'other football supporters, ordinary kids who couldn't afford to get into all that King's Road shit'.[31] And as punk began to fragment into competing tendencies, so bands like the Angelic Upstarts and the Cockney Rejects came to stand for what Garry Bushell in *Sounds* contended was the 'Real Punk', not 'the tail end of a decaying, fatally flawed movement, but the start of something newer, realer and harder than the rest'.[32]

The term 'Oi!' itself was taken from a Cockney Rejects song, 'Oi! Oi! Oi!', though it held a wider cultural significance. Not only was it a cockney shout that reflected the street-level focus of the bands and their audience, it served also to affirm Oi!'s working-class heritage.[33] This, in turn, was given expression in its appeal to skinheads, the overtly proletarian youth culture that first emerged in Britain during the later 1960s.[34] The original skins had fused a 'hard mod' style with images and sounds derived from the newly arrived Jamaican rude boys to forge a starkly working-class alternative to the so-called swinging sixties of the mainstream pop and hippy counter-culture. Their 1970s equivalent seized on the aggressive urbanity of punk, aligning themselves with bands such as Sham 69 to prompt a skinhead revival that continued into the 1980s (and beyond). More than that, however, the term 'Oi!' referred back to music hall and variety; it complemented the repeated references to working-class culture – pubs, football, boxing, the bank holiday beano, Butlin's, the betting shop – that peppered Oi! releases, interviews and articles.[35] Like 2-tone, which Bushell also championed and which shared an audience with Oi!, it comprised a fusion of youth cultural forms: where 2-tone combined punk, ska and early reggae in a cross-racial alignment of skinheads, mods and rude boys, so Oi! sought to integrate punk music with terrace culture in an amalgam of punks, skins and 'herberts' (meaning ordinary working-class youth, often proto-football casuals).[36] As a result, some ambiguity existed as to just what differentiated punk and Oi!, though the term mostly applied to bands that were avowedly working-class and included a non-punk, often skinhead, contingent amongst their audience. Oi!, Lee Wilson of Infa Riot insisted, was punk made by and for 'ordinary geezers … punks, skins, bootboys. It ain't about safety pins and rainbow hair anymore'.[37]

Initially, the bands most closely associated with Oi! were located in and around London. The Cockney Rejects, as their name suggests, were based in the East End, while the Angelic Upstarts had relocated to London from the north-east by 1980. In terms of gigs and meeting places, pubs such as the Bridge House in Canning Town, the Ancient Briton in Poplar, the Lord

Northbrook in Lee, the Barge Aground in Barking and the Deuragen Arms in Hackney formed hubs of the emergent scene, where bands such as the 4-Skins, Cock Sparrer, The Business and Infa Riot played or were regulars. Just off Petticoat Lane, too, the Last Resort skinhead emporium became a site of information and exchange, giving its name to a band formed out of Herne Bay in Kent. Following a *Sounds* article designed to promote this 'new breed' of punk, coverage of Oi! then extended further afield to encompass bands from the north of England (Blitz, Red Alert), the Midlands (Criminal Class, Demob), Wales (The Oppressed, The Partisans) and Scotland (The Strike). *Sounds* also published an irregular 'Oi! – The Column' from 1981, alongside Oi! charts compiled by pub DJs and readers. By mid-1981, some forty bands were aligned to Oi! in one way or another, making it an integral part of what was a resurgent punk scene in 1981–82.[38]

Musically, Oi! was best sampled on the series of albums compiled between 1980 and 1984.[39] These featured a mix of bands and poets, serving to showcase both Oi!'s roots and the new groups that defined its sound and stance. Each came replete with short essays, stories and poems designed to locate Oi! within a distinct cultural milieu; on *The Oi! of Sex* (1984), for example, a series of definitions were listed: Oi! is 'having a laugh and having a say', 'sharp in brain and dress', 'proud to be working class', '2-tone with bollocks', 'proud to be British, but not xenophobic', 'kiss me quick hats', 'turning council houses into mansions', etc.[40] An Oi! Organising Committee was also established, comprising Garry Bushell, Lol Pryor, Dave Long and John Muir, which helped compile the albums, arrange gigs, link bands to labels and convene conferences in order to provide a sense of point and purpose for the fledgling movement.[41] At the latter, held in January, May and June 1981, bands, writers and fanzine editors committed to arranging benefits for the unemployed and prisoners' rights organisations. The music, by general agreement, should be direct and accessible; lyrics were to deal with everyday life and aimed at the 'kids on the street'. Political affiliation was firmly rejected, though Lol Pryor was charged with contacting the Right to Work campaign initiated by the Socialist Workers' Party (SWP) to discuss holding gigs in support. More generally, existing parties on the left and right were dismissed in favour of self-organisation and the prioritisation of issues deemed relevant to working-class youth.[42]

Not surprisingly, the Southall riot served to derail much of the momentum gathered behind Oi! prior to July 1981. Thereafter, major label interest cooled (the first two Oi! compilations had been released by EMI and Decca respectively), gigs became harder to book, and bands previously happy to be associated with Oi! began to distance themselves amidst the ongoing media storm.[43] In the short term, attention turned away from cultivating a movement of working-class punk to repeated disavowals of racism or association with the far right. Blitz, The Business, Infa Riot and The Partisans undertook an 'Oi! Against Racism and Political Extremism But Still Against the System' tour; Bushell penned regular articles for *Sounds* seeking to demonstrate that neither Oi! nor skinhead culture was inherently racist or right-wing; contacts with street-fighting anti-fascist groups on the far left (who later formed Red Action) ensured that the accusations levelled against Oi! did not lead to gigs being targeted for bloody reprisals.[44] Even then, Oi! bands continued to top the independent singles and album charts complied by the British Market Research Bureau.[45]

By late 1983–84, Oi! – and punk more generally – appeared to have run out of steam. Record sales began to fall; street-level (and musical) fashions continued to evolve; the bands split up, changed direction or resigned themselves to playing small-scale gigs to a dwindling audience. Within the skinhead subculture, the question as to its politics led to rancour and division, provoking a crisis of identity that manifested itself in disputes over the true essence of skinhead. The 'sussed' skin, as promoted by fanzines such as *Hard as Nails*, was contrasted with the 'bonehead': a sense of style and recognition of the culture's origins were set against 'tatty' flying jackets, glue-sniffing and far-right politics.[46] Bushell, too, had begun to lose heart by late 1982, writing a provocative article for *Sounds* that suggested punk had become formulaic, ghettoised and fatalistic, losing its way to the libertarian sensibilities of anarchists like Crass that he felt ignored the 'class realities of contemporary British society'.[47] Thereafter, he continued to support bands fuelled by the same sense of working-class anger that he had first recognised in punk, be it the furious anarcho-thrash of Conflict or the soul-inflected agit-pop of The Redskins, before eventually moving away from *Sounds* to become a controversial figure in tabloid journalism. As for Oi!, its influence would gestate, later re-emerging to infuse burgeoning scenes in the USA, Europe and Asia over the 1990s and into the twenty-first century. Back in the early 1980s, however, the 'beat of street' looked set to be buried beneath the din of dissenting voices.

'Looking at us but not talking to us': interpreting Oi! from the outside

Much of the furore that enveloped Oi! was informed by a wider debate rooted in the social and cultural upheavals of the 1950s to 1960s.[48] For the mainstream media, Oi! became another in a series of 'moral panics' linked to the emergence of youth culture as a recognisable component of contemporary society. In other words, it was seen to represent a threat to prevailing societal values and interests as defined by the media and the wider establishment.[49] Simultaneously, it fed into political antagonisms on the left and right of British politics. Initially, both the far left and the far right displayed antipathy towards the rise of teenage consumption and evolving youth cultural styles that helped distinguish the post-war twentieth century. By the late 1960s, however, the growth of a politicised counter-culture and the tendency for popular musicians to engage with political issues led to discussion as to the meaning of specific (youth) cultural forms and their use as a medium for social and political change. This took place across an intersecting political and academic terrain that comprised the varied contours of the new left, the CCCS and, eventually, the Communist Party of Great Britain (CPGB) and its assorted revolutionary rivals.[50] It also found its way into the music press, the writers for which often registered counter-cultural and/or political backgrounds that informed their understanding of popular music.[51] By the late 1970s, youth culture was recognised as a site of hegemonic struggle – part of a Gramscian 'war of position' that saw activists lay claim to popular music and its associated cultures as a portent for either revolution or reaction. Most successfully, members of the International Socialists (from 1977, the SWP) helped initiate Rock Against Racism (RAR) as a means of reclaiming popular music as a progressive force in the wake of controversial comments on race and fascism by Eric Clapton and David Bowie respectively. This, in turn, combined with the Anti-Nazi League (ANL) to forge a cultural weapon designed to thwart the advance of an NF that was threatening to become the third party of British politics by the mid-1970s.[52]

Simultaneously, the far right itself moved to contest and usurp the left's cultural turn. Initially, this meant providing bookshops, clubs and amenities, but was further complemented by efforts to recruit young working-class members from the football terraces, at gigs and in schools.[53] Unlike the left, which tended to focus its attention on the content and production of youth cultural forms, the far right's approach was applied more in spatial terms; that is, the colonisation of spaces in which young people gathered and lived.[54] Organisations such as the NF and British Movement (BM) fixed their efforts on street-level recruitment and, for a time, met with limited success. In areas where growing youth unemployment, ill-conceived urban redevelopment and notable levels of immigration combined with the wider economic problems facing Britain in the 1970s and early 1980s, as in London's East End, parts of the West Midlands and Yorkshire, so the NF and BM made inroads.[55] Significantly, too, the politicisation of youth culture led to some cultural identities being bound up with an affinity to the NF or BM. In particular, an element within the revived skinhead movement aligned itself to the far right, sometimes out of a distorted sense of nationalism or racial prejudice, sometimes simply as an anti-social provocation designed to intimidate, irritate and affirm a feeling of detachment from mainstream society.[56]

Punk emerged in the midst of all this, its meaning contested by political activists from the left and right. Where eager revolutionary socialists recognised punk as 'a protest against the frustrations and conditions that afflict working-class youth', so some neo-Nazis interpreted punk's use of the swastika as evidence of young people 'becoming more aware of their white identity'.[57] On both sides, punk's sense of opposition suggested it provided a ready pool of disaffection for recruitment and, potentially at least, mobilisation. Indeed, Garry Bushell was in 1977 a young SWP member and among the first to enthuse about punk's being a youthful 'reaction to a society collapsing around them'. The left, he argued, had a responsibility 'to channel that rebellion into a real revolutionary movement'.[58]

Such attention brought conflict. In tandem with the success of RAR, under whose banner numerous punk bands played, so far-right interventions became commonplace at gigs over the course of 1977 to 1984. This, certainly, was the case with prototype Oi! bands such as Sham 69, The Ruts and the Angelic Upstarts, whose working-class ire was coveted by the left while also attracting a notable far-right contingent to their audience.[59] For Sham, it proved to be their undoing. As the band came under pressure to disavow the fascist element amongst its following, playing RAR gigs and condemning the far right, so their London gigs were regularly disrupted by the NF and BM.[60] More generally, however, punk tended to resist overt political affiliation; support for a cause did not necessarily translate into ideological commitment. So, for example, if the Sex Pistols' Johnny Rotten was outspoken in his condemnation of racism and the NF, then he also bemoaned the 'condescending attitude' of 'those hardline lefties' who sought to use punk for their own ends; a refrain oft-repeated by punk bands over the late 1970s.[61]

By 1980, therefore, the political aspirations that the left harboured for punk had failed to transpire. For the left, punk in and of itself was deemed either to have been appropriated by capitalism or transformed into a reactionary musical form through which its listeners' experiences and expectations were reinforced rather than challenged. In particular, punk's social realism was seen only to reaffirm the Sex Pistols' predicted 'no future'.[62] Given such a perspective, the left tended to dismiss Oi!'s protest as overly crude; its emphasis on class rejected as a 'cover' for reactionary attitudes.[63] For the SWP's Joanna Rollo, Oi!'s 'smattering of social awareness' was but part of a more general rhetoric of nationalism and violence that pointed towards Nazism.[64]

Such reasoning was reflected in the music press. Prior to Southall, *NME* writers such as Ian Penman and Chris Bohn had dismissed Oi! in much the same way as elder critics had dismissed punk: as the 'utter pits of rock 'n' roll'; as a celebration of 'empty-headedness and grubbiness'; as a 'caricature of "working-class culture"'.[65] After Southall, attention turned to politics, with the predominant motifs of Oi! being filtered through a cultural lens that served to confirm a hardening critique. Oi!'s class-cultural identity was equated with racism; its patriotism with nationalism; its masculinity with misogyny; its audience with the far right.

As already noted, it is undeniable that Oi! attracted far-right elements into and around it. Both Gary Hodges and Garry Hitchcock of the 4-Skins had been members of the BM in the mid-1970s; sections of Oi!'s audience were affiliated to the far right and ruined many a punk and 2-tone gig proving this to be so; the lead singer of Combat 84, Chris 'Chubby' Henderson, had swapped a Charterhouse education for fascist politics and Stamford Bridge by the late 1970s.[66] Most notoriously, the cover image for 1981's *Strength Thru Oi!* LP turned out to feature Nicky Crane, a fascist skinhead whose place in the BM Leader Guard drew attention to an album title that was generally read as a pun on the Nazi slogan, *Kraft durch Freude*, rather than The Skids' *Strength Through Joy* (1980) release of the previous year.[67] Oi!, too, seemed to revel in a violent image that although relating more to football and youth cultural rivalries nevertheless appeared sinister when seen from beneath the boot of someone like Crane. If, by framing Oi! within a culture of Saturday afternoon and bank holiday punch-ups, Bushell hoped to say 'don't smash other kids and fight them … go and smash the government and destroy Westminster', then he left himself open to criticisms of glorifying violence and pandering to a thuggish image that was often associated with the far right.[68]

But to thereby define Oi! as racist, right-wing or fascist is to offer a partial – if not wholly distorted – reading of its motivations and content. For a start, the far right's own attempts to claim Oi! were resisted by the majority of those involved. This was certainly the case with Bushell, who had previously lent support to RAR, contributed to its magazine, *Temporary Hoarding*, and whose writings made regular reference to 'twisted Nazis', the 'cretinous' BM, the 'fringe crackpots of the far right', and the 'pathetic Nazi elements no-one else wants'.[69] Bushell also refused to cover bands that supported or included card-carrying members of the NF or BM among their ranks, leading to his being physically attacked by the BM at an Angelic Upstarts gig in early 1982 and targeted by *Bulldog* magazine as the 'biggest enemy' of the NF.[70] Indeed, the two bands which formed the template for Oi!, the Angelic Upstarts and Cockney Rejects, could each boast anti-fascist credentials. While the Upstarts were stalwarts of RAR, with a lead singer (Mensi; Thomas Mensforth) whose lyrics and interviews espoused the virtues of the British labour movement and railed against the far right, so the Rejects' anti-politics stance extended to physically confronting members of the BM who sought to cause trouble at their gigs.[71] Just as they dismissed the 'wankers' handing out political leaflets at football matches, so they and their entourage took affirmative action to eject BM troublemakers from a gig at London's Electric Ballroom in 1979. Members of the Rejects and the 4-Skins were also among those who later did battle with a Nazi contingent in Barking, winning the turf war and keeping the BM away from their respective bands.[72]

As for racism, a number of Oi! bands followed the Upstarts' lead in playing anti-racist gigs designed to confirm their opposition to the NF, among them The Business, Criminal Class and Infa Riot. If The Oppressed's Roddy Moreno was responsible for later establishing Skinheads Against Racial Prejudice (SHARP) in Britain, then Garry Johnson had already made his position clear in 1981: 'Oi! ain't about black v white', the 'white working class [have] got more in common with [the] black working class than they have with [the] rich white middle class'.[73] Oi!, after all, claimed a kinship with 2-tone, which itself suffered from far-right interventions provoked by the contradiction inherent in the NF and BM's attempt to claim a subculture whose heritage was informed by ska, reggae and soul. As this suggests, the political affinities within Oi! (and within skinhead culture) were diverse.[74] As well as the Upstarts, those featured on the Oi! compilation albums included the Battersea-based League of Labour Skins choir (singing 'Jerusalem') and the militantly anti-fascist Burial.[75] Bushell himself had left the SWP by 1980, but he remained a 'socialist, a trade unionist, and a patriot' who in the run-up to the 1983 general election insisted that the assault of Thatcherism on British industry and working-class life meant the 'punk and Oi! line is "Kick out the Tories" – Vote Labour'.[76] Johnson, meanwhile, explained his politics this way:

> If it was law [to vote] I'd vote Labour 'cos of its tradition and what it stood for when it was formed – power to the people, defenders of the poor and all that. But it ain't that now, it's not working class. It's a middle-class social club! I'm a Militant at heart. I like their policies of, like, the abolition of the House of Lords and the monarchy, but I don't like their leaders. They ain't working class are they? They might be in Liverpool but not London.[77]

More generally, the majority of bands aligned to Oi! rejected formal politics in all its shape and forms, seeing it as divisive, deceitful and delusional, particularly those organisations on the far left and right that sought power by 'climbing on the backs of the working class'. As Cock Sparrer put it:

Everybody's talking about revolution/ Everybody's talking about smash the
state/ Sounds to me like a final solution/ Right wing left wing, full of hate/
We don't wanna fight/ Because you tell us too/ So watch your back when you
attack/ Cos we might just turn on you ... [78]

Despite the events in Southall, therefore, NF and BM attempts to claim Oi!
as a means to express the 'frustrations of white youths' made limited headway.[79]
Although, as Tim Brown has argued, Oi! cemented the connection between
skinhead and punk to provide a musical form through which skins could
express their ideas, it did not thereby follow that the far right gained control of
its political agenda.[80] For this reason, the NF moved to establish an alternative
in the form of White Noise Records, the forerunner of the Blood & Honour
franchise that later served to distribute neo-Nazi music worldwide. The NF
had already tried to project a racist voice onto punk through the formation of
Rock Against Communism (RAC) in 1978.[81] This had failed to attract more
than a handful of bands, though the NF continued to encourage its members
to attend, disrupt and distribute literature at gigs into the 1980s. By 1982,
the reformation of Skrewdriver – a Blackpool punk band that had nurtured a
skinhead following while playing London gigs in 1977–78 – allowed for the
revitalisation of RAC with a group whose singer, Ian Stuart, openly committed
to the NF. It was from here that an overtly fascist music scene emerged, with
Skrewdriver at the centre of a network of bands that included Brutal Attack,
The Ovaltinees, Die-Hards, and Peter and the Wolf.

To sum up, popular references to Oi! have tended to be filtered through
competing interpretations as to its point and purpose. In other words, meanings have been projected onto Oi! rather than drawn from it. This was most
obvious in the 'moral panic' initiated within the mainstream media, but was
also true of readings framed by the cultural politics of the left and right. Indeed,
the left's understanding of Oi! was partly informed by a gradual realignment in
its relationship with the working class evident from at least the 1960s. If, during
the early 1980s, workers were still seen as the bedrock of industrial struggle,
then the cultural continuities and patterns of life that had typically defined
working-class communities since the nineteenth century were increasingly
regarded as incubators of sexism, racism, homophobia and parochialism. In
effect, the 'white' working class was seen to have become part of the problem
rather than the solution, a bulwark against radical socio-cultural change that
was seemingly embodied in Oi!'s territorialism, masculinity, patriotism and
refusal to adopt the language of progressivism. Simultaneously, such characteristics opened Oi! up to approaches from the far right. These, however, were
blunted by the fact that Oi!'s emphasis on class, locality and lived experience

allowed for convivial as well as contentious modes of interaction to exist within the working-class communities from which it emerged – hence the history of much British youth culture, including skinheads.[82] As a result, the far right's attempts to racially define Oi! were rejected and the NF and BM were forced to develop a distorted variant of a pre-existing youth culture to carve out a cultural space. To quote Cock Sparrer once more:

> We don't wanna be part of no new religion/ we don't need a boot or a switchblade knife/ We don't wanna be part of a political dream/ We just wanna get on living our lives ...[83]

'The East End is all around': Oi!, class and locality

Attempts to apply a political label to Oi! were bound to fail. As a form of street-level punk, Oi! encompassed a range of perspectives that could not be contained within a framework of 'left' and 'right'. That said, it remained a forum for protest and a means by which those typically denied a public voice could engage with the world of which they were part. What gave Oi! a sense of coherency was its overlapping emphases on class, locality and youth.

Broader historical context is important here. The post-war period was characterised by a range of socio-economic developments that combined to challenge existing patterns of British life. Full employment, growing affluence and technological breakthroughs in mass media and production each served to facilitate an age of consumption. This, in turn, was complemented by demographic shifts occasioned by expanding educational provision, immigration, patterns of employment and, to 1960, national service. By the 1970s, however, fault lines were beginning to appear.[84] If talk of 'classlessness' and 'consensus' had always tended to mask tensions bubbling beneath the surface of consumer-based 'prosperity', then these were revealed once inflationary pressures gave way to the industrial unrest, rising living costs and unemployment that have since become totems of the 1970s to 1980s. In response, the political certainties of the post-war period were seemingly undermined, provoking realignments in both Conservative and Labour politics (towards Thatcherism and, eventually, New Labour) and simultaneously providing space for new political formations – often issue or identity-based – to emerge. Economically, British policy moved away from the broadly Keynesian principles that had underpinned the economy from the 1940s towards a monetarist strategy that was extended by the Conservative governments led by Margaret Thatcher following her election in 1979.

The implications of all this would become clear in time. The structural changes ongoing within the British economy – away from industrial production towards the service sector – were accelerated. The power of the trade unions was curtailed via a mixture of legislation and set-piece industrial disputes epitomised by the bitter miners' strike of 1984–85. Large-scale unemployment, which peaked at 3,278,000 (11.9 per cent) in 1984, became a permanent feature of Britain's economic landscape, while old industrial regions fell into a decline from which many have yet to recover.[85] More generally, the collectivist, egalitarian principles of the welfare state were replaced by those of individualism, as the nationalised industries were sold off and the private sector blossomed on the back of cheap credit and government incentive. In the long term, Britain was to emerge rebranded as a financial centre geared towards the interests of the entrepreneur. In the short term, the country was beset by inflation, inner-city riots and intense social conflict as the 'popular authoritarianism' that Stuart Hall recognised as the kernel of Thatcherism buried itself in the national psyche.[86]

Oi!'s 'protest', therefore, was both a reflection of and response to these realignments. It stood opposed to Thatcher's assault on the industrial and cultural cornerstones of British working-class life while simultaneously baulking at the stultifying bureaucracy of Labour social democracy and rarefied identity-politics of the left. Class and locality, rather than formal politics or ideology, served as the prism through which the prevailing concerns of Oi! were viewed and understood. Most obviously, Oi! expressed a class identity that was rooted in the politics of everyday life: in work, the weekend, the community, street and home. This, perhaps, had been best realised on Sham 69's *That's Life* (1978), which provided a twenty-four hour snapshot of a working-class lad who gets up late, argues with his parents, gets sacked from work, wins on the horses, goes to the pub, meets a girl, has a fight, and wakes up with a hangover. It captured, as Paul Morley noted in his review of the album, youth's social and domestic claustrophobia; the sense of someone struggling to control their own life.[87] But numerous Oi! songs focused on similar topics, recounting low-level struggles with authority and the adventure of a night out or an afternoon on the terraces. Oi! songs reverberated with the sound of concrete and steel; they moved through the backstreets to reveal both the empowerment and the tensions inherent in the adoption of a youth cultural style; they described local characters – Jack-the-lads, plastic gangsters, clockwork skinheads – evocative of the environments from which they emerged. Oi! rarely moralised, concentrating instead on the documentation – sometimes serious, sometime humorous – of a life being lived.

At its most effective, Oi! set the drama of a residual working-class culture against the limited prospects afforded by boring jobs, unemployment and impending adulthood. Cock Sparrer, for example, contrasted the fear of boredom with the thrill of 'Runnin' Riot', while Prole's 'Generation Landslide' depicted the amphetamine-fuelled joy of youth being buried beneath the socio-economic dislocations of the early 1980s and the broken promises of the 'swinging sixties'. The Business, too, fused boisterous sing-a-longs with pointed social commentary in a kind of celebratory protest. As for the 4-Skins, their set-list combined dystopian depictions of a society descending into chaos with blunt affirmations of defiance mediated through a hyper-working-class skinhead identity.[88]

In political terms, Oi! concentrated its ire on those socio-economic and establishment forces that served to limit or encroach upon working-class life. The police, government officials and would-be politicians were berated, while overt class warfare was declared in songs such as The Cockney Rejects' 'Hate of the City', The Business's 'Sabotage the Hunt', Garry Johnson's 'Land of Hope and Glory' and The Exploited's 'Class War'. The lack of a job or a perceivable future was, perhaps, the most recurrent theme of Oi! A barrage of songs were directed against a Tory government accused of trying to 'kill the spirit of the working-class man', most of which demanded work or some kind of future vision be provided for the young unemployed.[89] Indeed, the ennui of unemployment was typically presented as the fuse-wire of the violence depicted in Oi!'s lyrics and the primary cause of the riots that broke out across Britain's cities in the summer of 1981. In the lexicon of Oi!, working-class youth were 'human hand-grenades'; the clockwork orange made flesh; a ticking time-bomb ready to explode.[90]

Not that formal politics was seen as a solution. Most of those involved with Oi! had come of age under the besieged Wilson–Callaghan governments of 1974–79, an experience more likely to have led to disillusionment than incipient support for Labour. 'We say bollocks to all politics, left, right, centre', said The Business's Micky Fitz, 'cos in practice it's always the working class who pay for the politicians' power games'. 'We've got nothing to do with [politics]', echoed the 4-Skins' original bassist, Steve Harmer, 'there's nothing worth voting for. They're all the same.'[91] There remained some affinity with grass-roots trade unionism, as evidenced in the Angelic Upstarts' paeans to the miners' strikes of the 1970s or The Business's exposé of the 'National Insurance Blacklist' wielded by construction industry employers to keep out militants.[92] But the left more generally was portrayed as a haven for middle-class liberals; students, teachers and social workers claiming to speak *for* the working class.[93] Put most succinctly by The Business via Garry Johnson's lyrics, the left was seen to comprise 'suburban rebels', 'middle-class kiddies from public school' who played at revolution but knew little of the inequities against which they campaigned.[94] This, in turn, fed into Oi!'s suspicion of organisations such as RAR. Where 2-tone was recognised as an organic, cross-cultural expression of racial unity focused on youth cultural style and the depiction of life in the 'concrete jungle', so RAR was dismissed as an organisation run by 'extremists' who 'didn't seem to be in touch with ordinary people'.[95] We should note, too, that such suspicions were also expressed by those involved in 2-tone, as with Pauline Black of The Selector's fear of being 'sucked into this sloganizing for whatever left-wing party [and] pandering to middle-class liberalism'.[96]

Oi!'s derision of the left no doubt contributed to the antipathy that fed the other way. The SWP's Right to Work campaign never replied to Lol Pryor's offer to arrange a benefit gig; a meeting between the Oi! Organising Committee and RAR in the wake of Southall did not convince the latter to lend its banner to any of the bands that played the Hambrough Tavern.[97] Equally, the forthright patriotism of most Oi! bands led its critics to reassert their ac-cusations of far-right sympathies. By the late 1970s, many on the left saw the Union Jack as synonymous with the NF; expressions of patriotism were read as covert racism or a nod to either fascism or British imperialism.[98] Integral to Oi!, however, was the interconnection of class and place: a sense by which identity was forged, in part at least, within the landscape that a person lived and worked.[99] As this suggests, Oi!'s patriotism was mediated through the socio-economic and political crises afflicting Britain in the 1970s to 1980s, which in turn were related to the experience of an increasingly beleaguered working class. Like punk in 1976–77, Oi! bands responded to the sense of decline that hung over Britain in the 1970s and early 1980s, embodying and reflecting back the fears of a media and political establishment that framed the nation within a narrative of decline, decay and dereliction.[100] But whereas punk dramatised the crisis, Oi! claimed to speak for the people most affected by it. To take a classic example, Cock Sparrer's description of a nation's pride being symbolised in 'the dirty water on the river' evoked the changing landscape of their east London roots, wherein the dockyards were closing and the old working-class communities were being dispersed. 'No one can take away our memory', they sang, 'England belongs to me'.[101]

Not dissimilarly, Oi! bands tended to present their patriotism as a chal-lenge to both the establishment's and the NF's claims on national symbolism. The Union Jack was 'our flag', Bushell insisted, 'not the rich's ... [it's] our work that makes them wealthy, our suffering [that] lines the fat scum pockets'.[102] If the ghost of the British 'Tommy' often found his way into Oi! songs, then he did so as a signifier of working-class sacrifice: a 'dead hero' sent to defend his country at the bequest of a ruling class far from the field of battle.[103] More positively, The Angelic Upstarts' 'England' was an ode to those who fought fascism in the Second World War, prefaced with a poem that asked: 'don't cross my love with views of hate and forget what those thousands died for'. For Mensi, being English and playing anti-racist gigs complemented each other.[104]

That a sense of national pride could bleed into jingoism and racism was recognised. Bushell, at least, argued that patriotism on its own was an ideological cul-de-sac. 'What happens when you're threatened with expulsion from school or the sack from work', he asked, 'you can't just wave a Union Jack, you've got to have more to say than that'.[105] Similarly, Oi!'s patriotic claims ran parallel to the sort of heroic-masculine tendencies that typically underpinned the hard right. But the prevailing sentiment that comes through in the songs and interviews around Oi! was that of a refusal to apologise or feel ashamed of either who you were or where you came from: that is to be English/British and working-class.[106]

Such affinities also worked at a local level. Bands built up local followings (Poplar Boys, Tucker's Ruckers, football mobs and other nameless groups of mates), with gigs serving as a meeting point that provided a good night out while emphasising the fact that those on stage were an extension of the audience. Local references ('the 69 bus down to Canning Town'), acknowledgements and photos of the bands' entourage and audience were a typical component of Oi! records. In such a way, locality served as a focus for working-class identification within Oi!, providing social connections that actually and symbolically affirmed common interests, experiences and concerns.

That said, such localised loyalties were sometimes a source of tension. Though the association of class identity with locality provided a sense of belonging and community, it also lay down a territorial claim that was exclusive as well as inclusive. Oi!'s 'voice', too, was primarily London-centric, suggesting its conception of both class and place was often rooted in the capital's traditional working-class communities. So, for example, the Cockney Rejects' adoption of football and the East End as symbols of class-cultural identity won them support from West Ham's notorious Inter-City Firm while simultaneously drawing the wrath of rival football fans in and outside of London. As a result, the band's gigs sometimes descended into territorial violence, as on 6 June 1980 at Birmingham's Cedar Club.[107] And although Oi! bands recognised the lesson of keeping football 'out of it', associated trouble would occasionally blight gigs thereafter.[108] By the same token, the Oi! Organising Committee's objective of 'pro-youth cult unity' was undermined by bands such as The Last Resort or The Exploited placing their respective skinhead and punk identities against those of soul boys and mods to rather grim effect.[109]

UNIVERSITY OF WINCHESTER
LIBRARY

Ultimately, Oi! was an expression of youthful, working-class revolt. In the context of the early 1980s, this tended to revolve around 'keeping what you've got, holding onto what you've gained, because if Thatcher had her way, we'd lose it all.'[110] As a result, Oi! had a defensive nature to it; its worldview combined a fatalistic vision of a deteriorating present with a commitment to fight back and salvage the class-cultural signifiers deemed to give life a sense of purpose and excitement. Like punk, it was anti-social; its proponents saw themselves outside of society and refused entry into it. Simultaneously, Oi! aspired to retain the basic principles of the original skinhead subculture: 'being proud of your working-class heritage, being clean and tidy, and having a respect for people around you.'[111] It was, therefore, class-orientated and localised; it was based on group loyalties forged amongst its immediate milieu; it communicated via a sense of style, class and common reference points located within a residual working-class culture.

Conclusion

Oi! was far closer to what its adherents claimed it to be than it was to what its critics accused it of being. That is, Oi! provided a cultural form that gave voice to the experiences of a particular milieu of British working-class youth in a period of socio-economic and political change. Such a milieu was primarily, but not exclusively, white, male and working-class. Though typically associated with punks and skinheads, Oi! drew from a wider range of cultural resources that both predated and followed on from punk. It referred back to the irreverent and bawdy comedy of the musical hall; to the sense of style and attitude of 1960s mod and skinhead culture; to the territorial pride of the terrace and the street corner. By 1980, it related closely to the 'new mod' and 2-tone scenes that had evolved out of punk's scrambling of pop history. In class terms, it was imbued with a collective sensibility of mutual defence and support that fed into a localised culture based around football, pubs, clubs, shops, clothes and streets.

With regard to politics, Oi! encompassed a range of opinion. Many of those involved came from traditional Labour and trade union families, born into the close-knit working-class communities that formed an integral part of Britain's labour tradition. Simultaneously, an affinity to class and locality allowed for a conservatism resistant to – or suspicious of – aspects of cultural and social change. Indeed, such a reconciliation of progressive and conservative perspectives had proven essential to the Labour Party's rise over the twentieth century, before the ongoing processes of socio-economic and cultural development served to strain such a balance from at least the 1960s.[112] Partly as a result of this, the far right did make inroads into Oi!'s core audience, serving to divide the scene and reaffirm certain stereotypes perpetuated in the media. But the emergence of 'white power' music was in many ways a product of Oi!'s resistance to organised politics of any stripe, left or right. As for racism, Oi! bands tended to reject such accusations but acknowledged that racial conflict existed within the communities of which they were part. The Oi! 'debate' of January 1981 recognised tensions between black and white youth as a by-product of socio-economic forces, a diversion that prevented working-class youths from uniting against the 'real enemy'.[113] Cuts and unemployment, Bushell argued, were 'the two main evils facing the British working class, regardless of creed or colour, and evils which make the fringe crackpots of the ultra-right look as insignificant as they undoubtedly are'.[114]

For the historian, Oi!'s significance rests on its providing insight into socio-economic, political and cultural trends beyond the remit of youth culture. First, those associated with Oi! communicated a very real sense of disengagement from politics in general and mainstream politics in particular.[115] In other words, Oi! expressed a form of anti-politics that opened the way for contact with organisations on the political fringe but more typically led to an expression of class-cultural identity rooted in the local community. In seeking to make sense of Oi!'s politics, Bushell recognised in it the 'seeds of a Clockwork Orange future', whereby anger and resentment could lead to 'volatile violent nihilism'. In effect, therefore, Oi! was an attempt to refocus the frustrations of working-class youth away from the 'demagogues' and towards more 'purposeful rebellion' – hence its early conferences and commitment to playing benefits and celebrating the culture from which it evolved. If politics no longer offered a solution to 'social injustice', then it was up to the young working class to find their own.[116] 'Sod the system', Garry Johnson argued, 'gotta rise above it'.[117]

Second, then, Oi! revealed some of the anxieties and concerns of a section of working-class youth at a time of rising unemployment and continuing socio-economic change. Not only were traditional working-class industries in decline, slowly giving way to service sector and, by the early 1980s, IT-focused jobs, but the shift to monetarism ensured that unemployment became a permanent and deep-rooted problem in British society.[118] Add to this cuts in public spending, and songs such as the 4-Skins' 'Bread or Blood', which evoked the East Anglian peasant revolt of 1816 to forewarn a return to the stark poverty and social inequalities of the early nineteenth century, captured the sense of unease that ushered in the 1980s for many British youths. Punk, after all, had been the first post-war youth culture to form in a period of economic depression rather than one of steadily rising living standards. By 1980–81, Johnny

Rotten's prophecies of 'no future' and 'anarchy in the UK' were even more resonant than in 1976–77.

Third, and related to both the above points, Oi! demonstrated the way by which class identities were forged out of culture and community just as much as in the workplace. Oi! bands recognised themselves as working-class, but did so primarily on account of their family backgrounds, locality and cultural choices. This, too, was an evolving process, with boundaries flexible enough to adapt to wider changes in society. Particular forms of pop music and sartorial style became emblems of working-class youth culture from the 1950s onwards. Oi! was thereby a street-level expression of working-class punk, but its protagonists were often equally enthused by a cultural lineage that took in ska, soul and reggae as well as punk's rockier precedents (Small Faces, Slade, etc.).[119] This, in turn, allowed racial boundaries to be crossed and therefore inform a generational shift in the construction of class identity. Almost paradoxically, it may be argued that in those areas of society where racial tensions were at their most acute, so the processes of interaction and integration were also most able to advance.

Finally, the way in which Oi! and its adherents were castigated in the media forms an early example of what has recently been labelled the 'demonisation' of the working class.[120] There had, of course, always been cultural snobbery and political opposition directed against working-class people. But the shifting political contours of the 1960s and 1970s led to two new offensives being opened up: one in terms of breaking the collective identity of the working class and its organisational resistance to the tenets of the 'new right'; the other through a reading of cultural-political struggles that cut across – or eclipsed – questions of class inequality. Initially, at least, punk's *threat* had stemmed in large part from the Sex Pistols' working-class belligerence and irreverence. The Pistols were depicted as 'foul-mouthed yobs'; it was Steve Jones, very much an Oi!-prototype, who sparked the moral panic that lifted punk out of the music press and into the wider public consciousness by swearing on live television. Any tendency to see in punk the seeds of working-class revolt soon gave way once the young tearaways 'having a laugh and having a say' refused to articulate a suitably prescribed script. For this reason, perhaps, Oi! – like the football hooligans and 'dead-end yobs' it spoke to – has resisted assimilation into the 'respectable' narrative that now binds punk more generally into the nation's cultural fabric.

Acknowledgements

Matthew Worley, 'Oi! Oi! Oi!: Class, Locality and British Punk', *Twentieth Century British History*, 24:4 (2013), 606–36, by permission of Oxford University Press. Research for this article forms part of the Leverhulme Trust funded project 'Punk, politics and British youth culture, 1975–85'. Many thanks to Iain Aitch, Angela Bartie, Tim Brown, Garry Bushell, Kev Clark, Jon Garland, Keith Gildart, Tom McCourt, Ray Morlham, Gary O'Shea, Andrew Perchard, Lol Prior, Lucy Robinson, Andrew Smith, John Street, Paul Stott, Toast, Coleen Weedon, Tim Wells and David Wilkinson for their help and insight.

Notes

1 John Lydon, quoted in C. Coon, 'Public Image', *Sounds* (22 July 1978), pp. 14–15.

2 G. Johnson, *The Story of Oi!: A View from the Dead End of the Street* (Manchester: Babylon Books, 1982), p. 16 (reissued by New Breed Book, Romford, 2008, p. 63).

3 G. Bushell, Sleevenotes, *Oi! The Album*, EMI, 1980; G. Bushell, 'Oi! – The Column', *Sounds* (17 January 1981), p. 11; G. Bushell, 'The New Breed', *Sounds* (1 November 1980), pp. 32–3.

4 G. Bushell, 'Oi! – The Debate', *Sounds* (24 January 1981), pp. 30–1.

5 D. Renton, *When We Touched the Sky: The Anti-Nazi League, 1977–81* (London: New Clarion Press, 2006), pp. 136–55.

6 See, for example, 'Terror in Southall', *Daily Mail* (4 July 1981), p. 1; 'Race Riots', *Daily Mirror* (4 July 1981), p. 1; 'Firebomb Rampage', *Daily Express* (4 July 1981), p. 1; 'Race Fury', *The Sun* (4 July 1981),p. 1; 'Blood On Our Streets', *News of the World* (5 July 1981), p. 1. The Southall riot, which coincided with disturbances in Liverpool and followed incidents in Brixton and Coventry, helped pave the way for a prolonged period of inner-city rioting over the summer of 1981.

7 P. Donovan and P. Evans, 'Exposed: The Racist Thug on the Cover of this Evil Record', *Daily Mail* (10 July 1981), p. 3; M. Duffy, 'Playing with Fire – And Other Skin Problems'; L. Hodges, 'Racists Recruit Youth Through Rock Music', *The Times* (3 August 1981), p. 3; S. Kinnersley, 'The Skinhead Bible of Hate from an Establishment Stable', *Daily Mail* (9 July 1981), pp. 18–19; N. Spencer 'Oi! – The Disgrace', *NME* (11 July 1981), pp. 4–5; and J. Rollo, 'Sounds Familiar', *Socialist Worker* (18 July 1981), p. 4.

8 See, for its quick dismissal, J. Savage, *England's Dreaming: Sex Pistols and Punk Rock* (London: Faber & Faber, 1991), p. 584; also C. Heylin, *Babylon's Burning: From Punk to Grunge* (London: Viking, 2007), p. 462; D. Laing, *One Chord Wonders: Power and Meaning in Punk Rock* (Milton Keynes: Open University Press), p. 112. For Oi! and 'white noise', see T. S. Brown, 'Subcultures, Pop Music and Politics: Skinheads and "Nazi Rock" in England and Germany', *Journal of Social History*, 38:1 (2004), 157–78; J. M. Cotter, 'Sounds of Hate: White Power Rock and Roll and

the Neo-Nazi Skinhead Subculture', *Terrorism and Political Violence*, 11:2 (1999), 111–40; N. Lowles and S. Silver (eds), *White Noise: Inside the International Nazi Skinhead Scene* (London: Searchlight, 1998).

9 See, for example, M. Bracewell, *England is Mine: Pop Life in Albion from Wilde to Goldie* (London: Flamingo, 1998), p. 95; D. Haslam, *Young Hearts Run Free: The Real Story of the 1970s* (London: Harper Perennial, 2007), p. 234; P. Long, *The History of the NME* (London: Portico, 2011), p. 146; G. Marcus, *In the Fascist Bathroom: Writings on Punk, 1977–92* (London: Viking, 1993), pp. 187–9; A. Smith, *No Such Thing as Society: A History of Britain in the 1980s* (London: Constable, 2011), p. 177.

10 Skinheads neither invented nor were the sole exponents of racial violence; nor, of course, were – or are – all skinheads racist. For a balanced overview of the skinhead subculture, see G. Marshall, *Skinhead Nation* (Dunoon: ST Publishing, 1996). The association of skinheads with 'paki bashing' was in part fuelled by the media, the BBC documentary 'What's the Truth about Hell's Angels and Skinheads', broadcast in 1969, and the *Skinhead* novellas by Richard Allen. But to thereby align racism with skinhead culture is far too simplistic. See, for a pre-history, G. Pearson, '"Paki-Bashing" in a North East Lancashire Cotton Town: A Case History of its History', in G. Mungham and G.Pearson (eds), *Working Class Culture* (London: Routledge, 1972), pp. 48–81.

11 Such an argument was best expressed in J. Clarke, S. Hall, T. Jefferson and B. Roberts, 'Subcultures, Cultures and Class: A Theoretical Overview', in S. Hall and T. Jefferson (eds), *Resistance Through Rituals: Youth Subcultures in Post-War Britain* (London: Hutchinson & Co., 1976), pp. 9–74. See also P. Cohen, 'Subcultural Conflict and Working Class Community', *Working Class Papers in Cultural Studies*, 2 (1972), 4–51.

12 Approaches within the CCCS could vary, ranging from Paul Willis's ethnographic study of working-class secondary-school pupils (*Learning to Labour: How Working Class Kids Get Working Class Jobs* (London: Gower, 1977)) to Dick Hebdige's semiotic reading of post-war style (*Subculture: The Meaning of Style* (London: Methuen & Co, 1979)).

13 For a good overview of the debate, see P. Hodkinson, 'Youth Cultures: A Critical Outline of Key Debates', in P. Hodkinson and W. Deicke (eds), *Youth Cultures: Scenes, Subcultures and Tribes* (London: Routledge, 2007), pp. 1–22. For criticism of the CCCS from a historical perspective, see D. Fowler, *Youth Culture in Modern Britain, c.1920–c.1970* (Basingstoke: Palgrave Macmillan, 2008.

14 This point is well made in B. Osgerby, *Youth in Britain Since 1945* (Oxford: Blackwell, 1998), pp. 73–4.

15 For youthful disengagement with mainstream politics, see R. Jowell and A. Park, *Young People, Politics and Citizenship: A Disengaged Generation* (London: Citizen Foundation, 1998); G. Parry, G. Moyser, N. Day, *Political Participation and Democracy in Britain* (Cambridge: Cambridge University Press, 1992). For the left and the 'cultural turn', see D. Dworkin, *Cultural Marxism in Post War Britain: History, the New Left and the Origins of Cultural Studies* (Durham, NC: Duke University Press, 1997); M. Kenny, *The First New Left: British Intellectuals After Stalin* (London: Lawrence &

Wishart, 1995); M. Waite, 'Sex 'n' Drugs 'n' Rock 'n' Roll (and Communism) in the 1960s', in G. Andrews, N. Fishman and K. Morgan (eds), *Opening the Books: Essays on the Social and Cultural History of the British Communist Party* (London: Pluto Press, 1995), pp. 210–24. For how this process fed into leftist politics in the 1980s and beyond, see J. Callaghan, *The Far Left in British Politics* (Oxford: Blackwell, 1987); E. Hobsbawm, 'Identity Politics and the Left', *New Left Review*, 1: 217 (1996), 38–47; L. Robinson, *Gay Men and the Left in Post-War Britain: How the Personal got Political* (Manchester: Manchester University Press, 2007); E. Smith and M. Worley (eds), *Against the Grain: The British Far Left, 1956 to the Present* (Manchester: Manchester University Press, 2014).

16 See, for example, D. Cook, 'The British Road to Socialism and the Communist Party', *Marxism Today* (December 1978), p. 371.

17 Quotes from Hobsbawm, 'Identity Politics and the Left', pp. 38–47; *British News* (January 1979), p. 2.

18 J. Clarke, 'Capital and Culture: The Post-war Working Class Revisited', in J. Clarke, C. Critcher and R. Johnson (eds), *Working Class Culture: Studies in History and Theory* (London: Hutchinson, 1980), pp. 238–53.

19 The Gymslips were the most well-known female Oi! band of the period. Much, of course, could and should be written on the gender politics of punk and related youth cultures.

20 C. Coon, 'Punk Rock: Rebels Against the System', *Melody Maker* (7 August 1976), pp. 24–5; C. Coon, 'Rotten to the Core', *Melody Maker* (27 November 1976), pp. 34–5; J. Ingham, 'The Sex Pistols … ', *Sounds* (24 April 1976), pp. 10–11; J. Ingham, 'Welcome to the (?) Rock Special', *Sounds* (9 October 1976), pp. 22–7; N. Spencer, 'Don't Look Over Your Shoulder, the Sex Pistols are Coming', *NME* (21 February 1976), p. 31.

21 T. Parsons, 'Go Johnny Go', *NME* (2 October 1976), p. 29.

22 T. Parsons, Review of *The Clash*, *NME* (9 April 1977), p. 13; M. Perry, 'The Truth', *Sniffin Glue*, 9 (April–May 1977), p. 9.

23 J. Burchill, '1976', *NME* (1 January 1977), pp. 17–20. See also J. Burchill and T. Parsons, *The Boy Looked at Johnny: The Obituary of Rock and Roll* (London: Faber & Faber, 1987, originally published by Pluto, 1978).

24 The most comprehensive and articulate account of punk's emergence remains Savage, *England's Dreaming*, pp. 105–261.

25 See S. Frith, 'The Punk Bohemians', *New Society* (8 March 1978), pp. 535–6; S. Frith and H. Horne, *Art into Pop* (London: Methuen, 1987), pp. 123–61.

26 *Anarchy in the UK*, 1 (1976), 8. 'There is only one criteria: Does it threaten the status quo?'

27 See, for example, the pre-punk t-shirt designed by Malcolm McLaren and Bernie Rhodes, 'You're gonna wake up one morning and *know* what side of the bed you've been lying on', and the second, unissued, edition of the 'Anarchy in the UK' fanzine held in the Jon Savage archive at Liverpool John Moores University. The latter celebrated the 1972 miners' strike.

28 M. Perry, 'The Sex Pistols for Time Out', *Sniffin Glue*, 6 (January 1977), p. 3. For punk's division into avant garde and social realist camps, see S. Frith, *Sound Effects: Youth, Leisure and the Politics of Rock 'n' Roll* (London: Pantheon, 1981), pp. 158–63; D. Laing, 'Interpreting Punk Rock', *Marxism Today* (April 1978), pp. 123–8; Laing, *One Chord Wonders*, pp. 104–5; Savage, *England's Dreaming*, pp. 277–9 and pp. 396–9. See also G. Bushell, 'Night of the Punk Undead', *Sounds* (11 July 1981), pp. 26–7, which placed Oi! in the populist tradition of the Sex Pistols, The Clash, Sham 69 and UK Subs, as opposed to the 'arty school' of bands such as Magazine, Television and Public Image Ltd.

29 For example, 1977–82 saw mod, skinhead and rockabilly revivals, futurism and new romantics, 2-tone, new pop and the varied permutations of post-punk. Much of this is covered in S. Reynolds, *Rip it Up and Start Again: Post Punk, 1978–84* (London: Faber & Faber, 2005).

30 Angelic Upstarts, *Teenage Warning*, Warner Bros, 1979 and *We Gotta Get Out of This Place*, Warner Bros, 1980; Cockney Rejects, *Greatest Hits Vol. 1*, EMI. 1980 and *Greatest Hits Vol. 2*, EMI, 1980; Cock Sparrer, *The Decca Years*, Captain Oi!, 2006 (compilation); Menace, *GLC*, Captain Oi!, 1994 (compilation); Sham 69, *Tell Us the Truth*, Polydor, 1978 and *That's Life*, Polydor, 1978.

31 R. Gurr, 'Runnin' Riot Wiv the Sparrer', *NME* (4 February 1978), p. 18. See also Cock Sparrer advert in *NME* (26 November 1977), p. 46: 'football hooligans, skinheads & clockwork orange lookalikes all welcome'.

32 The quotes come from a singles review of the Angelic Upstarts' 'Out of Control', in *Sounds* (19 January 1980). See also G. Bushell, 'Harder than the Rest', *Sounds* (8 March 1980), pp. 32–4; G. Bushell. 'The Angelic Upstarts are all Washed Up', *Sounds* (3 May 1980), pp. 21–2 and 50.

33 G. Bushell, *Hoolies: True Stories of Britain's Biggest Street Battles* (London: John Blake, 2010), p. 156.

34 G. Marshall, *Spirit of '69: A Skinhead Bible* (Dunoon: ST Publishing, 1991); Osgerby, *Youth in Britain*, pp. 64–81; Bushell, *Hoolies*, Chapter 3. See also Brown, 'Subcultures, Pop Music and Politics', 157–60.

35 Oi! often referred back to variety and musical hall performers (Jimmy Wheeler, Max Miller, Billy Cotton, Flanagan and Allen), many of whom had used the phrase in one way or another. The music hall and variety side of Oi! was given expression in the form 'punk pathetique', a jokey off-shoot of punk that revelled in bawdy humour. See 'Jaws', *Sounds* (12 July 1980), p. 10; G. Bushell, 'Oi! – London Loonies', *Sounds* (31 January 1981), p. 35. The cover of *Carry On Oi!*, Secret Records, 1981, was designed like a saucy seaside postcard, and each of the Oi! albums came with a billing, e.g. 'for your titillation, edification and enjoyment' – that recalled music hall stage announcements. *Oi! Oi! That's Yer Lot*, Secret, 1982 was named after a Jimmy Wheeler catchphrase.

36 G. Bushell, *Dance Craze* (London: Spotlight Publications, 1981).

37 Bushell, 'Oi! – The Debate', pp. 30–1.

38 G. Bushell, 'Carry on Oi!', *Punk's Not Dead*, 1 (1981), p. 30. For the punk resurgence, see I. Glasper, *Burning Britain: The History of UK Punk, 1980–84* (London: Cherry Red, 2004). A glance at the charts, both national and independent, reveals regular incursions by punk bands formed circa 1979–80, such as Anti Pasti, Blitz, The Business, Crass, Conflict, Discharge, The Exploited, Flux of Pink Indians, the 4-Skins, GBH, Peter and the Test Tube Babies, Subhumans and Vice Squad.

39 The six Oi! LPs were *Oi! – The Album*, EMI, 1980; *Strength Thru Oi!*, Decca, 1981; *Carry on Oi!*, Secret, 1981; *Oi! Oi! That's Yer Lot*, Secret, 1982; *Son of Oi!*, Syndicate Records, 1983; *The Oi! of Sex*, Syndicate Records, 1984.

40 Sleevenotes, *The Oi! of Sex* (1984).

41 'G. Bushell', *Hard as Nails*, 4 (1985), pp. 14–15. Pryor was sometimes known as Ron Rouman.

42 G. Bushell, 'Oi! – The Debate', pp. 30–1; Bushell, 'Oi! – The Column', *Sounds* (30 May 1981), p. 14; 'Skunk Rock', *Sounds* (11 July 1981), p. 16. The first debate was part of the 'New Punk Convention', held in Southgate in January 1981; the second 'New Punk Conference' was attended by 57 people and held at London's Conway Hall in July 1981. An All London Oi! Conference was held in May 1981.

43 Paul du Noyer, 'Oi! – The Backlash', *NME* (18 July 1981), pp. 3–5.

44 For Red Action's defence of Oi!, see *Red Action*, 10 (1984), p. 3.

45 The key Oi! records for this period, including 7 inch singles, can be found on the Captain Oi! reissues of 4-Skins, *The Good, The Bad and the 4-Skins*, Secret, 1982; Angelic Upstarts, *Two Million Voices*, EMI, 1981.The Business, *Suburban Rebels*, Secret 1983; Cock Sparrer, *Shock Troops*, Razor, 1983; The Exploited, *Punk's Not Dead*, Secret, 1981; Infa Riot, *Still Out of Order*, Secret, 1982, The Last Resort, *A Way of Life – Skinhead Anthems*, Last Resort, 1982; The Partisans, *The Partisans*, No Future, 1983. See also, Blitz, *Voice of a Generation*, No Future, 1982 and Peter and the Test Tube Babies, *Pissed and Proud*, No Future, 1982. Various other groups were included under the Oi! umbrella and released singles between 1981 and 1984.

46 *Hard as Nails*, 2 (1984), p. 2. See also fanzines such as *Backs Against the Wall, Bovver Boot, Croptop, Skinhead Havoc, Spy-kids, Stand Up and Spit* and *Tell Us The Truth*. The argument reversed was presented most stridently in *Blood and Honour* publications from 1987.

47 G. Bushell, 'Punk is Dead', *Sounds* (4 December 1982), p. 11.

48 For an overview, see Osgerby, *Youth in Britain*, pp. 16–103.

49 S. Cohen, *Folk Devils and Moral Panics: The Creation of the Mods and Rockers* (London: MacGibbon and Kee, 1972).

50 See Waite, 'Sex 'n' Drugs', pp. 213–16; S. Woodbridge, 'Purifying the Nation: Critiques of Cultural Decadence and Decline in British Neo-Fascist Ideology', in J. Gottlieb and T. Linehan (eds), *The Culture of Fascism: Visions of the Far Right in Britain* (London: I. B. Tauris, 2003), pp. 129–44.

51 P. Gorman, *In Their Own Write: Adventures in the Music Press* (London: MPG Books, 2001).

52 D. Widgery, *Beating Time: Riot 'n' Race 'n' Rock 'n' Roll* (London: Chatto & Windus, 1986); I. Goodyer, *Crisis Music: The Cultural Politics of Rock Against Racism* (Manchester: Manchester University Press, 2009).

53 See, for example, D. Holland, 'The National Front – A Youth Wing?', *Spearhead* (June 1977), p. 9; E. Morrison, 'Why the Left is Winning', *Spearhead* (May 1980), pp. 15 and 19.

54 M. Worley, 'Shot By Both Sides: Punk, Politics and the End of "Consensus"', *Contemporary British History*, 26:3 (2012), 333–54.

55 M. Walker, *The National Front* (London: Fontana, 1978 edn); N. Fielding, *The National Front* (London: Routledge, 1981); R. Hill and A. Bell, *The Other Face of Terror: Inside Europe's Neo-Nazi Network* (Glasgow: Grafton, 1988).

56 I. Walker, 'Skinheads: The Cult of Trouble' (1980) and P. Harrison, 'A Quiet Day at the Match' (1979), in P. Barker (ed), *The Other Britain: A New Society Collection* (London: Routledge & Kegan Paul, 1982), pp. 7–17 and pp. 227–38. See also comments by Madness about NF skinheads in D. Pearson, 'Nice Band Shame About the Fans', *NME* (24 November 1979), pp. 6–8.

57 A. Wall, 'Punk', *Comment* (5 March 1977), pp. 72–4; A. Critic, 'Rock and Reich', *British Patriot* (January–February, 1977), pp. 3–4.

58 G. Bushell, 'Sex Pistols: Whose Finger on the Trigger?', *Socialist Worker* (18 December 1976), p. 11.

59 Alan Weatherley on the Angelic Upstarts, in *Red Rebel* (January–February 1979), p. 5; J. Ross, 'If the Kids are United: The Giro Generation Fights Back', *Socialist Worker* (12 August 1978), p. 5; 'Youth Unite at Upstarts Gig', *Young Socialist* (19 August 1978), pp. 6–7. See also references to Sham 69 in *Challenge*, especially April–May 1978, p. 7.

60 The culmination of this was the BM's violent disruption of Sham's 'Last Stand' at the Rainbow Theatre in London in July 1979. See 'Nazi Nurds Wreck Sham's Last Stand', *Sounds* (4 August 1979), p. 10.

61 *Temporary Hoarding*, 2 (1977); C. Salewicz, 'Johnny's Immaculate Conception', *NME* (23 December 1978), pp. 21–4; P. Morley, 'Chaos and Concern', *NME* (22 July 1978), pp. 7–8; P. Du Noyer, 'Taking Tyne-Age Wasteland', *NME* (21 April 1979), p. 25; S. Clarke, 'The Rise of The Ruts', *NME* (14 July 1979), pp. 7–8.

62 For leftist critiques of Oi! and its punk precedents, see S. Frith, 'Post-Punk Blues', *Marxism Today* (March 1983), pp. 18–21; N. Halifax, 'Second Wave', *Socialist Review* (April 1982), p. 35; M. Lynn, 'Music and Politics', *Challenge* (December 1979), p. 7; L. Toothpaste and T. Allcock, 'The Sham in Sham 69', *Socialist Worker* (25 November 1978), p. 10.

63 M. Kohn, 'Hip Little Englanders', *Marxism Today* (November 1983), pp. 37–8. Chris Dean and Steven Wells, two SWP skinheads, critique Oi! in X. Moore [Chris Dean], 'Guerrilla Verses England's Grey Unpleasant Land', *NME* (6 February 1982), pp. 15–16.

64 Rollo, 'Sounds Familiar', p. 4.

65 I. Penman, Review of *Oi! The Album*, *NME* (1 November 1980), p. 41; C. Bohn, Review of *Strength Thru Oi!*, *NME* (20 June 1981), pp. 36–7.

66 For Hitchcock, see G. Bushell, '(Sk)in the Beginning … ', *Sounds* (2 August 1980), p. 27; K. White, '4-Skins Manager Boasted of Being a Thug for Nazis', *The Observer*, 12 July 1981, p. 3. For Hitchcock's continued involvement in far-right politics, see N. Lowles, *White Riot: The Violent Story of Combat 18* (London: Milo, 2001). For Henderson, see 'Skinheads', *Arena*, BBC Documentary, 1982. A few minor right-wing skinhead bands existed in 1980–82, such as The Afflicted, The Elite and Public Enemy.

67 Donovan and Evans 'Exposed', p. 7.

68 Kinnersley, 'The Skinhead Bible', p. 19.

69 Sleevenotes to *Strength Thru Oi!*; 'Nazi Fartsy', *Sounds* (13 December 1980), p. 10; 'Garry: For the Record … ', *Sounds* (25 July 1981), p. 10; G. Bushell, 'Staying Alive', *Sounds* (21 November 1981), pp. 32–3.

70 *Bulldog*, 33 (1983), p. 3; *Bulldog*, 34 (1983), p. 2. The latter included Bushell's address, leading to him and his family being threatened by NF activists. Garry Johnson was also beaten up by fascists in the aftermath of Southall.

71 See, for example, Du Noyer, 'Taking Tyne-Age Wasteland', p. 25. See also Mensi's documentary on the Tyne shipyards for *Play At Home*, Channel 4, 1984.

72 J. Turner, *Cockney Reject* (London: John Blake, 2010), pp. 56–60 and pp. 186–7; 'Fighting in the Streets' from Cockney Rejects, *Greatest Hits Vol. 1* (1980). For Oi! songs that attack the far right, see, see Blitz, 'Propaganda', *Voice of a Generation* (1982); Angelic Upstarts, 'Their Destiny is Coming', *We Gotta Get Out of This Place* (1980); Cock Sparrer, 'Run With the Blind' and 'Price Too High To Pay', on *Runnin' Riot in '84*, Syndicate Records, 1984. The Barking incident was, in part, a reprisal for the BM's attacking a black skinhead in Beacontree.

73 Garry Johnson, 'United', *Carry On Oi!* (1981); Johnson, *The Story of Oi!*, pp. 10–12. For SHARP, see Marshall, *Spirit of '69*, pp. 138–43.

74 Chris Dean of The Redskins made this clear: 'we come from up north where there is a strong left-wing tradition amongst skinheads'. See P. Wellings, 'Scalp Hunter', *Sounds* (14 August 1982), p. 23; Moore, 'Guerrilla Verses England's Grey Unpleasant Land', pp. 15–16.

75 The League of Labour Skins was organised by John McAvoy; as its name suggests, it comprised Labour-supporting skinheads. See also the letter from Paul Cousins of the Poplar Skins to *Socialist Worker* (9 December 1978), p. 9 and the SWP-aligned Redskins (formerly known as No Swastikas): while critical of Oi!, their name was a deliberate attempt to reclaim the skinhead tradition for the left. Alongside The Burial, Red London and Skin Deep were two overtly left-wing skinhead bands to emerge in the early 1980s. From the right, only ABH, a punk band from Lowestoft, featured on any of the six Oi! albums. See 'Rocking the Reds', *Bulldog*, 39 (1984), p. 3.

76 'Garry – For the Record', *Sounds*, 25 July 1981, p. 10; G. Bushell, 'Last (Dis)orders', *Sounds* (4 June 1983), p. 27.

77 G. Bushell, 'The Voices of Britain', *Sounds* (29 January 1983), pp. 22–3.

78 Cock Sparrer, 'Watch Your Backs', words and music by Bruce, Burgess, McFaull and Beaufoy, reproduced by permission of Orange Songs Ltd. 'I Got Your Number', on the same album (*Shock Troops*), makes a similar point. See also 'Manifesto' by the 4-Skins on *The Good, the Bad, and the 4-Skins* (1982).

79 'We are the New Breed', *Bulldog*, 24 (1981), p. 3.

80 Brown, 'Subcultures, Pop Music and Politics', 158.

81 For RAC, see *British News* from September 1978 through 1979; D. Brazil, 'Spittin' Hate at the Future of Rock 'n' Roll', *The Leveller* (October 1979), pp. 18–19; V. Goldman, 'Seeing Red', *Melody Maker* (25 August 1979), p. 9.

82 For a discussion of this, with reference to recent lectures by Paul Gilroy and Stuart Hall, see R. Harris and B. Rampton, 'Ethnicities Without Guarantees: An Empirical Approach', in M. Wetherell (ed.), *Identity in the 21ˢᵗ Century: New Trends in Changing Times* (Basingstoke: Palgrave, 2009), pp. 98–100. See also Osgerby, *Youth in Britain*, pp. 64–9; Hebdige, *Subculture*, pp. 54–9.

83 Cock Sparrer, 'Watch Your Backs'.

84 See, for example, C. Brooker, *The Seventies: Portrait of a Decade* (London: Allen Lane, 1980); D. Sandbrook, *Seasons in the Sun: The Battle for Britain, 1974–79* (London: Allen Lane, 2012); D. Sandbrook, *State of Emergency: The Way We Were: Britain, 1970–74* (London: Penguin, 2011); F. Wheen, *Strange Days Indeed: The Golden Age of Paranoia* (London: Fourth Estate, 2009); P. Whitehead, *The Writing on the Wall: Britain in the Seventies* (London: Michael Joseph, 1985). For interesting reassessments of the period, see L. Black, H. Pemberton and P. Thane (eds), *Reassessing the Seventies*, Manchester: Manchester University Press, 2013; C. Hay, 'Chronicles of a Death Foretold: The Winter of Discontent and Construction of the Crisis of British Keynesian', *Parliamentary Affairs*, 63:3 (2010), 446–70; J. Moran, '"Stand Up and Be Counted": Hughie Green, the 1970s and Popular Memory', *History Workshop Journal*, 70: 1 (2010), 173–98; N. Tiratsoo, '"You've Never Had it so Bad": Britain in the 1970s', in Tiratsoo (ed.), *From Blitz to Blair: A New History of the Britain since the 1970s* (London: Weidenfield & Nicolson, 1997), pp. 163–90.

85 *Labour Market Review* (Basingstoke: Palgrave Macmillan, 2006), pp. 52–4; S. Glynn and A. Booth, *Modern Britain: An Economic and Social History* (London: Routledge, 1996); R. Coopey and N. Woodward (eds), *Britain in the 1970s: The Troubled Economy* (London: UCL Press, 1995).

86 S. Hall, 'The Great Moving Right Show', *Marxism Today* (January 1979), pp. 14–20. For a historical account, see A. Gamble, *The Free Economy and the Strong State: The Politics of Thatcherism* (Basingstoke: Palgrave Macmillan, 1994 edn). For a comprehensive overview, see B. Harrison, *Finding a Role? The United Kingdom, 1970–1990* (Oxford: Oxford University Press, 2010).

87 Sham 69, *That's Life*, Polydor, 1978; Morley, *NME* (4 November 1978), p. 37.

88 Cock Sparrer, 'Runnin' Riot' backed with 'Sister Suzie', Decca, 1977; Prole, 'Generation Landslide', *Son of Oi!* (1983).

89 The quote is from The Last Resort, 'We Rule OK', *A Way of Life* (1982). Hear also, for just a few examples, Angelic Upstarts, 'Two Million Voices' and 'Woman in Disguise';

The Business, 'Work or Riot' and 'Product'; 4-Skins, 'Norman' and 'Seems to Me'; Infa Riot, 'Each Dawn I Die' and 'Riot Riot'; The Partisans, 'No U-Turns'.

90 For example, Bushell, 'The New Breed', pp. 32–3; Angelic Upstarts, 'Teenage Warning' backed with 'The Young Ones', Warner Bros, 1979; Blitz, 'Time Bomb', *Voice of a Generation* (1982).

91 G. Bushell, 'Minding Their Own', *Sounds* (27 February 1982), pp. 18–20; Bushell, 'New Breed', pp. 32–3. See also J. Waller, 'Where Now for Oi!?', *Sounds* (19 September 1981), pp. 24–5.

92 See, for example, the cover of Angelic Upstarts, *We Gotta Get Out of This Place* (1980) and the track 'King Coal'. Also 'Heath's Lament' from *Two Million Voices* (1981) and 'Geordie's Wife' from *Reason Why?*, Anagram, 1983. The Business, 'Harry May' backed with 'Employers' Blacklist, Secret Records, 1981.

93 Johnson, *The Story of Oi!*, p. 10.

94 The Business, 'Suburban Rebels', *Carry on Oi!* (1981); also Cockney Rejects 'On the Waterfront', *Greatest Hits Vol. 2* (1980).

95 Bushell, 'Staying Alive', pp. 32–3; J. Street, *Rebel Rock: The Politics of Popular Music* (Oxford: Blackwell, 1986), pp. 77–8.

96 Quoted in *Big Flame* (April 1981), p. 13. Other punk bands expressed similar concerns. In particular, anarchist bands such as Crass offered stinging critiques of the left. See Worley, 'Shot By Both Sides', 345–6.

97 Kohn, 'Hip Little Englanders', pp. 37–8.

98 For a discussion of left-wing attitudes to patriotism, see R. Samuel (ed.), *Patriotism: The Making and Unmaking of British National Identity* (London: Routledge, 1998. See also 'Racism' in *Temporary Hoarding*, 1 (1977).

99 See, for example, P. Cohen, 'Subcultural Conflict and Working Class Community', in S. Hall, D. Hobson, A. Lowe and P. Willis (eds), *Culture, Media, Language* (London: Routledge, 1980), pp. 78–87; J. Bourke, *Working Class Cultures in Britain, 1890–1960* (London: Routledge, 1994), pp. 170–212.

100 This was captured in such 'state of the nation' texts as R. Clutterbuck, *Britain in Agony: The Growth of Political Violence* (London: Penguin, 1978); S. Haseler, *The Death of British Democracy* (London: Paul Elek, 1976); I. Kramnick, *Is Britain Dying? Perspectives on the Current Crisis* (New York: Ithaca, 1979).

101 Cock Sparrer, 'England Belongs to Me' backed with 'Argy Bargy', Carrere Records, 1982.

102 Sleevenotes to *Strength Thru Oi!*; also Johnson, 'National Service', *Strength Thru Oi!* (1981).

103 For example, Angelic Upstarts, 'Last Night Another Soldier', 4-Skins, 'Remembrance Day', The Samples, 'Dead Hero'.

104 D. McCulloch, 'The Charm of Mensi', *Sounds* (20 June 1981), p. 22. Oi! bands tended to see the Falklands crisis in these terms, as a war against fascism or foreign aggression rather than an exercise in British imperialism. It did not, however, quell Oi!'s rejection of either Thatcherism or the Conservative government. See the comments of

Mensi in G. Bushell, 'Upstate with the Upstarts', *Sounds* (26 June 1982), pp. 16–17. For Bushell and Mensi, the line was 'fascists off the Falklands and Thatcher out'.

105   Bushell, 'Staying Alive', pp. 32–3.

106   The definitive statement is by the 4-Skins, 'Sorry', *Strength Thru Oi!* (1981).

107   G. Bushell, 'Rejects … ', *Sounds* (5 July 1980), pp. 15–16.

108   Bushell, 'The New Breed', pp. 32–3; G. Bushell, 'Let There Be Ruck', *Sounds* (17 January 1981), p. 49.

109   'Oi! Rides Again', *Sounds* (14 August 1982), p. 8; The Last Resort, 'Soul Boys', *Skinhead Anthems* (1982); The Exploited, 'Fuck A Mod', *Army Life* EP, Secret, 1981.

110   Bushell, 'The Voices of Britain', *Sounds* (29 January 1983), pp. 22–3.

111   The quote is by Rob Hingley, an original 1960s skinhead, in Marshall, *Skinhead Nation*, p. 26.

112   For the way in which Labour could encompass a radical-socialist and a popular-patriotic tradition, see M. Pugh, 'The Rise of Labour and the Political Culture of Conservatism', *History*, 87:288 (2002), 514–37. See also, F. Lindop, 'Racism and the Working Class: Strikes in Support of Enoch Powell in 1968', *Labour History Review*, 66:1 (2001), 79–100.

113   See, for a study of racism and the working class, A. Phizacklea and R. Miles, *Labour and Racism* (London: RKP, 1980). Most Oi! and proto-Oi! songs that referred to race urged black and white unity, as with Sham 69's 'Song from the Streets', the Angelic Upstarts' 'Kids on the Street' and 'I Understand', and Garry Johnson's 'United'. The 4-Skins' 'One Law for Them' was more ambivalent, evoking the spectre of Enoch Powell in the context of a song that more broadly depicted Britain's class-ridden society driven to the brink of collapse.

114   'Garry – For the Record', p. 10.

115   This fed into a fluctuating but general trend of declining political identification and voter turnout from the 1950s. See P. Norris, *Electoral Change since 1945* (London: Sage, 1977).

116   Bushell, 'New Breed', pp. 32–3; Bushell, Review of the Angelic Upstarts' *We Gotta Get Out of This Place*, *Sounds* (29 March 1980), p. 31.

117   Garry Johnson, 'Dead End Yobs', on *Strength Thru Oi!*

118   See R. Drewett, J. G. Goddard and N. Spence, 'What's Happening in British Cities?', *Town and Country Planning*, 44 (1976), 14–24 ; R. D. Dennis, 'The Decline of Manufacturing Employment in Greater London', *Urban Studies*, 15 (1978), 63–73; A. Marwick, *British Society Since 1945* (London: Penguin, 1996 edn), pp. 278–324; S. Glynn and A. Booth, *Modern Britain: An Economic and Social History* (London: Routledge, 1996).

119   For an insight into this, see the 4-Skins' Hoxton Tom McCourt's top ten in *Ready to Ruck*, 3 (1981), p. 20, which includes Ben E. King, Iggy and the Stooges, Cock Sparrer, Dusty Springfield, the Four Tops and the Cockney Rejects.

120   O. Jones, *Chavs: The Demonization of the Working Class* (London: Verso, 2011).

3

Playing a-minor in the punk scene? Exploring the articulation of identity by older women punks

LAURA WAY

Punk has retained its presence in the subcultural literature that has flourished since the Birmingham University Centre for Contemporary Cultural Studies (CCCS) was established in the 1960s. But while theoretical shifts away from the assumed link between youth and subcultural participation have drawn attention to ageing within a subculture, there continues to be a notable absence of women in such analysis. To help rectify this, I intend here to utilise research based on qualitative interviewing to consider the experiences of four older punk women. In so doing, it will be argued that women were and continue to be both active and public in their participation in the punk subculture; and that punk continues to form a fundamental part of their respective identities.

The opening chords

My earliest punk memory is whirling around the living room like a demented dervish to 'Rock the Casbah' by The Clash with my security blanket in tow. My childhood was punctuated throughout by music, from The Smiths on school mornings to my dad teaching me Nirvana guitar riffs. Pictures of my dad at seventeen show a gangly youth in bondage trousers, ripped shirts, studded belts and candyfloss hair and as I got older he passed down to me leather belts, studded wristbands and old band t-shirts. By my early teens I had been exposed ıy dose of punk and grunge with many an eighties classic thrown in measure. By age twenty-one, in 2005, I had been playing bass guitar ... ıerground punk band for five years and gigged extensively within the thriving punk scene. At the time of this research I was twenty-three, finding my feet in a second punk band and realising that punk had become far more than just the music I listened to and played.

In many ways, therefore, this chapter stems from my own commitment to punk as a genre of music, as a lifestyle, and as a way of thinking. Coupled with my feminist convictions, I wanted to make known the voices of older women punks who had been largely ignored in the existing academic research on subcultural participation, fandom and ageing. I also saw such research as a means of understanding my own relationship with punk, engaging with the issues that lay ahead of me as I, in turn, became an older punk woman.

Background

There is not the space here to provide an in-depth background history of punk. However, it is necessary to acknowledge what is meant by the term in the current context. For writers such as Dick Hebdige, punk is a subcultural movement expressed predominantly through particular clothes and graphics.[1] For others, 'punk rock' exists primarily as a 'music-based and music-centred phenomenon'.[2] In the work carried out under the auspices of the CCCS, emphasis tended to be placed on groups of youths with shared behaviours, musical tastes and stylistic choices.[3] In the context of working-class dissatisfaction, the CCCS conceptualised punk as a 'spectacular' subculture engaged in 'intentional communication' and obvious fabrication.[4] Punk and similar subcultural groups were viewed predominantly in terms of aesthetics, with style seen to provide a form of resistance to class subordination. In so doing, however, such an emphasis on the 'meaning of style' meant that the musical aspect of the subculture (what was listened to, what records were bought) tended to be neglected. Yet punk arguably remains a predominantly music-based subculture. Its adherents tend to share anti-authoritarian, anarchist and nonconformist beliefs that are complemented by a DIY ethic in terms of music-making, style, activism and so forth.[5] Punks today may not always adopt the shock-style tactics of their earlier counterparts, but they continue to hold fast to ideas and an image that reflects a perceived resistance to mainstream fashion and capitalist production. For all the claims that 'punk is dead', a modern punk underground continues to thrive, with Clark going so far as to suggest that punk faked its own death, shrugging off the assumptions imposed on it by subcultural theorists to embody the anarchism to which it always aspired.[6]

More recently, debate has turned to the suitability of 'subculture' as a recognisable concept, with 'scenes', 'lifestyles', 'proto-communities' and 'neo-tribes' raised as alternative definitions of youth cultural formation.[7] Even then, however, the focus has remained concentrated on 'youth', leaving us to wonder how age affects a person's commitment and affiliation to a particular identity, however defined.

This chapter seeks to engage with such questions by focusing on four women punks from across the UK. The women came from different back-grounds and, while all were born within the space of a decade, they were of different ages. Jett was the oldest woman at forty years of age; she lived with her partner and had a number of children. Cica, thirty-two, was married with a child. Buckfast was married and thirty-three years of age; Abitbatty was thirty-nine and single. Their pseudonyms were self-chosen. While Buckfast, Cica and Jett had 'joined punk' in their teens (at fourteen, fifteen and thirteen years respectively), Abitbatty did not 'find' punk until her thirties. The sample was achieved through utilising existing contacts (band members and music promoters who themselves were older punks) within the scene. A minimum age of thirty was set for the project; to avoid exclusion, no upper age limit was applied, with the term 'older' used to distinguish the thirty-and-above-year-olds from the younger women punks who usually feature in popular accounts and academic research. Crucially, too, all four women self-identified them-selves as punks, so avoiding the imposition of a punk identity.

The interviews covered a range of subjects. For the purpose of this chapter, however, the emphasis is on exploring what punk meant to the women; how they expressed and maintained a punk identity; and how their experiences relate to Andes' concept of a 'punk career'.[8]

Being punk

For Hebdige and the CCCS, 'being punk' entailed engaging in a spectacu-lar visual style that resisted both the parent culture (working-class) and the dominant, hegemonic culture (bourgeois) through the adoption of particular symbols.[9] This could include, for instance, taking everyday objects such as a safety-pin or a bath plug and using them as clothing accessories. Historically, therefore, punk has tended to be associated with a sartorial style, be it 'spec-tacular'[10] or more subtly expressed,[11] that serves as a resistance to conventional modes of dress.[12] Moreover, such resistance may be implicit not only in the clothes punks choose to wear, but in their hairstyles and body modifications (piercings and tattoos).

Recent research, however, suggests that being punk does not merely rely on wearing, say, a studded leather jacket or sporting a Mohican.[13] To this end, I shall briefly outline how our older punk women became involved in punk, before examining how they 'do' punk in relation to three principal areas: music, lifestyle practices, attitude. This chapter concludes by considering my findings alongside academic work on the concept of commitment in subcultures.

How it all began

In terms of becoming involved with punk, three out of the four women had been exposed to punk during their teenage years. This exposure came from going to a punk gig, listening to friends' punk tapes, going to school discos or from being around older people who were interested in punk. All their initial experiences of punk were connected to music:

> I left primary school in 1978 and … it was, a lot of the, you were sort of exposed to it from older people and also things like um, sorta junior discos and stuff. [Jett]

> [At] 15 I went the first time to a punk gig, DOA with Jello Biafra … and, uh, I knew exactly that was my thing. [Cica]

> I was around 14, um, and there was a car park down the road from us which had an abandoned mini in it … and, um, a sorta like couple of lads that I was knocking around with that were into skateboarding and stuff and they brought a couple of tapes down to the car park. [Buckfast]

Somewhat differently, Abitbatty came to punk later in life through her involvement in the rockabilly/psychobilly music scene. She was 'too young to be an original punk', but was eventually attracted both by the music and what she described as a 'total feeling of freedom'. Indeed, all of the women spoke of a freedom they saw as inherent within punk. For Cica, punk gave her an opportunity to express herself, while Jett said it was the sense of being different that attracted her to punk.

Contrary, then, to the suggestion made in previous literature that older women's relationship to punk becomes a somewhat private affair,[14] going to gigs and watching bands was of the utmost importance to all four women. According to Buckfast, 'gigs and … pubs is basically what me and my other half do'. Abitbatty even admitted that she went a 'bit stir crazy' if she did not get to see a live band every week, while travelling to gigs and participating in punk festivals such as Rebellion were also noted.[15] Crucially, perhaps, going to a gig was not just about watching a band, but about being able to find opportunities to meet new people and share ideas. For Cica, gigs enabled her to 'exchange news or exchange new thoughts … new views', while another participant spoke of getting involved in the rough pits in front of the stage. As this suggests, both music and a sense of community were important to our older women punks, echoing the findings of research into ageing within other subcultures.[16]

Lifestyle practices

As noted, previous research on punk – including women punks – has placed much emphasis on style.[17] The CCCS certainly regarded clothing as an important means of showing subcultural belonging. Interestingly, however, our punk women sometimes disputed that there was a link between the clothes they wore and the punk identity they assumed. Cica saw clothes as a means of 'expression', but went on to say that 'punk is more in your mind'. Whether this was a contradiction in itself or whether Cica was commenting on how dress can be a secondary rather than a primary form of expression was unclear. Far more specific were Cica's feelings towards the acquisition of clothes: 'It doesn't matter if it's the jacket, you know, I did it on my own … it's not bought, you know, for a hundred and twenty quid'. Cica did not follow disposable fashion; she did not 'spend any money for clothes at all', let alone 'punky looking ones'. In so saying, Cica resisted punk's commodification and reaffirmed her conviction that punk was more a state of mind: a punk identity was not something to be bought; wearing 'punky' clothes did not make someone a punk.[18]

For Buckfast and Jett, the way they dressed and the relationship between clothes and punk had changed over time. Jett acknowledged having 'done' all the classic punk styles: 'I've been through the, like I've had the Mohawk, had the Siouxsie and the Banshees hair, you know and, er, the … sorta gothic look, the bondage trousers … I've done the lot basically.' Not dissimilarly, Buckfast acknowledged changing her dress style, though she did not see her earlier years as characterised by a classic punk style: 'I think the punk I was when I was younger was mixed up, it wasn't what anyone would call, I mean, visually it wasn't what anyone would say was the classic style.' Jett described what she wore now as 'either tight, like, skin-tight trousers or combats and baggy, you know, the sorta baggier jeans and leather jacket, t-shirt.'

As photos provided by the interviewees made clear, all four women displayed recognisable elements of punk style, either in terms of haircut or clothing. Certainly, all four would have been viewed by a lay audience as 'alternative', in the sense they did not adopt mainstream fashions or appearance. If their 'punkness' was internalised, then style evidently still held a significance for the women.

More problematic was the relationship between employment and sub-cultural affiliation. While Buckfast acknowledged having to keep an eye on her choice of outfits for work, Abitbatty was the only woman to completely avoid a punk style for work: 'unfortunately I'm not one of these punks that can be, um, punky all the time if you like, I've got a proper job and have to wear a suit'. Though her hair is dyed a red hue, Abitbatty necessarily hid her undercut style at work. As this suggests, style formed only a part of her 'punkness'. But like Bennett's older male punks, who refined their image while keeping some essence of their original punk style, even Abitbatty retained a visual distinctive-ness via her hair colour if nothing else.

In terms of appearance and femininity, Holland's work on alternative women, femininity and ageing has helped fill something of the academic void noted by Schilt and Giffort.[19] In particular, her chapter 'Defying the Crone' ex-plored how her interviewees began 'toning down' their image as they got older, a process most thought to be involuntary.[20] Significantly, however, most of Holland's interviewees felt they remained the same person as they had always been (i.e. an 'alternative woman'), despite their visible changes in style.[21]

Such sense of accommodation was evident among the older punk women too. Buckfast noted that she had refused to compromise her look when younger, but that 'as you get older you kinda realise that you kinda do'. This she linked to having to work, pay the rent and the bills. Abitbatty's relatively late entry into punk meant her situation was somewhat different, and we have already seen how she toned down her image for work. In many ways, however, such accommodation reaffirms the extent to which punk for these women was not just a fashion, but an ideology for living life. That said, a certain resentment at having to compromise was clear. Talking about the younger punks she saw at gigs, Abitbatty admitted to being 'jealous that they have nice brightly coloured hair and … I think I wish I could have mine like that'. The choice of dressing to shock was seen to have been left behind with the ageing process.

Linked to this, perhaps, is the extent to which women can feel expecta-tions about their appearance during different times of their lives. Abitbatty's comment that she wore 'skirts that are too short for my age' all but acknowl-edged that short skirts were more the preserve of a younger generation. In so doing, Abitbatty defied Holland's crone: she recognised the dress expectations of an ageing woman and ignored them.

But Holland also found a second contradiction in the way that 'alternative women' spoke of their increased self-confidence at the same time as they hinted at regretting their loss of youth. Buckfast, in particular, spoke extensively on the subject, accepting that her punk look had 'kinda disappeared but um ... still there on a Saturday night sometimes'. In reference to my own age at the time (twenty-three), Buckfast spoke wistfully of time past: 'it gets worse in ten years' time [laughter] twenty-three was, uh, I think the best time for me'. It was 'amazing how much you try and hold on to it', she continued, 'amazing how much you drift when you get older'.

Attitudes

Punk ideology is often viewed as highly individualistic and anti-authoritarian. In terms of attitude, a strong sense of individualism was expressed by all four of the women interviewed. Cica observed that 'I do what I wanna do', 'I do my own stuff' and 'punk is for me, just be myself'. Abitbatty said that for her punk was 'partly the music that I like, partly I guess the way I dress, um, but probably not conforming to what everybody wants me to be, just trying to be myself.' Similarly, when asked what it was about herself that made her a punk, Jett answered: 'I think it's because I don't want to follow what everyone else does, I never have, I never will ... I've always seen myself as a bit of an outsider, not in a nasty way but, you know, a nice way. I just don't want to be like everybody else.'

Both Buckfast and Jett mentioned the term 'outsider' or 'outcast' in the course of their interviews. For them, punk was something alternative to the mainstream; something other than following 'the crowd'. It offered an alternative to a culture which people felt they did not fit into. Or, as Jett put it, 'it's up to me how I want to ... dress or whatever, what music I want to listen to'. For Buckfast, it was 'the way I'm just me'.

In the same way that Holland's interviewees expressed disapproval of women engaged in traditional femininities that they saw as inappropriate at their age, the women I interviewed were happy to voice their opinions of their own reference group.[22] Abitbatty regarded a lot of women her own age as being 'stuck in a rut'; their getting married and starting a family was contrasted with the feeling of freedom that she herself had found through punk. In the same breath, Abitbatty, who herself was single and had no children, admitted that she did not 'know many single women who've not been married that are my age to be honest ... not had kids'. In other words, she sensed that she did not fit in with other women her age, but simultaneously felt she had good reasons for not wanting to. This, however, was not a sentiment shared by all four women interviewed. Both Cica and Jett had families, and both spoke positively about this.

There was general agreement as to punk's providing what Abitbatty described as an 'alternative lifestyle' and an 'attitude'. For Cica, punk was a 'life attitude' and an 'ideology'. Jett, meanwhile, saw punk as imbued with certain ethics, particularly do-it-yourself. According to Buckfast, punk was an 'an attitude; it's a way of life, it's a way of thinking, an outlook on life that I think's different from other people's.' Punk, therefore, was understood as a community of people following a particular way of life. And yet, such a sense of community appears – ostensibly at least – to contradict the individualism that all the women interviewed claimed to feel. How do we explain this?

Commitment and the 'punk career'

Commitment, in the context of a subculture, is here taken to refer to the depth and degree of a member's participation. For our purposes, it is applied in relation to the notion of 'being punk' and Andes' concept of a 'punk career'. Indeed, Andes argues that commitment is a process that varies over time and can be experienced in different ways by different individuals.[23] Thus, commitment is maintained through an individual acting in accordance with their own individual standards of punk, standards which are informed by an ideal type. The ideal type, in turn, is informed by the individual's reference groups and, as reference groups change, so too does the individual's understanding of what it means to be punk. From this, Andes presents a three-stage model of the 'punk career': stage one is rebellion; stage two is affiliation; stage three is transcendence. Individuals, however, may not necessarily pass through or adopt all of the behaviours typical of each stage.

The predisposition before each of the three stages is 'difference'. For Andes, this difference is described as a 'felt difference' by individuals from those in their immediate reference group. Thus, for example, a difference from those classed as 'normal others' or from other, existing punks.[24] With regard to the women interviewed, Jett certainly felt that what first attracted her to punk, aside from the music, was a sense of being different. She contrasted punk music ('angry', 'rebellious, 'liberating', 'noisy') with the music prominent at the time ('disco was a big thing then and basically was a lot of crap'). In so doing, she differentiated punk and herself from that which she considered mainstream. Abitbatty, too, recalled a felt difference while at school: 'I had a lot of trouble because of the music that I liked; 'cause I never liked the mainstream music I was always getting picked on, being weird you know.' Andes herself notes the difficulty in measuring 'the extent to which the informants are reinterpreting and reconstructing their pasts in terms of their current identities'.[25] Yet there is no doubt that entry into punk was understood by the four women as relating to a sense of difference that complies with Andes' model.

The first stage of the punk career is rebellion, when an individual begins to actively participate in the punk subculture. Here the reference group is still normal others, with members of the subculture constructing their idea of themselves as punk in relation and opposition to their reference group.[26] Initially, then, an individual's identification with and understanding of punk is immersed in the notion of deviance. For stage two, affiliation, the reference group shifts from normal others to members of the punk subculture. Individuals recognise that there are standards of dress and codes of behaviour that enable punk to be seen as a distinctive lifestyle. Thus, each of the older women punks recalled adhering to a more defined notion of punk dress in their youth than they did subsequently. Buckfast, for example, talked of the dreadlocks she once had and her distinctive style of dress; Jett, as we have seen, worked her way through numerous spectacular styles of punk dress.

The third and last stage of the punk career is transcendence. This, according to Andes, is when individuals within the punk subculture become concerned with expressing an ideological commitment to punk. In other words, punk becomes a system of beliefs and values maintained whether or not individuals participate in certain lifestyle practices such as going to gigs, dressing in a punk style, listening to punk records, etc. The outward display of being punk has been transcended and commitment to the subculture internalised.

Bennett's study of older male punks seems to support Andes' thesis. Not only were the older male punks seen to tone down their style of dress as they aged, but their ongoing commitment to punk led them to express their 'punk-ness' in ways that went deeper than clothing.[27] Attitude was deemed most important here, which chimes with the feelings expressed by the older punk women of punk being a lifestyle and a state of mind.

Essential, too, to the transcendence stage is a feeling of autonomy. A sense of non-conformity remains, but has extended to an unwillingness even to identify as 'punk', never mind being part of a social group.[28] While all four of the women interviewed self-identified themselves as punks, there remained a current of individualism and non-conformity running throughout. Here, then, lay the contradiction of individualism within a recognised community or subculture. The punk community was seen as a group of people all following a punk way of life, an alternative culture for those who felt they did not fit in. Punk provided an alternative to the mainstream and a means of not following 'the crowd'. But in defining themselves as different and individual, the punk women created lifestyles for themselves that fitted into the punk subculture and provided them with a sense of belonging to complement their punk identity.

Such a contradiction was recognised. Buckfast described punk being for 'the people who ... wanna be individual but it's not completely individual, but it is to the mainstream'. It may also be argued, too, that there are two ways of understanding such an apparent contradiction. First, by reflecting back on Andes' proposition of a punk career, which by stage three was defined via the individual's feeling a sense of autonomy. That is, a sense of individualism, or of being unique, that resists even a willingness to identify as punk. Yet, the older punk women remained happy to identify as punk and express an affinity to the punk subculture, while also retaining a right to individualism that fitted with the autonomy specified by Andes.

Second, therefore, may the contradiction be explained by the centrality of 'individualism' to punk's typical rationale? From the outset, punk's non-conformity was expressed in terms of individuality. Accordingly, the women's sense of individualism may be read as yet another component of the punk lifestyle they had adopted. Although it follows that being an individual cannot be truly realised while being a member of a subcultural group, a *sense* of individualism can be adopted as an inherent punk trait. That a tension still exists between a commitment to 'being punk' and 'being me' may be apparent from outside the subculture, it is reconciled within via the identification of punk with personal autonomy: 'the way I'm just me' (Buckfast), 'being myself' (Cica).

Conclusion

While the experiences of the older punk women considered here support Bennett's work on older male punks in terms of their toning down of their punk style, they appear to differ with regard to the continued importance attached to subcultural membership. Toning down was sometimes viewed as a means of accommodation; a way of adjusting to meet current situations or demands. But there was evidently some resentment at having to do so, and it was viewed as something almost intrinsic to ageing. Similarly, while the women seemingly confirm the subcultural literature on ageing and internalisation, they evidently continued to engage in outward displays of subcultural commitment. None of the women had privatised their fandom; all were active and visible participants in the punk subculture. There did, however, appear to be a contradiction at the heart of women's punk identity; that is, between individualism and a sense of belonging to a collective.

Most recent work on post-youth subcultures does now presume – or recognise – continuing participation amongst ageing members within the subcultural community they affiliated with in their youth.[29] However, the sample of older women punks here included one who had 'joined' the subculture in adulthood. Perhaps, therefore, the relationship between youth and subculture,

even when continued affinities are recognised, is more problematic than discussed hitherto?

Lastly, Andes' work on commitment contributes much to our understanding both of ageing within a subculture and the various ways of 'being punk'. By
arguing that punk is an achieved status, however, Andes suggests that having
become a punk, then one must eventually cease to be so. This is followed by the
argument that those who pursue their punk identity from their late twenties
onwards tend to feature more on the organisational and creative level of the
subculture (such as musicians and promoters). Against this, the punk women
interviewed demonstrated the extent to which older punks found ways to
negotiate their age and punk identity without having to fall back on an organisational or creative role. In other words, they retained a sense of participation
and autonomy that helped give meaning both to themselves and to the punk
community of which they felt part.

Notes

1 D. Hebdige, *Subculture: The Meaning of Style* (London: Routledge, 1998 edn).
2 D. Huxley, 'Ever Get the Feeling You've Been Cheated? Anarchy and Control in The
   Great Rock 'n' Roll Swindle', in R. Sabin (ed.), *Punk Rock: So What? The Cultural
   Legacy of Punk* (London: Routledge, 1999), p. 81.
3 D. Clark, 'The Death and Life of Punk, the Last Subculture', in D. Muggleton and R.
   Weinzierl (eds), *The Post-Subcultures Reader* (Oxford: Berg, 2003), pp. 223–36.
4 Hebdige, *Subculture*, p. 100.
5 C. O'Hara, *The Philosophy of Punk: More Than Noise!* (San Francisco: AK Press,
   1995).
6 Clark, 'The Death and Life of Punk', p. 231.
7 A. Bennett, 'Subcultures or Neo-Tribes? Rethinking the Relationship between Youth,
   Style and Musical Taste', *Sociology*, 33:3 (1999), 599–617.
8 L. Andes, 'Growing Up Punk: Meaning and Commitment Careers in a Contemporary
   Youth Subculture', in J. S. Epstein (ed.), *Youth Culture: Identity in a Postmodern World*
   (Oxford: Blackwell, 1998), pp. 212–31.
9 Hebdige, *Subculture*, pp. 100–12.
10 *Ibid.*
11 A. Bennett, 'Punk's Not Dead: The Continuing Significance of Punk Rock for an
   Older Generation of Fans', *Sociology*, 40:2 (2006), 219–35.
12 O'Hara, *The Philosophy of Punk*, p. 27.
13 Bennett, 'Punk's Not Dead', 219–35.
14 *Ibid.*

15   The Rebellion festival is a regular punk music festival that took place in Amsterdam (May 2007) and Blackpool (August 2007) during the year of the research.

16   P. Hodkinson, 'Ageing in a Spectacular Youth Culture: Continuity, Change and Community Amongst Older Goths', *The British Journal of Sociology*, 62:2 (2011), 262–82.

17   See, for example, L. Leblanc, *Pretty in Punk: Girls' Gender Resistance in a Boys' Subculture* (London: Rutgers University Press, 2002).

18   Such opinion supports Bennett's study of male punks, which suggested older male punks had no need to externally communicate their 'punkness' (as younger punks did), because their 'sustained commitment to punk over time had resulted in them literally absorbing the "qualities" of true "punkness"'. See Bennett, 'Punk's Not Dead', 225.

19   K. Schilt and D. Giffort, 'Strong Riot Women and the Continuity of Feminist Subcultural Participation', in A. Bennett and P. Hodkinson (eds), *Ageing and Youth Cultures: Music, Style and Identity* (London: Berg, 2012), pp. 146–58.

20   S. Holland, *Alternative Femininities: Body, Age and Identity* (Oxford: Berg, 2004).

21   *Ibid.*, pp. 152–4.

22   *Ibid.*, p.121.

23   Andes, 'Growing Up Punk', pp. 212–31.

24   *Ibid.*

25   *Ibid.*, p. 223.

26   *Ibid.*, pp. 212–31.

27   Bennett, 'Punk's Not Dead', 219–35.

28   Andes, 'Growing Up Punk', pp. 212–31.

29   See Bennett and Hodkinson (eds), *Ageing and Youth Cultures*.

4

Immigrant punk: the struggle for post-modern authenticity

IVAN GOLOLOBOV

I know, I'm stranger in your land
I know, ladies and gentlemen
I know, I am coming here to stay
And take your jobs away.[1]

Punk is often regarded as a subculture essentially based on the principles of authenticity.[2] In most general terms, following Taylor, authenticity is understood as an ability to break external impositions and to express one's own Self.[3] The reverse of this term is coined by Adorno who regards inauthenticity as a situation where 'something broken is implied'; he considers the inauthentic 'an expression which is not immediately appropriate to what is expressed' and by whom.[4] Being 'a call to arms to the kids who believe that rock and roll was taken away from them' and a 'statement of self-rule' and 'ultimate independence',[5] punk indeed can be seen as a quest for authenticity aiming at expressing the Self which cannot be appropriately expressed by other means. However, in practical studies of punk this concept is not an easy one with which to operate. In spite of all its implied honesty, sincerity and truthfulness, punk as a broad cultural movement somehow does not seem to fit with this concept. Regular subversion of meanings, elements of self-destruction, self-abasement, nihilism, the clear anti-foundationalist stance and revolutionising potential of punk, all make it difficult to locate something uncontroversially authentic. This creates a tension that is further amplified by regular associations of punk with post-modernism,[6] where, according to Jameson, the rules of 'new superficiality' and 'depthlessness' make the very distinction between authenticity and inauthenticity obsolete.[7]

Is it wrong to say that punk had initially made a strong authentic claim? Or were these associations incorrect, and, as some authors suggest, was punk only marginally related to postmodernism in the moment of its early crossover with the artistic visions of Andy Warhol, Malcolm McLaren and Vivienne Westwood?[8] This chapter argues that punk is not wrongly seen as a postmodern phenomenon, and that it is deeply rooted in this movement, aesthetically and ideologically. However, at the same time, it clearly also drifts away from the 'superficiality' and 'depthlessness' of postmodernism, and actively seeks ways of being authentic, honest, sincere and true, not only to itself, but also to the audiences with whom it speaks. As an example of new postmodern authenticity I analyse the question of selfhood and discuss the way it is represented in immigrant punk, and argue that immigrant punk, being postmodern in its language, appears to be anti-postmodernist in its appeal, which makes it capable of expressing a particular message and able to objectify a particular postmodern identity. In so doing, I will first review the argument that associates punk with postmodernism. Then I will attempt a critique of this approach and show why some authors convincingly argue that unlike other genres of popular music, punk is rather a reaction, and to a certain extent a revolt, against the postmodern condition. Discussing this paradox I introduce a response given to the tension between the postmodern attitude and a search for authenticity by the immigrant punks. This response is analysed in relation to the rebellious, revolutionary and transformative potential of punk, so crucial to its cultural identity, and the chapter concludes by situating the aforementioned inauthenticity of immigrant punk in a theoretical framework of the postmodern subject.

Punk as a postmodern cultural practice and as a reaction to postmodernism

Postmodernism, within the frame of this research, is understood as a set of discursive attitudes inherent to a particular historical moment. Such a moment is characterised by the devaluation of grand- or meta-narratives of modernity such as religion, philosophy and elaborate political programmes based on abstract truths. It defies such narratives in contextual, direct, action-based or performative practices of validating identities and social relations.[9] According to Baudrillard the state of postmodernity is also defined by the loss of connection with the real world, which comes to be substituted by the hyperreality of its representations, or simulacra.[10] The growing value of image has a profound effect on all spheres of our life, including economics, politics, social relations, and art.

> Art produced under its [postmodernism's] reign is characterised by a peculiar depthlessness, a draining away of any emotional content; instead, it celebrates the disintegration of the subject and offers mere pastiches of a historical past nostalgically reduced either to a lost world of political commitment or to a source of glossy retro-style images; the strange exhilaration postmodern art induces is an instance of the 'hysterical sublime', of the excitement and terror with which we respond to the realisation that the workings of the global economic system can no longer be represented or imagined.[11]

This inability to realise or imagine the workings of the global system is expressed in postmodernist art through various means. With regard to music, Kramer argues that musical expressions of the 'hysterical sublime' do not comprise a style but rather an attitude that, among other qualities, is ironic, embraces contradictions, and actively includes citations from other styles and musical traditions.[12] Albright indicates that postmodern musical language tends to rely on bricolage, polystylism and randomness.[13] Thus, we see the de-valuation of musical proficiency; the combination of various styles and genres, such as reggae, rock, metal, ska; the famous punk safety-pins and toilet chains transformed into the trappings of fashion; highly provocative lyrics, as well as a vocal irony, all clearly relate punk to this cultural moment. In addition, punk can be considered ideologically postmodern. It openly declares its anti-foundationalism; it not only frequently attacks metanarratives but also raises its fists against the very possibility of such narratives by assaulting institutions of authority, religion and corporate business. Nihilism, self-abasement and self-destruction show complete disregard to the future and indifference to one's own life.[14] The slogan 'No Future!' translates into a celebration of violence, war, destruction, catastrophe and decay, and breaks with the linear time of modernity, throwing the audience into a timeless loop of the postmodern moment.

Yet, as Moore writes: '[w]hereas the first [punk] response to postmodernity appropriates signs, symbols, and style for the purposes of shock and semiotic disruption, the second attempts to go "underground" and insulate punk subculture from the superficiality of postmodern culture'.[15] The culture of DIY, independent labels and self 'punk productions',[16] and the organisation of autonomous space and alternative economies all developed within punk communities, each propose to construct a real alternative to postmodernist popular culture. As Clark writes:

Long after the 'death' of classic punk, post-punk and/or punk subcultures
coalesce around praxis. For contemporary punks subcultural membership,
authenticity, and prestige are transcended through action internal to the
subculture ... Against the threatening purview of mass media and its capacity
to usurp and commodify style, punk subcultures steer away from symbolic
encounters with the System and create a basis in experience.[17]

This impulse shifts the accent from denial or the 'corrupt' reality of early
punk to constructive opposition in action, practices and the alternative teleology of 'Do or Die'.[18] 'Rock Against Racism', 'What Are We Going to Do About
the USA?',[19] 'We Need a New America',[20] the anti-Bush campaign, 'Another
World is Possible' and other political initiatives developed within the punk
scene show the degree to which it can actually be involved in constructing,
rather than destroying, social order. Alternatives and strategies of everyday
resistance, such as the street confrontations with ideological opponents celebrated by Red and Anarchist Skinheads (RASH) and Skinheads Against
Racial Prejudice (SHARP), straight edge and the idea of 'clean living',[21] veg-
anism and the aforementioned idea of autonomy declared in hardcore and
anarcho-punk, are just a few examples. According to Moore, these movements
are a part of the 'quest for authenticity' that gives punk an independence from
the cultural industry and allows '[renunciation of] the prevailing culture of
media, image, and hypercommercialism'.[22] In its attack on postmodern culture,
punk builds up ideological foundations to secure its oppositional and protest
identity. These foundations include, for instance, narratives of working-class
solidarity assumed in Oi! and the moral imperative of gender equality advo-
cated by punk-feminism,[23] or the militant agnosticism of hardcore which in
the 1980s came out with a highly structured project of political atheism and
an elaborate defence of critical reason celebrated by the pleiad of bands signed
to Epitaph records. Articulation of punk ideologies came hand in hand with
crystallisation of specific punk styles: New York hardcore; Californian hardcore; anarcho-punk; old-school punk; Oi! and street punk. These were less
and less engaged with irony, contradictions, bricolage, randomness and polystylism, and increasingly focused on elaborating their own musical language,
fashion, performance and behavioural practices. 'The authentic punk holds
the accepted values, supports the agreed upon norms, and correctly hates the
inauthentic *poseur* [original emphasis].'[24]

In this way, paradoxically enough, punk can be seen as striving for authenticity in the relevant artistic expression of its ideological stance and resistant
to authenticity in its moment of nihilism and denial of its own identity, as

brilliantly coined by Penny Rimbaud of Crass in his remark: 'I've got the answer to [the question] what is punk. And it is very simple. It isn't. Period.'[25]

Punk-as-style and punk-as-event

Moore believes that postmodernist deconstruction and substantive stylisations of punk form an ongoing tension inside the punk culture.[26] He seems to think that these two vectors form a dialectical contradiction which divides periods in the history of punk, and defines the identities of particular scenes. This implies that there can be little or no authenticity in what may be called postmodern punk and, on the contrary, there is little of postmodernism in the scenes built upon articulate values, rules and identities. I believe that this approach does not reveal the whole complexity of punk as a cultural movement. Contrary to such an approach I suggest that the tension between postmodernist deconstruction and a search for the Real in punk may not necessarily be divided by time or space. Moreover, I argue that certain interpretations of punk effectively combine both. In this regard it would be more appropriate to single out various approaches to punk not as postmodernist versus authentic, but as those which tend to avoid this tension by appropriating punk as a style, and those which essentially rely on it in their cultural identity and appropriate punk as an event.

Understanding style as a certain set of aesthetic norms, punk-as-style can be seen as a practice to which self-definition, establishing and maintaining itself within certain norms is central. In this dimension punk aims at securing its differential identity.[27] As Azerrad writes:

> Hardcore punks were happy, even determined to limit their appeal. The music was resolutely unmelodic, humbly recorded, and vastly unsexy. It was a point of honor not to reach out beyond their nationwide tribe. It was not only a way to cement a fledgling community, but … it was also a way to feel powerful at a time in life when one can feel particularly powerless.[28]

Contrary to hardcore, punk-as-event avoids limiting its appeal and resists closing itself down within certain norms. It deconstructs surrounding discourse, and un-defines the stylistic and cultural identities it is placed within. This, according to Bakhtin, breaks the mutual isolation of a culture that objectifies our activities and a life in which these activities take place.[29] Unlike culture, which is oriented towards repetition, life allows an experience that is unique, unrepeatable and happens only once. Punk-as-event is essentially oriented towards this singularity, uniqueness, and unrepeatability of experience and the moment of its being. This, in turn, also offers a prospect for authenticity, albeit of a different kind. Roberts, analysing cultural postmodernism, gives us a hint:[30]

> We might want to compare the actual, directed anger of 'punk rock' as manifested in an album such as the Sex Pistols' Never Mind the Bollocks with the postmodern directionless emotion of Nirvana's album Nevermind (an album whose very title seems a laconic, wearied shortening of the Pistols' original). Kurt Cobain layers the 'raging' of punk-influenced guitar noise underneath an ironically detached vocal persona, 'ah well, whatever, never mind'. The Sex Pistols parodied British patriotism ('God Save the Queen, the Fascist Regime'), where Nirvana are all about pastiche.[31]

According to Bannister, Kurt Cobain clearly speaks from the position of a 'postmodern subject': unsure, ironic, contradictory, depthless and empty.[32] This subject, nevertheless, does not only un-define its substance, but also creates the field of equivalence to itself, and manages to express the voice of its generation, externally described as 'lazy, listless baby busters':

> Beavis and Butt-head were their icons; Beck's 'Loser' was their song … ; Richard Linklater's 'Slacker', with its Austin, Texas, deadbeats, was their movie. … Net surfing, nihilistic nipple piercers whining about McJobs; latchkey legacies, fearful of commitment. Passive and powerless, they were content, it seemed, to party on in a Wayne's Netherworld.[33]

Such powerlessness, passivity and fear are difficult to express as the very act of expression and naming this state implies a certain power, an active stance, and the courage of the artist. This would be inauthentic to that subject. The way this lack of agency can be expressed is through enacting the gap. Cobain does this in his absent narrative and in the blurred and confusing messages of his songs. Colliding emotions and musical languages; depleted, highly melodic and, one might even say, sentimental verses crushing into the power of over-driven guitar, solid rhythm, noise and screaming: it all serves to amplify the confusion and contradictions of Nirvana's aesthetics. This contradiction enacts the despair and anger[34] of Cobain's own generation and the situation in which it finds itself, something he formulated off-stage in a clear political appeal:

> We and you can do so much more. I'm disgusted by my own and my generation's apathy. I'm disgusted at what we allow to go on, by how spineless, lethargic and guilty we are of not standing up against racism, sexism and all those other 'isms' that the counterculture has been whining about for years while they sit and enforce those same attitudes every night on their televisions and in the magazines. It's the ism-attack bought off by consumerism.[35]

However, unlike in hardcore, Oi! and other punk styles, this attack is not that of one against the other. There is no existential enemy. This war is waged inside: inside the generation; inside the popular culture to which Nirvana belongs and which it simultaneously hates; inside Kurt Cobain himself. This split of the subject is translated into a particular aesthetic language that enacts the incomplete identity of the postmodern Self. This virtual absence, the un-achieved fullness of the Self accentuated by Cobain, does not however imply that it is impossible to stay true to such a Self in a particular artistic expression. But this expression would be different from the voices of a fixed subject. It would not refer to the discursive position,[36] a social identity which provides the fullness of the Self but, as Penny Rimbaud asserts, it would be the 'voice of the individuals expressing themselves as individuals'.[37] This is the voice of an individual who is yet to find who they are. It is a voice of the absent Self, of the Self in search. And this search 'cannot be viewed. It can have no overview … [it] defies the definition. It is beyond definition. The moment it is defined then it ceases to be. That has been the case of all great cultural movements'.[38] The defiance of definition suggests that in this particular instance the incom-plete Self does not seek to fill its emptiness with a positive symbolic context; on the contrary, it strives to gain its recognition and discursive rights exactly in its absence, incompleteness and openness. The more the openness and in-completeness of the Self disappears in the 'text' of popular culture, the less content the postmodern subject becomes. In the end Cobain chose to 'burn out' instead of 'fading away', stating that his 'ethics involved with independence and the embracement of [the] community' came into unsolvable contradic-tion with the need to 'rip people off by faking [excitement] and pretending [to be] having 100% fun',[39] a problem which he, personally, could not solve in any other way than taking his own life.

A decade later Beavis and Butthead were taken off the air, MTV stopped being a music channel and 'Loser' was out of the charts, leaving the floor for the stars of X Factor and American Idol. McDonalds changed its design and the youth no longer needed to bother about McJobs: they were successfully filled by immigrants.

Immigrant punk

As Roger Sabin shows, immigrants were a difficult topic to discuss, especially in early British punk.[40] Remaining the music of the 'white minority'[41] and 'white noise' made by 'white boys',[42] punk only marginally touched on the issues of immigration and the problems of immigrants until these problems were articulated in punk by the immigrants themselves. This articulation resulted in the formation of a new genre of 'immigrant punk', a term coined after a song by the New York-based band Gogol Bordello. As Rebecca Jablonsky writes, the band:

> [i]ntroduce the term 'immigrant punk' definitively and self-consciously, particularly in the last two lines 'You got a dictionary kickin' around? Look up the immigrant, immigrant, immigrant punk!' This challenges the listener of the song to recognise the label 'immigrant punk' as official, which effectively plays on (and possibly mocks) the struggle for cultural and legal legitimacy that immigrants experience upon arrival to the United States.[43]

The struggle for the legitimacy of immigrants in the West defines the ideology of the immigrant punk. Aesthetically, it is formed on the intersection of national music traditions, punk rock, and other styles and genres of popular music:

> This is a new wave post-punk sound. More melodic than the original punk ... A passionate humor and a cocky sweetness winks behind a back to basics anti-authoritarian melange of international sound. It's a circus of Gypsy music, tango, polka, dub, rock 'n' roll, flamenco, hora, reggae, Afro-Eastern European with a backbeat of working-class intellectual left-wing heart.[44]

Immigrant punk is a fluid, ex-territorial, and tendentious supra-national scene which among others includes such bands and performers as Manu Chao (France/Spain, playing with Mano Negra since 1987, and performing solo from 1995 onwards), Asian Dub Foundation (formed in 1993, UK), Babar Luck (playing with King Prawn from 1993 till 2003, and then performing solo, UK), Kultur Shock (active since 1996, USA), and Gogol Bordello (formed in 1999, USA).[45] Sharing similar appeal for the cultural legitimacy of the immigrants and recognition of cultural diversity this scene is, however, rather diverse aesthetically.

Manu Chao's 'musical vocabulary ... [is] bracing punk rock, folkloric pop, lilting reggae, frenetic ska, sinewy salsa ... Immigrant songs and those about the world's disenfranchised, dispossessed and "disappeared" are a key part of Chao's repertoire'.[46] He sings in French, Spanish, English, Italian, Galician, Arabic, Portuguese and occasionally in other languages, such as Wolof.

Babar Luck performs acoustic but still rather aggressive punk-rap-reggae. According to Punkoiuk.org, his performance absorbs 'his native culture and music, alongside reggae, hiphop, acoustic music, classic rock, punk, underground music and the sights and sounds of London town'.[47]

Asian Dub Foundation play electronic rapcore heavily influenced by South Asian traditional music. Their performance is often described as 'a combination of ragga, garage punk and traditional Indian ragas',[48] or as a 'multicultural Clash or Sex Pistols, carrying the torch of punk rebellion ... with an album titled Punkara – a conflation of "punk" and "Bhangra"'.[49]

Kultur Shock acknowledge the multicultural nature of their performance by singing in Bosnian, Bulgarian, English, French, German, Italian, Spanish and Arabic, and play music which 'falls outside most definable genres':

> Its Gypsy punk rock combines the aggression of heavy metal with the defiance of punk music and the yearning of Balkan folk music. Heavy-metal riffs crash into complex Balkan violin melodies; Gypsy singing floats above driving bass lines. The band's music and lyrics strike this listener as a frenetic, heartfelt resistance to racism, nationalism and fanaticism of any kind.[50]

Their record, released in 2006, has been described as 'an exhilarating journey into a world inhabited by people too many Americans would like to just send back where they came from'.[51]

Gogol Bordello fuse Russian rock, Ukrainian folk, traditional Gypsy and Jewish music into a sparkling punk cabaret, adding English, Russian, Ukrainian, Gypsy, Spanish, Italian and Romanian languages into a quasi-pastiche of immigrant punk.

Yet, in spite of all this variety in aesthetics, the scene demonstrates a certain degree of organic coherence. Gogol Bordello and Kultur Shock supported each other on some of their American tours. Members of Gogol Bordello are good friends with Manu Chao. In 2005 they covered his song 'Mala Vida',[52] originally performed by Mano Negra.[53] Manu Chao and Asian Dub Foundation headlined the compilation *Another World Is Possible* released by Uncivilized World in 2005. In 2007 Asian Dub Foundation were joined by Al Rumjen the former singer of King Prawn, where Babar Luck was playing bass guitar prior to starting his solo career.

The bands and performers associated with immigrant punk also share a profound similarity in the 'ideology' of their music making. To a greater or lesser degree they all tell the stories of their lives and their music comes from the lived experience of cultural alienation.

Gogol Bordello were formed in 1999 by Ukrainian-born Eugene Hütz and later joined by other immigrants from Russia, along with Romanians, Israelis, an Ethiopian, an Ecuadorian, and several British and American musicians. In their songs Gogol Bordello explicitly discuss the place of immigrants in Western society, their segregation and marginalisation.[54] 'I had to give up my citizenship in the Ukraine in order to get out and I was not accepted as a citizen of the US until 1996. So I know how that feels,' said Eugene Hütz, the band's singer.[55]

Kultur Shock were founded in Seattle in 1996 by Srđan Gino Jevđević a Bosnian immigrant who relocated to the USA after fleeing the siege of Sarajevo), Val Kiossovski and Boris Iochev, both immigrants from Bulgaria. Gino specifies some aspects of what it is to feel yourself an immigrant:

> I am driving, and I have a Bosnian passport. A passport of the Republic of Bosnia. [In the US] it's pretty much like a toilet paper, and your picture on it, and nobody gives a fuck for you, nobody, I mean my band is waiting for me for ages on the borders … while I am right there questioned about who the fuck knows what. All the visas are there but … and it's not the way I look you know, even when I had full dreadlocks and my hair covered the head … I was questioned all the time, short hair long hair, doesn't matter. So, having that passport is bad, in Europe – directly bad.[56]

Babar Luck was born in Pakistan and moved to London at the age of eight. He described his experience of growing up in London as a 'wonderful experiment and oppression':

> We had to build up our own little street culture and stand up for ourselves. I remember going to Drew Road Primary School in E16, and I was the only brown boy. Jaswinder Singh was the only brown girl. Even the teachers used to make fun of us. In our comprehensive school, we had 20 per cent black, 20 per cent Asian, and 60 per cent white and/or mixed up. Our school was the only one in the area that had coloureds. Every day there used to be battles. You'd hear cries of, 'Get the Pakis, get the Pakis!'[57]

> When I was in my teens I moved to another area that was more multicultural, and I rediscovered qawwali singers, Hindi films, the Bollywood films I'd grown up watching. Then I got into reggae music. … I'd hang out with these old Rastamen, who talked about history … They'd sing songs and we'd all clap hands. There would be people of black background, Asian background; my friend would bring down a sitar, and another friend would play electric guitar, and another friend would play bhangra beats.[58]

Asian Dub Foundation emerged out of a community project designed to teach Asian kids music technology. The band was formed in East London by a tutor Aniruddha Das (aka Dr Das), a youth worker John Pandit (aka Pandit G), a Bengali rapper Deedar Zaman (aka Master D), and later joined by Steve Chandra Savale (aka Chandrasonic) and Sanjay Tailor (aka Sun-J). They were all born into families of South Asian immigrants. 'Their debut album *Facts and*

Fictions (Nation Records) came out in 1995 and was largely overlooked by a country obsessed with retro guitar pop. To be "Asian" was yet to be considered "cool"'[59] and, as Banerjea notes, it was still a time of 'vilification of and violence against people of colour, "guest workers" or immigrants, struggling to establish themselves on that continent'.[60]

Manu Chao was born in Paris in a family of Spanish immigrants. His mother is Basque, his father is Galician. They left Spain in 1956 to escape Franco's dictatorship. Soon the family moved to the city's suburbs, where Chao grew up in an environment of working-class immigrant communities. 'After two decades of global trekking, Chao has firsthand experience with the immigration debate that has become so loud and controversial around the world'.[61]

From a position of first-hand experience, immigrant punk speaks of a misrecognised identity. Gogol Bordello clearly reflect this misrecognition in 'Immigrant Punk': 'Upon arriving to the melting pot/ I get pencilled in as a goddamn white/ Now that I am categorised/ Officer gets me naturalised ... Legalise me! Realise me!'[62] Asian Dub Foundation, too, in their 'Real Great Britain', describe the de-facto status of the immigrant inner-nation, pointing at the divide of the nation into three parts where the 'bottom third' is the one 'you never see'.[63] Indeed, the discursive invisibility of the 'bottom third', with its incomplete and 'unrealised' identity, is a central moment of the immigrant Self, an individual who has been externally 'categorised' and denied their independent selfhood. This misrecognition is especially evident in the stylistic identities of the immigrant communities. Sharma has referred to the problematic of Asian rap, which for many years could not find a place in the black-and-white divide of the rap scene,[64] while Annirudha Das of Asian Dub Foundation has further commented on the oppressive orientalism experienced by Asian youth: 'we're [the Asian people] expected to have a certain type of sound. First we're not expected to make music at all, then people expect to hear sitars and tablas'.[65] Babar Luck echoes this misrecognition in his own way, pointing at the oppressive system of race division: 'King Prawn weren't brown enough, black enough or white enough. I'm not black enough or white enough for this society, but that's just how it is'.[66]

The oppression of external stratification depriving the immigrant Self from its power to make its own decisions is also extensively noticed by Manu Chao in his 'Clandestino' mentioning the experience of being regarded by the authorities as 'a ghost in the city', and therefore, living a 'prohibited life'.[67]

'It's more about frustration, more about wanting to be recognised as a person on the Earth. It's like we need to come up with our own generational chants to define us', comments Hütz on this situation.[68] Kultur Shock are also raging against this misrecognition imposed by the system of divisions and limitations that blocks the immigrant 'person' from realising itself. Gino explains in one of his interviews:

> We do not recognise borders, passport … Being free by the Webster
> Dictionary is the access to move … all access. Right? Access to all sides, so
> how can a guy with a moustache or a girl without a moustache stand on the
> border of some country to tell me if I'm good enough to get there, some
> kind of immigration police of some country. If I'm good to go somewhere
> and somebody else is not and so on I do not think that's legal. Freedom and
> borders … that's not legal. That's limitation of your national born right … [69]

Borders depriving a person from the 'natural born right' of movement are a common point of attack for immigrant punks. Gogol Bordello stress this problem in a number of their songs, notably 'Your Country' and 'Not a Crime'.[70] Babar Luck does it in his 'World Citizen' and 'One World',[71] Asian Dub Foundation raise the issue in their 'Fortress Europe'[72] and Manu Chao points to the hypocrisy of Western anti-immigration policies in one of his interviews:

> It's very curious because all the governments say they are fighting against
> immigration and building big walls all around the first world, and that's one
> fact. But a second fact, also really curious, a big part of the economy is going
> good just because of the 'clandestinos.' That's the big hypocrisy, you know,
> [because] an illegal immigrant cannot integrate, cannot say if he is happy or
> not with his job, can be paid less than anybody else, and that's perfect for the
> economy … In Spain 20 years ago, Spanish people were the immigrants. They
> used to go to find work in France, Germany and Switzerland, and now they
> fight against immigration – it's quite silly, no? No memory. Even in United
> States, it's the same – a country of immigrants, and now they try to avoid
> immigration.[73]

The attack on the borders and oppressive anti-immigration policies of the Western states does not only defend free movement, it also identifies a situation where real immigrants and the reality of immigrant lives appear to be externally substituted by their popular representations:

> Everybody football, everybody France/France, love the Africans/But when
> they riot they're not so much fun/Why can't everybody be like Zinedine
> Zidane?

> Mexicans are everyday feeding, building USA/ But when they're done, kick
> them out all/ Build a wall, build a wall!

Everybody does Balkan folk/ Everybody Kultur, everybody Shock/ They love
our talent, artistic touch/ Us? Not so much.[74]

The attack on the value of representations imposed on individual experience
is clearly a counter-postmodernist move. It radically un-defines postmodernism. It deconstructs its deconstruction and shows its metanarrating nature. In
this denial of overrepresentation immigrant punk creates an articulate prospect
of authenticity which 'correctly hates the inauthentic' postmodernist poseur.[75]
Asian Dub Foundation, for instance, attack fashion, which is seen as the ultimate representation of postmodernist substitution of reality by an image. In
'Real Great Britain' they clearly relate the hypocrisy of establishment to the
'fashion-tashion' behind which there is nothing else to see.[76]

Gogol Bordello criticised the bohemian culture of the creative class, associating it with 'revolutionaries who sleep with no compromise'.[77] The New York
band also vocally attacks another iconic symbol of the postmodern evasion of
the original. In particular, they point at the 'Karaoke dictatorship', 'posers and
models with guitars', and suggest that they are going to 'make a better rock revolution alone with my dick!'[78] Criticising inauthentic 'posers', Gogol Bordello
undermines the lack of real experience lost in the endless representations and
repetitions. Eugene Hütz says: 'I think … that Western civilization and culture
had kind of exhausted itself or maybe repeated itself too many times at this
point …'[79] Moreover, in an artistic statement made at the Whitney Museum
Biennial in 2002, Gogol Bordello declared: 'Gogol Bordello's task is to provoke
audience out of post-modern aesthetic swamp onto a neo-optimistic communal movement towards new sources of authentic energy [sic]'.[80]

Artistically, however, it is a deconstructing move which, according to
Hebdige, mobilises 'the cultural forms of lived experience and resistance embedded in the streets, the shops and clubs … to make the crisis *speak* [original
emphasis]'.[81] The crisis and cultural mobilisation of lived experience is expressed by the immigrant punk in a clear postmodernist language.

It is full of citations. Asian Dub Foundation, for instance, integrate a cut 'n'
mix approach into their music, 'sampling … other songs and borrowing from
many different styles'.[82] Gogol Bordello use multiple music and poetic quotations from Russian rock. The song 'Nomad Chronicles' from *Voi-la Intruder*[83],
for example, clearly borrows its chorus from the song 'Nikto ne uslyshyt/Oi-yo'
of the Russian rock group Chaif, initially released in 1990.[84] The chorus 'Mama-
diaspora papa v Gogol Bordello' in 'Dogs Were Barking'[85] is a paraphrase of
'Mama-anarkiia' initially performed by another famous Russian rock group
Kino.[86] The songs of Gogol Bordello contain numerous references to other
music such as the Stooges, Zvuki Mu, a Russian avant-punk band, as well as

to Soviet films and literary classics, of which 'Start Wearing Purple' is the most famous. Apart from the aforementioned 'Mala Vida Gogol', Bordello covered several traditional songs, such as 'Tu Jésty Fáta',[87] and used traditional motifs which, for instance, inform 'Super Taranta!'[88] and 'Mishto!'[89] Kultur Shock, too, make regular reference to Balkan folk melodies.

Musically, immigrant punk tends to avoid the traditional composition of popular song and is often rather random, even for punk rock. The visual image of immigrant punk is deliberately unfashionable and often rather dissimilar to the expected punk outfit. Asian Dub Foundation look more like rappers. Gogol Bordello have quite a distinctive visual style of basking travellers, and Babar Luck performs in traditional Islamic clothes.

Moreover, aesthetics of immigrant punk have no references to a particular alternative metanarrative. It is not a celebration of a particular national culture, alternative to the West. Gino says that Kutur Shock in no way play a particular Serbian or Bosnian music.[90] Babar Luck expresses his 'trials and tribulations of growing up as a British Asian' not in the 'safe' aesthetics of Asian music, but through 'a vibrant backdrop of punk rock riffs, rock steady ska, acoustic soul, and hip hop'.[91] Gogol Bordello coin their deconstruction in a 'chaotic clash of cultures'[92] which is fixed by neither a particular ethnic flavour nor a style of folk, nor even their polyglot lyrics, but by a 'cacophonous' and 'unstable hybrid'.[93] This hybrid, nevertheless, is seen as the most appropriate way to express the incomplete immigrant Self:

> Kultur Shock doesn't sing about broken hearts and flowers, but about everyday existence and faith that it might get better. Or worse. Punk describes our will to fight for what we believe in, Balkan melodies are the voice of the people we are part of and representing, and finally, metal adventures are our way to rage against the machine.[94]

The deconstructive rage of the immigrant punk against the machine of postmodernism is integral to the global punk scene. Unlike a style which essentially relies on maintaining a difference with other styles to secure its authenticity in a particular language of artistic expression, immigrant punk creates artistic and cultural space inclusive to various styles and audiences. Babar Luck regularly plays traditionally 'white' punk venues. Asian Dub Foundation are hugely successful in Eastern Europe, Manu Chao and Gogol Bordello are international stars. The desire to reach a wide audience is clearly acknowledged by immigrant punk.[95] Sometimes it results in rather unexpected collaborations where, for instance, Pakistan-born Babar Luck can perform with the Siberian folk collective Yat-Kha, or Gogol Bordello, much to the dislike of many in the immigrant punk scene, with Madonna. These collaborations, paradoxically enough, fall in line with the unachieved fullness of the immigrant Self, which neither refer to a particular style of musical expression nor to an ethnic or diasporic Self of a people in exile.

Authenticity in immigrant punk is not about being true to some 'home', a culture, a particular community, style or even a scene. It is about the lack of those and the impossibility of being oneself in a particular context. This context is not just the West but also, and mostly, the postmodern condition which is seen as an external imposition to one's true Self. The experience of this impossibility to achieve the fullness of the Self is impossible to define or to describe. The voice of this incomplete subject can only be expressed through the incompleteness itself, through the very lack produced in the act of musical performance. It is a performance which, as *Metal Hammer* comments, 'isn't "pure" or "authentic" enough'[96] but may be regarded by Jello Biafra as 'punk rock as it should sound like'.[97]

Conclusion

The inauthenticity of the immigrant punk to the available styles and genres of popular music and its impurity in relation to particular folk traditions translates the dislocation of the immigrant subject. Laclau and Mouffe understand dislocation as a disruption of the symbolic organisation invoked by the real events which cannot or can be hardly symbolised within a given discursive order.[98] Being devoid of its symbolic recognition, the dislocated subject becomes excluded from the structure of social organisation. By this exclusion it loses its place of speaking from which it can express its demands and realise socially accepted practices. Exactly due to this misrecognition in the post-Marxist theoretical tradition, the dislocated subject is regarded as marginal and subaltern.

In this rupture the immigrant Self finds a new substance, which is not cultural but, as Žižek and other contemporary discourse theorists would suggest, political.[99] In the moment of its dislocation:

[t]he subject is forced to take decisions, or to identify with certain political projects and the discourses they articulate – when social identities are in crisis and structures need to be recreated. It is in the process of this identification that the process of political [emphasis added] subjectivities are created and formed. Once formed and stabilised, they become those subject positions that turn individuals into social actors with certain characteristics and attributes.[100]

The projects and discourses of immigrant punk to which the immigrant Self subject identifies are expressed in the very aesthetics of performance. The 'troubadours of neo-authentic trans-global art syndicate family' mix 'Gypsy, Cabaret and punk' into the chaos and spontaneity of a musical act. Such an act is clearly carnivalesque and in this moment forms a substantial counter-point to the postmodern simulacra. It dismantles the discursive structures this condition contains, notably the qualities of emptiness, depthlessness and, para-doxically enough, performativity of discourse. It annihilates the very discursive condition of the postmodern spectacle as, according to Bakhtin:

> Carnival doesn't know footlights, in the sense that it does not acknowledge any distinction between actors and spectators. Footlights would destroy a carnival, as the absence of footlights would destroy a theatrical performance. Carnival is not a spectacle seen by the people; they live in it, and everyone participates because its very idea embraces all the people. While carnival lasts, there is no other life outside it. During carnival time life is subject only to its laws, that is, the laws of its own freedom. It has a universal spirit; it is a special condition of the entire world, of the world's revival and renewal, in which all take part.[101]

The inner laws of carnival and the laws of its own freedom are the laws of chaos.[102] In this chaos, carnival is embracing indecision, contingency and the possibility of emancipation.[103] Marginalised in styles of punk for the sake of their consistency and the credibility of political engagement, in immigrant punk carnival is brought forward as a real alternative to postmodern irony, challenging its superficiality and depthlessness and discrediting the value of the postmodernist representation of a representation in both its practice and its results.

This research demonstrates that the question of authenticity in punk rock is more complex than a discussion of supposedly authentic hardcore and inauthentic postmodernist punk suggests. Wiseman-Trowse argues that authenticity is ultimately a relationship between cultural expression and lived experience.[104] Immigrant punk demonstrates that postmodernist language of music performance may translate an absolutely counter-postmodernist appeal that expresses a culturally unrepresented experience of the immigrant Self. This suggests a principally new, one may call it postmodern, form of authenticity.

Such authenticity obviously demands a special attention and it is not possible here to explore this concept in full. However, it possible to see that this authenticity is formed in a different arrangement of cultural space where depth and substance are sought not within a particular artistic language, ide-ology and cultural environment of various scenes, styles and genres, but in the moment of their mutual distortion. It is this all-embracing moment, con-necting the multiplicity of languages, styles, and cultures in a singularity of a particular experience which demands active relation to the historical moment of its emergence. This demand resists the safety of postmodern simulacra, and keeps the nerve of punk open to the here-and-now of its experience. As Eugene Hütz puts it:

> The immediacy is what guides and is the guiding force. That's not to say it's a mindless, 'live now' [type of thing] … [This] moment is more precious than you think. This idea is recurrent in many philosophies – the key is not to be ahead of time or to be retro. The key is to be with the motherfucking times. That's where the shit is, that's where it's happening.[105]

Acknowledgements

The article is written with the financial support of the Arts and Humanities Research Council (AHRC ref: AH/G011966/). The opinions expressed in this article are, however, those of its author.

Notes

1   Kultur Shock, 'God is Busy, May I Help You?', on *We Came to Take Your Jobs Away*, KoolArrow Records, 2006. All lyrics used by kind permission of Kultur Shock.
2   B. Cogan, 'What Do I Get? Punk Rock, Authenticity and Cultural Capital', *CounterBlast.org*, http://www.nyu.edu/pubs/counterblast/punk.htm, accessed 28 March 2014; A. Gordon, 'The Authentic Punk: An Ethnography of DIY Music Ethics' (PhD Thesis, Loughborough University, 2005); P. Lewin and J. Patrick Williams, ''The Ideology and Practice of Authenticity in Punk Subculture', in P. Vannini and J. Patrick Williams (eds), *Authenticity in Culture, Self, and Society* (Farnham: Ashgate, 2009), pp. 65–84; S. Widdicombe and R. Wooffitt, '"Being" Versus "Doing" Punk: On Achieving Authenticity as a Member', *Journal of Language and Social Psychology*, 9:4 (1990), 257–77.
3   C. Taylor, *The Ethics of Authenticity* (Cambridge, MA: Harvard University Press, 1992), p. 27.
4   T. Adorno, *The Jargon of Authenticity* (London: Routledge 2003), pp. 1–136.
5   Malcolm McLaren quoted in Chris Salewicz, 'The Grand British Punk Revolution', *D.O.A.: The Official Filmbook, a Punk Magazine* (1981), www.punkmagazine.com/vault/vault-doa_grand.html, accessed 28 March 2014.
6   S. Connor, *Postmodernist Culture: An Introduction to Theories of the Contemporary* (Oxford: Blackwell, 1997, second edition), p. 65; J. Cypher, 'Ruder Than You: Punk's Postmodern Aesthetic', *Canadian Review of Comparative Literature*, 3:21 (1994),

371–81; D. Muggleton, *Inside Subculture: The Postmodern Meaning of Style* (Oxford: Berg, 2002).

7   F. Jameson, 'Postmodernism, or the Cultural Logic of Late Capitalism', *New Left Review*, 1:146 (1984), 61–2.

8   J. Davis, 'The Future of "No Future": Punk Rock and Postmodern Theory', *The Journal of Popular Culture*, 29:4 (1996), 2–25; R. Moore, 'Postmodernism and Punk Subculture: Cultures of Authenticity and Deconstruction', *The Communication Review*, 7 (2004), 305–27.

9   J. F. Lyotard, *The Postmodern Condition: A Report on Knowledge* (Manchester: Manchester University Press, 1984).

10   J. Baudrillard, 'Simulacra and Simulations', in Mark Poster (ed.), *Jean Baudrillard: Selected Writings* (Stanford, CA: Stanford University Press, 1998), pp. 166–84.

11   A. Callinicos, *Against Postmodernism: A Marxist Critique* (Cambridge: Polity Press, 1989), pp. 128–9.

12   J. Kramer, 'Postmodern Concepts of Musical Time', *Indiana Theory Review*, 17:2 (1996), 21–62.

13   D. Albright, *Modernism and Music: An Anthology of Sources* (Chicago: University of Chicago Press, 2004), p. 12.

14   S. Colgrave and C. Sullivan, *Punk: The Definitive Record of a Revolution* (New York: Thunder's Mouth Press, 2001), p. 171.

15   Moore, 'Postmodernism', 307.

16   S. Thompson, *Punk Productions: Unfinished Business* (Albany, NY: SUNY Press, 2004).

17   D. Clark, 'The Death and Life of Punk: The Last Subculture', in D. Muggleton and R. Weinzierl (eds), *The Post-Subcultures Reader* (Oxford: Berg, 2003), p. 233.

18   Dropkick Murphys, *Do or Die*, Hellcat Records, 1998.

19   This was a slogan that appeared on a poster for Anti-Flag, an American punk band known for their active support of progressive political action.

20   Bad Religion, 'New America', *The New America*, Atlantic Records, 2000.

21   R. Haenfler, *Straight Edge: Clean Living Youth, Hardcore Punk, and Social Change* (New Brunswick, NJ: Rutgers University Press, 2006).

22   Moore, 'Postmodernism', p. 307.

23   L. Leblanc, *Pretty in Punk: Girls' Gender Resistance in a Boys' Subculture* (New Brunswick, NJ: Rutgers University Press, 1999).

24   L. Kristiansen, J. Blaney, P. Chidester and B. Simonds, *Screaming for Change: Articulating a Unifying Philosophy of Punk Rock* (Plymouth: Lexington Books, 2012), p. 36.

25   Penny Rimbaud, speech at the 'Rottenbeat: Academic and Musical Dialogue with the New Russian Punk Workshop', University of Warwick, Pushkin House, London, 4 May 2011.

26   Moore, 'Postmodernism', p. 307.

27 On logic of difference and logic of equivalence, see E. Laclau and C. Mouffe, *Hegemony and Socialist Strategy: Towards a Radical Democrat Politics* (London: Verso, 1985), pp. 127–34; S. Žižek, *The Sublime Object of Ideology* (London: Verso, 1989), p. 95.

28 M. Azerrad, *Our Band Could Be Your Life: Scenes from the American Indie Underground, 1981–91* (New York: Little Brown & Co., 2001), pp. 13–14.

29 M. Bakhtin, *Towards the Philosophy of the Act* (Austin, TX: University of Texas Press, 1993), pp. 2–3.

30 Although Nirvana are often considered to be the most prominent band of grunge and are not unequivocally associated with punk by critics, Kurt Cobain himself made clear that what they were doing may be seen as punk rock. '"Punk is a musical freedom", says Nirvana's guitarist-singer Kurt Cobain. "It's saying, doing and playing what you want." www.livenirvana.com/documents/bioDGC.html, accessed 28 March 2014.

31 A. Roberts, *Frederic Jameson* (London and New York: Routledge, 2000), p. 126.

32 M. Bannister, *White Boys, White Noise: Masculinities and 1980s Indie Guitar Rock* (Aldershot: Ashgate, 2006), pp. 146–9.

33 M. Hornblower, 'Great xpectations: slackers? Hardly', *Time* (9 June 1997), p. 58.

34 N. Nehring, *Popular Music, Gender, and Postmodernism: Anger is an Energy* (London: Sage, 1997).

35 F. Andrick, Interview with Kurt Cobain, 26 October 1991, San Francisco, CA, www.livenirvana.com/interviews/9110fa/index.html, accessed 28 March 2014.

36 M. Foucault, 'The Order of Discourse', in M. J. Shapiro (ed.), *Language and Politics* (Oxford: Blackwell, 1984), pp. 108–38.

37 Rimbaud, speech at 'Rottenbeat'.

38 *Ibid.*

39 Kurt Cobain suicide note, http://kurtcobainssuicidenote.com, accessed 28 March 2014.

40 R. Sabin, '"I Won't Let that Dago By". Rethinking Punk and Racism', in R. Sabin (ed.), *Punk Rock: So What? The Cultural Legacy of Punk* (London: Routledge, 1999), pp. 199–218.

41 D. Traber, 'L.A.'s "White Minority": Punk and the Contradictions of Self-Marginalisation', *Cultural Critique*, 48 (Spring 2001), 30–64.

42 Bannister, *White Boys*, pp. 146–9.

43 R. Jablonsky, 'Russian Jews and "Gypsy Punks": The Performance of Real and Imagined Cultural Identities within a Transnational Migrant Group', *Journal of Popular Music Studies*, 24:1 (2012), 3–24.

44 D. Monet, 'Immigrant Punk, Gypsy Punk and the Post New Wave Sound of Gogol Bordello', http://doloresmonet.hubpages.com/hub/ImmigrantPunkGypsyPunkandthePostNewWaveSoundofGogolBordello, accessed 28 March 2014.

45 Kultur Shock and Gogol Bordello are often labelled as Gypsy punks, and this definition is also sometimes attached to Manu Chao.

46 R. Harrington, 'Seeing the World Through Manu Chao's Eyes', *Washington Post* (22 June 2007).

47 'Babar Luck: Care in the Community (Rebel Records)', review in *Punk and Oi in the UK* (March 2006), www.punkoiuk.co.uk/reviews/reviewmonth. asp?lstMonth=March+06, accessed 28 March 2014.
48 'Asian Dub Foundation', C. Larkin (ed.), *The Encyclopaedia of Popular Music* (Oxford: MUZE 2006), p. 276.
49 L. Pattison, 'There is Some Incendiary Fund to Have With. Asian Dub Foundation: Punkara', BBC review (13 October 2008), www.bbc.co.uk/music/reviews/6zvr, accessed 28 March 2014.
50 D. Adamek, 'Kultur Shock Plays the Balkans', *The New York Times* (7 April 2011).
51 J. Greene, 'We Came to Take Your Jobs Away. Review', *Allmusic.com (2006)*, www. allmusic.com/album/we-came-to-take-your-jobs-away-mw0000555686, accessed 28 March 2014.
52 Gogol Bordello, 'Mala Vida', *East Infection*, Rubric Records, 2005.
53 Mano Negra, 'Mala Vida', *Patchanka*, Boucherie Productions/Virgin France, 1988.
54 Gogol Bordello, 'Santa Marinella', *Gypsy Punks: Underdog World Strike*, SideOneDummy Records, 2005.
55 R. Cooper, 'An Interview with Eugene Hutz of Gogol Bordello: Talking about the Gypsy Punk Revolution', *About.com*, http://punkmusic.about.com/od/interviews/a/Eugenehutz_2.htm, accessed 28 March 2014.
56 Gino on American people at *Storypipe.com* (21 December 2006), www.youtube.com/watch?v=rRjYEhxGx7U, accessed 28 March 2014.
57 'Philosophising with Babar Luck', www.youtube.com/watch?v=fFGqlvPfk1o, accessed 28 March 2014.
58 C. Nickson, 'Babar Luck: A Pakistani Cockney Cross between Billy Bragg and Spike Milligan?', *fRoots*, 274 (April 2006), p. 16.
59 Asian Dub Foundation official biography, www.asiandubfoundation.com/?page_id=204, accessed 28 March 2014.
60 K. Banerjea, 'Sounds of Whose Underground?: The Fine Tuning of Diaspora in an Age of Industrial Reproduction', *Theory, Culture and Society*, 17:3 (2000), 65.
61 Harrington, 'Seeing the World Through Manu Chao's Eyes'.
62 Gogol Bordello, 'Immigrant Punk', *Gypsy Punks: Underdog World Strike*, SideOneDummy Records, 2005.
63 Asian Dub Foundation, 'Real Great Britain', *Community Music*, Ffrr, 2000.
64 S. Sharma, 'Noisy Asians or "Asian Noise"?', in S. Sharma, J. Hutnyk and A. Sharma (eds), *Dis-Orienting Rhythms: The Politics of the New Asian Dance Music* (London: Zed Books, 1996), pp. 32–60. See also A. Dawson, '"This is the Digital Underclass": Asian Dub Foundation and Hip-Hop Cosmopolitanism', *Social Semiotics*, 12:1 (2002), 27–44.
65 R. Huq, 'Asian Kool? Bhangra and Beyond', in Sharma, Hutnyk and Sharma (eds), *Dis-Orienting Rhythms*, p. 71.
66 P. Meadey, 'Babar Luck: "I use brains – and fists"', *The Independent* (26 May 2006).
67 Manu Chao, 'Clandestino', *Clandestino*, Ark21/Virgin Records, 1998.
68 Cooper, 'An Interview with Eugene Hutz'.

69 'We Do not Recognise Borders: Judith Gennet Talks to Kultur Shock', *RootsWorld. com*, www.rootsworld.com/interview/kulturshock.html, accessed 28 March 2014.

70 Gogol Bordello, *Gypsy Punks*.

71 Babar Luck, *World Citizen Frankenstaanee*, Babar Label, 2007.

72 Asian Dub Foundation, 'Fortress Europe', *Enemy of the Enemy*, Ffrr, 2003.

73 Harrington, 'Seeing the World Through Manu Chao's Eyes'.

74 Kultur Shock, 'Build a Wall', *Integration*, Kultur Shock Records, 2009.

75 Kristiansen, Blaney, Chidester and Simonds, *Screaming for Change*, p. 36.

76 Asian Dub Foundation, 'Real Great Britain'.

77 Gogol Bordello, 'Future Kings', *Multi Kontra Culti vs. Irony*, Rubric Records, 2002.

78 Gogol Bordello, '60 Revolutions', *Gypsy Punks*.

79 Cooper, 'An Interview with Eugene Hutz'.

80 Hutz and GB, Mission, GB official website, www.gogolbordello.com/the-band/mission/, accessed 28 March 2014.

81 D. Hebdige, 'Digging for Britain: An Excavation in Seven Parts', *The British Edge* (Boston: Institute of Contemporary Arts, 1987), p. 48.

82 J. Ervine, 'Citizenship and Belonging in Suburban France: The Music of *Zebda*', *ACME: An International E-Journal for Critical Geographies*, 7:2 (2008), p. 203.

83 Gogol Bordello, 'Nomadic Chronicles', *Voi-la Intruder*, Rubric Records, 1999.

84 Chaif, 'Nikto ne uslyshit/Oi-yo', *Davai vernemsia*, 1990/Feelee, 1992.

85 Gogol Bordello, 'Dogs Were Barking', *Gypsy Punks*.

86 Kino, 'Mama-anarchiia', *Noch'*, Antrop, 1985/Melodia, 1988.

87 Gogol Bordello, 'Madagascar-Roumania (Tu Jésty Fáta)', *East Infection*.

88 Gogol Bordello, *Super Taranta!*, SideOneDummy Records, 2007.

89 Gogol Bordello, *Gypsy Punks*.

90 '"This is the capital of the Serb Republic and mostly Serbs," said Mr. Jevdjevic. "But I won't play only for Serbs. I wouldn't play Sarajevo only for Muslims. I wouldn't play Mostar only for Croats. They have to all be together for me to play."' Quoted in Adamek, 'Kultur Shock Plays the Balkans'.

91 Meadey, 'Babar Luck'.

92 B. Sisario, 'Gypsy Punk Cabaret', *New York Times* (14 April 2002).

93 *Ibid.*

94 Kultur Shock, *Ministry of Kultur*, Kultur Shock Records, 2011.

95 'Asian music is very much part of the World Music scene, but we make music – the music we hear every day. It provides us with a medium to talk to people, to get social and political ideas across, to get the attention of youth', Anirudha Das quoted in Huq, 'Asian Kool?', p. 68.

96 Kultur Shock Record Review, Kultur Shock official website, www.kulturshock.com/press?id=2076, accessed 28 March 2014.

97 'Kultur Shock is what punk rock should sound like', Jello Biafra on *Gigmaven.com*, 2012, http://gigmaven.com/kulturshock?f=c, accessed 28 March 2014.

98 See also D. Howarth and Y. Stavrakakis, 'Introducing Discourse Theory and Political Analysis', in D. Howarth, A. Norval and Y. Stavrakakis (eds), *Discourse Theory and*

Political Analysis: Identities, Hegemonies and Social Change (Manchester: Manchester University Press, 2000), pp. 1–24.

99 E. Laclau and L. Zac, 'Minding the Gap: The Subject of Politics', in E. Laclau (ed.), *The Making of Political Identities* (London: Verso, 1984), pp. 11–39; J. Butler, E. Laclau and S. Žižek, *Hegemony, Contingency, Universality: Contemporary Dialogues on the Left* (London: Verso, 1999).

100 D. Howart, *Discourse* (Buckingham: Open University Press, 2000), p. 109.

101 M. Bakhtin, *Rabelais and His World* (Bloomington, IN: Indiana University Press, 1985), p. 7.

102 T. Todorov, 'L'Heritage de Bakhtine', in M. Carel (ed.), *Les Facettes du dire. Hommage a Oswald Ducrot* (Paris: Kime, 2002), p. 341–7.

103 E. Laclau, 'Constructing Universality', in Butler, Laclau and Žižek, *Hegemony, Contingency, Universality*, pp. 281–307; J. Torfing, *New Theories of Discourse: Laclau, Mouffe, Žižek* (Oxford: Blackwell, 1999), p. 113.

104 N. Wiseman-Trowse, *Performing Class in British Popular Music* (Houndmills: Palgrave Macmillan, 2008), pp. 1–173.

105 E. Broadley, 'Gogol Bordello', *SuicideGirls.com* (2 October 2007), http://suicidegirls. com/interviews/Gogol+Bordello/, accessed 28 March 2014.

5

Crass, subculture and class: the milieu culture of DIY punk

This chapter presents an account of the activities and social formation of the DIY punk band Crass in order to develop a critique of the notion of 'subculture' employed at the time of the group's existence (1977–85) by the Birmingham University Centre for Contemporary Cultural Studies (CCCS). It supplies a narrative of how the band and the cultural movement known as `anarcho-punk' provided a 'milieu' where class identities could blend and develop hybrid forms of cultural and social capital.[1]

The central planks of my argument are, firstly, that the notion of subculture developed by the CCCS took its theoretical understanding of the structural position of class too literally, thus making it difficult to identify the differing effects of class on actors within a particular milieu. Secondly, that in present-ing subcultures as a response to a loss of identity and community rooted in social class – and the reading of subcultural style, activity, argot and creativity as part of a class response from a subordinate social position – the CCCS was too rigid in its theoretical framework. In particular, it failed to explain the more heterogeneous, complex and hybrid cultures that emerged across the UK as processes of migration, globalisation and broader influences on previously more stable identities began to take effect. By contrast, it is argued here that subcultural spaces and sites of production and creativity opened dialogues *between* people from different class backgrounds with shared interests in such things as popular music and a critical understanding of modern life. These processes presented opportunities for new and hybrid cultures and forms of cultural capital to emerge. Indeed, Crass may be seen as a part of this process, with both middle-class and working-class members drawing from influences that ranged from the 1960s counter-culture to school teachers, harsh home environments, access to art school and the emergence of punk as an oppositional youth culture.

The chapter begins by discussing the CCCS's theorisation of subculture and my development of the concept of ' milieu' as a different starting point for an analysis of these types of phenomena. It then moves on to examine Crass, the individuals within the band and what their musical, biographical and social activities tell us about punk as a milieu and as a site for the blending of cultural and social capital.

Subcultures, milieu and identity: from Birmingham to North Weald, Epping Forest!

Subculture, as a concept and a descriptive term that conveys a sense of sociality outside of the norm, has been argued over and debated keenly by academics and social commentators alike. Most famously, perhaps, the CCCS developed over the 1960s and 1970s a theory that located subculture as a site of 'resistance' to prevailing socio-economic structures, class relations and cultural hegemony.[2] This, typically, was defined in class terms, but did not thereby assert that subcultures provided a solution to the position of a subordinate class group. Rather, the CCCS suggested that class tensions and relations were played out in the imagination and displaced by an emphasis on symbolic goods, style, violence and knowledge of particular fields of activity (e.g. popular music).

Phil Cohen identified four modes for the generation of subcultural style: dress, music, ritual and argot.[3] These were all constructed by the subcultural group in circumstances that reflected their position in the social order. Through them, Cohen suggested, it was possible to read the subcultural group's experience of and response to their prevailing social positioning. In other words, the CCCS argued that youth subcultures (and, indeed, working-class cultures more generally) were a response to the 'socially organised positions and experiences of the class in relation to the major institutions and structures'.[4] They provided spaces where meaningful collective and individual actions were constructed, though each generation tended to build new responses or variations on the past. In terms of an individual's life history, this was seen to develop within the confines of the experience of class relations.

Such analysis may be proven partially correct and relevant to very particular subcultural forms in specific historical periods. However, the theories of the CCCS fail to take into account the ways in which subcultural spaces open up dialogues and communication between disparate individuals from different class positions. Following Bourdieu, the subcultural 'field' of popular music and, specifically, punk may be seen as providing various sites of development and engagement. With regard to Crass, the band lived collectively at Dial House in North Weald, Epping Forest. Within this setting they formed a *milieu* that drew its musical, cultural and political references from diverse sources (hippy culture, counter-culture, the wider punk movement).[5] Thus, the subcultural spaces inhabited by Crass facilitated hybrid identities that moved individuals and groups or collectivities beyond their starting position into new and diverse territory. This, in turn, not only challenges the idea of punk as a working-class response to structural changes in the social order,[6] but also suggests the possibility of a subcultural 'solution' via the emergence of counter-hegemonic forces. Organic intellectuals, in the Gramscian sense, emerged from this milieu (e.g. Penny Rimbaud of Crass, Dick Lucas of the Subhumans), enabling them and others to engage with different ideas and explore different practices that led to a change in perception of their class outlook.[7] By replacing the CCCS version of subculture with the more dynamic concept of milieu, we can understand the social trajectory of individuals through their biographical narrative, stocks of knowledge and typifications as well as their historical class position.

In some ways, this relates to the work of John Irwin, whose 1977 book, *Scenes*, made the case for lifestyle or subcultural 'scenes' providing ways of coping with the complexities of modern life.

> Scene activities are not irrelevant because if the societies of the future are to survive in a world which is rapidly being shrunk and damaged by technology and overpopulation, and if they are to preserve the values of freedom and individualism, their citizens will have to be capable of coping with heterogeneity and change, and of negotiating new values and rules for changing situations. This will require a heightened capacity for voluntary action and the skills of mixing with strangers. Scenes, which may at present seem excessively hedonistic, are helpful preparations for this future mode of behaviour.[8]

If ideas of community are changing, then the concept of milieu gives us some tools to look more microscopically at this. In relation to Crass, we can see how its members – specifically Penny Rimbaud (Jeremy Ratter) and Steve Ignorant (Steve Williams) – developed a politics that tried to deal with a hybrid class identity in relation to ideas of anarchism, humanism and transcendentalism.[9]

Such a politics, moreover, was at least partially a response to the variety of organised and programmatic political groupings on the far left and far right that sought to engage with the band at their gigs and through articles in papers and fanzines.

Crass, punk and class

George McKay was one of the first academic writers to take the Crass phenomena seriously. As his starting point, he cited one of the only references to Crass in the existent scholarly writing about punk: Jon Savage's *England's Dreaming* (1991):

> Their *Feeding of the Five Thousand* (Small Wonder, EP, 1978) was the first
> of a sequence of media (records, slogans, books, posters, magazines, films,
> actions and concerts) so complex that they deserve a book to themselves, and
> so effective that they sowed the ground for the return of serious anarchism
> and the popularity of CND in the early eighties. It is also possible to trace the
> current popularity of the travelling lifestyle to Crass's huge success in the early
> eighties.[10]

Mckay describes the internal variation in Crass's line-up in terms of class background and a mixture of so-called subcultural forms. The age range of the band meant that some members (Rimbaud, Gee Vaucher) had roots in the hippy subculture of the 1960s, while others came of age in tandem with punk's subcultural formation. Rimbaud's father was a Colonel in the army and fought in the Second World War. He sent his son to public school and expected great things, but was soon to be disappointed by the ever-questioning and rebellious Jeremy. Two expulsions from public schools, horror from Jeremy at the fact that there were `haves' and `have-nots' in society, an affection for rock 'n' roll, the angry young men writers of the 1960s and the delights of sex and smoking, soon sent Rimbaud on a very different path to that which his middle-class parents expected.[11]

Steve Williams, by contrast, grew up in Dagenham after his mum moved back to where her wider family was located having left his dad while they had been trying to build a new life in Stoke. He grew up in a very working-class family, living with his nan, grandad, mum, brother and sister in a council house. His early life was fairly stable; his mum found a new partner, although Williams didn't get on with him. He hated school, but he nevertheless found an interest in literature and film through his English teacher who encouraged him to read things like Keith Waterhouse's *Billy Liar* and works by John Osborne,

Stan Barstow, Alan Sillitoe and Barry Hines. Books and the enthusiasm of his teacher fired Williams's imagination, as did a teenage love for music (especially David Bowie). The two sat well together and prepared him for a position as a lyricist and vocalist in Crass.[12]

Dial House, the open house that Rimbaud found and paid minimal rent on from 1965, became a meeting point for a variety of people. Key to the formation of Crass, however, was the arrival of Williams. His older brother, David, had visited a few times with friends and eventually invited Steve, who became a regular visitor thereafter. Steve seemed to grow in confidence and began to experiment with new ideas, books, music and skills. He describes being introduced to the work of Hubert Selby Junior, Jack Kerouac and Walt Whitman, music that he had never heard of in the areas of jazz and classical, mad-cap moments playing pots and pans, lighting trees from underneath at night time, learning screen printing and art techniques from Penny and Gee Vaucher (who became Crass's visual artist). He likens the experience to the feeling and excitement he got from his English teacher at school, but this was more 'real'; he felt listened to and respected by those around him who were often many years his senior (Rimbaud was twenty-nine to Ignorant's fourteen when they first met). These lines from Ignorant's biography are pertinent in this respect:

> What I looked forward to most was that whenever I visited Dial House I'd be growing. Experimenting with something new. And whatever I tried, whenever I was there, Pen and the others would be going *Go for it – do it!* After so many years of indifference from mum and Stan, Dial House gave me all the encouragement I could want. In spades … I'd never seen anything like Dial House, or met anyone like the people who lived there … But whenever I was there I knew I wanted to live like this, I knew I wanted some of it. I just didn't think it was going to happen, but as it turned out, soon I was going to move in. And stay for twenty years.[13]

Dial House was a place outside of the norm that meant that people from different class backgrounds could potentially meet and share ideas and experiences on the basis of a mutual interest in music, literature, film and art. They also tended to share an antipathy for the way that society was organised. Their different class backgrounds gave them different windows into Britain's class-ridden social order, but their desire to respond to it creatively was similar.

When the backgrounds of a large number of punk's key protagonists are examined, it becomes clear that their class origins were diverse. Punk was not the easy-fit working-class subculture imagined by the CCCS. Throughout his influential text, *Subculture: The Meaning of Style* (1979), Dick Hebdige has a difficult time trying to tease out the working-class elements of early punk. In the chapter on 'style as homology', for example, he starts by stating the case for subculture as a 'symbolic fit between the values and lifestyles of a group, its subjective experience and the musical forms it uses to express or reinforce its focal concerns'.[14] Bricolage (the use of objects, clothing and symbols to assemble subcultural form) is also presented as a part of this process. He cites skinhead as a good example; a subculture represented by hardness, masculinity and working-class identity.[15] Punk, though, presented a different problem:

> There was a homological relation between the trashy cut-up clothes and spiky hair, the pogo and amphetamines, the spitting, the vomiting, the format of the fanzines, the insurrectionary pose and the soulless frantically driven music. The punks wore clothes that were the sartorial equivalent of swear words, and they swore as they dressed – with calculated effect, lacing obscenities into record notes and publicity releases, interviews and love songs.[16]

From here, Hebdige treads a fine line between identifying the symbolic nature of the subculture with actual working class-ness. The safety-pins and bin-liners worn by punks are recognised as signifiers of a relative poverty that was 'either directly experienced and exaggerated or sympathetically assumed, and which in turn was made to stand for the spiritual paucity of everyday life',[17] but Hebdige also seems aware of too literal a reading of the conjectural relationship between punk and mainstream culture. To make sense of this, he delves deeper into theory and the framework of homology, referring to writers around the French journal *Tel Quel* who used the concept of signifying practices to analyse the deconstruction of the meaning of symbols and their reconstruction within specific cultural and subcultural artistic work. In particular, he cites the work of Julia Kristeva, the Bulgarian-French psychoanalytical philosopher, whose understanding of radical signifying practices that 'negate and disturb syntax' and disrupt meanings are easily read from an ordered class position. From this, Hebdige is able to suggest that punk, instead of reflecting the position of its class background to reconcile and recreate a sense of traditional class community, dislocates itself from its class position to reform meanings to the extent that it moves outside the knowledge of ordinary people. Punks emphasised their 'otherness'; they tried to escape their class background by disfiguring and masking themselves. Even then, however, Hebdige remains convinced that the working-class element was the root of the form, despite the fact that it 'refused to make sense, to be grounded, [and] read back to its origins'.[18]

For Hebdige, then, punk represented the 'pre-categorical realities of bourgeois society – inequality, powerlessness, alienation', but in a way that dislocated itself from its parent culture.[19] It represented the contradictions of modern life rather than trying to 'magically' resolve them. It was a form of rupture with modern life, existing in a constant state of flux and assemblage.

Within the confines of his theoretical framework, Hebdige struggles to resolve the contradictions between class culture, parent culture and a sense of unity or homology. If, however, he had thought of punk as a different type of subculture to skinhead, one that was fed by both working-class as well as middle-class youth, he may have come closer to reconciling the diverse backgrounds of those involved. Music, as a form of popular culture, has the ability to reach a wide range of people. Punk seems to have formed through a mixture of class backgrounds and identities – but key to its inception was an attitude that despised what was going on socially, either in terms of popular music alone or more generally in the context of the sense of crisis that developed over the 1970s. Joe Strummer (John Mellor) and John Lydon came from very different class backgrounds, but their shared disgust for the general picture of life in Britain in the 1970s converged to help define what became known as punk. Similarly, as punk developed as a social and cultural movement beyond London, it spread to a wide variety of individuals and groups. Crass, as a band and an idea, grew within this hybrid culture, reflecting the mixed-class origins of its members while also breaking clear from the more fixed identities of previous subcultures.

There is no authority but yourself

The milieu inhabited by Crass, and the diverse ideas contained within it, enabled those of different class positions to acquire more complex types of cultural capital than those experienced in previous social spaces and groupings.[20] This, as noted by George McKay in his discussion of Crass's political position, has been described by some as being 'up shit creek'.[21] In a number of interviews, including one with myself, Rimbaud has explained his take on anarchism as being one informed by libertarianism and humanism, but also – via the work of Walt Whitman – transcendentalism. Transcendentalists believed in the inherent goodness of human beings and nature and despised the influence of the state and church. They saw the church as corrupting the true nature of the individual, which must be embraced in order for a real community to develop. For Rimbaud, the family, church, state and all professional institutions are constructs that serve to constrain what we really are.

As the Jesuits acknowledged, in the first seven years of your life you are impregnated with vile thinking, be it the thinking of the family, the thinking of the church, the thinking of the state, the thinking of professional institutions. You are simply a pawn to that. I'm 67 now and I'm still thinking uh uh, another one! They are like viruses; they are like viruses on the soul. I can say that lightly and yet I am having to repress an absolute rage. It is a cheating of life. I don't feel that I have lived. You know I have a far more interesting and far more exciting life than many people, but that was Jeremy, that was my father's son that has done that. I, in my own right, haven't yet existed because 'I in my own right' is a complete question mark in itself. That is why Quantum and modern physics fascinates me because that is the case: we don't exist as isolated individual organisms, we can't do, we are actually mutually dependent; we're symbiotic.[22]

According to Rimbaud, there is a deeper state of the soul, an untouched area where 'I am they and they are me' – a type of universality which modern individualism, the Cartesian self, cannot comprehend. He sees himself as a part of a universal humanity that can only be expressed by poetics and creative work.

Crass, as a project, certainly presented a highly critical view of modern British life in the 1970s to 1980s and it is intended here to examine key songs to illuminate the politics and hybrid cultural capital that developed within and around the group. 'Reality Asylum', the proposed opening track of Crass's first record, outlined one of the pillars of the band's – and especially Rimbaud's – disgust: organised religion. Christ and the crucifixion are painted as being responsible for the fear that humans have of their own being, sexuality and, ultimately, humanity. Woman as a figure is portrayed as being stripped of her central being by becoming the source of sin for the Christian religion:

> You carry the standard of our oppression
> Enola is your gaiety
> The bodies of Hiroshima are your delight
> The nails are the only trinity,
> Hold them in your corpsey gracelessness
> The image I have had to suffer
> The cross is the virgin body of womanhood that you defile
> You nail yourself to your own sin
> Lame-arse Jesus calls me brother
> There are no words for my contempt
> Every woman is a cross in his filthy ideology
> His arrogant delight …

Share nothing, you Christ
Sterile, impotent, fucklove prophet of death
You are the ultimate pornography
In your cunt fear, cock fear, man fear, woman fear,
Unfair, warfare, warfare, warfare, warfare,
Jesus died for his own sins, not mine.[23]

Religion is thus lambasted for its ignorance of humanity, sexuality, love, desire and its message of fear and guilt for human feeling. The record is powerful; its message recited over a harsh avant-garde soundscape. Indeed, the track was refused pressing at the plant used by Small Wonder Records and was initially left off Crass's debut EP, *The Feeding of the Five Thousand* (1978).

Religion features throughout Crass's work, like a black cloud haunting the every move of fearful humans cowering in the shadow of popes, priests, vicars, archbishops and deacons. But *The Feeding of the Five Thousand* also turned its attack on mundane existence and the monotony of work. Significantly, the focus is as critical of the idea of the working class holding value in certain types of collective workplaces as it is to the modernist idea of factory production:

I hate the living dead and their work in the factories
They go like sheep to their production lines
They live on illusions, don't face the realities
All they live for is that big blue sign
It says … FORD
I'm, BORED, BORED, BORED[24]

Such sentiment clearly exposed the difference between Crass's political position and the prevailing leftist politics of the period, a distinction further developed on the band's second album, *Stations of the Cross* (1979). The album starts with 'Mother Earth', Rimbaud's musing on Myra Hindley as an anti-mother, a figure of complexity whose image revealed the hypocrisy of tabloid readers who 'wanted her dead' but were also appalled by her crimes. The story is intimated as a drooled-over pantomime that the good 'Christian' public devoured at will. They would rip her 'limb from limb', which Rimbaud suggested was the result of a hypocritical idea of violence as an end to 'solve' social problems.[25] But 'White Punks on Hope' came next; a track that rejected the politics of both the left and right. Rimbaud's lyrics suggest that punk had offered hope after 'years of crap', but questions of politics and class had intervened to produce dead ends: the restriction of thought rather than freedom of thought. Rock Against Racism (RAR) is the principal target of the track, with Rimbaud insisting that white liberal demonstrations in parks with bands like

The Clash playing were not an answer to racism. Where The Clash, in 'White Riot', sang 'black man's gotta a lot of problems, but he don't mind throwing a brick', Crass and Rimbaud argued 'Black man's got his problems and his way of dealing with it, so don't fool yourself that you're helping with your white liberal shit'. Racism, for Rimbaud, was dealt with by practice: not the political practice of argument but the practical application of acceptance of people on a day-to-day level. He positioned The Clash as going back on the sentiment of their original song by playing the RAR festival, concluding by dismissing left-wing and right-wing politics as boring and regressive. The song ends with the line 'Anarchy and Freedom is what I want'.[26]

Crass had used the anarchy symbol at their gigs from mid-1978, mainly because they were attracting an audience that comprised both far-left elements (be it the Socialist Workers Party, Militant, Workers Power or Revolutionary Communist Group) and members of the far right (including British Movement skinheads). The symbol served to distance the band from each while also signalling a willingness to communicate with individuals on both sides and present a different set of political reference points. Crass had no clear theoretical basis to their anarchism, Rimbaud going so far as to say that if someone had mentioned Bakunin to him at that time he would have thought they meant a type of vodka![27] Simultaneously, Crass used the CND symbol as a peace sign to suggest that they were not into violence; though it also referred to their support of anti-nuclear campaigns.

Over time, Crass's understanding of anarchism and its historical position sharpened. The band sought to develop an alternative to the programmatic and, as they saw it, dogmatic politics of the organised left (and right) – an alternative that emerged out of the band members' own backgrounds and the way they creatively responded to events unfolding around them. Thus, Rimbaud began to make reference to the losses of the anarchists in the Russian Revolution, the Spanish Civil War and the rejection of libertarian thinkers and activists by French socialists in the revolts of the 1960s. His version of anarchism effectively restated the key Crass slogan, 'There is no authority but yourself', suggesting anarchism as the right of an individual to make their own decisions in life and that such a right is a fundamental freedom. Communism and socialism to Rimbaud represented just another face of the will to power, but with a dictatorship of the proletariat rather than a dictatorship of capital.[28]

Other themes covered on *Stations of the Crass* include the hypocrisy of religion and the possession of love, as juxtaposed by Eve Libertine (Bronwyn Jones) in 'Darling'. The song starts with the lines, 'they sell us love as divinity, but it's only a social obscenity, hello hero, hero hello'. Pete Wright, on 'Fun Going On', sings of the pointlessness of wanting a job, saying he would be described as a 'shirk' but he never wanted 'in' on the employment game. He addresses religion, war, work and family life, suggesting all are a con and a direct contrast to the idea of 'having fun when you are young'. Gee Vaucher, meanwhile, offered 'Heard Too Much About', a song that suggests the working class and the ruling elite both work in their respective factories and offices aware that something is missing in their lives. Domestic violence, family, church and school are evoked as providing 'no choice at all' for those who continue to live without trying to question their lives.

All these tracks have echoes in the literature, plays and ideas that members of Crass were reading and engaging with. Steve Ignorant talks about the effect of reading Alan Sillitoe's *The Loneliness of the Long Distance Runner*, a story about a boy who, after a short life of petty crime, is sent to a Borstal and tries to find solace and a purpose in long distance running. He is offered early release if he wins a cross-country race against a local public school. But after being ahead for most of the race, he stops just short of the finish line and allows the other runners to pass him before giving a defiant gesture to his Borstal captors. Hard labour is the result, but he is happy that his independent spirit gave him a small victory over the hypocrisy of the guards.[29]

Others in Crass saw such acts of rebellion as a challenge to live up to. John Osborne's *Look Back in Anger* is continually evoked within the band's lyrical themes. A working-class and upper middle-class relationship portrayed as a fault-line of antagonism, not necessarily because of the class difference but because of the character, Alison, the wife of Jimmy Porter, wanting to maintain a normal domesticity that strangles the life and creative impulse out of her husband. He ends up having an affair with his wife's middle-class actress friend, rejecting his wife before finding a strange truce-like reconciliation at the end. Indeed, the figure of Jimmy Porter and his desire to have something more than the banality of everyday life is a theme Crass evoke again and again in their lyrics and the artwork of Gee Vaucher.[30]

Walt Whitman is another writer whose work had a definite influence on Crass. His humanism, realism and open discussions on sexuality, prostitution and American life evidently informed Crass's ideas on transcendentalism. The band did, however, offer a more critical view of modern sexuality with their third album, *Penis Envy* (1981), sung entirely by Eve Libertine, Joy De Vivre (Joy Haney) and Gee Vaucher (as Gee Sus). In the sleevenotes to the 2010 re-release of *Penis Envy*, Libertine discusses the way in which sexual division and the cementing of what it is to be feminine and masculine remain every bit as hypocritical and constraining in the contemporar era as when the album was first released. She outlines where she feels feminism has gone:

Thirty years on: pink for girls, blue for boys. So what's new? It may be more
sexy, princess pink, and a blue inkling towards army camouflage, but the
effects are just the same: an earlier than necessary separation from the wonder
of our being: a conformity to centuries of female oppression. Yes, what's new?
The heels of Bata Motel are now so high that women wearing them stagger
along with the flock on burning feet, clumsy-legged and tight arsed, calling it
'female power'.

Libertine's (and Crass's) feminism was radical, but not in the sense that
feminist writers of the late 1960 and 1970s would have imagined. The debates
between second-wave feminists (Dworkin, Mackinnon, *et al.*) and the emergent third-wave feminism dominated the feminist theoretical and political
landscape of the 1980s and early 1990s. Crass, with *Penis Envy*, contributed to the idea of moving beyond a unified feminism. They were concerned
with a sexual politics and women's rights that fed directly into the Greenham
Common women's peace camps. Libertine's ideas fit into the individualistic approach to anarchism and feminism that Rimbaud applies in his broader analysis
of society. The songs on *Penis Envy* deal with the bondage of high heels and the
fashion accessories of mainstream femininity ('Bata Motel'); growing up in a
family tied to work, mortgage payments and reproduction of gender stereotypes ('Systematic Death'); the traps and perils of the beauty myth and beauty
products, including surgery to re-shape appearances to fit in with mainstream
versions of sexuality ('Poison in a Pretty Pill'). There are also songs that deal
with familiar Crass themes, such as an antipathy and opposition to organised
politics and ideology. 'Where Next Columbus?' is Libertine's narrative against
the politics and ideas of Marx, Mussolini, Jung, Sartre, Einstein and Jesus, suggesting their respective ideologies have been developed and carried forward
by an army of followers looking for something (and someone) to lead them
out of their own psychologically and socially fragile predicament. Again, the
inference is that a form of self-awareness, a do-it-yourself philosophy and the
realisation that only you can make changes through your own practice provides
the core message of the work.

The themes that dominated Crass's early albums reveal a band trying to
argue against and move beyond the rigidity of class politics and personal class
position. By the time Crass had started work on their fourth album, *Christ:
The Album* (1982), however, Margaret Thatcher's new-right regime had taken
a firm hold on the UK. Mass unemployment had reached 3 million; there were
riots in many of Britain's major cities, trade union disputes, H-Block protests
in Ireland and an economic recession. Crass, though, had been creating a large
audience for the anti-war movement. The band's anarchism was being taken

seriously and debated by many; Greenham Common had become a focus for the women's movement; squatting and turning empty buildings into low-rent housing through the setting-up of housing co-ops or creating social centres was also beginning to blossom. Given this, Crass were optimistic about their ability to affect society and build areas of pressure and practical activity that made a difference. Accordingly, *Christ: The Album* was their most ambitious project to date. They spent far more time on it than on previous albums (around six months) and developed a 15-track record, presenting it as a double LP in a black box with a live recording of a gig at the 100 Club in London and a booklet entitled *A Series of Shock Slogans and Mindless Tantrums*.

Taken generally, the album continued the themes that peppered Crass's previous records: the first track, 'Have a Nice Day', bemoans pop's star system while the 'Iron ladies and steel men, [wait] for their fucking war to start again', positioning Crass as the screaming critic of the social order that won't go away. 'Mother Love' attacks the notion, authority and suffocation of the family; 'Nineteen Eighty Bore' presents a damning account of a population kept in line and happy to accept the drip-feed diet of TV entertainment. Rimbaud was the architect of the first and third tracks, while Ignorant wrote 'Mother Love'. At times, Rimbaud verges on elitism, wanting to shake anyone who will listen out of his or her cathode ray addiction:

> Fantasise and dream about what you might have been.
> Who needs controlling when they've got the cathode ray?
> They've got your fucking soul now they'll fuse your brains away.
> Mindless fucking morons sit before the set, being fed the mindless rubbish
>   they deserve to get.[31]

The rest of the album deals with subcultural wars, consumerism, macho punk and includes a number of anti-war and anti-violence songs. It finishes with the track 'Major General Despair', an anti-war song that fades out to be replaced by an E. P. Thompson speech at a CND rally that suggests people together can make a difference against what he describes as a tide of barbarity and the threat of annihilation occasioned by nuclear war: 'Now, looking at you, I know one thing, we can win, we can win, I want you to sense your own strength'.

Within a few weeks of finishing the record, however, Margaret Thatcher sent a fleet of ships down to the Falkland Islands to engage in a war that killed approximately 900 people, cost millions of pounds, and had a profound effect on the British public. Crass, whose optimism was rising before the release of *Christ: The Album*, felt they had lost a battle and been caught unawares by the war. Having not recorded a song directly about the Falklands conflict for the album, the band set about releasing a single. The result, 'How Does it Feel to

UNIVERSITY OF WINCHESTER
LIBRARY

be the Mother of a Thousand Dead?' (1982), was a direct, simple and non-complex attack on Thatcher and her government for taking the country to war:

> Your arrogance has gutted these bodies of life, your deceit fooled them that it was worth the sacrifice.
> Your lies persuaded people to accept the wasted blood, your filthy pride cleansed you of the doubt you should have had.
> You smile in the face of the death cause you are so proud and vain, your inhumanity stops you from realising the pain that you inflicted, you determined, you created, you ordered – It was your decision to have those young boys slaughtered.

The record caught the attention of the mainstream press and was mentioned in parliament. It was used by opposition Labour MPs at Prime Minister's questions to ascertain whether Margaret Thatcher had listened to the record and what her response was. None was forthcoming. Crass, meanwhile, were beginning to realise that their politics, though hugely affective at an individual level, lacked the power to effectively intervene in large-scale events. As a result, the band's politics became more interventionist. Its members participated in three 'Stop the City' events and organised a two-day squat gig in London. Stop the City was described as a 'protest and carnival against war, oppression and exploitation' that encouraged people to come to the financial district of London and use a range of creative and innovative practice to protest against capitalism and war. The demonstrations were wonderfully carnivalesque and successful in the first two instances. They can definitely be seen as the forerunners to the Anti-globalisation movement of the 1990s and 2000s, and the Occupy movement of 2010–11. By the third, however, the police had got used to the tactics employed by the protestors and more effectively contained the protest, making hundreds of arrests. Crass were aware at this point too that their phones were being tapped. They would get visits from the police and MI5; they were feeling the intense stare and controlling gaze of the state. In response they made one more album, the almost avant-garde *Yes Sir, I Will* (1983), and two more singles; 'Whodunnit' (1983) and 'You're Already Dead' (1984), all of which continued the rabid critique of Thatcher's government. They also produced, in secret, a cut-up tape of a supposed conversation between Margaret Thatcher and Ronald Reagan. The 'conversation' presented Thatcher as admitting responsibility for sinking a retreating Argentine ship, the *Belgrano*, and admitting that she had let HMS *Sheffield* be sunk to protect Prince Andrew (who was aboard HMS *Invincible*). It finished with Reagan saying he was prepared to launch nuclear missiles in mainland Europe to protect American interests.

Crass had secretly mailed the tape from Amsterdam to a large number of press associations across the world in the hope of causing embarrassment and damage to Thatcher. For six months nothing happened and then a media storm was created. American press and media started by blaming the Kremlin and the KGB but the British paper, *The Observer*, somehow got hold of the information that Crass were the source of the tape. Such an outcome increased the tensions within the band themselves. They knew that they had been watched and had their phones tapped, but this situation led to a new level of paranoia. Finally, the band kept their promise of breaking up in 1984. Although further releases came out under the Crass name, these tailed off and the band threw themselves into different projects and work.

Conclusion

What is clear from this discussion of Crass is that they were a band that broke relatively successfully with the class politics of the 1970s and provided an alternative set of ideas and reference points that were incredibly potent because of their use of a popular music milieu to communicate with a wide and diverse social audience. Their version of anarchism, viewed through the lens of an individual's responsibility for their own actions, and their presentation of anti-war, pacifist, vegetarian, squatting and DIY cultural ideas, meant they broke permanently from both the mainstream political and radical left–right political ideas that helped shape the post-war period. This, of course, coincided with Thatcher's own breaking of 'consensus', replacing it with Sir Keith Joseph's monetarism and free market principles.

Crass were an alternative response to the traditional class politics of the UK. Their cultural and political work forged a hybrid class identity that developed a cultural capital that moved individual perceptions and horizons to a new level.

The band's version of anarchism, based on a DIY philosophy and individual responsibility, moulded a new and influential anti-political response to the post-consensus landscape. The band posited a position that went against organised politics with a mantra of 'There is no authority but yourself' that referenced anarchism, humanism, poetry and transcendentalism. They put forward a set of ideas that had been evident before in various types of literature and music, but which now coalesced in a unified and focused shift that fed into the consciousness of literally thousands of kids from a variety of backgrounds, towns and cities.[32]

In terms of 'subcultural theory', Crass made a difference through a milieu that tried to get people to think beyond the confines of the socio-economic and cultural positions they had grown up inhabiting. The band formed part of a break in structured class politics and presented ideas that communicated to a number of people across class positions. In so doing, the anarcho-punk associated with Crass therefore necessitates a revision of CCCS theory to appreciate the evolving nature and hybridising of class and knowledge associations facilitated through the vehicle of a popular music milieu.

Milieu, as a concept, provides a tool to help us understand this via its attention to biography and the ways in which the world inhabited by an individual can change their outlook. In the case of Crass, the politics of the (DIY) independent punk scene of the late 1970s and early 1980s provided a social space for a distinct political outlook to develop. Such a politics may be seen to be directly linked, on the one hand, to the colliding worlds of the class positions of the different individuals involved and, secondly, to their creative response to that interaction. This chapter has suggested that Crass provide an example of how the CCCS's subcultural theory is too rigid a formula to understand the different trajectories of class groupings within a subculture such as punk. Moreover, it demonstrates how attention to the detail of the creative work, social network and interactions within the social space of a subculture can illuminate the effects of class, cultural capital, social knowledge, economic capital and politics on a specific subculture. This, then, provides researchers with a challenge: that in order to understand these groupings, an intensive research process and historical tracing of not just the events and their appearance but the individuals involved must be undertaken. The concept of milieu can help us with that process; Crass, meanwhile, provide us with a particularly useful example of its relevance.

Notes

1   Milieu as a concept is set out in my book *Exploring the Networked Worlds of Popular Music* (2010). The concept looks at the stocks of knowledge that an individual develops in relation to their particular family and class background, before then trying to assess how these develop and change with interaction with the groups an individual engages with. It also attempts to locate actors in relation to their structural position or (in Bourdieu's terms) 'field' in order to understand how they interpret and act on events.

2   See, for example, J. Clarke, S. Hall, T. Jefferson and B. Roberts, 'Subcultures, Cultures and Class: A Theoretical Overview', in S. Hall and T. Jefferson (eds), *Resistance*

Through Rituals: Youth Subcultures in Post-War Britain (London: Hutchinson & Co., 1976), pp. 9–74; P. Cohen, 'Subcultural Conflict and Working Class Community', *Working Class Papers in Cultural Studies*, 2 (1972), pp. 4–51.

3 *Ibid.*

4 Clarke, Hall, Jefferson and Roberts, 'Subcultures, Cultures and Class', p. 57.

5 P. Webb, *Exploring the Networked Worlds of Popular Music: Milieu Cultures* (New York: Routledge, 2007).

6 D. Hebdige, *Subculture: The Meaning of Style* (London: Routledge, 1979).

7 I. Glasper, *The Day the Country Died: A History of Anarcho Punk, 1980–84* (London: Cherry Red, 2006); G. Mckay (ed.), *DIY Culture: Party and Protest in '90s Britain* (London: Verso, 1998); R. Wallace, *The Day the Country Died – The DVD* (London: Cherry Red, 2006).

8 J. Irwin, *Scenes* (London: Sage, 1977).

9 A. C. Rose, *Transcendentalism as a Social Movement, 1830–50* (New Haven, CT: Yale University Press, 1981).

10 J. Savage, *England's Dreaming: The Sex Pistols and Punk Rock* (London: Faber & Faber, 1991), p. 584.

11 P. Rimbaud, *Shibboleth: My Revolting Life* (Edinburgh: AK Press, 1999).

12 S. Ignorant and S. Pottinger, *The Rest is Propaganda* (London: Southern Records Books, 2010).

13 *Ibid.*, p. 211.

14 Hebdige, *Subculture*, p. 127.

15 J. Clarke, 'Skinheads and the Study of Youth Culture' (University of Birmingham: CCCS Working Papers, 1975).

16 Hebdige, *Subculture*, p. 114.

17 *Ibid.*, p. 115.

18 *Ibid.*, p. 121.

19 *Ibid.*

20 P. Bourdieu, *The Field of Cultural Production: Essays on Art and Literature* (London: Polity Press, 1993).

21 McKay, *DIY Culture*, p. 77.

22 Interview with author, 21 September 2010.

23 All lyrics quoted with permission of Penny Rimbaud. Records cited: 'Reality Asylum', Crass Records, 1978; 'Bored', from *Feeding of the Five Thousand*, Small Wonder Records, 1978; 'Mother Earth', 'White Punks on Hope', 'Fun Going On', 'Darling', 'Heard Too Much About', from *Stations of the Crass*, Crass Records, 1979; 'Bata Motel', 'Systematic Death', 'Poison in a Pretty Pill', 'Where next Columbus?', from *Penis Envy*, Crass Records, 1981; 'Have a Nice Day', 'Mother Love', 'Nineteen Eighty Bore', 'Major General Despair', from *Christ The Album*. Crass Records, 1982; 'How Does it Feel (to be the Mother of a Thousand dead)', Crass Records, 1982; 'Who Dunnit?', Crass Records, 1983; 'You're Already Dead', Crass Records, 1984.

24 'Bored', *Feeding of the Five Thousand*, Small Wonder Records, 1978.

25 'Mother Earth', *Stations of the Crass*, Crass Records, 1979.

26 'White Punks on Hope', *Stations of the Crass*, Crass Records, 1979.
27 Rimbaud, *Shibboleth*, p. 109.
28 *Ibid.*, p. 158.
29 Ignorant and Pottinger, *The Rest is Propaganda*, pp. 45–6.
30 G. Vaucher, *Crass Art and Other Pre Post-Modernist Monsters* (Edinburgh: AK Press, 1999).
31 'Nineteen Eighty Bore', *Christ the Album*, Crass Records, 1982.
32 Interview with author, 21 September 2010. Rimbaud talked of a working-class kid who 'bought wholemeal bread, went to a library and got out an interesting book, thought about squatting an empty house, thought about the nature of religion, the state and the family'.

11

Transmission: punk and place

'Flowers of evil': ecosystem health and the punk poetry of John Cooper Clarke

JOHN PARHAM

The 'punk poetry' of John Cooper Clarke displays a keen awareness of its environment. 'The Day the World Stood Still' freezes, for a day, a world of traffic noise, dirt, flies. The curiously named 'I Travel in Biscuits' opens with a bombardment of the dirge disharmonies of the city:

> the sound of the daylight
> the smell of the urine
> the rain on the drainpipes
> the filthy two-two time
> i should know better
> how an animal feels;[1]

Across his descriptions of these 'garden[s] of cement' ('Limbo (Baby Limbo)'),[2] lie recurring motifs of rats, flies, germs, disease and death that signal the intertwined, mutually constitutive elements – the filth of the natural and built environment – and of the society that created them definitively captured in 'Evidently Chickentown':

> the fucking view is fucking vile
> for fucking miles and fucking miles
> the fucking babies fucking cry
> the fucking flowers fucking die

the fucking food is fucking muck
the fucking drains are fucking fucked
the colour scheme is fucking brown
everywhere in chicken town.[3]

Punk is many things:[4] a state of mind; a strategy for living; a 'spectacular subculture' that ripped the ephemera of consumerism – dog collars, bicycle chains, safety-pins – out of their everyday context;[5] absolute nihilism; or, as Greil Marcus argues, a more politicised *negation* which marked an 'underlying refusal to give up on imagining something other than the world as it is'.[6] Most of all, perhaps, it represents a generalised state of alienation.[7] While this has been recognised as encompassing almost anything – social and political marginalisation, religion, gender inequality, the common pop theme of teenage, sexual frustration – relatively little attention has been paid to punk's environmental alienation and discernible sense of place.

The argument of this chapter is that place is both a central source of punk's alienation and a significant component of its subcultural engagement with and resistance to 'the world as it is'. Furthermore, this alienation is embedded so deeply in some punk artists as to have engendered a complex sense of the interrelationship between physical environment and social and political disadvantage akin to Marx's concept of social metabolism. Discussed below, this describes networks of material 'interchange between organisms and their environment',[8] including humans, and sees these partially, but significantly, as determined by wider political and economic processes. Particularly in the city, the central location of punk, such processes are often hostile or at least neglectful towards the physical environment and its people. Consequently, I will argue that punk's resistance to those processes engendered a broadly eco-critical sense of place which intuited certain fundamental ecological concepts – including the centrality of place to human identity and an awareness of 'environmental injustice', the idea that colourless, polluted, toxic physical surroundings both mirror and help constitute equivalent urban, social conditions (e.g. slum housing or ill health), leaving some people victim to a disproportionate impact from environmental hazards.

Lastly, it will be argued that punk developed aesthetic forms ideally placed to articulate environmental injustice, forms epitomised and extended by John Cooper Clarke. His work is exemplary here for two reasons: an acute sensitivity to place which will be explored, with reference to local history, in the context of his growing up in Salford. This was a city wedged, at that time, between two countervailing, external forces – the Victorian, industrial past that had shaped Marx's metabolic concept; and the gradual erosion of that past by creeping, late twentieth-century globalisation. Secondly, the concordance between Cooper Clarke's own experience of place, gleaned here from newspaper interviews, and his practice. Through examples from the poems, and concluding with an analysis of the recorded version of 'Beasley Street', I will discuss how a poetic practice shaped and transformed by punk articulates, not least when set to music, what Laurence Buell has called a 'toxic discourse' of place.

Music and the environment

Punk's negation encompasses forms of environmental engagement and re-sistance that stem from a sensitivity to place. This can be conceptualised, in the first instance, with reference to ecocriticism, the field of study which ad-dresses how cultural forms might encompass ecological or environmental perspectives on nature and/or advocate green social-political positions. Punk does, admittedly, rather deviate from central emphases within an ecocriticism largely dominated by pastoral perspectives. John Elder, in his landmark study *Imagining the Earth* (1985), advances the notion of 'Reinhabitation', arguing that a return to places seemingly 'harmonious with the cycles of nature' is a prerequisite for environmental awareness.[9] David Ingram remarks that pastoral forms such as country or folk have tended to be the 'main mode by which the eco-utopian potential of [popular] music has been articulated'.[10] An example would be John Denver's celebrations of inhabiting rural America in songs like 'Take Me Home, Country Roads' or 'Wild Montana Skies'.[11] Ingram's closest British equivalent, Rob Young's *Electric Eden: Unearthing Britain's Visionary Music* (2011), tells a similar tale about folk music which has, over the decades, repeatedly summoned up the age-old 'dream of Albion' in the service of a 'myth of the natural life'.[12]

Yet punk's eco-critique is consistent with recent shifts in ecocritical per-spective, developed mainly within postcolonial or environmental justice ecocriticism, in which it has been recognised that an ecological insistence upon the centrality of 'belonging in place' to human identity must, nevertheless, always be coloured by a complex amalgamation of broader (social, political, global economic, ecological) forces, many of which have left people, not least in cities, subject to rather less affirmative feelings of place – displacement, alienation, injustice, risk. A central message of any number of punk tracks – The Saints' 'I'm Stranded'; X-Ray Spex's 'Let's Submerge'; The Jam's 'Down in the Tube Station at Midnight' – this reassertion of 'place', but with caveats of contingency and contestation offered up by the paradigm of 'space', is also evident both from recent analyses of place in popular music and classic sub-cultural readings of punk.

Andy Bennett, for instance, has described music, subculturally, as 'the product of local knowledges and sensibilities and a form of independent cultural territory'which, 'highly contested', operates in 'perpetual dialogue with [...] the social and spatial organisation of a given locality'.[13] Dave Haslam illustrates this in *Manchester England: The Story of the Pop Cult City* (1999), arguing that the source of Manchester's 'cultural alienation' lies in its opposition to an English national identity bound up with nature (i.e. pastoral), the fine arts, country houses, etc. and, consequently, that Manchester music has more of an affinity with 'outlaw American culture'.[14] According closely with connections Cooper Clarke has made between his experience of Salford and a practice informed, notably, by the American punk of The Ramones, this fits, furthermore, with the idea that British punk, as conceived in central texts such as Iain Chambers' *Popular Culture: The Metropolitan Experience* (1986), represents a 'reassertion of placed identities'.[15]

Chambers regarded punk's semiotic disruption of everyday signifiers as, for all its polysemic qualities, a conscious response to hegemonic, conventional social values, that, furthermore, was grounded in the city, 'home', he argued, both of consumer society and subcultural forms of resistance.[16] 'Living in the city we inherit its physical structures and cultural conditions while also challenging *and* exploring this inheritance, a process within which our urban "sense" and "self" is formed' [original emphasis]. The signs generated by punk were, that is, 'inhabited'; they 'sharpened the comparative sense of the immediate, the local and the particular'.[17]

While Chambers wrote, primarily, from a theoretical context, regarding the city as 'a psychological as well as ... physical reality',[18] Cooper Clarke, grounded in the conjunctures of post-war Salford, was as interested in the material environment that punk could articulate. His Manchester was, as Cooper Clarke has suggestively put it, 'a kind of magical realist place, a bit like Macondo in Gabriel Garcia Márquez's *One Hundred Years of Solitude*'.[19] Yet while his work, as we shall see, takes on surrealist or magical realist properties parodying, or making 'unreal', consumerism, everyday life, authority and bureaucracy this has nevertheless always been leavened by depictions of environmental ugliness, dirt, ill health, disease and death. Cooper Clarke recognises that concealed beneath what Chambers calls the 'dirty sign' of the city are metabolic, social-ecological patterns of relationship that have consequences for the working class in particular.

His approach is similar to how Mikita Brottman describes punk in connecting it to Bakhtin. Brottman suggests that Bahktin's concept of *polyglossia*, the expression of a diversity or 'multiplicity of social voices and their individual expressions', is 'most radical and significant at times of festivity or social unrest' where it assumes the mode of 'carnival'. This she defines as a reduction whereby 'everything authoritative, rigid, or serious is subverted, loosened and mocked'.[20] Forged in the folkloric traditions of a pre-industrial society, carnival reduces 'all false sublimations back to their earthy, earthly roots' and is characterised by features such as parody, mockery, violence, swearing and crude humour, attributes conventional to punk. She goes on to suggest that by highlighting the intimate connection of all things, the carnival mode exposes the interrelationship of the base to the political structure, though she concludes that these 'ritualistic violations' have all too often, all too easily been subsumed into the ironies of postmodern consumer culture.

Earthiness is largely meaningless, therefore, unless it really does reveal the material consequences – social, human, environmental – that the political structure has on the ground.[21] Brottman suggests that 'textual carnival' has never really done justice to the actual 'dialogical struggle' of 'social carnival'.[22] Perhaps bearing this out, punk has often been seen as fragmented by a divide between a deconstructive (carnivalesque) first wave (the Sex Pistols, X-Ray Spex etc) and a reconstructive 'second wave' (later Clash, The Jam).[23] The first, while 'shocking' and 'apocalyptic', was also, often, Jude Davies argues, 'severely limited' in its 'ability to envision social change'; the second, though more 'communicative' and 'consensual', and more directly engaged with political themes, was, arguably, musically conservative and easily assimilated.[24] Cooper Clarke, however, is a rare example of an artist who has been able to blend punk's deconstruction with new wave's more reconstructivist elements. Specifically, he has harnessed punk's performative energies towards a clear articulation of environmental blight and social injustice. That articulation is grounded, and derives its force from, the poet's own 'sharpened' sense of place.

Salford: context

Roy Bullock's collation of newspaper stories from the *Salford City Reporter* documents the city in the years from Cooper Clarke's birth to the onset of punk and the beginnings of his performing career.[25] The stories presented bear out the extent to which Salford remained a byword – as in the title of another book – for *The Classic Slum*.[26] For example, in 1956, seven years after Cooper Clarke's birth, the *Reporter* noted that:

Despite an appeal by Dr J L Burn, the Medical Officer of Health, that the feature should show something of the good side of Salford, the BBC presented the same old 'Darkest Salford' to the nation in its 'Special Enquiry' TV programme on Wednesday 4 January. There were the same old shots of Hanky Park and Primrose Hill, with relief shots of back entries. A brief shot of one small block of flats was all the publicity that modern Salford got.[27]

While vigilant, then, to such stereotyping, local history sources such as Bullock's do, in this period, construct a narrative largely shared by Cooper Clarke that foregrounds a prevailing sense of environmental injustice, experienced as a consequence of the twin, colliding processes of Victorian industrialism and incipient global capitalism.

Remnants of the Victorian industrial city remained, therefore, even as punk approached: the last gas lamp only came down in 1972;[28] green space was scarce ('there's not much grass in Hanky Park');[29] and parts of the old industrial slums survived. Housing, described as 'relics of the darkest period of the Industrial Revolution and deemed to be beyond improvement', was only slowly being demolished;[30] old-fashioned, flush-less 'tippler toilets' only disappeared in 1970. Of these, a local history website records, 'waste would remain in an open sewer until the tippler filled with the waste kitchen sink water would then tip, sending a couple of gallons of water through the system flushing the waste away. This had a habit of creating a bad odour in warm weather'.[31]

Nevertheless, Victorian Salford was gradually receding from view. Prefaced by comments such as 'Another bit of Salford's industrial history is about to vanish',[32] the *Reporter* was full of stories about the loss of the infrastructure of an industrial working-class community – in the closures of traditional manufacturing and industry, countless pubs, churches and chapels, cinemas, traditional shops (grocers or watch repairers or drapers) and public baths. Socially and environmentally some things did change for the better. There were many building or refurbishment programmes for schools, colleges and hospitals; 'Operation Eyesore' grants were put in place in 1973 to clean grime off churches;[33] in 1974 it was announced that there may soon be fish in the River Irwell as a result of anti-pollution laws;[34] the first section of a new riverside walk opened in 1976;[35] and by 1978 there were even two low-energy houses being built![36] At the same time, there were emergent signs of a large-scale, global capitalism. Salford got its first supermarket in 1961 followed quickly by the appearance of Tesco, Marks and Spencer, and Asda; 'Containerisation' reached the docks in 1968; Salford gained the UK's first 'urban motorway' in 1971. Such urban renewal was, however, characterised by the same callousness towards the inhabitants that had marked the city's industrial past, whether in terms of heritage or a sense of community. On the planned demolition of Peel Park College, Library and Art Gallery, the chair of the education committee is quoted as saying: 'Perhaps there is a little nostalgia, but we cannot afford to have ancient monuments in Salford. The Art Gallery and Library will be out of position.'[37] Correspondingly, the demolition of housing and pubs was often marked by an 'old-fashioned street party'.[38]

What one can glean, then, from local history accounts in this period is an ongoing narrative of environmental injustice. The central insight of environmental injustice is that while the degradation of the physical landscape runs parallel to that of the built environment, more fundamentally, material, metabolic processes connect human with nonhuman. In any conception of environmental injustice, key signifiers therefore will be the physical environment, the built environment (notably housing) and, especially, human health. For a 'toxic' physical environment will metabolise into health implications for the urban poor, a notion encapsulated in the paradigm of 'ecosystem health'. A concept that initially applied medical terminology – 'stress', 'syndrome', 'dysfunction', etc. – to describe the risks that society can impose upon ecosystems, it has since expanded to encompass a recognition that human health is itself subject to such risks, thereby foregrounding the 'fundamental connections … between human and ecosystem health'.[39] All these elements – environment, housing and health – are, indeed then, the central focus of local history narratives about Salford as they are of Cooper Clarke's personal reflections and poetry about place.

Bullock's anthology records the loss of green space alongside a house-building programme in the 1950s and 1960s which – reflecting a period of transition in Manchester from terraced houses to high-rise blocks or prefabricated, lower-level, 'deck access homes' ('streets in the sky') – engendered social, environmental and health risks.[40] A *Manchester Evening News* publication records, of the Hulme development in Manchester, that 'little thought' had been given to:

> basics such as cleaning public areas of litter or adequate waste disposal.
> Walkways soon became litter traps, stairwells stank of urine and vermin
> infestation was endemic. On top of all this, it transpired that there had been
> widespread use of asbestos in the construction.[41]

This was a pattern that recurred in Salford. 'Revolutionary prefabricated building methods' were introduced, though replaced by the end of the 1960s because 'although efficient in terms of cost it is realised that high living is anti-social and productive of much unhappiness'.[42] Chillingly, back in 1945, the

Housing Committee had agreed, albeit 'under protest', to fifty prefabricated houses that were to have 'double asbestos sheeting instead of concrete walls'.[43]

Health, however, was a mixed picture. For Cooper Clarke's youth actually coincided with an active public health policy driven by the aforementioned John Lancelot Burn, the area's Medical Officer of Health between 1941 and 1969. In that period, Salford became the first city in Britain to wipe out diphtheria while also attempting to tackle tuberculosis by a mass X-ray of its population.[44] 1964 saw the lowest death rate in Salford for twenty-five years with heart disease, its traditional 'No.1 killer', down 25 per cent.[45] Yet social illnesses did persist. Salford had the highest death rate from lung cancer out of twenty comparable cities in Britain in 1957 and throughout the late 1950s it also had the highest drunkenness rate.[46]

Growing up at this precise historical moment, Cooper Clarke's experience and perception of Salford was much the same. While reticent about his upbringing – his social class remains unclear; his father was an engineer; his mother an 'unpublished poet' – Cooper Clarke was close to the city's industrial landscape. On leaving school, he worked as a fire-watcher on Salford docks, an apprentice engineer, a lab technician and a compositor (setting print type). While interviews imply a certain nostalgia for the period – references to the Rialto Cinema, across the road from his house, or the recollection that 'we were all happy under Harold Wilson'[47] – the narrative his work develops is of Salford as a place of profound environmental injustice, one particularly instructive in understanding the degree to which environmental and historical context shapes subcultures as well as recognising the substantial element of place awareness and eco-critique in punk's subcultural resistance.

Consequently, the core signifiers of physical environment, housing and health are central, too, to Cooper Clarke's sense of place. Green space, for example, was unfamiliar and, where it did appear, potentially toxic:

> I used to think trees were dirty because when I was a kid in Salford you'd climb them and come off filthy, it was like you'd been up a chimney ... And even if you got a stretch of park you just had to scrape the grass and there were, like, cinders, underneath ... it was horrible.[48]

Streets and houses are recalled, likewise, as exemplifying environmental degradation or as a focal point for social problems. Answering a much repeated question as to the real location of 'Beasley Street', Cooper Clarke has said: 'The nearest thing that comes to mind is Camp Street [in Broughton] as it was in those days, big houses split into flats with *a lot of different things going on*' [emphasis added].[49] His work likewise displays a marked attentiveness to health founded on personal experience. He attributes his remarkable slimness to tuberculosis contracted as a child. The disease killed his aunt, in a period Cooper Clarke refers to as a 'heartbreak upon heartbreak' of habitual death in the family.[50] His writing came to articulate, then, a troubled experience of place, one contextualised within the buffeting, distorting and reorganising forces of both late industrialism and emergent globalism.

Social metabolism

For Marx, the most significant regulatory process, beyond nature itself, shaping both the physical and human environment was the dynamic of social relations that work to 'metabolise' human and nonhuman natures into forms symptomatic of the society surrounding them. Yet though social processes beget their own physical (as well as social) environments, according to metabolic (and ecological) logic, 'nature' can, at any time, rebound upon the society that produces it. While that might impact upon anyone – one could cite Disraeli fleeing a cholera outbreak in London – these self-induced environmental impacts more often than not mirror the inequalities of the social system.

One can see this in Marx's related concept, 'metabolic rift'. This refers to the carrying away of soil nutrients (in food, fibre production, etc.) which strips the land of its essential nutrients and perpetual fertility. Whereas postcolonialist ecocritics have discussed this in relation to the processes of colonialism and globalisation, in industrial capitalist societies, that configuration has been, and often still is, centred upon the city:

> Capitalist production collects the population together in great centres, and causes the urban population to achieve an ever-growing preponderance. This has two results. On the one hand it concentrates the historical motive power of society; on the other hand, it disturbs the metabolic interaction between man and nature i.e. it prevents the return to the soil of its constituent elements consumed by man in the form of food and clothing; hence it hinders the operation of the eternal natural condition for the lasting fertility of the soil. Thus its destroys at the same time the health of the urban worker and the intellectual life of the rural worker.[51]

While a US-centred environmental justice ecocriticism has recently drawn upon literary texts to alert attention to just such interconnections,[52] in the UK a similar understanding has been most apparent in the literature of Marx's own historical period. For as Bruce Haley has argued, no topic more occupied the Victorian mind than health, as dominant a concept to them as nature had been to the Romantics.[53] Yet an argument can also be made that punk has its own intuition of urban metabolic processes, an intuition no more obvious than in the work of John Cooper Clarke. And this is largely because his encounter with Salford left Cooper Clarke knowingly shaped by the same industrial past that had informed both Marx's concept of social metabolism and the Victorian literary preoccupation with health and environment. Indeed, the journalist Robert Chalmers has described 'Beasley Street' as 'like Engels' prose accounts of the Mancunian slums crossed with Bob Dylan's "Desolation Row",[54] while Paul Morley has remarked 'I get the feeling he was around in the latter part of the nineteenth century'.[55] The clearest evidence, however, for a 'Victorian' outlook can be gained from Cooper Clarke himself.

He has, for example, repeatedly spoken of his admiration for Baudelaire, the archetypal poet of the nineteenth-century city. He bonded with his wife over Baudelaire, has described the poet as 'my hero', and can recite his verse effortlessly.[56] Cooper Clarke has, furthermore, compared himself to the character Adam Adamant from a 1960s BBC drama *A Vintage Year for Scoundrels*, a time traveller who, in 1902, is transported 'into modern London with his Victorian values system'.[57] And, when asked in a recent *Guardian* interview whether it feels strange to still be doing what he does in the early twenty-first century, Cooper Clarke replies 'It does. I feel like a nineteenth-century phenomenon transplanted to the present day. I have quaint values, sure, but I like to think that I have a little bit of retro charm too'.[58]

If those 'quaint values' include an attunement to urban metabolism, an obvious precursor to Cooper Clarke's work lies, as Chalmers indicates, in Friedrich Engels' descriptions of the working-class areas of Manchester in *The Condition of the Working Class in England*. Engels' analysis culminates in Salford. A passage describes an old man working to sustain himself by removing dung while 'puddles of excrement lay close about' the cowshed in which he lived.[59] Steven Marcus has summarised that account, suggesting that Engels unconcealed the metabolic relations of the Victorian industrial city:

> The old man has been productively used up and discarded as refuse. Yet he, too, is part of the life of the city and his life has a meaning … It is Manchester itself in its negated and estranged existence. This chaos of alleys, courts, hovels, filth and human beings is not a chaos at all. Every fragment of disarray, every inconvenience, every scrap of human suffering has a meaning. Each of these is inversely and ineradicably related to the life led by the middle classes, to the work performed in the factories, and to the structure of the city as a whole.[60]

Describing in detail, Marcus continues, 'the ecological relations of the various parts of the district to the rivers, streams and flats amid which they are situated;

to the factories that surround them; and to the middle-class residential districts that begin at their outskirts', Engels revealed a 'hidden ground of things, a substructure'. This was that the working-class districts lay 'at the very center of things, yet out of sight' signifying, once revealed, a social system for which the middle class and their political representatives were culpable.[61] Yet Engels despaired of his inability to communicate the 'phenomenological quality of this reality' and regarded his accounts as 'by far not nearly strong enough … to convey vividly the filth, ruination and uninhabitableness, the defiance of every consideration of cleanliness, ventilation and health that characterise the construction of this district'.[62] What follows will argue that Cooper Clarke specifically evolved, from punk's own sense of 'negated and estranged' existence, an aesthetic practice that, however preposterous this may sound, bypassed the limitations of the more discursive, rational framework that Engels had struggled to work with.

Punk, Cooper Clarke, and a metabolic aesthetics

Engels' frustration bears out the geographer Neil Smith's observation that, given that the 'notion of metabolism sets up the circulation of matter, value and representations as the vortex of social nature', this very complexity necessitates 'both analytical and poetic exploration'.[63] Evading, in other words, the full capacity of analytic prose, one must ask, as Michael Niblett has done, 'is it possible to identify an aesthetics of the metabolic rift […]?' Niblett, too, concludes that realist modes cannot properly accommodate the fluidity of the metabolic metaphor. From Michael Löwy's work, he proposes instead an 'irrealist' aesthetics which without entirely opposing the real nevertheless includes 'elements of fantasy, the oneiric and the surreal': 'the eruption into a text', Niblett writes, 'even if otherwise broadly realist of irrealist elements'.[64] While he is concerned with forms of the postcolonial novel, such a description also fits well with Cooper Clarke's poetic practice.

Describing the chief influences on his work, he has frequently spoken of his English teacher, Mr Malone, who 'used to read old nineteenth-century stuff and say "just do it like that but only write about what you know"'.[65] Cooper Clarke has insisted, consequently, upon the conventional poetical qualities of his work, citing, for instance, their 'very strict metre', learnt from Palgrave's Victorian anthology the *Golden Treasury of English Songs and Lyrics* (1861).[66] Nevertheless, what he knew was Salford, and that environment was one that he rendered through punk.

Cooper Clarke is ambivalent about having routinely been labelled the 'punk poet'. While he describes this in one interview as 'a horrible over-simplification', to Chalmers he concedes, 'punk poet, it's a good enough term'.[67] Artists like The Ramones and Patti Smith did articulate his experience, he has said, rather better than mainstream 1970s rock. He makes the point in a foreword written for an anthology of *Sniffin' Glue*, the punk fanzine, and again in an interview at the 2010 Edinburgh Festival:

> He always liked American music. 'Glasgow is the same as Manchester and Liverpool – west-facing ports. We had R&B years before London … I knew I didn't like all these people that were around at the time; people like Genesis and Yes. I didn't even have to listen to them, I knew from the names I didn't like them'.[68]

Though Cooper Clarke had already been performing on the traditional circuit of Northern working-men's clubs, punk reactivated his poetry. His mode of performance was, up to a point, that of first wave punk. Qualifying ecocriticism's emphasis on affirmative environmental language, Lawrence Buell has suggested that polluted environments like the city demand more negational modes such as what he calls toxic discourse, 'expressed anxiety arising from the perceived threat of environmental hazard'.[69] I have argued, in turn, that first wave punk's generic features – speed of delivery, distortion, brutal three-chord structures, over-amplified bass guitar and drums, harsh, abusive or nonsense vocals – constitute, themselves, a 'toxic' discourse.[70] Cooper Clarke's punk poetry offers, however, an even more developed version of that.

His mode has been well captured in statements of Paul Morley's that though Cooper Clarke perceived the inherent surrealism and Dadaism of punk, his performance is, in fact, an amalgamation of 'unsavoury syllables and stewed surrealism'.[71] That combination – surrealism and toxicity – is the aesthetic Cooper Clarke developed out of punk. Here, irrealist (or surreal) *deconstructive* elements help circumvent the complexity of the metabolic paradigm. Correspondingly, the carnivalesque reduces the evocation of place back to its earthy roots, a *reconstruction* that brings fully to life the toxic horror of the city. In his work, the latter takes noticeably Bakhtinian forms – frequent swearing, crude humour, the underlying violence or baseness of his imagery and, above all, a sharp, harsh, regional accent – about which, Chalmers notes, while 'there's nothing affected', he nevertheless 'luxuriates in its extremes'. As Haslam concludes, Cooper Clarke 'pinned down life in the local environment', even though he

> seemed out of place most places … especially among the pantheon of post-punk icons; up close to the everyday, the detail of dismal daily life, yet with his

head mangled like a Martian with a bad education ... If Joy Division walked the shadowed side of the street, John Cooper Clarke provided the crazy paving.[72]

With his surrealism churning up the 'hidden ground' of urban environmental injustice, Cooper Clarke's work brought social observation back down to earth. In 'Sleepwalk', 'no guardian angel intercepts the sleepwalking kid/who sleepwalks the fractured steps to the sleepwalking skids'; while, of a woman reduced to prostitution, 'you're gonna find her on the midnight shift/ standing in the dirt' ('Midnight Shift'). The critique is given particular force by Cooper Clarke's own metabolic perception that the social state will ultimately inhabit one's physical being. For that reason, infection, disease, illness and death habituate his verse.

> every fucking sentence complains about the damp
> a bad break, a slight ache is every ones complaint
> back in the slums
> desire burns like chicken pox underneath the thumbs
>
> ('Limbo (Baby Limbo)')

> the ups and downs of times like these
> fucking around is a social disease
> when the public at large don't know they've got it
> conditional discharge a sticky deposit
>
> ('Conditional Discharge')[73]

In the counteraction of Victorian-industrial and incipient global forces, 'new urban natures'[74] were being created, fixed within often concealed patterns of social injustice. Cooper Clarke's poems un-conceal, however, revealing not only the physical but also the psychological consequences, the 'vacancy' of urban lives (centrally constructed by punk) brought fully alive by the intonation and rhythm of his verse. Yet he then builds this into a searing critique of a social state and a political class callous to the needs of people it would rather hide away:

> their lives are a mystery they make it their career
> in the single file of history fall and disappear ...

> [they] violently sleep
> or steal from cigarette machines just for the change
> to get back to where they've been: a doorway in the rain ...

saint Margaret dies intact she hardly seems alert
the marble glance denies the fact her face hurts
the extra legal image the cold cream skin
the regal gimmicks did you in
look through heaven's windows you can see the powder blue veil
the cover girl of limbo and sweetheart of the jail ...

a hero rides to heaven the public merely rot
for a fraction of forever in a designated spot
eternally paralysed the morbid orbit shifts
halfway to paradise stuck in the lift

('Limbo (Baby Limbo)')

This conjunction of an irrealist aesthetics that brings alive environmental injustice while narrating and diagnosing its source reaches its culmination, however, with the musical arrangement given to 'Beasley Street'.

Beasley Street

Cooper Clarke made three recorded albums – *Disguise in Love*; *Snap, Crackle and Bop*; and *Zip Style Method*. Opinion on the arrangements of those albums – by Martin Hannett, producer of Joy Division – have been, to say the least, mixed. Cooper Clarke has said that he had 'no idea' what Hannett was doing; fellow poet Mike Garry objects that 'his words are musical enough'.[75] Others, though, such as Jarvis Cocker and the music writer Simon Reynolds, have been more positive.[76] An implication of these more favourable verdicts is, perhaps, that as music is central to the estranged aesthetic of punk, Cooper Clarke drew upon that resource to cement his own toxic discourse. Indeed, the arrangements seem particularly appropriate to the magical realist Manchester that he sought to convey. Working at variance, Colin Sharp writes, with a tradition of song writing built around 'guitar (often acoustic to begin with) and voice'[77] – i.e. a tradition of pop which, according to Rob Young, has developed out of folk – Hannett developed a predominantly percussive sound, double-tracked bass rhythms and 'subsonic' or 'depth-charge' drums, which, alongside disorienting and unconventional pop instruments – viola, piano, synth, other 'unsettling' sound effects – created the sense that 'something is sonically "wrong"'.[78]

'Beasley Street' (1980) offers up, in this context, a quite literal *sense* of place in which the city is audibly present. Cooper Clarke is 'perfectly placed in the middle of the mix, in the middle of the street. Peripheral noises colour and underline: strange disembodied sounds appear and disappear, like passers-by'.[79] An experience of Salford, alienated rather than affirmative, the poet draws upon the devices of first-wave punk, specifically in his hard-edged, confron-tational accent. Heavy emphasis is placed on the end of lines, on phrases or rhymes: 'breath … death'; or, drawled with a Salford intonation,' a baby *dies*'.[80] All this is heavily underscored by Hannett's musical accompaniment. The track begins with indistinct background noise. This slowly gives way to a discomfort-ing, underlying rhythm accompanied by ongoing, and increasing, discordant noise. The rhythm is percussive and 'subsonic', an underlying bass line connot-ing the dark, uneasy, irregular beat of the city that is loudly supplemented by various aural signifiers of the environment's disharmony – an irregular drum pattern, horror film sound effects, an insistent tambourine, replaced, just before the end, with what sounds like someone banging on a pipe. A buzzing guitar riff (which appears suddenly at the end of verse 3) and a discordant piano, which plays throughout, gradually ratchet up the noise and, with it, the sonic sense of 'something … wrong'. The track becomes increasingly more chaotic and cacophonous.

While, however, the sound of 'Beasley Street' is primarily that of first-wave punk, the rich descriptiveness of Cooper Clarke's lyrics suggests the rhetori-cal qualities of the second wave. Though there is no 'story' as such, and the track has little obvious trajectory, he does, nevertheless, in this snapshot of an archetypal 'dirty afternoon' in Salford in the 1970s, narrate an understanding of place. In the first instance, we find the beauty of nature itself grounded and polluted – a 'rainbow in the road' seemingly referring to spilt oil or petrol. Greater emphasis falls, secondly, on the human environment, housing or the street itself. He rapidly builds up an inventory, rich with toxic description, of fleas, rats, 'fecal [*sic*] germs', excrement, 'the perishing stink of squalor', dead canaries, yellow cats, 'shitstopper drains'. The result of inhabiting this particular environment – alongside, that is, crime, poverty, hopelessness, despair – is the additional penalty of never-ending, interbred, epidemic ill health, to the foreground in the assonant rhyme that gives to the poem its fictional name:

> people turn to poison quick
> as lager turns to piss
> sweethearts are physically sick
> every time they kiss
> it's a sociologist's paradise
> each day repeats
> uneasy cheesy greasy queasy beastly beasley street

Ultimately, however, the poem also constructs an understanding and experience of environmental injustice. In a social context in which both the physical environment and its population are 'null and void' – and yearning, indeed, for the vacant nihilism of punk: 'if I could have just one wish/ I would be a photograph' – these are people, put simply, whose 'common problem/ is that they're not someone else' and who are rarely able to escape a pervasive, perpetual cycle of environmental degradation and health risk where, as 'the dirt blows out, the dust blows in'. Yet, more than just read about it, we are made to *feel* this hopeless incarceration within the toxic environment through the structure of the poem itself. While it never reaches a narrative conclusion – the penultimate verse's description of 'eyes dead as viscous fish' and 'yellow cats' simply augmenting the images from before – the relentless (anti)lyricism and rising percussive levels do leave us feeling aurally imposed upon, incarcerated, ourselves, within this barrage of almost seven minutes. 'Beasley Street' is not designed to be easy listening. As Cooper Clarke puts it in 'Evidently Chickentown', 'it fucking hurts to look around'. Yet ingrained with the angry, empty despair of punk, the track still nevertheless achieves a critique of a political class callous to people it would rather sink into obscurity. For there is, lastly, an attribution of culpability, a brief gesture towards political statement, directed at Thatcherism and carried in the still rather shocking line: 'Keith Joseph smiles and a baby dies in a box on Beasley Street'.

Signifying his bittersweet relationship to the sometimes mythologised entity of punk, Cooper Clarke, in a poem commissioned for the *Sniffin Glue* anthology, satirises how the figure of the punk would: 'Affect the look of a man obsessed/ Predisposed to the predistressed'.[81] Yet, immersed as he was in Salford, there is no affectation in his work. He understood only too well the metabolic processes that shape physical and social environment alike. If punk, too often, has neglected the former, ecology often forgets the latter. Cooper Clarke's work demonstrates the reach that a fundamental ecological concept such as the shaping influence of place can have even on urban subcultures seemingly far removed from 'nature'. Yet it also suggests, more radically, that punk might just offer an aesthetic well placed to unravel the metabolic complexity of an urban environmental injustice so harsh – whether in the slums of the Victorian city or the callous expansion of post-industrial global capitalism – as to have, until punk, defied adequate representation.

Notes

1 All references from the poetry are taken from John Cooper Clarke, *Ten Years in an Open Necked Shirt* (London: Arena, 1983). 'I Travel In Biscuits', words and music by John Cooper Clarke, Martin Hannett and Stephen Hopkins © 1982, reproduced by permission of Dinsong Ltd/ EMI Songs Ltd, London W1F 9LD.

2 'Limbo (Baby Limbo)', words and music by John Cooper Clarke © 1979, reproduced by permission of Dinsong Ltd/ EMI Songs Ltd, London W1F 9LD.

3 'Evidently Chickentown', words and music by John Cooper-Clarke, Martin Hannett and Stephen Hopkins © 1980, reproduced by permission of Dinsong Ltd/ EMI Songs Ltd, London W1F 9LD.

4 R. Sabin (ed.), *Punk Rock: So What? The Cultural Legacy of Punk* (London and New York: Routledge, 1999), pp. 2–3.

5 I. Chambers, *Popular Culture: The Metropolitan Experience* (London and New York: Methuen, 1986), p. 183.

6 See S. Thompson, *Punk Productions: Unfinished Business* (Albany, NY: SUNY Press, 2004), p. 4; and G. Marcus, *Lipstick Traces: A Secret History of the Twentieth Century* (London: Faber & Faber, 1989), p. 9.

7 J. Davies, 'The Future of "No Future": Punk Rock and Postmodern Theory', *Journal of Popular Culture*, 29:4 (1996), 12–13.

8 J. Bellamy Foster, B. Clark and R. York, *The Ecological Rift: Capitalism's War on the Earth* (New York: Monthly Review Press, 2010), p. 160.

9 J. Elder, *Imagining the Earth: Poetry and the Vision of Nature* (Urbana, IL: University of Illinois Press, 1985), pp. 37–8.

10 D. Ingram, *The Jukebox in the Garden: Ecocriticism and American Popular Music* (Amsterdam and New York: Rodopi, 2010), p. 52.

11 *Ibid.*, pp. 92–3.

12 R. Young, *Electric Eden: Unearthing Britain's Visionary Music* (London: Faber & Faber, 2011), pp. 477, 606.

13 A. Bennett, *Popular Music and Youth Culture: Music, Identity and Place* (Basingstoke: Macmillan, 2000), pp. 53–67.

14 D. Haslam, *Manchester England: The Story of the Pop Cult City* (London: Fourth Estate, 1999), pp. 256–7.

15 A. Leyshon, D. Matless and G. Revill (eds), *The Place of Music* (New York/London: The Guilford Press, 1998), p. 20.

16 Chambers, *Popular Culture*, p. 17.

17 *Ibid.*, pp. 183–7.

18 *Ibid.*, p. 183.

19 R. Chalmers, 'A Life of rhyme', *The Independent on Sunday* (8 November 2009), www.independent.co.uk/arts-entertainment/books/features/a-life-of-rhyme-john-cooper-clarke-the-punk-poet-laureate-grants-robert-chalmers-his-first-major-interview-in-more-than–20-years–1814712.html, accessed 11 September 2012, n.p.

20 M. Brottman, *High Theory/Low Culture* (New York and Basingstoke: Palgrave, 2005), p. 2.
21 *Ibid.*, p. 12.
22 *Ibid.*, p. 19.
23 See Davies, 'The Future of "No Future"'; M. Brake, *Comparative Youth Culture* (London: Routledge & Kegan Paul, 1985), p. 77.
24 Davies, 'The Future of "No Future"', 9 and 22.
25 R. Bullock, *Salford 1940–1965: Twenty-Five Years in the History of the City of Salford* (Manchester: Neil Richardson, 1996) and *Salford 1966–1990: Twenty-Five Years in the History of the City of Salford* (Manchester: Neil Richardson, 1998). As the volumes are ordered chronologically, subsequent references will be by date to which the entry refers.
26 R. Roberts, *The Classic Slum: Salford Life in the First Quarter of the Century* (Manchester: Manchester University Press, 1971).
27 Bullock, *Salford 1940–1965*, 6 January 1956.
28 Bullock, *Salford 1966–1990*, 8 December 1972.
29 Bullock, *Salford 1940–1965*, 3 April 1959.
30 *Ibid.*, 2 January 1959.
31 http://menmedia.co.uk/middletonguardian/community/nostalgia/s/1240500_tippler_toilets_left_a_lot_to_be_desired, accessed 7 November 2012.
32 Bullock, *Salford 1966–1990*, 1 June 1973.
33 *Ibid.*, 23 March 1973.
34 *Ibid.*, 1 November 1974.
35 *Ibid.*, 6 August 1976.
36 *Ibid.*, 16 June 1978.
37 Bullock, *Salford 1940–1965*, 24 March 1961.
38 *Ibid.*, 18 June 1976.
39 R. T. Di Giulio and E. Monosson (eds), *Interconnections Between Human and Ecosystem Health* (London: Chapman & Hall, 1996), p. 3.
40 Bullock, *Salford 1966–1990*, 11 February 1972.
41 Manchester Evening News, *The Changing Face of Manchester in the Seventies* (Altrincham: At Heart Publications, 1997), p. 31.
42 Bullock, *Salford 1966–1990*, 4 October 1968.
43 Bullock, *Salford 1940–1965*, 16 February 1945.
44 Bullock, *Salford 1966–1990*, 5 January 1973.
45 *Ibid.*, 1 January 1965.
46 *Ibid.*, 4 July 1957.
47 S. Hattenstone, 'John Cooper Clarke: "It's diabolical how poor I am"', *The Guardian* (29 May 2012), n.p. www.guardian.co.uk/music/2012/may/29/john-cooper-clarke-punk-poet-interview, accessed 11 September 2012.
48 See www.salfordstar.com/article.asp?id=105, accessed 11 September 2012.
49 www.salfordstar.com/article.asp?id=106#16365, accessed 11 September 2012.
50 Chalmers, 'A Life of Rhyme', n.p.

51 K. Marx, *Capital: A Critique of Political Economy, Vol. 1* (Harmondsworth: Penguin, 1976), p. 637.
52 See, particularly, J. Adamson, M. M. Evans and R. Stein (eds), *The Environmental Justice Reader: Politics, Poetics and Pedagogy* (Tucson, AZ: The University of Arizona Press, 2002).
53 B. Haley, *The Healthy Body and Victorian Culture* (Cambridge, MA and London: Harvard University Press, 1978), p. 3.
54 Chalmers, 'A Life of Rhyme', n.p.
55 *Evidently … John Cooper Clarke*, dir. John Ross, BBC Four (2012).
56 Chalmers, 'A Life of Rhyme', n.p.
57 N. McCormick, 'John Cooper Clarke: punk's poet laureate returns', *The Daily Telegraph* (27 July 2010), www.telegraph.co.uk/culture/music/7912033/John-Cooper-Clarke-punks-poet-laureate-returns.html, accessed 11 September 2012.
58 Hattenstone, 'John Cooper Clarke', n.p.
59 Cited in S. Marcus, 'Reading the Illegible', in J. Dyos and M. Wolff (eds), *The Victorian City, Vol. 2* (London, Henley and Boston: Routledge and Kegan Paul, 1978), p. 272.
60 *Ibid.*, p. 272.
61 *Ibid.*, pp. 270–1.
62 *Ibid.*, p. 270.
63 N. Smith, 'Foreword', in N. Heynen, M. Kaika and E. Swyngedouw (eds), *In the Nature of Cities: Urban Political Ecology and the Politics of Urban Metabolism* (Abingdon: Routledge, 2006), pp. xiii, xiv.
64 M. Niblett, 'World-economy, World-ecology, World literature', *Green Letters*, 16 (2012), 20–1.
65 www.salfordstar.com/article.asp?id=106#16365, accessed 11 September 2012.
66 *Evidently … John Cooper Clarke* (BBC).
67 Rob Fitzpatrick, 'Manic Street Preacher', *The Guardian* (5 September 2009), n.p. www.guardian.co.uk/music/2009/sep/05/john-cooper-clarke-interview, accessed 11 September 2012.
68 www.edinburgh-festivals.com/viewpreview.aspx?id=1535, accessed 12 November 2012.
69 L. Buell, *Writing for an Endangered World: Literature, Culture, and Environment in the U.S. and Beyond* (Cambridge, MA and London: The Belknap Press, 2001), pp. 30–1.
70 J. Parham, 'A Concrete Sense of Place: Alienation and the City in British Punk and New Wave 1977–1980', *Green Letters*, 15 (2011), 80.
71 *Evidently … John Cooper Clarke* (BBC); P. l. Morley, 'Review, Kings Hall, Manchester', *New Musical Express* (3 March 1979), pp. 53–4.
72 Haslam, *Manchester England*, p. 123.
73 'Conditional Discharge', words and music by John Cooper Clarke, Martin Hannett and Stephen Hopkins © 1980, reproduced by permission of Dinsong Ltd/ EMI Songs Ltd, London W1F 9LD.
74 Heynen, Kaika and Swyngedouw, *Nature of Cities*, p. 4.
75 Cited in *Evidently … John Cooper Clarke* (BBC).

76 Cocker cited in *Evidently ... John Cooper Clarke* (BBC); S. Reynolds, *Rip it Up and Start Again: Post-punk 1978–84* (London: Faber & Faber, 2005) p. 192.

77 C. Sharp, *Who Killed Martin Hannett? The Story of Factory Records' Musical Magician* (London: Aurum, 2007), p. 123.

78 *Ibid.*, p. 33.

79 *Ibid.*, p. 123.

80 'Beasley Street', words and music by John Cooper-Clarke, Martin Hannett and Stephen Hopkins © 1980, reproduced by permission of Dinsong Ltd/ EMI Songs Ltd, London W1F 9LD.

81 M. Perry (ed. T. Rawlings), *Sniffin' Glue: The Essential Punk Accessory* (London: Sanctuary, 2000), p. 7.

7

Distortions in distance: debates over cultural conventions in French punk

On 6 May 1968, a cadre of French police entered the Sorbonne to restore order, called by administrators in response to the alleged destruction of audi-torium chairs, three to be exact, caused by the student occupation that began earlier that weekend in protest against the actions of administrators at the Nanterre campus. The subsequent mêlée between the police and students sparked broader protests, as young workers instigated a series of strikes through France during the months of May and June 1968 which threw into question the authority of the French government of President Charles de Gaulle. The events of May in Paris drew the attention of the world, especially from likeminded student groups in Italy, Mexico, the USA, and Great Britain, as evidence of the revolutionary potential of young people. Although no political revolution occurred in France the events remained afterwards a potent symbol for young people as proof of the power of protest. About a decade later, a concert was held in Paris, a festi-val of French punk bands, at the famed Olympia theatre. All of the important groups of the nascent French scene – including Stinky Toys, Métal Urbain, Bijou, and Les Guilty Razors – performed that night, and the so-called 'La nuit de punk' was recorded for release to capitalise on the growing popularity of punk rock in France. The recording's cover photograph captures the nearly 300 seats that were destroyed during the concert, as if to underscore its significance by referencing the earlier destruction.[1] Just as the students destroyed the seats in the Sorbonne to protest the administration establishment, so too did the punks destroy those in one of the historical halls of French popular song as an expression of cultural protest. When it appeared in France in the late 1970s, punk was often equated with the events of 1968. However, in terms of social impact the two events could not be further apart, as punk's development in France lacked the same critical power as the protests from a decade earlier or its British antecedent.

Why did the punk subculture, which was so significant across the Channel, have less of an impact in France? What was, in essence, lost in translation? How did the social conventions developed in one context change as cultural practices moved into new contexts? As punk increasingly became an indigenous phenomenon in late 1970s France, it contained a number of critical differences that marked it as distinct from its Anglophone counterpart, especially in terms of its political meaning. Punk subculture developed in Britain as an expression of cultural protest concerning the failure of British society to fulfil the equity promise of post-war affluence, but in France this same issue had manifested itself earlier in the events of May 1968.[2] The student protests in France signified the rejection of the existing social and cultural norms, which subsequently energised the French counter-culture in the early 1970s. By the time punk developed as a youth subculture in France, much of this conflict had been played out in the counterculture, throwing into question the meaning of French punk for both its observers and participants. Furthermore, the cultural challenge punk presented – *épater les bourgeois*, so to speak – already had other voices in France prior to 1976, with the most obvious example being Serge Gainsbourg. The looming presence of such a figure provided a form of cultural competition that was lacking in the contexts of British and American popular music. Most important, however, were the different conceptions of subcultural authenticity in the French context, what subcultural identities represented in their efforts to articulate authentic forms of living in contrast to cultural norms, and how French critics and musicians understood those identities. The seemingly rapid establishment of cultural conventions within the punk subculture led many observers in France to define it as a distinctly British phenomenon that had been merely transplanted, and as a result punk had a more limited impact in France than it had in Britain during the 1970s. Nevertheless, there were French young people who still found personal meaning in the punk subculture despite the critical consensus against its French iteration. The debates among French musicians and music critics concerning punk in its initial phase in the late 1970s and the responses of French youths illuminate how the conventions that defined the punk subculture failed to translate into the French national context, pointing to how subcultural meanings dramatically change as they move through national boundaries especially as 'authentic' versions become more easily accessible with cultural globalisation.

During the twentieth century, youth subcultures became increasingly visible social phenomena, and in the post-war period, they had served as a cultural challenge to the political consensus of the Western world. Developments in popular culture in the late 1950s appeared to offer an expression of defiance against social norms, especially rock 'n' roll with its emphasis on rhythm, noise and innuendo, and the reactions against rock 'n' roll in the USA, France and West Germany suggest that political and cultural elites took the music's critical potential seriously.[3] Rock 'n' roll and other genres of popular music were central to the construction of subcultural identity, serving as a form of social cohesion among audiences. Often perceived as a revolt based in style, subcultures gained the interest of scholars in the 1960s and 1970s as an avenue of social protest for young people. Subcultures were predicated on the rejection of existing values – for example, *Die Halbstarken* in both of the post-war Germanys, the *Vittorio* in Italy, the Teddy Boys in Great Britain, and *les blousons noirs* in France were defiant in their embrace of roll 'n' roll music and style – but ultimately they were accepted within their respective societies.[4] These different youth communities shared values and characteristics despite the varied cultural contexts: an affinity for leather jackets, dancing, and public consumption of rock 'n' roll. Although the values of these different youth groups became part of broader social norms, the increased manifestation of these subcultures led scholars to formulate schema to understand the broader meaning of these socio-cultural groups.

The most well-known academic work on subcultures was done during the 1970s at the University of Birmingham's Centre for Contemporary Cultural Studies (CCCS), which focused on various expressions of British youth identity, including punk, which was growing in significance after the Centre's inception. The scholarship of this cohort of academics, led by Stuart Hall, brought together elements of sociology, anthropology and Marxist theory to formulate a methodology of studying subcultures and ascertaining their meaning as a form of protest. According to the scholars of the Birmingham School, subcultures were inherently expressions of cultural resistance against dominant cultural norms in post-war Britain, and researchers understood these expressions of social identity as part of a general revolt against society. In these works, the construction of subcultural identities revealed a search for authentic communities in response to the anomie of modern life. For these scholars, the examples that CCCS studied – the punks, the Teddy Boys, and the Mods, among others – signify authentic communities, although these communities' values are continually threatened by society's co-opting of style.[5]

According to the formulations of the CCCS, the inherent revolt of subcultures was the rejection of this co-optation and the spectacular refusal to live within cultural norms, illustrating a more aesthetic form of protest within the realm of culture. Implicitly linked with popular musical styles, British subcultures, especially punk, provided examples of new identities and influenced young people throughout the world to create their own communities through the consumption and production of music.

While the Birmingham School's theorisation of subcultures remains influential among contemporary scholars, numerous critiques of its particular vision of subcultural identity point out the lack of objectivity concerning the importance of subcultural protest, an emphasis on masculine communities of youth, and the centrality of Marxist notions of class consciousness (or lack thereof) within the conclusions of these researchers.[6] These critiques have produced new and fruitful works seeking to reevaluate the formulation of subcultural theory, leading to more nuanced works such as those by Sarah Thornton and Hilary Pilkington, which seek to move beyond the initial formulations of the Birmingham School. Thornton's *Club Cultures* importantly assesses subcultural identity through Pierre Bourdieu's concept of cultural capital and moves beyond the semiotics central to Hebdige's *Subculture*. Instead, Thornton applies Bourdieu's concept to illustrate the wide divergences within the seemingly singular solidarities of subcultures and the processes of negotiation within these communities. She also provides a critique of the emphasis on class identity by examine how subcultures, at least in the case of rave culture, imagine a post-class collectivity in which class boundaries are subverted.[7] Pilkington's work on Soviet and post-Soviet youth cultures stresses the importance of sociological field work in studying subcultural activity, recentring the investigation of subcultural meaning to a more localised context.[8]

The most significant critique of the CCCS comes from David Muggleton, who challenges the modernist assumptions that structure much of the group's subcultural theory. Muggleton's *Inside Subculture* points to the importance of postmodernist theory in undermining the essentialist tendencies inherent in the work of the Birmingham School by pointing out the complexity and ambiguity within the system of signs that signify the boundaries of subcultural identity. Muggleton attempts to recover the lived experiences of subcultural subjects, who often feel that the existing formulations of subcultural theory fail to reflect their own viewpoints and feelings, which are obscured by totalising tendencies of Marxist cultural studies. Like Pilkington, Muggleton suggests the importance of looking at the activities of subculturalists rather than the concept of subculture itself, as the latter is fraught with over-determined analysis that often conceals the meaning of expressions of subcultural identity.[9]

Nevertheless, the emphasis on semiotics in Hebdige's analysis still offers a framework for thinking about the transformation of subcultural conventions as they operate in different contexts and how the conventions established in one situation might affect the articulation of a subculture elsewhere. His focus on aesthetics and their shifting meaning helps to illustrate the difficulties of interpreting meaning for those outside of the community. While Hebdige certainly understood the concept of social belonging within notions of class identity, gender and national identity also serve to alienate individuals and foster desires to emulate subcultural activities. Punk, as a spectacular expression of subcultural identity, had numerous symbols – ripped clothing, safety-pins, swastikas and Mohawks, to name the more obvious ones – that observers equated with the community but could certainly be misconstrued outside of it. The swastika, for example, confounded many observers over its meaning among punks. The global movement of punk culture, from the USA and Britain to France, Mexico, the Soviet Union and Australia, was predicated on the perceived value of these symbols to represent a punk style, even if individual subculturalists understood them differently. These different national contexts would eventually offer their own symbols in establishing a local punk community, but the initial distortions of punk culture in its translations, as the French case reveals, were due to the values attributed to the origins of its style, underscoring the importance of aesthetics in its global movement.

Punk appeared in Great Britain during the mid-1970s as a culmination of post-war subcultures with its confrontational stance against all social norms. However, punk took the critical logic of subculture to its end by defying the progressive assumptions of British consensus society. Punk was a manifestation of this utopian sense of negation against all social conventions, including the idea of subcultural acceptance. While its origins remain the focus of much argument among music critics, punk for many was associated with the formation of the Sex Pistols in 1976. In response, punk subcultures developed throughout Britain, France, West Germany and beyond. Both as an aesthetic and a musical genre punk challenged broadly accepted British values. Reliant upon an idealisation of the rebellion of early rock 'n' roll, punk combined this sound with post-Marxist critiques of post-war consumer culture, especially those associated with Situationist ideas, which developed in the 1960s among young French intellectuals in tandem with artistic movements. Situationists asserted that culture was a critical arena to combat the deleterious effects of post-war consumerism, which had come to dominate much of Western society.[10] Greil Marcus has famously emphasised the links between the punk subculture and the ideas of Situationism, especially those evident during the events of 1968, even if punks themselves were often critical of such conclusions.[11] The slogans plastered on the walls of Paris suggested a revolt of the imagination, one which punks in Britain, rooted in the intellectual milieu of the national art schools, embraced. The international roots of punk – American rock 'n' roll, French Situationism, Dada, and British subcultural traditions – implied the possibilities of the subculture to traverse national boundaries and operate in numerous contexts, and the presence of a punk community in the USA illustrates how punk operated in different locations.[12] Rock 'n' roll had found a home throughout the world and so too would punk, although with different results.

In Britain, punk evoked the spirit of 1968 in its confrontational attitude towards norms and willingness to channel this energy into new creative outlets. The relationship between punk and the ideas of the student protests suggests the potential for punk to serve as an instrument to challenge the cultural consensus in France. The events of May 1968 remained a symbolic moment for political protest in contemporary French society, even as their meanings and outcomes continued to be debated by participants, politicians and scholars. The demonstrations, which began within the university system in the spring of 1968, revealed the difficulties in maintaining the political consensus that had defined Western European politics since the end of the Second World War.[13] Students protested against the educational establishment, the continued class division between students and workers, and the conservative social mores of Gaullist France. While efforts among small protest groups – *groupuscules* – continued into the 1970s, the idea of revolutionary political change gave way to attempts at cultural revolt instead. The French counter-culture, akin to those of Britain, West Germany, and the USA, articulated a culture of sex, drugs, and rock 'n' roll as expressions of liberation in the spirit of 1968. The preferred genre of the counter-culture, progressive rock, emphasised musical sophistication to challenge French norms, but this approach was gaining acceptance among broader audiences, in effect weakening its critical power. Yet even as this subculture weakened, another was developing that took a different aesthetic approach.

The first stirrings of a French punk subculture appeared in Paris. There, a number of important antecedents were in place prior to the seminal Sex Pistols' concert in September 1976. One was the opening of the Open Market, a record store specialising in American and British imports, in 1972. The Market's proprietor, Mark Zermati, established the Market as an important conduit for foreign musical styles to reach French audiences. He was a rabid supporter of American musical counter-culture and tried to ensure that French consumers had access to the recordings of the newest sounds from New York and London. Zermati's musical taste vacillated between the raw sounds of early rock 'n' roll and the more experimental music at the fringes of the progressive rock movement. Importantly, the Open Market offered a locus for French youths disaffected with progressive rock, and the store's racks were full of alternatives from points beyond France: British glam, American garage rock and German space rock, among others. The Market, like CBGBs in New York or Malcolm McLaren's various King's Road shops in London, was a physical space that permitted likeminded youths to congregate and form a punk community centred on music.

Zermati also founded Skydog Records, which released and distributed titles by the Stooges, MC5, and Flamin' Groovies beginning in 1973 and would later release several seminal French punk singles. Skydog, again analogous to British independent labels such as Stiff Records and Rough Trade, was the first record label to bring together the various musical elements that would form the foundation of a punk musical aesthetic: the Stooges' and MC5's distorted anti-politics and the Groovies' stripped-down emulation of the Beat bands of the early British scene. Skydog kept these examples of proto-punk in circulation in France, meaning that French audiences had access to important releases that would shape the sound of punk. With both the Open Market and Skydog, Zermati's influence on the development of punk in France (and in general) cannot be understated.

Zermati's efforts to promote these groups and this new sound were soon joined by music critic Yves Adrien, who, in his 1973 essay 'Je chante le rock électrique [I sing the rock electric]', asserts the importance of the developing musical style of punk in reconnecting rock music with its rebellious origins. Adrien regularly wrote in columns in French music monthly *Rock & Folk*, as well as counter-cultural publications such as *Parapluie*, offering his views on the changing meaning of popular music in 1970s France. Presenting a history of rock 'n' roll music that emphasises its inherent defiance, Adrien observes that rock 'n' roll's anti-establishment nature was still apparent in the music of the Stooges, Kim Fowley and MC5, the same groups Zermati supported.[14] Adrien's 'Je chante' details the emergence of this new type of rock that challenges the accepted values of Western society, a type of music that was gaining an audience on the cultural margins in New York and London. Unlike the more serious and brooding nature of progressive rock, this new style was more interested in fun. Adrien's articulation of the importance of this new music as an expression of youth revolt suggests that French observers, at least music critics, understood its potential as a new form of protest. Other prominent French music journalists, such as Alain Pacadis and Patrick Eudeline, also lent their support to this emerging subgenre of roll 'n' roll bands in their columns in the leftist newspaper *Libération* and the music monthly *Best*.

Outside of these literary examples, the records of glam-rock groups such as Les Frenchies and Au Bonheur des Dames reveal how more popular French bands were following similar trends as groups in the USA and the UK. The glam subculture, with its emphasis on theatre and performance, was a crucial precedent for punk by providing examples of cultural subversion at once subtle and spectacular. In the early 1970s, glam broke through as a form of popular music in Britain with the commercial successes of T. Rex, Slade and David Bowie. As Philip Auslander observes, some French music critics often saw the genres of punk and glam as part of a broad reaction to counter-cultural rock.[15] The appearance of a glam rock subculture in France was much like that of other subcultures – hippies, beatniks and rockers, for example – indicating the lack of significant internal debate over the various aspects of the subculture. With the recordings of the glam rock groups, the cultural and musical antecedents were in place to prepare French young people for the development of punk.

The first recognised punk musicians to perform in France – Patti Smith, The Sex Pistols and The Clash – were all fêted by journalists as the future of popular music. However, many French youths already had an idea of what was to come. For example, Parisian artist Elodie Lauten was connected to the New York art scene, which had taken an increased interest in the music coming from CBGB's and Max's Kansas City. Lauten had traveled to New York in 1972 before returning to Paris in 1974, loaded down with vinyl from the nascent punk scene. Subsequently, she brought musicians to her loft for listening parties, and several of her guests were important participants in the French punk scene.[16] By the summer of 1976, several bands had formed in France that emulated the musical styles associated with British punk, the most notable being Stinky Toys, a group that garnered the attention of Pistols manager Malcolm McLaren. McLaren hoped to pair the French group with his infamous band for the latter's British tour in 1976. Although this tour was mostly aborted due to the negative press the Pistols received, Stinky Toys performed at the 100 Club in London as part of a punk festival in September of that year. Prior to this festival, however, Zermati had organised the first punk rock festival in Mont-de-Marsan in August 1976, bringing together British and French bands for an audience of nearly 2,000, whose success led to a larger festival in 1977 that featured The Clash and The Damned as headliners.

Stinky Toys played a brand of music similar to many British bands and wrote original music in English rather than French, aping the mod sound of the Yardbirds and the Who. Their stripped-down arrangements contrasted with the musical complexity of progressive rock. Progressive musicians believed themselves to be carrying on the conflict of May 1968 within the realm of culture, an idea many punks believed to be representative of their genre.[17]

Musically, punk was a reaction against the sophistication and intellectualism of progressive rock and an attempt to democratise music through the concept of do-it-yourself.[18] Inspired by the general attitude of punk, Stinky Toys began performing in 1976. Despite the obvious connection between her band and the British punks, singer Elli Medeiros rejected that label for her band: 'We always said to journalists that we were not [punk] but they always labeled us as such … we hate the English [punks].' Medeiros stressed the differences between her group and the British punks, not only in musical style but also in fashion, as the Toys favored a 'clean image'.[19] These two reactions suggest that the band understood punk in a somewhat stereotypical fashion as a distinct look and sound and ultimately as an explicitly 'English phenomenon'.[20]

Critics generally agreed with the band's rejection of its punk identity, using the group as an example of the limitations of punk in France. For example, Stéphane Pietri and Alexis Quinlin, two journalists who immediately wrote a comparative history of the punk scenes in Britain, France, and the USA, asserted that Stinky Toys were 'not authentic punk rockers' and that the group's simplistic English lyrics merely copied the worst examples of punk. Two other journalists, Jean-Dominique Brierre and Ludwik Lewin, saw Stinky Toys as evidence of the fetish for foreign culture that was characteristic of French music in general.[21] French pop music had been long dominated by translations of American and British music, and to critics French punk was just another example of musicians with a 'completely artificial manner without invention or originality'.[22] Undoubtedly, the long-practised tendency of French musicians to borrow the sound and style of Anglophone bands wholesale had soured critics and audiences alike. As Patrick Eudeline observed, 'Rock and Roll in France [is] blocked by its linguistic problems, by a national image. Our local punks often do not hesitate to carry a Union Jack'.[23] Consumer trends in France began to change in mid-1970s, with audiences increasingly rejecting translations in favour of the original songs in English.[24] While covers were a common practice in punk in general, French punks wrote instead many original songs, but in English. Stinky Toys were but one of several groups, which also include Guilty Razors, The Lous, The Dogs, and Electric Callas, who recorded exclusively in English. For these groups, English was the language of rock 'n' roll, thus by extension, punk, and French was inherently foreign to it. As Fabienne Shine, lead singer for the French group Shakin' Street, bluntly stated: 'French just isn't authentic', and looking at the decisions made by many French groups this idea was not uncommon.[25]

Rock & Folk, in many ways, contributed as well to the perception of punk as something happening outside of France. Certainly the magazine's focus on Anglophone music suggests that it would follow a similar line as that of other critics, but *Rock & Folk* also introduced a regular column, 'Beret punk', in June 1977 that specifically covered French groups, illustrating how the magazine tried to link the punk phenomenon to the French context. The one-page column briefly covered concerts and releases by French groups, often in contrast to the more extensive articles on British groups during 1977. For example, in the July 1977 issue, critic Alain Dister crafted a discography of seminal punk recordings, highlighting the work of American groups such as the Ramones and the Dictators and British groups such as the Jam and the Clash, while even recognising the Australian band the Saints. Not one French group was listed among Dister's list (nor referenced in the article), again reifying the foreignness of the genre.

Beyond language, authenticity was also equated with the belief in British punk's honest articulation of the social problems facing young people. As the post-war economic miracle faded in the early 1970s, unemployment and inflation stimulated punk's rejection of social norms, as the social consensus that had been part of the post-war economic boom unraveled. British youths, seemingly discarded by their society, railed against the political and social establishment and imagined a different type of living – one that shocked observers. The central idea of punk was the articulation of an authentic culture that represented the marginalised youth and voiced its concerns. As the Situationists asserted, the expression of authentic art was a pathway to revolution in the post-industrial society, and punk's ability to 'never mind the bollocks' was an example of this sort of speaking truth to power.[26] However, French youths and critics at times emphasised the national differences between themselves and British punks. Again, Brierre and Ludwik crystallise this viewpoint: 'Here [in France], one finds a cultural and political terrain that is vastly different. Punk in France is imported. Unlike in Britain, in France punk has never been a social phenomenon … The French groups are not driven by the hordes of young unemployed, and in the absence of such a dynamic situation, they had to cling to the pre-existing cultural and political stereotypes in punk. The result is often artificial but allows one to see [punk] from a different perspective.'[27]

Yet the situation in France was remarkably similar, as unemployment had reached the one million mark in 1978 and inflation sapped the growth of the French economy.[28] Some punks tried to address these issues at their performances. For example, Asphalt Jungle's singer Patrick Eudeline shouted out 'Chomage! [Unemployment!]' between songs at the Mont de Marsan festival in 1977 to draw attention to the economic situation facing his audience. However, this action elicited a critique from Francis Dordor, a music reporter in attendance: 'What does Eudeline know about unemployment? Is he going to establish a chapter of the CGT [Confederation General du Travail, the national workers' union] at la Couple or the Gibus Club [two Parisian nightclubs]?'[29] While Dordor was dismissive of Eudeline's sincerity, Alain Pacadis questioned all of the punk groups, except the British band the Damned which 'were the only group possessing a true punk energy'.[30] Other critics asserted that the appearance of punks in France illustrated the existence of the same social tensions as in Britain.[31] Even supporters, such as Yves Adrien, suggested that punk's foreignness was its value to help French society out of the stale culture of the 1970s.[32] This pervasive belief in the alien nature of punk reveals why French punks failed to have success in their homeland, especially when 'authentic' punks were performing on the same stage.

One group that overtly rejected the emphasis on Britishness for punk authenticity was Métal Urbain, arguably the most accepted group among British audiences. Unlike the other French groups, Métal Urbain attempted to integrate new instruments and influences into punk, to create a distinct musical sound. Using synthesisers and drum machines, Métal Urbain anticipated the acceptance of electronics in post-punk. Emphasising the importance of punk as an expression of discontent, the group sang about the things that occupied French society, namely the Occupation and the social divide between the wealthy city centres and the poor suburbs. The group was rewarded for such innovations by becoming the first release of the pioneering British independent label Rough Trade, which was their 'Paris Maquis' single.[33]

Since these were issues that concerned France, the group sang in French. In contrast to others in their cohort, Métal Urbain rejected the link between the English language and punk authenticity. Instead, singer Clode Panik stressed that the connection with the audience, and not foreign conventions, defined authenticity in punk. Indeed, Panik stated that many French groups used English to hide their bad lyrics and their lack of message.[34] Their connection with the audience, not the fact that British groups used the English language, was what made British punk authentic. Speaking to fellow punks in France, Panik asserted: 'You write your lyrics in French so that they can be understood by French youth'.[35] Despite this approach, the band still looked to British examples to define their approach. For example, Métal Urbain recorded a translation of the Pistols' 'Anarchy in the UK', appropriately rechristened 'Anarchie en France', which included references more pertinent to French audiences. Panik recognised the influence of the Pistols, noting that he wanted to 'say the same things [but] in French'.[36] Even with these efforts, Métal Urbain did not connect with a broader French audience, and while the group did get some recognition from British audiences it broke up by 1979.

Other French groups such as the Olivensteins, Gazoline, and Marie et les garçons followed Métal Urbain's lead and recorded original songs in French.

These groups often formed not in the capital but in provincial university towns, following a similar pattern to the development of punk in Britain. Nevertheless, the divide between the two conceptions of linguistic authenticity confounded the attempts to create a unified punk movement in France. The eventual commercialism and rigid aesthetic of British punk led to the emergence of what has been dubbed post-punk, a varied collection of musical groups unconnected to a subculture. Similarly in France, the association between Britishness and punk fostered the exploration of new sounds, such as cold wave and *le rock alternatif* as part of French post-punk music.[37] Here, issues of language were not part of the discussion of the merits of these emerging genres. Additionally, the development of a French Oi! scene in the 1980s could reveal how the issue of authenticity was no longer part of the cultural discussion. Nationalist hardcore groups used the British-style punk of the 'Blood and Culture' movement to assert a white Frenchness without the whiff of irony concerning the 'alien' culture of punk.

With French groups divided it should come as no surprise that French audiences were similarly fractured. While it is difficult to ascertain the experiences of French punks, as Middleton suggests, there are some examples of young people expressing their ideas and thoughts about punk, albeit it within the framework of music periodicals. *Rock & Folk* invited its readers in February 1977 to submit letters about punk – whether they are 'punk ou pas [punk or not]' – and printed a collection of responses in the March issue, and the magazine's readership provides a glimpse of how French audiences tried to engage with punk.[38] The article, simply titled 'Punk?', is accompanied by a Serge Clerc cartoon that illustrates many stereotypes of punk fashion in the form of a how-to-guide telling readers both what to wear and where to purchase them. The six pages of letters reveal young people both engaged with punk and skeptical of its meaning.

Those in favour of punk, often those who self-identified as punk, wrote of the importance of *punkitude*, a French term that illustrates the attempt to translate the concept of punk into the French context, as representing their desires for revolt and change. As it was for young people elsewhere, punk was a method of challenging the status quo of social isolation and economic trouble. For example, in a letter signed by 'A dozen kids from the HLM [Habitation à Loyer Modéré (low-income government housing)]', punk is described as the music of their environment, one of 'violence, brawls, hate, chains'.[39] The authors note that all music has a context, and the context of punk is the HLM. The alienation experienced among the young denizens of public housing certainly made punk an obvious form of expression – members of Métal Urbain lived in such housing. The letter suggests that French audiences understood the value of punk in articulating the chaos and anomie of late 1970s France, despite what critics asserted. Another respondent emphasised how the music of the Sex Pistols 'testifies to the urgency [of punk]', while another offered 'The Rights of Punk and Citizen', a riff on the foundational document of modern France.[40] In those letters where punk was celebrated, the issue of national authenticity does not appear to prevent these young people from embracing a punk identity. One letter writer even gave the editors the idea for the 'Beret Punk' column as a way to highlight French groups. Again, these letters pointed out the continuities between the French context and the British and American ones instead of differences.

However, not all readers were supportive of either the genre or the subculture and its place in France, echoing the critical consensus concerning punk. One respondent, Philippe Fossat, equated punk with the phenomenon of 'Salut les copains', a popular radio and television show in 1960s France built upon facsimiles of American rock 'n' roll, while another critiqued 'these groups of perverse intellectuals (the Sex Pistols) or fake teenagers (the Ramones) [that] produce a stereotypical music that shamelessly pillages the magical heritage of the Sixties'.[41] The same concern that made punk's transition into France difficult – the issue of authenticity – is not assumed for British punks either, illustrating how French listeners were not accepting of all new trends from across the Channel. Nevertheless, much of this critique hinged upon other British and American bands representing more authentic forms of popular music, thus still revealing the importance of foreign music in defining this central aspect of subcultural identity.

Even after the 'Punk ou pas' request, readers continued the debate about the meaning of punk in the letter columns of the magazine, with more and more readers identifying with the subculture. In December 1977, a letter writer, Simon Cussonal, lambasted the punk subculture as one of violence, fascism, and amateurism and something alien to the ideals of French youth.[42] In the very next issue, several readers responded in defence of the subculture, emphasising its place in France. For example, Laurent Faugerolas refuted all of these criticisms against punk while J. F. Pizzetta suggested that Cussonal listen to the Sex Pistols' 'God Save the Queen' – a telling choice – to understand the value of punk.[43] Readers continued to challenge other readers in the letter pages during 1978, railing against stereotypical assessments of punk. These exchanges between readers and the divergence of opinion of French music fans again point to the divisions concerning punk among French listeners.

The importation of punk ideals and musical practices was thwarted by internal dissent among the French concerning its aesthetic values. Musicians, critics and fans alike all revealed how their diverse interpretations of the meaning of punk prevented a unified and durable community from developing in France. The emphasis on authenticity – in which punk articulated an authentic notion of living – was conflated with Britishness, despite punk's cosmopolitan pedigree and the elements of French culture that influenced the philosophical underpinnings of the subculture. As a result, the development of a punk subculture in France could not find its own identity and became a caricature in terms of fashion and musical conventions, confounding its initial translation across the English Channel. While punk eventually bloomed in France, its initial aborted life in the 1970s illustrates how the perceptions of conventions that govern subcultures also confound their global movement.

Notes

All translations from the French, unless otherwise noted, are by the author.

1 Various artists, *Le Rock d'ici à l'Olympia*, EMI France/ Jurassik Punk JP 990404, 1999.
2 M. Seidman, *The Imaginary Revolution: Parisian Students and Workers in 1968* (New York: Berghahn Books, 2004).
3 G. Altschuler, *All Shook Up: How Rock 'n' Roll Changed America* (New York: Oxford University Press, 2003); U. Poiger, *Jazz, Rock, and Rebels: Cold War Politics and American Culture in Divided Germany* (Berkeley, CA: University of California Press, 2000); and P. Yonnet, *Jeux, modes et masses: La société française et le moderne, 1945–85* (Paris: Gallimard, 1985).
4 K. Maase, 'Establishing Cultural Democracy: Youth, Americanization, and the Irresistible Rise of Popular Culture', in H. Schissler (ed.), *The Miracle Years: A Cultural History of West Germany, 1949–68* (Princeton, NJ: Princeton University Press, 2001), pp. 429–50; Poiger, *Jazz, Rock and Rebels*; and A. Marwick, *The Sixties: Cultural Revolution in Britain, France, Italy, and the United States, c.1958–c.1974* (New York: Oxford University Press, 2000), pp. 95–8.
5 D. Hebdige, *Subculture, the Meaning of Style* (New York: Routledge, 1991), p. x.
6 On a full discussion of critiques of the CCCS, see K. Gelder, *Subcultures: Cultural Histories and Social Practice* (New York: Routledge, 2007), pp. 95–106.
7 S. Thornton, *Club Cultures: Music, Media, and Subcultural Capital* (Middleton, CT: Wesleyan University Press, 1996).
8 H. Pilkington, *Russia's Youth and its Culture: A Nation's Constructors and Constructed* (New York: Routledge, 1994), pp. 144–50.
9 D. Muggleton, *Inside Subculture: The Postmodern Meaning of Style* (New York: Berg, 2000), pp. 20–1.
10 S. Plant, *The Most Radical Gesture: The Situationist International in the Postmodern Age* (New York: Routledge, 1992), Chapter 1.

11 G. Marcus, *Lipstick Traces: A Secret History of the Twentieth Century* (Cambridge, MA: Harvard University Press, 1989). See also J. Savage, *England's Dreaming: Anarchy, Sex Pistols, Punk Rock and Beyond* (New York: St Martin's Press, 1993) for a nuanced challenge to Marcus's thesis.

12 There is a wealth of scholarship on American punk. For some examples, see T. Henry, *Break All Rules!: Punk Rock and the Making of a Style* (Ann Arbor, MI: UMI Research Press, 1989); C. Heylin, *From the Velvets to the Voidoids: A Pre-Punk History for a Post-Punk World* (New York: Penguin Books, 1993); P. Lentini, 'Punk's Origins: Anglo-American Syncretism', *Journal of Intercultural Studies*, 24:2 (2003), 153–74; L. McNeil and G. McCain, *Please Kill Me: An Oral History of Punk* (New York: Penguin Books, 1997); J. Miller, *Flowers in the Dustbin: The Rise of Rock and Roll, 1947–77* (New York: Fireside Books, 1999); M. Spitz and B. Mullen, *We Got the Neutron Bomb: The Untold Story of L.A. Punk* (New York: Three Rivers Press, 2001).

13 T. Judt, *Postwar: A History of Europe Since 1945* (New York: Penguin Books, 2006), Chapter 8.

14 Y. Adrien, 'Je chante le rock electrique', *Rock & Folk*, 73 (January 1973), 36.

15 P. Auslander, *Performing Glam Rock: Gender and Theatricality in Popular Music* (Ann Arbor, MI: University of Michigan Press, 2006), pp. 28–9.

16 A. Pacadis, *Un jeune homme chic* (Paris: Denoël, 2002 [1978]), p. 42; and A. Pacadis, 'Notes', *Façade*, 2 (1977), 5.

17 J. Briggs, 'A Red Noise: Pop and Politics in 1970s France', in T. Brown and A. Lison (eds.), *Sounds and Visions: Music, Counterculture and the Global 1968* (New York: Palgrave MacMillan, 2014), pp. 15–27.

18 S. Thompson, *Punk Productions: Unfinished Business* (Albany, NY: SUNY Press, 2004), pp. 13–15; and C. O'Hara, *Philosophy of Punk: More Than Noise!* (San Francisco: AK Press, 1999), pp. 27–8.

19 P. Eudeline, 'Amoureux solitaires', *Best*, 150 (January 1981), reprinted in *Gonzo: Écrits rock, 1973–2001* (Paris: Denoël, 2002), p. 153; and S. Pietri and A. Quinlin, *Punk: Seventeen Rock* (Paris: Régine Deforges, 1978), p. 127.

20 C. Eudeline, *Nos années punk: 1972–78* (Paris: Denoël, 2002), p. 168.

21 J.-D. Brierre and L. Lewin, *Punkitude* (Paris: Albin Michel, 1978), p. 14.

22 *Ibid.*, p. 13.

23 P. Eudeline, *L'aventure punk* (Paris: Sagittaire, 1978), p. 66.

24 C.-J. Bertrand and F. Bordat, *Les Médias américaines en France: Influence et penetration* (Paris: Belin, 1989), p. 115.

25 I. Birch, 'Street Heat: France, La Vie en Pose', *Melody Maker* (6 May 1978), p. 20.

26 H. Barker and Y. Taylor, *Faking It: The Quest for Authenticity in Popular Music* (New York: W. W. Norton & Co., 2007), Chapter 8.

27 Brierre and Lewin, *Punkitude*, p. 65.

28 R. Gildea, *France Since 1945* (New York: Oxford University Press, 1995), pp. 96–7.

29 F. Dordor, 'L'été punk', *Best*, 111 (October 1977), 11.

30 A. Pacadis, *Un jeune homme chic* (Paris: Denoël, 2002 [1977]), p. 168.

31 P. Manoeuver, 'Les martyrs', *Rock & Folk*, 128 (September 1977), 51.

32 Y. Adrien, *Növovision: Les confesssions d'un cobaye du siècle* (Paris: Denoel, 2002 [1980]), p. 166.

33 On the social significance of 'Paris Maquis', see J. Briggs 'Nazi Rock: The *Mode rétro* in French Pop Music, 1975–80', *Modern and Contemporary France*, 19: 4 (2011): pp. 11–13.

34 Clode Panik, 'Old Men', *Best*, 126 (January 1979).

35 Pietri and Quinlin, *Punk*, p. 150.

36 *Ibid.*, p. 141.

37 S. Reynolds, *Rip It Up and Start Again: Postpunk 1978–84* (New York: Penguin, 2006). For an overview of French post-punk culture in Paris, see B. Couturier, *Une scène-jeunesse* (Paris: Autrement, 1983).

38 'Punk ou pas', *Rock & Folk*, 121 (February 1977), 41.

39 'Punk?', *Rock & Folk*, 122 (March 1977), 72.

40 *Ibid.*, pp. 74–5.

41 *Ibid.*, p. 76.

42 'Courrier', *Rock & Folk*, 131 (December 1977), 23.

43 'Courrier', *Rock & Folk*, 132 (January 1978), 23–6.

8

Lo spirito continua: Torino and the Collettivo Punx Anarchici

GIACOMO BOTTÀ

The role played by industrial cities in the birth, consolidation and transmission of cultural scenes, sounds and rituals is a potentially fascinating field of research. Too often, however, such connections have been simplistically interpreted, with the greyness and harsh noise of the industrial city glorified as the true essence of a local culture.[1] But urban poverty or brutalist architecture are not enough in themselves to provide exciting new music or a counter-cultural awakening among youth. We cannot explain punk, for example, by simply asserting a deterministic link between young people and a decaying urban environment.

Industrial conurbations, from the post-war years through until the 1970s, offer a common paradigm for urban development in Europe.[2] They have provided the setting for many individual and collective destinies, though young people have more typically used popular music as a means of escape than a means to celebrate the environment in which they live. An examination of the Collettivo Punx Anarchici of Torino, meanwhile, suggests that punk served as an *Ersatz* for the lack of enjoyable public spaces in the city. The objective here, therefore, is to reveal the complex interaction between the (sub)cultural productions of a group of youngsters in an industrial city under economic duress. In so doing, punk is understood to represent a complex set of ideologies and practices that transcend any specific national culture. To focus on the local will allow us to address punk as a spatial and cultural articulation of resistance.

Torino into the 1980s

Torino lies in the north-east of Italy, the administrative capital of the Piedmont region. Its history is marked by two major events. First, as the seat of the Savoia royal family responsible for *Risorgimento*, it was briefly elected capital of independent Italy in 1861, before the title moved to Florence in 1865 and Rome in 1871. Second, Torino is the city of Fiat. When the national government left Torino, the urban elite felt the urge to provide a new point of supremacy for the city. In 1899, therefore, a group of noblemen, financiers and landowners established the Fabbrica Italiana Automobili Torino.[3]

In the economic boom that followed the Second World War, Fiat developed into one of Italy's major industrial concerns. As an employer of skilled and unskilled workers, it attracted many hundreds of citizens from the south and east of the country. This, unsurprisingly, had a major impact on Torino's urban development. Between 1951 and 1961, the city's population grew from 719,000 to over one million.[4] Such sudden migration, moreover, brought almost pre-modern conditions to the city; in the 1950s, many migrants were lodged in huts, shelters and military barracks on the fringes of Fiat's Mirafiori and Lingotto factories. Many simply alternated sleeping in beds according to the factory shifts, lived in overcrowded attics across the city centre, or even slept on benches in railway stations.

As a result, the municipality was forced to solve the problem of overcrowding by providing decent housing for the workers and their families in close proximity to the factories. From the 1960s on, workers were moved to monofunctional blocks of flats built on peripheral wasteland before even asphalted roads were completed or facilities and shops settled. But although living conditions improved considerably with these modern flats, social tensions and problems such as vandalism soon appeared. Migrants from the rural south of the country faced racism and sometimes had to adapt hastily to a city life of anonymity and coldness.

The late 1960s, in concomitance with the students' revolt, saw large sections of the Italian workforce politicised; strikes and demonstrations increased. By the 1970s, radicalisation led to violence and terrorism, with Torino becoming one of the main stages of the Italian *anni di piombo* ('years of lead'). Indeed, the 1970s was to be amongst the most violent periods of the city's history, with political demonstrations leading to confrontations between political rivals and the police. Riots, replete with Molotov cocktails, tear gas, weapons and wooden sticks were common. Popular music concerts, including those by The Clash, Siouxsie and the Banshees and The Police, ended in riots born out of political tensions, common rowdiness and claims to a 'culture for all'.

Concurrently, the global automobile industry entered into crisis, with huge repercussions for Torino in terms of forced exclusions from the labour force. Altogether, the radicalisation of students, youth culture and workers combined with police repression, terrorism and economic crisis to leave scars across the city's urban tissue that led to perceptions of danger and tension permeating its public spaces. It was in such a context that the Collettivo Punx Anarchici emerged.

Punx in space

According to De Sario's study of Italian radicalism, the 1980s represented an important moment in the history of Torino.[5] Already, in 1977, the city's communist mayor, Diego Novelli, had tried to initiate more positive forms of local activism in an attempt to curtail radicalisation, criminality and social isolation. Of course, Novelli was operating within a traditional leftist approach that sought to provide equal welfare across the city without discrimination. The Collettivo Punx Anarchici, however, developed a somewhat more culturally distinct response to the complex interaction of political, economic and cultural factors that shaped the city's history.

The Collettivo was formed in the early 1980s by a group of youngsters, most of them still in secondary education. Bands belonging to the Collettivo included Declino, Negazione, Quinto Braccio, Contrazione and Kollettivo. Though other punk bands formed in Torino, political and ideological differences meant that not all participated in the Collettivo's activities. For example, Blue Vomit were considered too much of a 'fun' band and too close to conventional British '77-style punk to be included in the Collettivo, despite associating with its members. If the roots of the Collettivo's punk identity may be found in early TV reports and magazine photos of the Sex Pistols and Ramones,[6] then the transition from music to related activism owed much to American (particularly Californian) hardcore punk bands perceived as an alternative to 'sell-out' British punk fashion:

> Everything revolved around music, it gave you another perspective. [But] as far as I'm concerned, my life didn't change when I listened to the Sex Pistols, but when I listened to Black Flag; that was my turning point.[7]

From the outset, making music was central to the scene-related activities of Torino's punks. However, the Collettivo was first and foremost a political group, meeting once a week in a small anarchist circle in Via Ravenna:

It was not until in 1983–84 that we began playing as Negazione. In truth, the thing started in the so-called Collettivo Punx Anarchici, which in those years met in a tiny room of the anarchist circle in Via Ravenna behind the railway station of Porta Nuova … There were, I would say, 20 to 50 people, sometimes more. We discussed what action to take, whether to boycott ATM [the municipal public transport company] in support of free public transport. But mainly we discussed organising gigs, where we had to do everything: get the PA, design the posters and print them, go around by night to hang them on walls, write the flyers. There were all these elements that could feed into political militancy, a musical scene or urban subculture; it was more like a mix of all of the above.[8]

Via Ravenna also provided an ideological link to pre-punk anarchist poli- tics and a physical space where the Collettivo was able to reflect on the political significance of what it was doing. This did sometimes lead to conflict with the older anarchist milieu. If some on the far left initially eyed the punks with sus- picion, then many older anarchists remained unconvinced of punk's potential to inform political activism:

Whenever we organised a gig, there would be huge discussions about the fact that gigs were useless, that we should organise something to deepen our position. I am talking about the older ones here. Me and the others, we were more like yes, right, we have our circled As and everything, but we also want to have fun, get drunk, play distorted fast music and scream this rage we have – to have a laugh.[9]

Given this, the consolidation of a politicised punk presence in Torino was further built on the *centri d'incontro* (meeting centres) introduced by Novelli in 1977.[10] These may well have been bound to a traditionally socialist view of citi- zenship and well-being, but one such centre, located in the remote Vanchiglia district, became a rehearsal and meeting place for Torino's punks. Indeed, the Collettivo soon organised a series of gigs there as a means to mesh their musical and political activities:

The social centre in Vanchiglia was used because we had an 'insider' working there. There was an opening, the chance to do things that brought us out of the discos, a very important step. It was also a rehearsal space, a room of two-square meters, with a drum-kit and mini PA: il Kollettivo, il Declino, Negazione and Contrazione all rehearsed there … and there was a place to have gigs. There were five or six gigs there, a very important one with MDC from San Francisco … At the time we were trying not to compromise and, theoretically, we shouldn't have been there because it was run by the municipality. But it was a smart compromise that allowed us to spend time together, to go from zero to one (which is better than nothing), and from there we moved to much more extemporary situations until 1987, when El Paso was squatted.[11]

Vanchiglia represented a kind of incubator of creativity, where music making was a social, collective and democratic action based on immediate feedback and response. Many of the bands' songs would be written and rehearsed there, 'born in a context of about 10 to 15 people' being present in the rehearsal space. As a result, songs were written 'not only by you and the band ..., but formed out of a socialising moment ... we hung out there all and each afternoon'.[12]

Politically, each of the gigs organised by the Collettivo in Vanchiglia supported a particular cause ('fighting urban apathy', 'against nukes'), the details of which were displayed on posters and xeroxed leaflets. These, in turn, were distributed at the door to raise awareness and targeted not only at the punks attending the gigs, but also the many other youngsters in Torino looking for something to do:

> The Collettivo started organising these gigs and they were crowded. In the city there was nothing going on, no one knew the bands that were playing, they were teenagers, but we were still going on stage in front of 4–600 people. At one famous gig, I don't remember, I think in February '83 with MDC from San Francisco, there were nearly a thousand people there.[13]

By 1983, compilation tapes and fanzines were circulating around the city. It was the release of Declino's debut EP (1983), however, that represented the Collettivo's first (and last) effort to produce an actual record. The EP was self-financed and self-released via *Contro Produzione Dischi*. Oliver, of the band Kollettivo, helped mix the recording. The cover, designed by Sergio of Quinto Braccio, depicted a streetscape dominated by cold, functionalistic architecture; in the street, a burning white flag hung on a broken pole. On the flipside of the cover, a political message was offered by the *Punx Anarchici Torino*, while the inner-sleeve comprised the lyrics and a long statement signed by the band.

Such a complete use of the record and its sleeve (graphics, pictures, lyrics, texts) to communicate a political message was reminiscent of much punk production of the time.[14] In the wake of Crass, bands conceived records as a multimedia form through which their message was not only conveyed by the music and the cover, but also via accompanying texts, pictures, prints, graphics, useful addresses and contacts. For both Crass and the Collettivo, such an approach sought to present cultural production as a networked alternative to the existing structures of the music industry. In other words, it offered a means of *Publizität* from below.

Popular music as *Publizität* from below

The Collettivo's positioning between political activism and cultural practice was common to hardcore punk across Europe and North America in the 1980s. Indeed, it is possible to talk of a transnational scene, with bands from Torino touring Europe while also corresponding and exchanging material at a national and international level. Negazione, for example, later moved to Amsterdam and toured the USA. But what is so striking about this is the predominance of industrial cities within the transnational network. Places such as Tampere (Finland), the Ruhr (Germany) and Gothenborg (Sweden) produced important bands and developed active local scenes. In many ways, hardcore punk became a 'public sphere' in the 1980s – a site of debate, conflict and resistance.

Following Jürgen Habermas's classic definition of *Öffentlichkeit*, the 'public sphere' relates to those social sites or arenas where meanings and identities are articulated, distributed and negotiated.[15] It is *on the street* that the various features of the public sphere materialise, co-exist and come together. As this suggests, the realms of the 'public' and the 'private' should be understood in spatial terms. For Doreen Massey, too, social relations are always spatial; space and 'the social' are inextricable from each other.[16] Whenever we talk about the private and public, we do so in ways that define social and spatial relations.

Such a conceptualisation may be read in hegemonic terms. Thus, the bourgeois public sphere can exist only via the suppression of whatever is felt to threaten or undermine it. This may include categories such as women, the poor, the ethnic or the religious 'other'. Not even in the idealised setting of the Italian renaissance *piazza* or the classic Athenian *agora* do we find a public sphere in which 'access is guaranteed to all citizens'.[17] Indeed, the notion of 'access' to the public sphere has numerous connotations. For instance, we can talk about it in relation to education, physical disability, 'capital' (in the Bourdieusian sense), ethnicity, religion, gender and age. The erosion of the public sphere is now, moreover, a significant topic of contemporary urban studies, particularly in relation to research on surveillance and social control, or on social justice and the 'right to the city'.[18] Actions that were once expected to take place in public, such as gathering, discussing and socialising, are seen to be taking place elsewhere (in shopping malls or social media).[19]

Back in the 1980s, Torino was systematically organised as a 'Fordist' city subordinate to industrial production. The public and the private were clearly demarcated. Private was home; the public constituted places of leisure and encounter (parks, squares), of transit (streets) and institutions (churches, schools, hospitals, prisons) where people gathered. The industrial spaces that encompassed great portions of the city were privately owned, but they could also be 'lived' as public spaces – as by the workers during a strike for example. This, in turn, caused spatial and social disruption, thereby placing the distribution of public and private into question. For Torino's punks, this had clear ramifications:

> [As the city] decayed, so the perspective changed from one of seemingly eternal development to reveal the city's physicality ... From being full of people, full of workers, full of life, it started to leak ... it was like an implosion. And this thing, we were not conceptualising it, but we felt it strongly in our own lives ... nothing special happened, but without doubt, we were all strongly marked by those things.[20]

Indeed, the Collettivo was able to transform private-but-vacant industrial spaces into public ones, both materially (by gathering in them) and at an imaginary level (by using them in pictures, lyrics and sounds). They also occupied public spaces and made them 'private', winning them as subcultural territories. Nonetheless, their main effort was directed toward the creation of counter-public spaces 'from below' situated in music itself. One seasoned activist recalled:

> The square was not working anymore; in the square you got beaten up, you got arrested. The usual channels of protest – for instance leaflets – seemed worn out. Nothing was working anymore, radios were already institutionalising themselves and so ... by trying to inject political content into cultural activity we found ourselves side by side with people, younger people with different points of views, but similar in method. [They were] doing things that started from yourself, from your condition, trying to run your life yourself and convey its political content. One thing that really impressed me about the punks was that their lyrics were like leaflets or like what we used to shout in demonstrations turned into football chants. These guys were so much younger than us, often ten years younger, but they were shouting from the stage in a very provocative way.[21]

It may be argued, therefore, that as Torino began to fall into decay, with vacant lots and empty properties, so people retreated to the private and left the public realm to be occupied by the unemployed, striking workers, student demonstrators and political conflict. Certainly, the heightened tensions of the 1970s continued to spill over into the subsequent decade. Torino, during the 'anni di piombo', was portrayed as a 'site of long and hard industrial conflict in which extra-parliamentary groups played an important role'.[22] The so-called '77 movement' brought violence and class war onto the streets via riots, shootings, bombings, sabotages and sedition. In response, the state used force, increased surveillance, arrests and legislation to ensure or restore 'order' to public spaces. According to one detailed history of Torino, more than a thousand violent attacks or confrontations took place between 1973 and 1981, with twenty-four victims killed by terrorists from either the Brigate Rosse or Prima Linea. As a result, the deep 'wounds' inflicted on the city through the 1970s into the 1980s remain unhealed today.[23]

Most obviously, the city's public sphere, especially in the city centre, was transformed. One interviewee remembered:

> Torino's first tram of the morning headed straight into Fiat and everything closed at 7.30 pm. From 7.30 pm it was curfew; it was a very 1970s kind of feeling when people feared going out … I lived in Via Turati, at Porta Nuova, in a student dormitory and when I met my punk friends to take the tram back at 11 pm there was no one else on the tram, it was very strange. Everyone lived and breathed Fiat.[24]

And as people retreated into private, so television began increasingly to serve as a substitute for the public sphere.[25] In Alberto Abruzzese's estimation, the television became a fake *Publizität* for a country without a 'metropolis'.

> The metropolis is a huge laboratory of social struggles and desires; it is a space which is deeply soaked in communication, in visual culture and in visibility, [but] a space which has not been experienced by Italians. We never had Paris, London, New York … Television has been for a long time the new [city] square.[26]

Even so, television's rise to cultural hegemony could not 'exhaust the full range of human practice, human energy, human *intention*'.[27] Indeed, punk critiques of the soporific effects of television are legion (hear, for just one example, Black Flag's 'TV Party'). But its relevance in Torino was perhaps compounded by the fact that the Italian public broadcasting company (RAI) had been founded in the city in 1924 as the Unione Radiofonica Italiana. Thus, the cover of Negazione's second EP, *Condannati a Morte nel Vostro Quieto Vivere* ('Condemned to Death in Your Quiet Life'), was especially potent. The artwork, designed by 'Dumbo' who collaborated with various punk bands in the early 1980s, portrays a man sitting on a couch in his slippers, pointing a gun to his head while lifting his hand to hide himself, as if captured by the lens of a camera. In front of him, a large television rests on a table. The setting is sparse, functional; a reproduction of the living room of many Italian families, with the television as its most important element. The critique is clear. But the Negazione cover may also serve as an example of the Collettivo's creating what Negt and Kluge define as 'a proletarian public sphere, a public from below':

> The masses won't let themselves be regulated anymore; they don't let themselves be told that they are not angry. Rather, they engage in fusions, they form connections. [This] for us is a process of igniting solidarity among people who might otherwise have very different ideas, about the question of foreigners, for example. A 'counter public' has its own process of learning … The bourgeois public sphere, in contrast, is prescribed. The newspapers, the media provide a prescribed view that filters experiences but does not render them.[28]

It is during 'historical fissures', Negt and Kluge argue, that 'proletarian publicity' comes to the fore. And because it is unable to control the public sphere, 'it has to be reconstructed from rifts, marginal cases [and] isolated initiatives'.[29] Torino's punks, therefore, provided an example of this process, articulating a protest born in but not solely out of their urban environment.

Punk as articulation

A better understanding of the Collettivo's relationship to Torino may be gleaned from the notion of 'articulation' developed within the Centre for Contemporary Cultural Studies (CCCS), and by Stuart Hall in particular. It may also help overcome a deep-rooted issue in the study of popular music and subculture; that is, the latter's relationship to a tangible heritage (such as architecture). The 'sound of the factory' or 'the rhythm of the assembly line' has often been used to reference disparate musical genres, from soul to heavy metal, from post-punk to house. But though Collettivo bands articulated themselves sonically within Torino, they did not simply reflect their urban-industrial context.

In *Resistance Through Rituals* (1976), the CCCS describe subcultures as containing a 'double articulation' that relates both to their parent culture (the working class) and to the dominant one (ruling class).[30] Building on the thought of Ernesto Laclau, Hall developed the concept further as a means to overcome Marxist reductionism. In other words, the term was used to refer both to a means of expression/enunciation and as a temporary structure formed between two elements. Such a concept is useful in explaining the con-textual constellation of cultural practices. As Jennifer Daryl Slack makes clear, 'the context is not something given out there, within which practices occur or which influence the development of practices. Rather, identities, practices and effects generally constitute the very context within which they are practices, identities or effects'.[31]

Punk subculture articulates itself as a heterogeneous mix of subjectivities (what Hall would call 'positionalities') and identities. The Collettivo, in practice, articulated itself through writings, drawings and music. But its critique of the socio-spatial structure of the city and the idea of individual and collective needs cannot be understood simply as deriving from a particular socio-spatial context. The Collettivo's members articulated themselves *within* such a context and were therefore at the same time able to change and to shape it.

Accordingly, any notion of punk as some kind of continuation of the workers' struggle falls somewhat short in relation to the Collettivo. For Mara, the female voice of Contrazione between 1983 and 1985, 'we always tried to express our needs. My need has never been to work in a factory and die there; my need has always been to live and be happy despite work'.[32] As this suggests, Contrazione were very much aware of the spatial articulation of their activities and the consequences thereof:

> Our aim was not to get used to desperation and greyness, but to use the sounds, colours and life of a city – coming everyday into our mind – as an incentive to build life and to fight. Fight for the present, against heroin, nuclear energy or things like life becoming subordinate to IT. [The awareness] of living in an urban landscape, which everyday revealed the symptoms of a progressive decomposition, gave Contrazione's music the power of a punch in the face and a means of projecting our conscience.[33]

Quite clearly, the CCCS's double articulation – based only on class relations – cannot adequately explain the activities of the Collettivo and its bands. For a start, punk, as a subcultural expression of youth, cut across social classes; the Collettivo comprised a diverse social mix. Nor were their activities connected to a specific class or generational identity, but to a far more cosmopolitan sense of rebellion that claimed public spaces and articulated itself betwixt and between politics and popular music.

This took an interesting turn in relation to lyrics. Punk lyrics were either built as political slogans, usually with refrains to be shouted *ad libitum* and resonant of the football terrace, or – later – imbued with an existential nuance that referred to social isolation, depression and sadness, sometimes in exaggerated emotional ways. Nonetheless, it was the articulation of these lyrics, mostly through shouts and growls, and their embedding within a fast and furious wall of sound, that determined their meaning. In recordings and especially in live situations, lyrics remained mostly unintelligible; however, they were photo-copied, distributed and translated into other languages. Any examination of the Collettivo's songs should therefore always refer to the way in which they were articulated.

'Mortale Tristezza', from Declino's debut EP, may be read as an articulation of the band's sound and subcultural standpoint within the material, social and historical context of Torino:

> Mortale tristezza in questa città/ poco borgehse, poco operaia/ un tempo reale, ora decadente ... mortale tristezza in questa città/ assale la gente che si sente derisa/ per i sogni svaniti d'ammucchiare denaro/ ma il robot non s'oppone e riprende a sognare.

> [Deadly sadness in this city/ not so middle class and not so working class/ once royal now decadent/ feeble resistance to this system ... deadly sadness in this city/ assaults people who feel derided/ for their broken dreams to pile up money/ but the robot doesn't rebel and starts dreaming once again.]

'Noi' by Negazione appears in *Condannati a morte nel vostro quieto vivere*, the band's second EP, recorded in an Amsterdam squat in 1985. Over an introduc-tory mid-tempo guitar riff, reminiscent of the Sex Pistols, Zazzo (the band's singer) begins to recite the lyrics. The song then accelerates, the guitar gets more intricate, the voice louder and the lyrics less understandable. 'Noi' is not constructed along a typical verse-chorus-verse pattern, but builds on a guitar riff that rises and falls before finally returning to the mid-tempo intro turned outro (and finishing). The lyrics provide a succinct articulation of the Collettivo, the band, and punk as a subculture located within Torino itself: 'Noi, noi rovesceremo l'orgoglio delle vostre automobili/ noi distruggeremo la felicità delle vostre domeniche'. ['We will overthrow your pride for cars/ We will destroy the happiness of your Sundays'.]

In their simplicity, the two sentences bring a certain context into focus. The first is about the manufacturing of cars and the pride associated with both the production and the ownership of them. The second is about the workers' condition and the traditional delights of Sunday, the day without work devoted to relaxation. There is an interesting dialectic progression from early punk: the idea here is not to burn cars and destroy Sundays, but to overthrow pride and destroy (false) happiness.

More broadly, the Collettivo should be understood as the articulation of several individual and collective forces, establishing precarious links and relations at different levels and under different circumstances with the social, cultural and spatial forces around them. It is impossible to understand the

Collettivo by merely referring to international, national or local socio-spatial
forces or, worse, to a tradition of political opposition fused with a musical/
fashion-related subculture. The songs embody a change in the status of the
individual musicians and listeners, both in their expression of subcultural
practice and in their relationship to their own environment. The music, as
an act of sounding out noise, seems to take on the role of public space: it is
no mere commodity; it becomes public with no copyright and distribution
through a democratic, non-commercial circuit. Its performative, or spectacular,
aspects (so rarely connected to music in subcultural studies) may be understood through Dick Hebdige's idea of dramatisation: 'Punks were not only
directly responding to increasing joblessness, changing moral standards, the
rediscovery of poverty, the depression, etc. they were dramatising what had
come to be called "Britain's decline"'.[34] Thus, dramatisation relates closely to
articulation, but emphasises aspects such as performance and mimesis. For
instance, the cover of Negazione's debut EP, *Tutti Pazzi* ('All Crazy'), shows
Zazzo sitting on the ground at a street corner next to a trash bin. The shot was
taken by Tax, the band's guitar player, while the band was hanging out close to
where Zazzo was living with his parents, in the *Lingotto* district. In the photo,
Zazzo plays the rejected, the mentally unstable, the unemployed, the heroin
addict. In his own words:

> [The picture] expresses a moment, a feeling of those times, not really
> desperation, because that is a big word, but anyway the scazzo ['don't give a
> fuck'] attitude, to use a more down to earth term. There was this feeling of
> impotence towards a lot of things that we could understand but could not
> handle or solve; the compromise of being forced to work. ... It's a very punk
> image: the guy seated on the ground. [But] we didn't want to present an image
> of the self-destructive punk, drunk and feeling sick ... We wanted to present
> the idea of madness, as in the title of the ep. All the text in the booklet was
> mine, [describing] episodes of daily madness, delinquency. The photo is really
> bound to the content of the ep.[35]

There are, too, clear subcultural references in the clothes (jeans, Chuck
Taylor shoes), pose and haircut, which refer to other punk covers such as the
Ramones' first album or Minor Threat's first EP. The trash-bin is a cheap piece
of functional urban design and can be read as a symbol of economic crisis
and cuts in public expenditure. In the background, there is a nearly ghostly
subconscious presence of a car, the hegemonic symbol in Torino. Finally, the
sleeve was presented via a xeroxed black-and-white aesthetic. Though this was,
in part, due to the band's available means of production, it also evoked a sense
of authenticity and a kind of humanism. In other words, dramatisation justified

the quest for authenticity and enabled Negazione to rearticulate the meaning of 'crisis' as a performative force.

Conclusion

Renewed interest in the 1970s and 1980s has not bypassed the Collettivo, whose members have recently issued memorial books, documentaries and anthologies.[36] Torino today is a very different place from the disrupted industrial town torn apart by political unrest in the 1970s and 1980s. Urban violence of either political or non-political origin has dissipated into *movida*, a trendy and gentrified night-life that has commodified the central river front (the *Murazzi*) into a strip of cocktail bars and lounges.

Nonetheless, as this chapter has shown, hardcore punk in Torino served as an expression of youthful resistance. Similar experiences were taking place in other industrial cities around the world, articulating punk in explicitly political and socio-economic contexts. Indeed, without punk's transmission into a global cultural phenomenon, much of the Collettivo's creativity would have detoured into violence, been heavily repressed, or simply left undeveloped.

This chapter has endeavoured to provide an analysis of local youth resistance, first as a form of *Publizität* from below, i.e. as an agency able to rebuild a public space of struggle, dialogue and politics. The Collettivo's cultural expression was produced and articulated within a definite socio-spatial context; the dramatisation of Torino punk enabled the Collettivo to emphasise spectacular elements of the crisis with which they engaged. In so doing, this chapter moves beyond a reductionist analysis of subcultural production towards a more complex reading of the interaction between identity, practice and materiality.

Acknowledgements

All lyrics quoted in the article are done so with permission of their authors and the bands. Thanks to Negazione, Franti and Declino for the permission to use their song lyrics. The songs by the above-mentioned bands quoted in the article are not subject to copyright.

Notes

1   Manchester immediately comes to mind. See D. Haslam, *Manchester, England: The Story of the Pop Cult City* (London: Harper Collins, 2000).

UNIVERSITY OF WINCHESTER
LIBRARY

2   P. Hall, *Urban and Regional Planning* (Harmondsworth: Penguin, 1975).

3   U. Levra, *Storia di Torino Vol. 7: Da Capitale Politica a Capitale Industriale* (Torino: Einaudi, 2001).

4   N. Tranfaglia, *Storia di Torino Vol. 9. Gli Anni della Repubblica* (Torino: Giulio Einaudi, 1999), p. 19.

5   B. De Sario, *Resistenze Innaturali* (Milano: Agenzia X, 2009).

6   R. Farano ('Tax'), interview with author, 12 March 2011.

7   M. Mathieu, interview with author, 19 February 2011. Similarly, G. Capra, interview with author, 18 March 2011, recalled: 'I was never interested in 1977 punk; my cultural step was directly from Genesis to Dead Kennedys; from Gentle Giant to DOA'.

8   Mathieu, author interview.

9   Farano, author interview.

10 De Sario, *Resistenze Innaturali*, p. 142.

11 Capra, author interview.

12 M. Bertotti, interview with author, 13 May 2011.

13 S. Bernelli, interview with author, 11 May 2011.

14 G. Berger, *The Story of Crass* (Oakland, CA: Omnibus Press, 2008).

15 J. Habermas, S. Lenox and F. Lennox, 'The Public Sphere: An Encyclopaedia Article (1964)', *New German Critique*, 3 (1974), 49–55.

16 D. Massey, *Spatial Divisions of Labour: Social Structures and the Geography of Production* (Basingstoke: Macmillan, 1984).

17 Habermas, Lenox and Lennox, 'The Public Sphere', 49.

18 H. Koskela, *Fear and its Others: Social Geographies* (London: Sage, 2010); D. Mitchell, *The Right to the City: Social Justice and the Fight for Public Space* (New York: Guilford, 2003).

19 H. Koskela, '"The Other Side of Surveillance": Webcams, Power and Agency', in D. Lyon (ed.), *Theorizing Surveillance: The Panopticon and Beyond* (Cullompton: Willan, 2006).

20 A. De Rossi, interview with author, 12 May 2011.

21 Radio interview with Vanni from Franti, included on Franti, *Estamos en todas partes* (Stella*near, 2006). The CD notes: 'No copyright/copyright is a fascist law protecting the ownership of ideas. The reproduction of this material is free, as long as the contents are fully respected and their circulation is kept outside logics of profit'.

22 Tranfaglia, *Storia di Torino*, p. 43.

23 *Ibid.*, p. 44.

24 Capra, author interview.

25 See, for example, J. Foot, *Milan Since the Miracle: City, Culture and Identity* (Oxford: Berg, 2001).

26 C. Antonelli, 'Cara Vecchia Italia sei un Paese nei Guai', *Rolling Stone* (30 April 2006), pp. 136–7.

27 R. Williams, *Marxism and Literature* (Oxford: Oxford University Press, 1977), p. 125.

28   Monica Krause, 'The Production of Counter-Publics and the Counter-Publics of Production: An Interview with Oskar Negt', *European Journal of Social Theory*, 9:1 (2006), 119–128.

29   O. Negt and A. Kluge, *Public Sphere and Experience: Toward an Analysis of the Bourgeois and Proletarian Public Sphere* (Minneapolis, MN: Minnesota University Press, 1993), p. xliii.

30   S. Hall and T. Jefferson (eds), *Resistance Through Rituals: Youth Subcultures in Postwar Britain* (London: Harper Collins, 1991), p. 15; Stuart Hall, 'On Postmodernism and Articulation: an Interview with Stuart Hall', *Journal of Communication Inquiry*, 10:2 (1986), 45–60.

31   J. Daryl Slack, 'The Theory and Method of Articulation', in D. Morley and K-H. Chen (eds), *Stuart Hall: Critical Dialogues in Cultural Studies* (London: Routledge, 1996), pp. 114–29.

32   M. Caberlin, interview with author, 22 April 2011.

33   S. Giaccone and M. Pandin, *Nel Cuore della Bestia* (Torino: Zero in Condotta, 1996), originally in *Yeti* fanzine (1983).

34   D. Hebdige, *Subculture: The Meaning of Style* (London: Routledge, 1979), p. 87.

35   G. Sassola, interview with author, 30 March 2011.

36   S. Bernelli, *I Ragazzi del Mucchio* (Milan: Sironi, 2003); Negazione, *Il Giorno del Sole* (Milan: Shake, 2012).

9

Shared enemies, shared friends: the relational character of subcultural ideology in the case of Czech punks and skinheads

HEDVIKA NOVOTNÁ AND MARTIN HEŘMANSKÝ

Punk in Czechoslovakia began to form prior to 1989, in a society substantially removed from that in which it had first been born. In other words, punk was imported into a Czechoslovakian society that was determined by a political system that claimed to be socialistic, was aligned to the idea of communism, and whose primary characteristics (regardless of the name) were built on repression, fear and conformity.[1] From within the same totalitarian regime, moreover, and very much linked to the emergent punk subculture, came the Czech skinhead.

Such a political system was soon to change. Nevertheless, punks and skinheads remain fellow travellers to this day; indeed, the relationship between the two subcultures, while taking different forms at different times in different places, may even be seen as essential to their survival. We would argue, too, that punk's development is always informed by the character of the dominant society of which it is part. Its subcultural identity is constructed in relation to the mainstream. Elements of mainstream culture, regarded by the subculture as symbolising key flaws in the dominant society, are reinterpreted and negated; the constitutive elements of the punk and skinhead subcultures are then formulated and internalised to determine the authenticity of its participants. That said, of course, it is impossible to discuss punk as an isolated phenomenon. In Czechoslovakia, the Czech Republic and Slovakia as elsewhere in the world, punk changed and evolved over time, drawing from different 'models', emphasising or suppressing elements of punk's original idea, creating new versions and variations.[2]

To explore this process analytically, we will use the concept of subcultural ideology as a kind of counterpoise to the subcultural style that also shapes subcultural identity. Simultaneously, we argue that subcultural identities are formed in relation to other subcultures, with which traditions are forged and to which actors from either side relate (either willingly or unwillingly). Finally, we argue for the importance of cultural diffusion, reinterpretation and even acculturation in understanding the development of subcultural styles, actions and relationships. To understand punk in Czechoslovakia, the Czech Republic and Slovakia, various intervening factors must be taken into account: the political regime into which punk was born; the changes to the dominant society that occurred thereafter; trends coming in from the West; relations with and between other subcultures. In this case, skinheads influenced punks and vice versa, meaning an analysis of both reveals much about the social phenomena and processes since characterised as post-socialist. The importance of the mutual relationship between both subcultures may best be demonstrated in the following two quotes:

> I remember one accidental meeting of a few punks and skinheads in the early nineties. I was sitting there wondering who was sitting in front of me, then acknowledging one of skinheads: 'Hey, I know you. I kicked you in the head at the Výstaviště[3] ... Sorry for that.' And he answered: 'Don't mention it, if you were lying on the ground, I would have kicked you too.' And then both of us continued our conversations with our own friends ... (Cook, male, 42)

> Trachta: Do you see any future for skinheads?
> Buqičák: ... As punks won't die out, so the skinheads won't die out – these are cultures with a tradition.[4]

Theoretical and methodological basis

Our interpretation of the formation and transformation of punk subculture in Czechoslovakia and, later, the Czech Republic, is based on the analytical categories of subcultural style,[5] capital[6] and identity,[7] with specific emphasis on subcultural ideology. While the first three concepts have been subjected to extensive theorisation, the last has been less so – primarily due to conflicting use of its meaning.[8] Here, though, we understand subcultural ideology to be a historically and culturally determined system of shared values, norms and attitudes that members of a particular subculture adhere to, approve and express.[9] In line with Thornton, we assert that ideology is developed via a dialogue with one's own and others' social formations.[10] We argue, too, that it is possible to follow such a development through three interconnected but analytically distinguishable levels: (a) in relation to the dominant society (how the dominant society is perceived); (b) in relation to a particular sub-culture (how a subculture perceives itself); (c) in relation to other subcultures (how subcultures perceive each other). These three levels provide a continual dialogue through which subcultural ideology is constructed, negotiated and reproduced, the relative importance of which may be determined by the pre-vailing historical and cultural context.

Our study is based on a relatively variable body of data. First, from in-terviews held with early Czech punks alongside observation and informal interview-conversations; second, from a re-analysis of qualitative research carried out by our students;[11] third, from publicly-accessible sources, both visual and written. Through this, we distinguish four types of formation ap-plicable to both the punk and skinhead subcultures, each of which corresponds to historical developments in Czechoslovakia and, subsequently, the two Republics. The chapter is organised chronologically into four periods: before 1989; early 1990s; late 1990s; after 2000. We are well aware that these periods are generalised, and we mean only to use them as an analytical framework in which to demonstrate our thesis. Our main research questions are as follows: what kind of subcultural ideology was constructed in each designated histori-cal period; to what extent is ideology important to subcultural identity; how is subcultural ideology constructed in relation to the mainstream, to others within a subculture, and to members of other subcultures?

The birth of punks and skinheads in Czechoslovakia

The form that punk and skinhead culture took in Czechoslovakia was shaped by the repressive character of the prevailing political establishment. Cultural in-formation from the West was acquired with difficulty. Though it was relatively easy – if sometimes illegal – to access Western music (via foreign radio broad-casts, street markets and, occasionally, on radio and television programmes tolerated by the government), wider cultural information breached the 'iron curtain' sporadically and devoid of its original context. The roots of punk in Czechoslovakia, therefore, date back to the late 1970s and were first tended by experimental musicians[12] and music journalists in the form of musical in-spirations.[13] It was, initially at least, far more intellectual than working-class.

Over time, punk music and style spread to a wider and younger audience. The 1980s saw a recognisable punk subculture emerge in Czechoslovakia, consisting not only of musicians but an audience that shared a kind of punk identity.[14] Evidently, however, the prevailing characteristics of the fledgling punk culture were informed by a regime that effectively isolated its citizens from the wider world, both physically (travel) and ideologically (censorship, jamming foreign broadcasts, education). It also sought to repress any manifestation of individuality.[15] To be different meant, at best, to give up on any career advancement. At worst, it might lead to oppressive intervention from the police or judiciary in the form of frequent and gratuitous ID checks, detention, and even imprisonment.

In terms of social composition, Czech punks in the 1980s were typically working-class youths from vocational schools with only the prospect of a factory job ahead of them. Because punks were seen as 'enemies of socialist regime', they possessed no chance of higher education, usually meaning they did not speak English and were therefore unable to understand the lyrics of their foreign idols, let alone any latent punk ideology. This, in turn, had an enormous impact on their understanding of what it 'meant to be a punk'. One enquiring punk later remembered:

> [We] were weirdoes among other punks, because we translated the lyrics and searched for the fundamental wisdom of life in them. They saw us as nutcases for concerning ourselves with it [ideology]; for them it did not matter."
> (Cook, male, 42)

The image of Western punk was more obvious and easily understood by its Czech 'imitators'. However, the clothing and artefacts that signified Western punk remained mostly inaccessible, allowing punk's DIY principle to quickly permeate the emergent culture via clothes and accoutrements adapted and adopted to replicate the fragments of information gleaned from the West.[16] So, for example, medical trousers were dyed and Czech military boots (called *kanady*) airbrushed to resemble Western styles. Creating a punk outfit necessitated much personal investment, in terms of imagination and time, but it also came at considerable risk. It was punk's image, far more than its music, that irritated the communist authorities. The strikingly visual difference between punk and the mainstream, alongside its apparent denial of 'positive' social values (as defined by the regime), was seen to have been imported from the 'enemy' West. By reason, therefore, punks were soon ascribed the role of 'opposition' and subjected to coercion.[17] If only a minority of Czech punks harboured conscious political intent, then they were stigmatised as so doing by the communist authorities by the late 1980s.

More typically, perhaps, Czech's punk subculture soon developed its own internal identity through the accumulation of subcultural capital and a style that displayed disinterest in mainstream values and disdain for the normative system of dominant society. This was often expressed in readily understandable symbolism, such as the circled A of anarchy. '[The] A in a circle, it was intelligible to everyone. Anarchy means chaos; everyone understands that, they knew it even from school' (Cook, male, 42). But while this simple reading was shared intuitively, it remained a form of ideological resistance to the regime (not to mention communism *per se*) that soon began to appeal as such. 'We wanted to be different, and this was the most different thing we knew' (Tuner, male, 43).

It was from this more consciously oppositional milieu that the first Czech skinheads emerged in the 1980s, a small but distinct part of the broader punk subculture.[18]

> Five of us always spent the weekend together. And one day, one of Duben cousin's [*sic*] appeared in a bomber jacket. I asked him: 'What's that jacket about?' And he answered: 'It's just a normal jacket.' And then we all knew that he was a skinhead now. But we continued to spend the time together … (Cook, male, 42)

As this suggests, both the punk and skinhead subcultures shared similar impulses. Both sought to provoke and differentiate themselves from mainstream society (personified by a communist regime that despised them and forced them to resistance); both adopted a style that reflected this; both listened to socially unacceptable music, be it termed punk or Oi! Little distinction between the two subcultures was made – due, in part, to the limited number of people involved and interpersonal relationships between the subcultures. Nor was attention paid to cultural and political differences commonplace in the West. '[It] was not unusual for someone to listen to The Exploited, The Clash or The Sex Pistols, and at the same time be racist and not see it as a problem' (Scribe, male, 41). Punks, for example, were often highly critical of the Roma population; some punk bands even had racist lyrics. The Slovak punk band, Zóna A, had a song entitled 'Cigánský problém' ('Gypsy Problem'). Not dissimilarly, one interviewee remembered: 'At that time, Šanov 1 sang how "We will tip the dustbins over and we will go after the blacks"' (Worker, male, 36).[19] Czech punk's and skinhead's subcultural ideology was, therefore, only remotely (if at all) inspired from abroad.[20] Rather, it took its cue from – and related to – issues and situations within contemporary society. It differentiated itself from the communist regime and so from the establishment. Indeed, such a position of resistance soon led it to adopt punk's most notorious signifier. 'The swastika was a symbol of resistance against communism, and was shared by all of us [punks and skinheads]' (Scribe, male, 41).

If you lose an enemy, you have to find a new one

The fall of Czechoslovakia's communist regime in 1989 constituted an important change for the punk and skinhead subcultures within the country. First, both subcultures lost their mutual enemy (the communist state). Second, the more relaxed social atmosphere brought with it greater tolerance to difference, as the normative system of Czechoslovak society began to recreate itself. Third, the fall of the 'iron curtain' enabled information from the West to flow freely into Czechoslovakia.

The loss of a common enemy (the communist regime) meant that Czech punks and skins had to find a new 'other' against which to base their subcultural identities. The early 1990s saw wholesale social, economic and political transformation, during which no clear – or intelligible – ideology was in place. Both subcultures, therefore, looked West for inspiration. As a result, specific subcultural ideologies were adopted. Czech skinheads quickly looked towards the German and British skinhead scenes, from which they adopted an ultra right-wing political position. Punks, meanwhile, began to flirt more openly with anarchism. Some formed or became part of an organised anarchist movement, initiating protests and demonstrations against racism, fascism, compulsory military service, US imperialism (as with the visit of President George W. Bush to Czechoslovakia in January 1991) and the opening of McDonalds' restaurants. They established links, too, with anarchists from mainly Italy, Germany and Spain.

The politicisation of both subcultures led to open and violent conflict between the two. This, initially, stemmed from their seemingly divergent political orientation, but soon bled into more basic (if presumed) subcultural antagonisms. If a punk prioritised anti-racism as their foremost political cause, then the skinhead became its personification. If the skinhead rejected anarchism, then that set them against punk. Such interpretation was further reinforced by the media, which throughout the 1990s depicted skinheads almost exclusively as neo-fascists or neo-Nazis, and punks as anarchists, deviants and junkies. Those punks and skins who swam against the prevailing current were, in turn, marginalised both within their respective subcultures and society more generally.

Crucial to the relationship between punks and skins in the early 1990s was the success of the skinhead band Orlík.[21] The band's popularity ensured that the skinhead style became more visible on the streets of Czech cities and in housing estates where 'kinder skins' (thirteen- to fifteen-year-old boys) listened to Orlík and adopted their 'patriotic' message. Punk, by contrast, remained on the margins. Indeed, the antagonism that grew between the two subcultures was reproduced in Orlík's songs. So, for example, 'Až nás bude víc' ('When There Will be More of Us') warns: 'Hey cock-a-doodle-doo,[22] beware of oi, don't go into streets, be afraid of skinheads'.[23] For a time, therefore, punks became fair game for skinheads and, in turn, saw skinheads as their principal enemy.

Of course, the so-called 'kinder skins' had no memory of the affinity that had previously existed between the two subcultures. There now existed, it seemed, a line demarcating those punks and skins who had come of age under communism and those emergent into the 1990s. For the former, many simply had to adapt to this new situation, though others did what they could to cross it.

> I [punk] was with my brother on Labour Day [demonstration], which we had helped organise. The skins were ready to assault us. We were all standing there: groups of skins and punks taunting each other, cops everywhere. And beside me appeared the Procházka brothers[24] who I knew from the past. So we began to chat. And then the cops came up, shouting, 'get away from each other'. And we all said 'Why? It's our business'; because we all still have an aversion to cops from before the [Velvet] revolution. So we argued with them [cops] for a while, then we decided to fuck off and go to the pub together. (Cook, male, 42)

As this suggests, punks and skinheads were associated with each other before 1989 via a simplified subcultural ideology based on resistance to a dominant society represented by the communist regime and an ignorance of their respective subcultural origins. After 1989, mutual antagonism built on politics and misinterpretation ensured punks and skins increasingly distinguished between each other and their respective subcultural ideologies. Rather than a shared subcultural ideology, born from an opposition to the dominant society, their respective ideologies by the 1990s were shaped more in opposition to each other. Subcultural capital was thus earned by a punk or skinhead who not only recognised the borders between the two subcultures, but who strengthened them. Equally, subcultural style was complemented by subcultural *practice*, meaning the active drawing of attention to the differences between the subcultures and the (physical) dangers they entailed.

Enemies within own ranks and rediscovered lost friends

Over the course of the 1990s, the transformation of Czechoslovakia (and even more the Czech Republic from 1993) moved it ever closer to Western society in terms of its structure, values and normative systems. The most important change in relation to our subcultures was the transformation of certain currents of thought into legitimate political formations acted out on the political stage. Simultaneously, conformity returned to become an appreciated value within the dominant society. Given this, political formations seeking mass appeal were weakened rather than strengthened by their actual, erstwhile or imagined associations with non-conformist elements such as punks and skins. Accordingly, the political overtures once made towards our subcultural groups began to weaken. The far right, in particular, found its progress hindered by its association with skinheads and their reputation as violent neo-Nazis.

At the risk of overstatement, both subcultures advanced from 'adolescence' to 'early adulthood' in the 1990s, through which their subcultural ideology of mutual differentiation was overcome. Punks and skins each reacted and responded to their distorted media image, leading to a growing emphasis on the 'traditional' form and roots of their respective subculture. An interest in the origins and history of the subcultures was evident, with fanzines giving space to debate as to their character in Czechoslovakia, the Czech Republic and Slovakia as compared to in the West. As a result, ideological currents within the subcultures polarised. Thus, the overtly anarchist punks gradually split away from the wider punk subculture, no longer feeling the need for a specific subcultural identity. Punks thereby tended to identify themselves with the punk subculture *per se* rather than active anarchism. Similarly, the skinhead subculture had split in two directions by the early 1990s: one, inspired by the West, towards neo-Nazism; the second, drawing from Czech history, forged a uniquely Czech variation of skinhead known as *kališníci*. The *kališníci* were radical and patriotic, but they were also strictly anti-Nazi.[25]

Simultaneously, the media representation of skinheads as primarily neo-Nazi or racist led many in the subculture to feel that their skinhead identity had been 'stolen' from them by the far right. In response, they began to trace their skinhead roots back to British working-class youth in the 1960s, rejecting identification with the far right and adopting a depoliticised version of skinhead subculture. Even then, there remained a distinction between those who accentuated skinhead-as-style and those who sought to assert a particular subcultural ideology. So, for example, anti-fascist skinheads – gathered in SHARP (Skinheads Against Racial Prejudice) and RASH (Red and Anarchy

Skinheads) – claimed continuity with the subcultural ideology of the original (British) skinheads. Alternately, of course, 'white power skinheads', particularly members of the *Bohemia Hammerskins* and, later, *Blood and Honour Bohemia*, retained their far-right affiliation. Accordingly, the skinhead subculture divided, with even former *kališníci* trying to align their patriotism with a 'traditional' style that bled into apolitical skinhead currents.

Style-wise, skinheads had begun to fuse their look with particular subcultural ideologies by the late 1990s. Rather than distinguish themselves from punk, they sought to distinguish themselves from other currents within the skinhead subculture. What had previously been a fairly uniform image, consisting of bomber jacket, army boots, jeans or army camouflage trousers, began to differentiate. Subcultural ideology had previously been transmitted almost exclusively through patches with select symbols. Now, those who considered themselves apolitical skinheads tended to wear 'traditional' skinhead-associated brands, such as Fred Perry, Lonsdale, Everlast and Ben Sherman; far-right skinheads wore their own brand, Thor Steinar; and 'red' skins demonstrated their subcultural identity via red braces or bootlaces. Punks, too, began to diversify their style to reflect their preferred sub-genre or subcultural ideology, a process enabled to some extent by the rise of clothes shops specialising in street wear.[26]

Between all this, some punks and skins sought to supress the distinctions between the two subcultures by referring back to their common historical roots in 1970s Britain and 1980s Czechoslovakia. The result was a blending of skinhead and punk style called 'skunx', a kind of hybrid subculture that enabled punks and skinheads to realign without changing their subcultural identity.[27] Such a phenomenon cannot be dismissed as the result of commodification, though most street-wear shops did sell clothes and accoutrements relating to both. Rather, the integration and 'use' of different styles may be interpreted as an intentional declaration of sympathy between the subcultures; an apolitical stance or, sometimes, a signal of anti-fascism.

Initially, at least, these changes were accepted with some hesitation. One skinhead remembered:

> Punks thought you were a Nazi; gypsies did as well, while Nazis called you left-wing. So for the classic [traditional] skinhead the situation was always worse than for a punk, because punk identity was clear and intelligible. But the classic [traditional] skinhead identity was not. (Merchant, male, 38)[28]

Yet, such diversification gradually broke through into both subcultures, once more bringing them closer together in recognition and knowledge (rather than ignorance) of their history. Such knowledge was then displayed (among apolitical skinheads) or demonstratively fused (among skunx), providing a form of subcultural capital that enabled for diversification and hierarchies to develop on either side. To be a skinhead or a punk did not demand following a current trend in subcultural style, but in choosing to follow this-or-that ideology. Subcultural identity was thus constructed on the basis of a particular subcultural ideology rather than a particular style. Among skinheads, in particular, this was primarily constituted in relation to their own subculture rather than in relation to dominant society or another subculture.

After subculture? Maybe not yet ...

As noted already, subcultural identity is, in part, determined by the nature of the dominant society in which it is situated. In the current period, this has ensured that (sub)cultures exist within blurred boundaries that are difficult to demarcate.[29] It is, in the twenty-first century, possible to think both of socially determined trans-local cultures and locally modified versions of global culture.[30]

In recent times, the ideology and style of both the punk and skinhead subcultures has become increasingly empty. The commodification of punk, for example, brought it into the mainstream to the extent that pop idols such as Madonna appropriated elements of punk style and commercial pop-punk bands like Green Day and Blink 182 found widespread success. As a result, punk's distinctive ideology and style has, at best, been diluted and, at worst, exorcised altogether. Punk has therefore lost much of its provocative power; as a point of opposition to the mainstream, it has become less interesting and effective. Indeed, punk's agitation has been overtaken by other subcultures such as ravers (*teknaři* in Czech), hip-hoppers or emos. These, in turn, have established themselves in Czech society and made ready use of globalisation's tools, such as virtual media.[31] Many original punks have themselves become ravers, so finding an alternate means to facilitate autonomy, freedom and escape from the 'system' (establishment).

The skinhead subculture has changed too. Those openly declaring an anti-racist affiliation have decreased in favour of apolitical skinheads. As the ranks of neo-Nazi skinheads diminish, and the media caricature becomes less prevalent, so skinheads appear to feel less need to declare themselves as active anti-racists.[32] Conversely, some recent studies have suggested an implicit racism continues to exist among those 'traditional' skinheads who declare themselves apolitical.[33]

Not surprisingly, the mass media continues to play an important role in defining the world of subcultures. As the punk and skinhead caricatures became less potent, so media attention turned elsewhere – to ravers, who are depicted as junkies or asocial individuals; to hip-hoppers, who signify vandalism; to emos, who self-harm and commit suicide.[34] Equally, of course, the 'anything goes' culture of late modernity means that punk and skinhead style no longer serves to challenge the dominant society, nor does it express any definite subcultural ideology. If people continue to feel the need to distinguish themselves from the dominant society or sections within it, then it is more likely to be ideology or lifestyle choice that demonstrates this. Ideology reaches through generations and is not based on social stratification. It is registered across a far more diverse terrain, be it organic food, natural childbirth or communal living, all of which are too diffuse or ambivalent to be seen as distinct subcultures. To the 'supermarket of style' we may add the supermarkets of ideology, music and behaviour.[35] In youth cultural terms, bands now consist of cross-subcultural members and play music not related to any of them. Indeed, the place of music as a constitutive element of subcultures has arguably been lessened to the extent that its ideological connotations are no longer apparent.

Even so, punk and skinhead subcultures remain and continue to exert an attraction for some. Nowadays, however, those who adopt the style tend to possess neither subcultural capital nor a shared subcultural ideology. There have, of course, always been people on the 'periphery' of the scene, but they tended either to move out of the subculture as they grew older or gained the subcultural capital necessary to move towards its 'centre'.[36] Today, their subcultural affiliation may fluctuate between one identity and another.[37] Or, following Muggleton, they exist as post-subculturalists; their identity fluid, permeable and hybrid.[38] It is, typically, older subcultural members who retain a strong sense of connection to ideology. Having accumulated subcultural capital, they continue to demonstrate this through a rather rigid adherence to style paraded at particular subcultural events such as concerts or festivals.[39] In many ways, therefore, punk and skinhead subculture in the Czech Republic exists now only as a residue. These are collectivities better suited for another world. Their potential members dissolve into the extensive choice of other subcultures; their distinctive ideologies are no longer clear; they no longer form the vanguard of oppositional style. Better, perhaps, to perceive punk and skinhead as a network of local idiocultures based primarily on personal relations.[40] They are localised, not simply in the physical sense, but also in terms of virtual space. They inhabit spaces where relationships are built and subcultural identities constructed. In such a way, punk and skinhead have acquired the form of trans-local scenes.[41]

What they retain in common is the notion of being embedded in the punk or skinhead tradition, but in practice they give rise to varied manifestations.

Conclusion

This chapter explored the processes through which subcultures are formed and reformed as social groupings with a distinct system of values, norms, behavioural patterns and lifestyle. The punk and skinhead subcultures of Czechoslovakia and the Czech Republic served to demonstrate that subcultures are not rigid or fixed social formations, but are greatly determined by their historical and cultural context. To understand subculture, attention must be given to those participating within the culture, to those against whom the respective subculture differentiates itself, and to the practices that form the subculture's meaning. We have thus focused on subcultural ideology as an analytical category negotiated through and against the norms and values of the dominant society. Moreover, we have done this across a period of political, socio-economic and cultural transformation, during which mainstream culture became both weakened and ill-defined. Within such a context, subcultures appear to seek out alternate 'others' to define themselves against. Indeed, such differentiation, the basic principle of subcultural existence, might often be founded in relation to another subculture. A conflict of ideology (understood as shared norms, values and attitudes) then becomes essential not only for the establishment of a subculture, but for its very existence.

As we have also shown, the most important element of subcultural ideology does not have to be its content, but its relationship to subcultures that differentiate against one another. In other words, the character of subcultural ideology is always negotiated in relation to another (sub)culture. But if the 'other' becomes unavailable, loses its distinction, or fails to 'co-operate' (respond), then the subculture begins to disintegrate. It will either divide within itself or blur its borders and blend into the dominant society. Conversely, if the ideology of its (sub)cultural opponent remains apparent and consistent, then the subculture unifies and creates ever more distinctive borders.

Acknowledgements

This chapter was supported by the Ministry of Education, Youth and Sports, and Institutional Support for the Long-term Development of Research Organizations, Charles University, Prague, Faculty of Humanities (Charles Univ., Fac Human 2012).

Notes

1 We are aware that 'communist' is – by political science standards – inadequate and even confusing as a term. However, 'communist' was the native (emic) term for the non-democratic totalitarian system of Czechoslovakia between 1948 and 1989 and will be used here as a kind of metaphor.

2 Czechoslovakia divided into two independent states, the Czech Republic and the Slovak Republic, on 1 January 1993. Though the Czech and Slovak subcultural worlds were always close to each other, our research relates primarily to the Czech region.

3 This was the first large-scale street fight between punks and skinheads. It occurred at an anarchist demonstration against the Jubilee exhibition that took place at Prague Výstaviště on 30 May 1991.

4 M. Trachta, 'Skinheads: Hrdost, styl a zábava', in Vladimír 518 and K. Veselý (eds), *Kmeny: současné městské subkultury* (Prague: Bigg Boss & Yinachi, 2011), p. 126.

5 M. Brake, *Comparative Youth Culture: The Sociology of Youth Cultures and Youth Subcultures in America, Britain and Canada* (London: Routledge, 1987); J. Clarke, 'Style', in S. Hall and T. Jefferson (eds), *Resistance Through Rituals: Youth Subcultures in Post-war Britain* (London: Routledge, 2003), pp. 175–91; D. Hebdige, *Subculture: The Meaning of Style* (London: Methuen, 1979); D. Muggleton, *Inside Subculture: The Postmodern Meaning of Style* (Oxford: Berg, 2000); T. Polhemus, 'In the Supermarket of Style', in S. Redhead (ed.), *The Clubcultures Reader: Readings in Popular Cultural Studies* (Oxford: Blackwell, 1998), pp. 130–3.

6 S. Thornton, *Club Cultures: Music, Media, and Subcultural Capital* (Middletown, CN: Wesleyan University Press, 1996); and 'Social Logic of Subcultural Capital', in K. Gelder and S. Thornton (eds), *The Subcultures Reader* (London: Routledge, 1997), pp. 200–9; O. Slačálek, 'České freetekno – pohyblivé prostory autonomie?', in M. Kolářová (ed.), *Revolta stylem: hudební subkultury mládeže v České republice* (Prague: SLON, 2011), pp. 83–122.

7 N. Božilović, 'Youth subcultures and subversive identities', *Facta universitatis - series: Philosophy, Sociology, Psychology and History*, 9:1 (2010), 45–58; T. H. Eriksen, *Antropologie multikulturních společností: rozumět identitě* (Prague: Triton, 2007); R. Jenkins, *Social Identity* (London and New York: Routledge, 3rd edn, 2008).

8 See J. B. Thompson, *Ideology and Modern Culture: Critical Social Theory in the Era of Mass Communication* (Stanford, CA: Stanford University Press, 1990).

9 See M. Heřmanský and H. Novotná, 'Hudební subkultury', in P. Janeček (ed.), *Folklor atomového věku. Kolektivně sdílené prvky expresivní kultury v soudobé české společnosti* (Prague: Faculty of Humanities, Charles University, Prague, 2011), pp. 89–110.

10 Thornton, 'Social Logic of Subcultural Capital', p. 201.

11 J. Dvořák, 'Vývoj vzájemného vztahu punkové a skinheadské subkultury od 80. let 20. století do současnosti na území Liberecka a Jablonecka' (Bachelor Thesis, Faculty of Humanities, Charles University, Prague, 2006); K. Klozarová, 'Vizuální atributy punkové subkultury v Československu, respektive v České republice a na Slovensku v 80. a 90. letech 20. století' (Bachelor Thesis, Faculty of Humanities, Charles

University, Prague, 2004); T. Novotný, 'S.H.A.R.P. – Skinheadi proti rasovým
předsudkům. Příklad současné Prahy' (Bachelor Thesis, Faculty of Humanities,
Charles University, Prague, 2011); J. Šarochová, 'Pohyb mezi subkulturami:
konstrukce subkulturní identity prostřednictvím biografického vyprávění' (Bachelor
Thesis, Faculty of Humanities, Charles University, Prague, 2011).

12 One of the first Czechoslovakian artists to play punk was Mikoláš Chadima and
his band Extempore (The New Rock and Joke Extempore Band), who incorporated a few punk covers into their repertoire. Their concert at the U Zábranských
club in 1979 is considered the first live punk performance in Czechoslovakia. See
H. Novotná and J. Dvořák, 'Punks vs. Skinheads – Historie jednoho vztahu', in D.
Bittnerová and M. Heřmanský (eds), *Kultura českého prostoru, prostor české kultury*
(Prague: Ermat, 2008), pp. 261–88.

13 For example, in May 1978 the music journalist Josef Vlček gave a lecture about punk
rock at VI. Prague Jazz Days festival in the Theatre of Music.

14 Among the first Czech punk rock bands were F.P.B. (Fourth Price Band), Kečup and,
later, Visací zámek.

15 For accounts of repression against long-haired people (called *vlasatci* or *máničky*),
see F. Pospíšil and P. Blažek, *Vraťte nám vlasy! První máničky, vlasatci a hippies v
komunistickém Československu* (Prague: Academia, 2010).

16 A similar trend happened in the 1960s, when the *vlasatci* (*máničky*) were inspired
by the visual attributes of ideologically different subcultures such as mods, rockers,
beatniks and hippies. See Pospíšil and Blažek, *Vraťte nám vlasy!*

17 For details M. Vaněk, *Byl to jenom rock 'n' roll? Hudební alternativa v komunistickém
Československu 1956–1989* (Prague: Academia, 2010).

18 K. Zástěra, 'K některým otázkám okrajových skupin dělnické mládeže (Punk a jeho
charakteristické rysy)', *Zpravodaj KSVI pro etnografii a folkloristiku*, 2 (1991).

19 Dvořák, 'Vývoj vzájemného vztahu punkové a skinheadské subkultury …', appendix,
interview no. 6. Šanov 1 was a Czech punk rock band from Teplice, formed in 1987.

20 An important source of inspiration was an article by Gerhard Kromschröder in the
magazine *100+1 Zahraničních zajímavostí* (100+1 Foreign Curiosities, 18, 1986)
called 'Holohlavci, to jsou, pane chlapci' (Baldheads are really great guys).

21 The success of Orlík is unparalleled to that of any other skinhead band. Even though
they released just two LPs (*Oi! Miloš Frýba for President* (1990) and *Demise!* (1991))
and broke up in 1992, they remain the most well-known Czech skinhead band today.
Orlík's ideology, evident in most of their songs, was based on radical patriotism,
nationalism and an aversion against anything non-Czech. It glorified the legacy of
the Hussite movement of the fifteenth century, which was seen as the greatest period
of Czech history. Though Orlík were radical nationalists, they were also strictly anti-
Nazi. The band's end was due to Nazi-skinheads doing Nazi salutes and chanting *Sieg
Heil* at their concerts.

22 Cock-a-doodle-doo ('kykyrý' in Czech), as in the sound of a rooster, refers to the
similarity between a rooster's crest and the mohawk hairstyle.

23 L. Ašenbrener, J. Fuchs, M. Šafář, *et al.*, 'Orlík - Live Delta (1989)', in *Encyklopedie čs. alternativní scény do roku 1993*, www.projektpunk.cz/obsah/O/Orlik/Live-delta/, accessed 12 December 2012.

24 The Procházka brothers were important figures in the skinhead subculture in the early 1990s.

25 *Kališníci* formed out of Orlík's audience. Their motto was 'Co je český, to je hezký', or 'What's Czech is good'.

26 So, punk circa 1977 (inspired by the Sex Pistols and the Clash), or punk circa 1982 (inspired by The Exploited and UK street punk). For a detailed account of punk's different styles, see Klozarová, 'Vizuální atributy punkové subkultury v Československu'.

27 See Dvořák, 'Vývoj vzájemného vztahu punkové a skinheadské subkultury'.

28 *Ibid.*, appendix, interview no. 4.

29 For anthropological critique of concept of culture see, for example, L. Abu Lughod, 'Writing Against Culture', in R. G. Fox (ed.), *Recapturing Anthropology: Working in the Present* (Santa Fe, NM: School of American Research Press, 1991), pp. 137–62.

30 For the concept of glocality, see A. Appadurai, *Modernity at Large: Cultural Dimensions of Globalization* (Minneapolis, MN: University of Minnesota Press, 1996); A. Gupta and J. Ferguson, 'Beyond "Culture": Space, Identity, and the Politics of Difference', *Cultural Anthropology*, 7:1 (1992), 6–23.

31 Heřmanský and Novotná, 'Hudební subkultury'; see also T. Holíková, 'Emo online: Struktura a funkce virtuální komunity serveru Emosvět'. (Bachelor Thesis, Faculty of Humanities, Charles University, Prague, 2012).

32 See Novotný, 'S.H.A.R.P. – Skinheadi proti rasovým předsudkům'.

33 P. Stejskalová, 'Subkultura skinheads – Kam až došly těžké boty', in Kolářová (ed.), *Revolta stylem*, pp. 159–99.

34 For moral panics on emo in Czech Republic, see M. Heřmanský, 'Emoce, žiletky a sebevraždy. Démonizace emo subkultury a morální panika v českém prostředí', in O. Daniel, T. Kavka, and J. Machek (eds), *Populární kultura v českém prostoru* (Prague: Karolinum, 2013).

35 Polhemus, 'In the Supermarket of Style', pp. 130–3.

36 Inspired by the skinhead fanzine *Bulldog*, Klozarová distinguished between those in the 'centre of the scene', those on the 'periphery of the scene' and those 'parasitising on the scene'. The first were usually older than eighteen years, active participants and aware of its history and style (i.e. they possessed the most of subcultural capital). The second were usually younger and saw punk as image rather than a lifestyle. The third abused the punk image. See also Novotná and Dvořák, 'Punks vs. Skinheads'.

37 See Šarochová, 'Pohyb mezi subkulturami'.

38 Muggleton, *Inside Subculture*.

39 See M. Pixová, 'Český punk za oponou i před oponou', in Kolářová (ed.), *Revolta stylem*, pp. 45–82.

40 G. A. Fine, 'Small Groups and Culture Creation: The Idioculture of Little League Baseball Teams', *American Sociological Review*, 44:5 (1979), 733–45.

41 R. A. Peterson and A. Bennett, 'Introducing Music Scenes', in A. Bennett and R. A. Peterson (eds), *Music Scenes: Local, Translocal and Virtual* (Nashville, TN: Vanderbilt University Press, 2004), pp. 1–15.

10

Ostpunx: East German punk in its social, political and historical context

AIMAR VENTSEL

> The availability of 'cultural and social means' is an obfuscating expression.
> In plain German, it should be put [as follows]: those who only have 'small
> cultural and social means' (to use politically-correct EU speak) are not
> sufficiently intelligent, educated or stable in their behaviour. Defined in this
> way by the EU, the poor are disburdened of responsibility for their situation
> and relieved of the moral pressure to try to alter it.[1]

The citation above comes from *Deutscland Schafft Sich Ab* (*Germany is Destroying Itself*), a scandalous book by the German politician and media personality Thilo Sarrazin, published in 2010. The work was much discussed in the German media and criticised for its xenophobia, primarily due to its argument that Turks and Arabs are genetically unable to integrate into German society. Ironically, however, another central argument of the book was ignored by both its supporters and its critics: that any German who is poor and unemployed is directly responsible for their failure. Throughout, Sarrazin argued that money received as social benefit was enough to buy healthy food; that free time should be used for educating oneself and not watching TV; and that there were people in Germany who earned less than the unemployed received from the state but who nevertheless did not give up working.[2] Looking for reasons as to why Germany's unemployed were overweight and poorly educated, he concluded that they had inherited the low intellect of what he termed the 'lower class' (*Unterschicht*) or 'education-distant population' (*bildungsferne Schichten*).[3]

Now, this may seem like a strange beginning for a chapter on punk, but many of the social issues highlighted by Sarrazin also concern German punks. Indeed, this chapter focuses on how the diminishing status of the working class is reflected in East German punk. Simultaneously, it argues that subculture can provide an alternative space for low-status people and the possibility of resisting public prejudices by applying irony and provocation.

Discussing the 'demonisation' of the working class is nothing new in the UK, whether in academic or leftist analytical literature.[4] It is not, however, commonplace in German academic or non-academic writing. This does not mean that prejudices against the unemployed are absent in Germany. In December 2010, a long-term unemployed punk from Berlin informed me that: 'Currently there is a new guilt complex (*das neue Schuldgefühl*) spreading in Germany. People believe that when you have no work, it is your own fault' (field diary, 2 December 2010). Nor is such discussion unbiased: unemployment is considered first and foremost a problem of the working class, or the 'lower class' as referred to in official terminology. It also tends to be linked to certain moral presumptions. A reading of various German academic works confirms the impression that the unemployed working class constitutes a passive mass of people who expect to be ushered out of their misery by state institutions.[5]

Class is an ambivalent concept in the sociology of subcultures. The linking of (working-) class origin to youth subcultural styles and music has been one of the main criticisms levelled against the Birmingham University Centre for Contemporary Cultural Studies (CCCS) by post-subcultural theorists.[6] In a punk context, various studies show how a middle- or working-class background can inform subcultural strategies and different interpretations of subcultural norms.[7] In the discourse of CCCS, however, little attention was paid to whether subculturalists defined themselves as members of a particular (usually working) class.[8] As for the CCCS's contention that subcultures provide a form of class-based resistance to the dominant society, it tends now to be argued that youth identities are centred more on consumption.[9] Others, however, continue to demonstrate the ways by which subcultural ideologies and practices include resistance to mainstream ideas, values and practices, with consumption (especially buying clothes and music) forming part of that resistance.[10] As a counter-argument to the post-subcultural approach, moreover, some have contended that theories of 'scene', 'neo-tribes' or 'lifestyle' overlook how social division and inequality continue to exist in socially and economically stratified societies and thereby continue to inform youth group identities.[11]

This article's data was collected during fieldwork conducted in the East German town of Halle (an der Saale) in 2006, 2007 and 2009–11.[12] Halle is a medium-sized city with some 230,000 inhabitants. It is located in the Saxony-Anhalt Bundesland and lies approximately 30 kilometres from Leipzig and 200 kilometres south of Berlin. As part of socialist East Germany, Halle's now mainly redundant chemical industry was of great importance. Today, Halle is establishing itself as centre for education and research. Even so, the unemployment rate of Saxony-Anhalt stood as the fourth highest in Germany in November 2012, with official unemployment in Halle comprising nearly 11 per cent of the working population and underemployment registering at 17.2 per cent.[13] In reality, the numbers are much higher. German statistics exclude those who participate in various re-education programmes (*Umschulung*) and people engaged in 'short-time' employment (*Kurzarbeit*). The fieldwork primarily consisted of participatory observation, though approximately forty interviews were conducted between 2006 and 2010 with both female and male unemployed or low-paid working-class punks aged between twenty-five and forty-five.

Punk in (East) Germany

Germany has one of the world's largest independent punk scenes, with several booking agencies, probably hundreds of clubs (focused exclusively or partly on punk), and a lively fanzine culture. Most of the scene is run on a DIY basis and brings very little commercial revenue to its organisers. Large German-based festivals, such as Endless Summer, With Full Force and Search and Destroy, are internationally renowned; foreign punk bands constantly tour the country. However, the punks of West and East Germany have rather different histories, due primarily to their respective Cold War origins.

Punk in 1980s West Germany was a visibly leftist movement. Punks took part in demonstrations, squatting and arranging benefit concerts. They were also involved in the Youth Centre movement (*Jugendzentrumbewegung*) that aimed to establish autonomous but council-financed youth centres, many of which still exist today and which served to provide the basis for the punk club network that emerged over the decade.

In the East, meanwhile, it is often argued that subcultures such as punk served as platforms – or 'enclaves' – for people who did not accept the social-ist ideology of the German Democratic Republic (GDR).[14] Punk culture in East Germany, therefore, has a long history of resistance and a clear anti-state position. It emerged in the 1980s as a seemingly spontaneous cultural protest against the socialist state and its ideology. In contrast to the West, punks in the GDR did not need an explicit oppositional or political ideology to reflect their position; the very fact that 'non-normative' youth existed was enough to irritate state officials.[15] However, both left- and right-wing sentiments existed within the GDR punk scene, leading to violent confrontations shortly before the end of socialist Germany.[16]

Punk in the socialist period formed part of a wider counter-cultural movement and existed in symbiosis with hippies, the oppositional left, the green movement, religious activists, early skinheads, heavy metal fans and other 'negative and decadent' groups.[17] Punk's link to these groups also resulted from them sharing the same space; in the GDR, only one autonomous institution hosted oppositional groups and cultural activities: the church. Although some punk concerts took place in schools, private houses or pubs, most 'non-normative' cultural events were organised on church premises.[18] As this suggests, being a punk in the GDR came with some risk; it was not uncommon for band members to be gaoled for offences such as 'parasitism', to be drafted into national service, or even forced to migrate to West Germany.[19] Alongside Berlin, Halle was one of the main centres for *Ostpunk*;[20] in 1984, the first punk festival in the GDR took place in the Christ Church of Halle (*Christuskirche*).[21]

After the German re-union, samplers of *Ostpunk* were released by West German punk record labels such as Hoehnie Records and Nasty Vinyl, but also by East German labels like Saalepower, which in turn helped spread East German punk across the country. Typically, however, East German punk remained a curiosity for the West German audience until the second half of the 1990s, when skinhead bands like Loikemie and Bierpatrioten, or punk bands such as Dritte Wahl, began to record regularly and gain a following throughout the German punk and Oi! scene. The term *Ostpunk* probably first appeared with the vinyl and cassette samplers that fed into the West from the GDR. The term then remained after 1989 for punk music made by bands from East Germany and today refers purely to geographical origin, there being little to distinguish the musical styles of West and East German punk bands.

The socio-economic transformation of (eastern) Germany

To discuss specifically *East* German punk, it is necessary to locate it in the wider context of the post-*Wende* transformation.[22] After the *Wende*, things did not go as smoothly as many enthusiastic German citizens expected. Since the early 1990s, Germany has been divided into *Ossis* (East Germans) and *Wessis*

(West Germans), an identity construction incited foremost by economic processes but also by cultural discrepancies. One reason for this division is the unfulfilled expectations of economic prosperity in the East and the steady decrease in living standards in the West. While the prognosis in 1991 was that 'the GDR will pay for unification ... from its own pocket', it soon became clear that West Germany would have to subsidise the restructuring of the East.[23] A 'solidarity tax' (*Solidaritätszuschlag*) was introduced in 1991 and the state (i.e. West Germany) plunged tax payers' money into unemployment programmes and schemes designed to modernise infrastructure. For many West Germans, therefore, the complaint was that 'we do not receive anything for our tax money'.[24] *Ossis*, meanwhile, were designated as people helped into the capitalist consumer society but who refused to work and instead enjoyed social benefits paid for by the *Wessis*.

The perspective from the East is more complex. It is well documented that scepticism among young people as to the benefits of unification was evident from the early 1990s.[25] As unemployment – unheard of in the GDR – increased in eastern Germany, and as enterprises closed and incomes failed to rise to the level of the West, so people became hostile to Western Germans and 'their' state. These sentiments were re-enforced, moreover, by the fact that West Germany did not undergo any visible change. The reunified Germany appeared to exist as a continuation of the Federal Republic of Germany, only with the former GDR now reformed and 'added'. Western administration, institutions and even police uniforms were simply introduced into the East, a process known as 'top-down reorganisation' that was accompanied by rapid deindustrialisation and the adoption of West German management models: in effect, the former GDR became 'an extended work-bench' of the West German economy.[26] Similarly, as industries were privatised, so top-level and management positions were appointed to people from Western Germany. Heike Solga has called it '*Westimport*', arguing that from 1996–97 only 2 per cent of senior managerial and administrative positions in eastern Germany were held by East Germans.[27] The West German managers soon received the nickname *Besserwessi* or the '*Wessi* who always knows better'.[28] And 'knowing better' did not simply mean managerial knowhow, but also a lack of respect and understanding of the erstwhile GDR's everyday culture. Thus, the *Besserwessi* found the East's architecture 'ugly', its furniture 'Eastern garbage' (*Ostschrott*), and its citizens 'brainwashed' (field diary, 15 December 2012).

In the transition period after the collapse of the GDR, punks in East Germany established a social space dominated for the first time by their own subculture. Within a few years of the *Wende*, East Germany had a very active DIY punk scene as squats, alternative (sometimes semi-legal) clubs and pubs appeared in virtually every town. This was possible due to unresolved property-ownership issues in the East, though the return of buildings to their (former) owners soon meant the number of punk squats and clubs declined. Even then, however, the East's punk network did not disappear. Most towns retained at least one club hosting punk and hardcore events into the 2000s, thereby providing a social and cultural space for its local punk scene.

For older punks and skinheads in Halle, the *Wende* period is remembered not as a rupture but as a 'golden era'. Squatting ensured that living costs were low and people earned good money by playing in bands or organising concerts. 'I had constantly 10.000 DM (5,000 euros) in my bank account', recalled one former promoter (Kai), now unemployed. But being busy on the alternative music circuits also meant people failed to find a 'respectable' profession or build up links into the labour market. When the squats and clubs closed, therefore, most had only one option: to apply for social benefits. Without being able to prove any legal income or recognisable working career during the 1990s, moreover, only the minimum rate of benefit was available. 'Suddenly I was not able to afford any new records or holiday trips', remembered Kai. It was from such disappointment that punks found common solidarity with other co-citizens.

According to Mike Dennis, the 'GDR legacy' is a product of dissatisfaction with life after reunification.[29] Daphne Berdahl, however, has demonstrated that the main reasons for the *Ossi–Wessi* divide stem from the West's constant ridiculing of the GDR's past and culture.[30] In order to conform to the new capitalist society, former GDR citizens were expected to change their mindset. In 2005, for example, the economist Robert Böhmer argued that the biggest obstacle to successful economic transformation was the continued existence of a 'GDR mentality'.[31]

Of course, economic inequalities cannot be ignored when discussing East and West German identities. Indeed, these have increased in recent years in line with the global economic recession, suggesting that widening wage differentials and alienation between eastern and Western Germany continues to grow. It has been estimated that 55 per cent of West Germans and 67 per cent of East Germans think there are psychological and cultural differences between East and West. Two-thirds of East Germans see themselves as neglected by society; 25 per cent think they are 'second rate citizens'.[32]

Resistance to such perceived colonisation and injustice has taken cultural form (among others). It has strengthened the regional *Ossi* identity and nostalgia for the GDR (*'Ostalgie'*), so that today an East German identity is expressed through the demonstrative use of East German symbols and consumption of East German products. Nevertheless, the 'GDR legacy' should not be reduced to nostalgia for a time when food and transport was cheap, work was done with 'honour', and everybody was guaranteed a job and welfare security.[33] Many of the young punks I interviewed were too young to remember the GDR. They see unemployment in the former GDR as the deliberate economic policy of Western German companies.[34] Thus, at a party I attended on the anniversary of reunification, one older punk's response to the official national holiday was one of anger: 'This was no reunification, this was a sell-out!' Less apocryphally, anti-West German sentiment fuelled a controversial discrimination case from 2010 where an East German woman was denied a job in a West German company because she was an 'Ossi'.[35] Many working-class punks and skinheads certainly bemoan the fact that traditional industries are declining and employers now prefer short-term employment. They see no future prospects for themselves or their children; the latter because there seems no possibility of affording the cost of a university education (field diary, 5 December 2012).

Certainly, several studies now exist to demonstrate how low social mobility is directly connected to educational attainment. German 'lower-class' students, they argue, tend to receive a poorer education than their middle- or upper-class equivalents, which thereby affects their chances of a successful career.[36] The patronising tone of some of these studies is surprising. Arguing that 'being unemployed is a fate', such studies basically conclude that existing class differences are deepening and there appears little chance of the 'lower class' attaining upward mobility.[37] 'Lower-class' schools, some German sociologists have argued, fail to teach their students the principles of *Leistungsphilosophie* (performance philosophy): that is, that everyone in Germany is individually responsible for shaping their own future.[38] As should be obvious, such rhetoric echoes that of Sarrazin. But if punks share the anti-West German sentiments of their social peer group, then they are also frustrated by direct and indirect social discrimination.[39] One skinhead girl complained: 'Everybody says that I am not stupid. But the company never promotes me, only these new middle-class employees. Despite all the training courses, I am never educated enough.' Not dissimilarly, a male punk described how: 'When I was fired, the boss told me it didn't matter whether I was on benefits or in work; in either case I'd end up as an alcoholic.' Such discrimination, it appears, comes from a belief that working-class people do not deserve better. 'Sure class differences are getting deeper', a mother and skinhead girl complained with bitter irony, 'we are the "lower class" … [and] if it is up to the rich, [then] we stay "lower class". To them, that is our place.'

Resistance, style and punk

Punk in twenty-first-century Halle is fragmented into several groups concentrated around individual clubs. Central to this study is a club called GiG that has a reputation of being the *Proll* club (as in prole or proletarian). Such reputation is based on the music: various ska-punk, Oi! and street punk bands perform there, drawing a masculine and aggressive skinhead or street punk audience. The term *Proll* is used proudly by regulars of the club to distinguish themselves from other punk groups of the city, who they see as 'hippie' or 'leftie'. Concerts in GiG are accompanied by excessive drinking and the occasional fight. Between concerts, the club functions as a hangout for regulars to come after work (be it legal or illegal).[40] While the late evening crowd is predominantly male, the concert audience usually includes a substantial number of women. Over time, the composition of GiG has changed. In 2010, the promoter of the club said: 'I don't know what has happened. We previously had a very mixed audience; students, artists, and so on. But now, only working-class kids [*Arbeiterkids*] come here.' In the evenings, visitors usually gather round tables to discuss music, politics and – more often – work. Because the core of the bar's regulars are blue-collar workers in their thirties, decreasing living standards, rising prices and social benefit cuts are central issues of discussion.

Dick Hebdige interpreted punk through a semiotic reading of style using the concept of 'bricolage'. One of his arguments was that identity, resistance and politics were manifested through clothes and other accessories.[41] Though such interpretation has been challenged, several more recent studies reassert the social and political meaning of youth cultural style. Kathleen Lowney, for example, has shown how consumption serves as a form of rebellion among teenage Satanists in a small southern US town.[42] Young people develop style as a means to shock their peers and adults; to manifest an opposition and create boundaries between them and 'ordinary people'. By using style as a means of juxtaposition, young people experience a feeling of power.[43] For J. Patrick Williams, 'the boundaries created and maintained *from inside* operate as a form of resistance and that is intentional'.[44]

One of the main criticisms made by post-subcultural scholars towards the CCCS is that youth cultural style is constantly changing; it cannot be fixed in relation to a particular group. Indeed, stylistic elements in German punk and skinhead subcultures are in constant fluctuation. The meaning of brands, key chains, buttons, the colour of a boot lace or musical tastes evolve and change periodically. But the complexity of style does not mean that style-as-expression loses its relevance for youth cultures.[45] In Halle, Ramones T-shirts can now be bought in coffee shops and former 'scene brands' (such as Lonsdale) in

Aldi. Such commercialisation changed the meaning of particular items, which were then replaced by other commodities (badges, certain colours, etc.) often only intelligible to other members within a scene. Combined with tradition and behaviour, style helps establish a group identity, creating a 'we-group' with its own aesthetics, rituals and power relations.[46] And nor is this only suggested by German youth sociologists, but also by interviewees in the current study.[47] Authenticity and identity are topics that concern most members of the local punk scene, irrespective of their stylistic preferences. 'You should look at details', was the comment of one punk girl as she explained the difference between rockabillies and goths, both sporting similar haircuts and denim jackets. Such stylistic differences establish both a common underground identity against the dominant mainstream and a more specific 'cluster identity' within the scene. The solidarity that exists in Halle between punks, skinheads, rockabillies, crusts and hardcore, metal and blues fans does not mean that distinctive group identities have disappeared, rather that a peaceful co-existence is maintained beneath the motto 'us against them'. Equally, style manifested as a political identity is evident in German fanzines and specialist internet forums.[48]

Youth culture's flexibility and creativity in re-creating through *bricolage* should not be underestimated.[49] In 2005, a new clothing brand, 'Hate you', became popular in Halle's punk clubs. Produced in Dessau, East Germany, one interviewee explained: 'If you wear "Hate you", everybody knows you come from the East'. Not dissimilarly, brands such as 'Randale' and 'Ostpunx' have in recent years made clear their East German origin. Both labels are produced by the same company, and their T-shirts, Harrington jackets or hooded sweatshirts are often created by printing or embroidering their logo onto existing sportswear brands (like Fruit of the Loom) or other clothes. By so doing, the clothes are transformed into a provocative manifestation of *Ossi*-identity that questions the assumed second-rate citizenship of those wearing them within the new German society.

An example of such 'symbolic resistance' may be discerned from a punk concert held at GiG in December 2011.[50] It was a DIY event organised by people living in the same building as the club is located. During the evening, two skinhead bands performed, drawing a large audience of punks and skins. The concert itself was a celebration of masculinity, typical of the tough streetpunk music style. The mosh pit consisted mostly of men, heavily tattooed and half-naked. The wild pogo included much hugging of each other, loud sing-a-long choruses and, at one point, a fight. The musicians of the headline band were older than the first, in their forties. They were dressed in typical skinhead style, with facial tattoos and heavily pierced. Most of their songs were narratives about their tough street life, being independent or 'staying skinhead forever'. When the concert ended, the promoter of the club moved to the DJ booth to play a 'punk disco' that comprised mainly songs from *Neue Deutsche Welle* (German new wave music from the 1980s). The songs were dark and existential; experimental electronic songs about alienation and unhappiness. The people danced with passion. Most were in their twenties or thirties, representative of the low-paid or unemployed 'lower class'. In front of me stood a rather drunk young girl unable – despite her efforts – to dance. On her T-shirt was the slogan '*Faulheit ist kein Verbrechen*' (Laziness is not a crime). Others wore badges, buttons or T-shirts that signalled their *Ossi* origin, their musical preferences or leftist anti-state position. The effect was quite dramatic. In my field diary I wrote:

> By 3 o'clock it became very grim. A dark empty room with a wet floor from spilled beer and covered with broken bottles. People were dancing and singing resolutely along to very dark music. I had a flash: street punk is about being subversive, demonstratively questioning social norms.

Those present at the concert were, taken generally, the embodiment of what in recent years has been described as the *prekariat* [precariat]; people at the bottom of society. Punks in Halle insist that they are still treated with distrust and encounter prejudice for their appearance. They regularly use words such as 'subversive' and often call themselves *Assis* (anti-social). With their facial tattoos, heavy alcohol use, fights and homo-social behavior, they ignore the norms of good behaviour, success and politeness. In so doing, the style and expression of Halle's punks and skinheads can be interpreted in the framework of a dual strategy; a combination of irony and a quest for authenticity.[51] The prejudice directed toward the unemployed 'lower class' is transformed into a virtue, becoming a platform for collective identity. Being provocative, subversive and *Assi* allows the punk/skinhead *prekariat* to exhibit their illusionary and short-lived independence from existing social hierarchies. Or, as J. Patrick Williams notes, 'studying the behaviour of subculture participants and coming to understand how they make sense of their own behaviour [sheds] light on how resistant they think they are.'[52] To place an ironic and emblematic emphasis on being lazy and anti-social is to claim authenticity within the scene.

Punk, then, has in the East German case become a platform for the 'lower class' to pass ironic social commentary on issues such as unemployment or lack of a perceived future. Keith Negus has used the concept of 'articulation' to analyse how the artist and audience create artistic identities and a sense of togetherness through music.[53] 'Articulation' seeks to explain how 'particular cultural forms become connected to specific political agendas and social identities'.[54] In the former industrial towns of the GDR, working-class youths have become targets for demonisation based on their social and regional origin. In response, East German street punks have developed a strategy to resist a 'new guilt complex' on two levels: as a member of the 'lower class' and through the regional semi-political identity of being *Ossi*. In so doing, they turn the mainstream's negative stereotype of the unemployed *Ossi* upside down, offering in the process a provocative demonstration of collective identity.

Conclusion

There is a strong element of opposition within youth culture, especially in punk.[55] Subcultural creativity thereby makes symbolic resistance possible through practice, objects and music. The flexibility of punk's framework enables it to constantly change and transform, which means its authenticity is periodically reframed and negotiated by members of the subculture.

By placing youth culture in its broader socio-economic context, the relationship between social processes and subcultural change cannot be denied. Class boundaries in German society are not only created by scholars; recent studies demonstrate that the German working class is aware of its group identity and its members consciously juxtapose themselves with 'higher' social groups.[56] Unequal access to resources and the demonisation of the 'lower class' accompanies specific interpretations of working-class youth as a source of social ills, making them 'strangers in this country'.[57] Nor should the regional identities of East and West Germans be overlooked. Eastern Germany's position as a problematic region within the German state is associated with a particular 'mindset' and a constant demand for national economic support. This makes being an *Ossi* less 'normal' and more 'different' from the West German majority. In order to become a fully recognised member of society, East Germans are expected to adapt to the Western way of thinking, to learn the 'right ways' of economic management, and to motivate themselves to break out of economic misery.

Punks in East Germany openly display their alienation from the mainstream society and its values. In so doing, they complement the classic subcultural sociology of the CCCS, which theorised how resistance to a dominant culture may be exercised in places such as dance halls, street corners, youth clubs and the street through stylistic practice. Such an approach, however, did little to explore the broader issues (unemployment, racism, social exclusion) expressed through the prism of subculture. East German punks demonstrate the ways by which youth can express solidarity within their social peer group(s), while also conveying the social and economic contradictions amidst which they live. Such a strategy establishes subcultural identity through common leisure practices and symbols that define their status within a scene. Punk does not exist outside of the society but within an existing framework of values, expectations and social norms. As this suggests, subcultural biographies reflect general social and economic processes and exist in direct relation to changes in society. Those who are described in the official rhetoric as *prekariat*, and who are doomed to a life of unemployment because of their 'fate', can find an alternative space in punk where they can be rock stars, friends or lovers. If recognition and solidarity does not exist on a societal level, then subculture becomes a refuge for the neglected.

Acknowledgements

Thanks to all the members of the AHRC 'Post-socialist Punk' project collective for the interesting workshops, discussions and inspiring insights into the punk life of their field regions. I am very grateful to Otto Habeck and the Max Planck Institute for Social Anthropology for use of the institute's facilities when writing this chapter. I am indebted to the anonymous reviewers for useful comments. And my profound thanks go to all the punks, skinheads and hardcore fans in Halle, Leipzig and Berlin for sharing their lives and thoughts with me. This research was supported by the European Union through the European Regional Development Fund (Centre of Excellence in Cultural Theory CECT).

Notes

1 T. Sarrazin, *Deutscland Schafft Sich Ab. Wie Wir Unseres Land Aufs Spiel Setzen* (Berlin: DVA, 2010), pp. 113–14.

2 *Ibid.*, pp. 112, 117 and 172.

3 *Ibid.*, p. 175.

4 A. Nayak, *Race, Place and Globalization* (Oxford and New York: Berg, 2003); J. Owen, *Chavs: The Demonization of the Working Class* (London: Verso Books, 2011).

5 See, for example, R. Böhmer, *Der Geist Des Kapitalismus Und Aufbau Ost* (Dresden: Thelem, 2005); M. Dennis, 'Perceptions of GDR Society and Its Transformation: East German Identity Ten Years after Unity', in C. Flockton, E. Kolinsky and R. Pritchard (eds), *The New Germany in the East* (London and Portland, OR: Frank Cass, 2000), pp. 87–105; W. Engler, *Die Ostdeutschen. Kunde Von Einem Verlorenen Land* (Berlin: Aufbau-Verlag, 1999); A. Fischer, Y. Fritzsche, W. Fuchs-Heinritz and R. Münchmeier, *Jugend 2000. 13. Shell Jugendstudie* (Opladen, Germany: Leske+Budrich, 2000); R. Kollmorgen, *Ostdeutschland. Beobachtungen Einer Übergangs- Und Teilgesellschaft*

(Berlin: VS Verlag, 2005); A. Willisch (ed.), *Wittenberge Ist Überall. Überleben in Schrumpfenden Regionen* (Berlin: Ch. Links Verlag, 2012).

6 A. Bennet and K. Kahn-Harris (eds), *After Subculture: Critical Studies in Contemporary Youth Culture* (Basingstoke: Palgrave Macmillan, 2004); D. Muggleton, 'From Classlessness to Clubculture: A Genealogy of Post-War British Youth Cultural Analysis', *Young*, 13:2 (2005), 205–19; D. Muggleton and R. Weinzierl (eds), *The Post-Subcultures Reader* (Oxford, New York: Berg, 2003).

7 P. Lamy and J. Levin, 'Punk and Middle-Class Values: A Content Analysis', *Youth & Society*, 17:2 (1985), 157–70; A. O'Connor, *Punk Record Labels and the Struggle for Autonomy: The Emergence of DIY* (Lanham, MD: Lexington Books, 2008).

8 One exception was Paul Willis, who demonstrated in his *Learning to Labour: How Working Class Kids Get Working Class Jobs* (Farnborough: Saxon House, 1977) that rebellion against mainstream society's norms does not exclude accepting and adopting those norms and class identities later in life. There are also numerous empirical studies that have suggested that subcultures are affected by the views and status of their members' parents. See R. Jenkins, *Lads, Citizens and Ordinary Kids: Working-Class Youth Life-Styles in Belfast* (London: Routledge and Kegan Paul, 1983); H. Pilkington, E. Omel'chenko and A. b. Garifzianova (eds), *Russia's Skinheads: Exploring and Rethinking Subcultural Lives* (London: Routledge, 2010); S. Verhagen, F. v. Wel, T. T. Bogt and B. Hibbel, 'Fast on 200 Beats Per Minute: The Youth Culture of Gabbers in the Netherlands', *Youth & Society*, 32:2 (2000), 147–64.

9 D. Hesmondhalgh, 'The Cultural Politics of Dance Music', *Soundings*, 5 (1997), 167–78; D. Muggleton, *Inside Subculture* (Oxford, New York: Berg, 2000), p. 198; S. Thornton, *Club Cultures: Music, Media, and Subcultural Capita* (Lebanon, NH: University Press of New England, 1996).

10 R. Haefner, 'Rethinking Subcultural Resistance: Core Values of the Straight Edge Movement', *Journal of Contemporary Ethnography*, 33:4 (2004), 406–36; R. Haefner, *Straight Edge: Clean-Living Youth, Hardcore Punk, and Social Change* (New Brunswick, NJ, and London: Rutgers University Press, 2007); H. Pilkington, 'No Longer "on Parade": Style and the Performance of Skinhead in the Russian Far North', *The Russian Review*, 69 (2010), 187–209.

11 T. Shildrick and R. MacDonald, 'In Defence of Subculture: Young People, Leisure and Social Divisions', *Journal of Youth Studies*, 9:2 (2006), 125–40; J. P. Williams, *Subcultural Theory: Traditions and Concepts* (Cambridge, MA, and Malden: Polity, 2011).

12 Support for my fieldwork came from the Department of Legal Anthropology of the Max Planck-Institute of Social Anthropology in Halle and the AHRC (as part of the 'Post-socialist Punk' project held at the University of Warwick).

13 www.pub.arbeitsagentur.de/hst/services/statistik/000000/html/start/karten/aloq_land.html, accessed 18 December 2012); http://statistik.arbeitsagentur.de/Navigation/Statistik/Statistik-nach-Regionen/Politische-Gebietsstruktur/Sachsen-Anhalt/Halle-Saale-Stadt-Nav.html, accessed 18 December 2012.

14   T. Kochan, *Den Blues Haben. Momente Einer Jugendlichen Subkultur in Der DDR* (Münster, Germany: LIT Verlag, 2003), p. 12.

15   M. M. Westhusen, *Zonenpunk. Punk in Halle (Saale) in Den 80er Jahren* (Halle (Saale): Verein für erlebte Geschichte, 2005).

16   I. Hasselbach, *Die Abrechnung. Ein Neonazi steigt aus.* (Berlin: AtV, 1993).

17   The GDR security service – Stasi – divided alternative and non-sanctioned movements into categories: 'negative decadent' and 'hostile negative'. While the first group consisted mainly of music-based subcultures, the second label was used to mark political groups such as peace and human rights activists. One of the major concerns of the Stasi was 'a possible coalescence between the "hostile negative" and the "negative decadent" strands and the potential of such development for "enemy" interference in the internal affairs of the GDR'. See M. Dennis and N. LaPorte, *State and Minorities in Communist East Germany* (New York, Oxford: Berghahn, 2011), p. 158.

18   T. S. Brown, '"1968" East and West: Divided Germany as a Case Study in Transnational History', *American Historical Review*, 114:1 (2009), 69–99; P. A. Simpson, 'Germany and Its Discontents: Die Skeptiker's Punk Corrective', *Journal of Popular Culture*, 34:3 (2004), 129–40; M. M. Westhusen, 'Zwischen Händel Und Chemie. Punk in Halle, Eisleben Und Dessau', in R. Galenza and H. Havemeister (eds), *Wir Wollen Immer Artig Sein … : Punk, New Wave, Hiphop, Independent-Szene in Der Ddr 1980–1990* (Berlin: Schwarzkopf & Schwarzkopf, 2005), pp. 334–47.

19   G. Hoekman, *Pogo, Punk Und Politik* (Berlin: Unrast, 2011), p. 45.

20   Today, the term *Ostpunk* is colloquially applied to bands from the formerly socialist East Europe.

21   Hoekman, *Pogo, Punk Und Politik*, p. 44.

22   The *Wende* means 'the turn' or 'change' from socialist to market-driven economy that took place after the collapse of the GDR in 1989–90.

23   *Wirtschaftswoche*, cited in J. Roesler, 'Privatization in Eastern Germany: Experience with the Treuhand', *Europe-Asia Studies*, 46:3 (1994), 505–17.

24   W. Engler, *Die Ostdeutschen Als Avangarde* (Berlin: Aufbau Taschenbuch Verlag, 2004), p. 57.

25   G. Leidecker, D. Kirchhöfer and P. Güttler (eds), *Ich Weiss Nicht Ob Ich Froh Sein Soll* (Stuttgart: J. B. Metzlersche Verlagsbuchhandlung, 1991), p. 91.

26   K. Koch, 'The Impact of German Unification on the German Industrial Relations System', in C. Flockton and E. Kolinsky (eds), *Recasting East Germany: Social Transformation after the GDR* (London: Frank Cass, 1999), pp. 52–68; Kollmorgen, *Ostdeutschland*; L. Turner, 'Unifying Germany: Crisis, Conflict, and Social Partnership in the East', in T. Lowell (ed.), *Negotiating the New Germany* (Ithaca, NY, and London: ILR Press, 1997), pp. 113–38; H. Solga, 'The Rise of Meritocracy?: Class Mobility in East Germany Before and After 1989', in M. Diewald, A. Goedicke and K. U. Mayer (eds), *After the Fall of the Wall: Life Courses in the Transformation of East Germany* (Stanford, CA: Stanford University Press, 2006), pp. 140–69.

27   Solga, 'The Rise of Meritocracy?', pp. 140–69.

28 W. Carlin and C. Mayer, 'The Treuhandanstalt: Privatization by State and Market', in O. Blanchard, K. Froot and J. Sachs (eds), *Transition in Eastern Europe, Volume 2* (Chicago: University of Chicago Press, 1995), pp. 189–214.

29 Dennis, 'Perceptions of GDR Society', pp. 87–105.

30 D. Berdahl, *On the Social Life of Postsocialism: Memory, Consumption, Germany* (Bloomington and Indianapolis: Indiana University Press, 2011).

31 R. Böhmer, *Der Geist Des Kapitalismus Und Aufbau Ost*, p. 265.

32 Dennis, 'Perceptions of GDR Society', pp. 87–105.

33 See, for example, Berdahl, *On the Social Life of Postsocialism*; J. R. Eidson, 'Cooperative Property at the Limit', in F. v. Benda-Beckman, K. v. Benda-Beckman and M. G. Wiber (eds), *Changing Properties of Property* (Oxford, New York: Berghahn, 2006), pp. 147–93; J. Eidson and G. Milligan, 'Cooperative Entrepreneurs? Collectivisation and Privatisation of Agriculture in Two East German Regions', in C. Hann and 'Property-Relations Group' (eds), *The Postsocialist Agrarian Question: Property Relations and the Rural Condition* (Münster: LIT Verlag, 2003), pp. 47–92; W. Engler, *Die Ostdeutschen. Kunde Von Einem Verlorenen Land* (Berlin: Aufbau-Verlag, 1999).

34 A. Ventsel, 'This is not my country, my country is the GDR: East German Punk and Socio-economic Processes after German Reunification', *Punk & Post Punk*, 1:3 (2012), 343–59.

35 www.spiegel.de/wirtschaft/service/diskriminierung-ossi-streit-endet-mit-verg-leich-a–723605.html, accessed 20 January 2013.

36 Jugendstudie 2010, *Shell Jugendstudie 2010* (Opladen, Germany: Leske + Budrich, 2010); K. Lenz, 'Lebenswege Durch Jugendphase. Ein Ost-West-Vergleich', in F. Ferchhoff, U. Sander and R. Vollbrecht (eds), *Jugendkulturen – Faszination Und Ambivalenz. Einblicke in Jugendliche Lebenswelten* (Weinheim and Munich: Juventa, 1995), pp. 146–60; W. Schubarth and K. Speck, 'Zwischen Annäherung Umd Spaltung – Soziale Probleme Ostdeutscher Jugendlicher Im Ost-West-Vergleich', in M. Busch, J. Jeskow and R. Stutz (eds), *Zwischen Prekarisierung Und Protest. Die Lebenslangen Und Dgenerationsbilder Von Jugendlichen in Ost Und West* (Bielefeld, Germany: transcript, 2010), pp. 155–74.

37 Jugendstudie 2010, *Shell Jugendstudie 2010*, p. 192.

38 K. Hurrelmann, *Lebensphase Jugend: Eine Einführung in Die Sozialwissenschaftliche Jugendforschung (Grundlagentexte Soziologie)* (Berlin: Beltz Juventa, 2012).

39 Ventsel, 'This is not my country', 349–51.

40 Many officially unemployed punks are engaged in illegal work. See A. Ventsel, 'Punx and Skins United: One Law For Us One Law For Them', *Journal of Legal Pluralism*, 57 (2008), 45–100.

41 D. Hebdige, *Subculture: The Meaning of Style* (London: Routledge, 2006 edn).

42 K. S. Lowney, 'Teenage Satanism as Oppositional Youth Culture', *Journal of Contemporary Etnography*, 23:4 (1995), 453–84.

43 Lowell, *Negotiating the New Germany*, pp. 113–38.

44 Williams, *Subcultural Theory: Traditions and Concepts*, p. 98.

45 Muggleton, *Inside Subculture*, p. 198.

46 G. Elwert, 'Boundaries, Cohesion and Switching: On We-Groups in Ethnic, National and Religious Form', in B. Brumen and Z. Smitek (eds), *Mess. Mediterranean Ethnological Summer School* (Ljubljana, Slovenia: Slovene Ethnological Society, 1995), pp. 105–21.

47 E. Müller-Bachmann, *Jugendkulturen Revisited. Musik- Und Stilbezogene Vergemeinschaftsformen (Post-)Adoleszenter Im Modernisierungskontext* (Münster, Hamburg and London: LIT, 2002).

48 For internal discussion about the political meaning of T-shirts, buttons and brands in German punk and skinhead culture one should read the leftist Internet site 'Oire Szene'.

49 P. Willis, J. Clarke, S. Hall and T. Jefferson, *Common Culture* (Milton Keynes: Open University Press, 1990).

50 J. Clarke, S. Hall, T. Jefferson and B. Roberts, 'Subcultures, Cultures, and Class', in S. Hall and T. Jefferson (eds), *Resistance through Rituals: Youth Subculture in Post-War Britain* (London: Routledge, 1976), pp. 9–74.

51 R. Moore, 'Postmodernism and Punk Subculture: Cultures of Authenticity and Deconstruction', *The Communication Review*, 7:3 (2004), 305–27; Brown, '"1968" East and West', 69–99.

52 Williams, *Subcultural Theory*, p. 95.

53 K. Negus, *Music Genres and Corporate Identities* (London and New York: Routledge, 1999).

54 *Ibid.*, pp. 134–5.

55 See, for example, G. Bushell, *Hoolies: True Stories of Britain's Biggest Street Battles* (London: John Blake, 2010); J. Lydon, *Rotten: No Irish, No Blacks, No Dogs* (London: Hodder & Stoughton, 1993); J. Savage, *England's Dreaming* (London: Faber & Faber, 1991).

56 B. Dewe and A. Scherr, 'Jugendkulturen, Lebenskonstruktionen Und Soziale Deutungsmuster', in F. Ferchhoff, U. Sander and R. Vollbrecht (eds), *Jugendkulturen – Faszination Und Ambivalenz. Einblicke in Jugendliche Lebenswelten* (Weunheim and Munich: Juventa, 1995), pp. 133–45.

57 *Ibid.*, p. 134.

When the punks go marching in: punk, communication and production

11

Silver screen sedition: auteurship and exploitation in the history of punk cinema

BILL OSGERBY

'Will your school be next?': mischief and mayhem at Vince Lombardi High

Teen rebellion is a force to be reckoned with at Vince Lombardi High School. The setting for the punk-musical-comedy *Rock 'n' Roll High School* (1979), Lombardi High has seen a succession of principals driven to despair by the recalcitrant students. Led by Riff Randell (P. J. Soles) – a nonstop party girl and fervid fan of punk stalwarts, the Ramones – the school kids are a font of adolescent abandon. As Randell pumps out Ramones songs through the school's PA, the hallways are jammed with teenagers bopping in a frenzy of delight. The arrival of a new principal, however, seems set to end the fun. An uptight disciplinarian, Miss Evelyn Togar (Mary Woronov) hates rock 'n' roll, and stamps out the high jinks with a burst of vindictive detentions. But, when she confiscates the students' tickets to see a big Ramones show, she pushes the kids too far. As Togar and a band of despotic parents begin a symbolic bonfire of the youngsters' favourite records (the Rolling Stones, Bob Dylan, the Ramones), Randell leads her pals in a euphoric takeover of the school. To Miss Togar's abhorrence, the Ramones themselves arrive on the scene ('Ramones? Do your parents *know* that you're Ramones?!') and help unleash a riot of rock 'n' roll revelry – dancing, food-fights and frisky antics in an overflowing bubble-bath. Finally, the film's finale sees the kids blow up the campus with a stash of dynamite, as the Ramones pound out the movie's theme song and the mutinous partying prevails.

Bankrolled by veteran cult filmmaker Roger Corman and directed by Corman's protégé, Allan Arkush, *Rock 'n' Roll High School* is a consummate pastiche of Hollywood high school movies. Of course, the film is notable for the Ramones' appearance, and their buzzsaw-paced numbers punctuate the picture like resonant machinegun bullets. But *Rock 'n' Roll High School* is also testament to Roger Sabin's observation that 'punk was not an isolated, bounded phenomenon, but had an extensive impact on a variety of cultural and political fields'.[1] Sabin's 1999 anthology went some way towards documenting punk's impact beyond the arenas of music and fashion, but he still observed that there 'is a long way to go before its contribution to other fields is properly recognised'.[2] Intervening time has seen this omission addressed in relation to at least some areas. Punk's impact on graphic arts and design, for example, has been documented by several expansive surveys.[3] And punk's close relationship with the cinema is also beginning to be acknowledged.

In his analysis of British punk films produced during the late 1970s and 1980s, Kevin Donnelly concludes, somewhat ruefully, that outside of a handful of movies either 'recording what happened or attempting to express the spirit of punk', the movement 'did not have widespread effects on other films, musicals or otherwise.'[4] But other writers recognise a more significant punk presence at the cinema. In their incisive guide to cult films, for example, J. Hoberman and Jonathan Rosenbaum highlight a wide range of both commercially produced and avant-garde movies that either feature punk or are influenced by its sensibilities.[5] And, in their monumental 'complete guide to punks on film', Zack Carlson and Bryan Connolly catalogue no less than 1,100 punk-related movies, from early European documentaries such as *Acceleration Punk* (dir. Robert Glassman, 1977) to visions of post-apocalyptic (and spiky-haired) gang-war such as *World Gone Wild* (dir. Lee Katzin, 1988).[6] A more analytic approach is taken by David Laderman, who explores the way 'punk musicals' such as *Breaking Glass* (dir. Brian Gibson, 1980) and *Smithereens* (dir. Susan Seidelman, 1982) meld the subversive spirit of independent filmmaking with the formulaic conventions of the Hollywood pop musical.[7] Other critics have been drawn towards the more experimental and overtly transgressive aspects of 'punk cinema'. Jack Sargent, for instance, delivers a comprehensive account of films produced by the New York art/rock underground of the late 1970s and early 1980s,[8] while both Nicholas Rombes and Stacy Thompson consider punk's enduring influence on generations of maverick filmmakers.[9]

Like the term 'punk', however, the concept of 'punk cinema' is slippery and contentious. For Thompson, 'punk cinema' is distinctively 'non-Hollywoodised' and 'must bear, aesthetically and economically, a filmic version of punk's de-mocratising dictum'.[10] Championing punk's 'do-it-yourself' ethos, Thompson insists that 'punk cinema must be produced without backing from the major studios'.[11] Additionally, he argues, 'punk cinema', should eschew orthodox forms of film narrative and structure which, he maintains, encourage audi-ence passivity and a lack of critical engagement. Instead, Thompson suggests, 'punk cinema' adopts a more challenging aesthetic, one that stands outside Hollywood convention, resisting narrative linearity and closure in favour of techniques that more actively engage the audience, so that 'the filmmaker ceases to be the creator of univocal meaning, and much of the labor of interpre-tation falls to the viewer'.[12] There are, though, a number of problems with this perspective. Not only does it struggle to differentiate 'punk cinema' from other 'alternative' filmmaking traditions, it also offers a somewhat overgeneralised caricature of mainstream cinema and its audiences as uniform and conformist. Thompson's anti-commercial criteria, moreover, effectively marginalises films such as *Rock 'n' Roll High School* from the 'punk cinema' canon.

Rock 'n' Roll High School certainly had a meagre budget ($300,000) and was shot at a breakneck pace (three weeks). But it was hardly the 'do-it-yourself' endeavour prized by Thompson. Executive producer Corman was a Hollywood legend. Since the 1950s he had specialised in low-budget, sen-sationalised movies geared to the youth market and, in 1970, had set up New World Pictures, a production and distribution company that became one of the USA's most successful independent film businesses. Corman's metier was squarely in the traditions of exploitation cinema – an approach to filmmaking that shuns dominant notions of artistic merit and narrative finesse in favour of cheap, quickly made product that cashes in on contemporary fads, pulling in audiences with the promise of spectacle and thrills. Rolling off the New World production line, *Rock 'n' Roll High School* exemplified this strategy, Corman luring young cinemagoers by tapping into the latest subcultural craze. The film, moreover, is hardly a solemn statement of avant-garde innovation. Rather than snubbing mainstream filmmaking conventions, *Rock 'n' Roll High School* play-fully sends them up. Its tongue-in-cheek tagline, 'Will your school be NEXT?', is a pointer to the movie's agenda of jokey silliness as it spoofs the stock clichés of teen cinema in a pageant of ironic humour and unfeasibly fast rock 'n' roll songs. But, despite their market orientation and taste for the goofball, the likes of *Rock 'n' Roll High School* should not be dismissed as simply a cheesy com-mercial rip-off of 'authentic' subcultural revolt.

Like its expression in music, fashion and design, punk's presence in cinema has been eclectic. Undoubtedly, a marked dimension of avant-garde auteurship has always featured in punk's relation with film. Rooted in subversive artistic sensibilities and positioned resolutely outside the mainstream, this tradition measures up to the economic and aesthetic imperatives Thompson sees as punk cinema's defining attributes. But this seditious auteurism has existed alongside – and has often intersected with – approaches more akin to the brash, irreverent practices of exploitation filmmaking. Like many of punk's creative manifestations, *Rock 'n' Roll High School* and its ilk revel in a taste for the camp and the carnivalesque, flaunting their artifice and exhibiting a flair for irony, pastiche and mockery. Such movies may not tally with Thompson's emphasis on DIY, 'non-Hollywoodised' aesthetics; but they should still be recognised as an inalienable facet of 'punk cinema' and underscore the unequivocal diversity of punk's relation with film.

Transgressive cinema from the blank generation

From the outset, punk had an affinity with cinema. New York's embryonic punk scene, for example, was quickly chronicled by Israeli filmmaker Amos Poe who collaborated with Ivan Král (Patti Smith's guitarist) to produce a pair of documentaries – *Night Lunch* (dirs Ivan Král and Amos Poe, 1975) and *The Blank Generation* (dirs Ivan Král and Amos Poe, 1976).[13] Lack of money and equipment meant a DIY aesthetic was inevitable, and Poe's films comprise grainy, shakily shot footage of Patti Smith, Blondie, Television, the Ramones, Talking Heads and other early punk bands playing at clubs like CBGB and Max's Kansas City. The sense of raw primitivism is especially pronounced in *The Blank Generation*, where the performance footage and soundtrack are slightly out of sync, a result of the music being dubbed from crude demos and recordings made at other performances. Rather than a sloppy flaw, however, this disjuncture is hailed by Laderman as 'a radical disjuncture' that challenges filmmaking conventions and gives the movie an edgy 'punk spirit'.[14] The style is shared by *The Punk Rock Movie* (1978), Don Letts's record of punk's early days in London.

Resident DJ for the Roxy – London's seminal punk club, opened in 1976 – Letts is often credited with introducing dub reggae to the British punk scene. But, while flipping the discs at the Roxy, Letts also began filming the bands performing, later assembling the footage as *The Punk Rock Movie*. Like *The Blank Generation*, the film represents a fascinating document of punk's beginnings, with early clips of The Clash, Generation X, The Slits, Siouxsie and the Banshees, and the Sex Pistols. The performances and off-stage footage (rehearsals, interviews and tour bus tomfoolery) were shot with a simple Super 8 camera, and a rough-and-ready version of the film ran for six weeks at the

ICA. Yet, despite being blown up to 35mm, the picture never secured a theatrical release.[15] Letts, however, remains sanguine about the lack of distribution, reflecting that it not only gave the film a 'cult status' but also meant 'I no longer had to show a film that technically made me cringe'.[16] For Thompson, however, the movie's lack of technical finesse is exactly what gives it cachet as a defining text of 'punk cinema'.

Applauding the non-corporate, DIY qualities of *The Punk Rock Movie*, Thompson acclaims the film 'as material proof that a fan need not remain wholly bound to consumption but can partake actively in the scene'.[17] He also champions the film's structural form as an embodiment of punk's egalitarian spirit. Drawing on the ideas of French semiotician Roland Barthes, Thompson suggests that 'punk cinema' is characterised by its 'writerly' potential. That is to say, the formal conventions of the text do not proscribe its meaning, but instead encourage active engagement and creative production on the part of the audience, making 'the reader no longer a consumer, but a producer of the text'.[18] For Thompson, *The Punk Rock Movie* embodies these traits. With no narrative, voiceover or subtitles to guide the viewer, the film's sole organising principle, he argues, becomes simply 'the punk song'. With this distinctly loose structure, Thompson suggests, *The Punk Rock Movie* 'opens itself out, encouraging and prodding the spectator to shift from the position of a passive (to a greater or lesser degree) recipient to that of an active producer of the film's possible significations'.[19] In these terms, then, the creation of the film's meaning lies largely in the hands of the audience.

There is, though, room to moderate some of Thompson's claims. For example, while the original print of *The Punk Rock Movie* was a crude affair, edited together with 'scissors and sellotape', the 35mm version ironed out many technical imperfections and added captions for the bands and songs.[20] Moreover, as Donnelly observes, the film was ultimately produced by Peter Clifton, a veteran filmmaker, whose directorial résumé included *The London Rock 'n' Roll Show* (1973), and Led Zeppelin's concert movie *The Song Remains the Same* (1975). As Donnelly drolly observes, 'while punk rhetoric may have been derided by the pillars of the music industry, for some of these pop music impresarios it was business as usual'.[21]

Nevertheless, many films related to the early punk scene evidenced an enthusiasm for the defiantly avant-garde. The challenging visual style forged by Jean-Luc Godard and the French *Nouvelle Vague* during the late 1950s and 1960s was a particular influence. Amos Poe, for example, drew on Godard's techniques as he shifted from documentary to a narrative film style with his 16mm movie, *The Foreigner* (1978). The film was financed by a $5,000 car loan but Poe, like Godard, made a virtue of his low budget. The cast were drawn

UNIVERSITY OF WINCHESTER
LIBRARY

from the director's friends and faces from the local punk fraternity (including The Cramps and Debbie Harry), while extensive location shoots cut costs but also leant a sense of gritty realism. Poe's hand-held camerawork, long takes and jump-cut editing were also indebted to Godard's approach, as was *The Foreigner's* narrative ambiguity. The film's anarchic plot sees European spy Max Menace (Eric Mitchell) arrive in Manhattan and tangle with assorted characters from New York street life as he tries to discover details of his mission. Meanwhile, an effeminate beatnik (Duncan Hannah) assembles The Bags – a squad of leather-clad punk assassins – to stalk and eventually snuff out the luckless agent, though the twists of the story are enigmatic and the characters' motives remain beguilingly obscure.

The *Nouvelle Vague*, together with Andy Warhol's film experiments, was also an influence on the 'No Wave' movement that flourished in New York's lower East side during the late 1970s and early 1980s. Its name a satirical wordplay on 'new wave' (the term that described punk's more market-friendly elements),[22] No Wave was a collaborative association of artists, musicians and filmmakers who embraced aesthetic styles deliberately abrasive and confrontational.[23] Musically, No Wave was epitomised by the angular, driving sounds of bands like D.N.A., Mars, and Teenage Jesus and the Jerks (fronted by Lydia Lunch). Cinematically, No Wave comprised a loose group of hipsters centred around the New Cinema screening room in the East Village. No Wave filmmakers such as Eric Mitchell, James Nares, Vivienne Dick and Nick Zedd defied cinema orthodoxy with short, stripped-down (often improvised) films which, like Zedd's *They Eat Scum* (1979), challenged audiences with images of violence, boredom and confusion.[24] The aesthetic was a significant influence on US independent cinema throughout the 1980s and 1990s, but Zedd and his associates themselves responded to the increasingly reactionary mood of Reaganite America by shifting to a more brutally confrontational approach in films that trafficked in extreme sex and violence. Dubbed the 'Cinema of Transgression' (a term coined in 1985 by Zedd, writing in his hand-xeroxed 'crudzine', the *Underground Film Bulletin*), the shift saw Zedd and figures such as Stephen Sayadian, Gregory Dark and Richard Kern deliberately push at boundaries of taste in work that combined black humour with a fascination for the grotesque and the offensive. Sayadian's *Café Flesh* (1982) and Zedd's *War Is Menstrual Envy* (1992), for example, both use the shock-value of violence and perversion to delve the depths of the illicit and the inflammatory; while Dark's *New Wave Hookers* (1985) courted outrage through its portrayal of low-life, porno sleaze set against an edgy, punk soundtrack (courtesy of LA Mexican-American punk band, The Plugz).[25]

Vulgarity and subversion also pervade Derek Jarman's *Jubilee* (1978). The British director's high-art, modernist sensibilities were debuted in *Sebastiane* (1976), a film that sparked controversy through its homo-eroticised portrayal of the martyrdom of St Sebastian, and in *Jubilee* Jarman drew on punk as an equally provocative theme. Living off Chelsea's King's Road, Jarman was familiar with London's punk scene from its earliest days, and was taken with its air of sedition. In 1977, Jarman had filmed *Jordan's Dance*, a Super 8 short featuring Jordan (Pamela Rooke), assistant and muse to punk grandees Malcolm McLaren and Vivienne Westwood, and the vignette became the foundation for *Jubilee*. Featuring assorted punk personalities (including Siouxsie Sioux, Jayne County, Adam Ant, Gene October and The Slits) and released just after the Queen's Silver Jubilee celebrations, *Jubilee* has a belligerent energy that would have genuinely shocked mainstream sensibilities of the time.

Described by Jarman as 'a determined, and often reckless analysis of the world which surrounded us',[26] *Jubilee*'s deliberately jerky narrative follows Queen Elizabeth I (Jenny Runacre) as she is transported from the sixteenth century to observe a desolate, broken-down Britain of a near-future 1970s. In this dystopic taste of things-soon-to-come, violence and lawlessness rule the streets. Elizabeth II is dead (mugged on Deptford waste ground) and Buckingham Palace serves as a recording studio for anarchic punk bands. Music, though, is tangential to the film. Aside from a punk-esque rendition of 'Rule Britannia' that accompanies Jordan's goose-stepping parody of patriotism, musical performances are cut short. Instead, the film centres on a girl gang of punk misfits – Amyl Nitrate (Jordan), Crabs (Nell Campbell), Chaos (Hermine Demoriane) and Mad (Toyah Willcox). Led by their own monarch, Bod (Jenny Runacre again), the gang lives a life of sexual degeneracy and casual violence; one especially visceral scene seeing a hapless lad exploited as a sex toy before being suffocated with a polythene sheet. The sordid violence and punk-themed chaos are deployed by Jarman as a metaphor for the social disintegration that seemed to infuse Britain during the late 1970s. The mood of crisis and alienation is underscored by the director's arresting imagery and reverse-angle shots, which disrupt realist filmmaking conventions and unsettle expectations. The bleak backdrop of 1970s London also accentuates the angry nihilism. As Jon Savage puts it:

> [With] its persistent air of disillusion and warning, *Jubilee* captured the mood of Punk England better than anyone could have predicted, not least in its locations: it remains one of the few places where you can see the 1977 London landscape.[27]

But the movie split the punk audience of the day. Some loved it; but others hated it. Vivienne Westwood was especially outraged at what she saw as a misrepresentation of punk, and quickly produced a T-shirt announcing her displeasure.[28] Undoubtedly, *Jubilee* was a vehicle for Jarman's fierce auteurism rather than any attempt to capture the 'spirit' of punk but, for Chris Barber, the contentious responses the movie elicited actually make it 'probably the finest punk film of all':

> Punk was a diverse movement from the start, full of unresolved contradictions and recognising difference as a virtue – this was integral to its creative energy. What could be more punk than provoking controversy even among punks?[29]

Britain's burgeoning punk scene also spawned a succession of documentaries. Directed by Wolfgang Büld, *Punk in London* (1977) was one of the first. In 1976 Büld was a film student studying in Munich when his excitement was sparked by news of British punk and, after blagging finance from a German TV station, he flew to London to record events. Shot in a rough, jerky style, Büld's film has a distinctive 'punk' feel, mixing interviews with raw performance footage of The Lurkers, X-Ray Spex, Subway Sect, Chelsea and The Adverts. A spate of other documentaries followed. Partly funded by the Belfast Arts Council, John Davis's *Shellshock Rock* (1979) captured the Northern Irish punk scene; Britain's later punk milieu was profiled in both *UK/DK: A Film About Punks and Skinheads* (dirs Christopher Collins and Ken Lawrence, 1979) and *Rough Cut and Ready Dubbed* (dirs Hasan Shah and Dom Shaw, 1982); while Wolfgang Büld explored the post-punk fallout in *Punk and its Aftershocks* (1980).[30] A documentary/narrative hybrid also appeared in the form of Jack Hazan and David Mingay's *Rude Boy* (1980).

As Savage observes, *Rude Boy* is configured as 'a tour through a society in terminal crisis'.[31] Filmed over three years, the movie follows Ray Gange (playing a character loosely based on himself), a young Brixton punk who quits his dead-end job to become a roadie for The Clash. Weaving through this storyline an additional sub-plot depicts police racism and corruption, while both narratives are punctuated by footage of National Front rallies, ranks of threatening police and other scenes portraying Britain as beset by social and political conflict. As the film progresses, Gange's life spirals downward as his drunken boorishness alienates the band and earns him the sack – a personal decline that the film juxtaposes to the rise of a right-wing Conservative Party, the movie's doom-laden conclusion closing with Margaret Thatcher's 1979 election victory.

Rude Boy's stark, docu-drama format is, as Philip Kiszely notes, rooted in the traditions of British realism.[32] The depiction of Gange's despondent, down-at-heel life harks back to the British New Wave of the 1960s and the 'kitchen sink' ambiance of *Saturday Night and Sunday Morning* (dir. Karel Reisz, 1960) and *A Taste of Honey* (dir. Tony Richardson, 1961). *Rude Boy's* grim *cinéma vérité* style, meanwhile, echoes the Free Cinema documentary movement of the 1950s and the work of directors such as Lindsay Anderson. For Stacy Thompson, the approach makes for an archetype of 'punk cinema'. Thompson praises *Rude Boy's* independent production credentials, but is especially enamoured of the film's refusal 'to proffer the usual pacing and structure of the dominant Hollywood aesthetic'.[33] *Rude Boy*, Thompson observes, 'moves slowly and meanderingly, without the linear structure and clear teleology that Hollywood cinema compulsively repeats'. The strategy, he argues, 'situates the spectator as an active interpreter of the text' by resisting orthodox expectations of narrative closure.[34] These same qualities, however, have alienated many audiences. The concert footage interspersing the film captures The Clash at their blistering best, but the narrative segments and 'political' juxtapositions have often been criticised as leaden.[35] US punk film encyclopaedists Carlson and Connolly express the view succinctly, concluding that *Rude Boy* offers a 'satisfying barrage of material' for Clash fans but, for anyone else, 'it's British people stumbling around and frowning'.[36]

Like the punk scene more generally, then, punk-related films of the 1970s and early 1980s were a confluence of creative styles. As filmmakers sought both to record and to express punk's rebellious energy they drew upon not only their own, auteurist vision, but also a battery of avant-garde traditions, from the *Nouvelle Vague* and *cinéma vérité* to docu-drama and 'kitchen sink' realism. At the same time, however, punk also had an affinity with the lowbrow and the trashy – and in 'punk cinema' this was epitomised by the influence of exploitation filmmaking.

A carnival of punksploitation

In the film industry, the term 'exploitation' is applied to cheaply made genres that shun dominant notions of artistic finesse, in favour of spectacle and sensational display. According to Eric Schaefer, exploitation films first appeared in the USA during the 1920s and embraced a variety of sub-genres – nudist and burlesque films, sex hygiene films, drug films, exotic and atrocity films – but all shared a common preoccupation with 'some form of forbidden spectacle that served as their organizing sensibility'.[37] Screened in seedy 'grindhouse' cinemas, exploitation films were akin to a carnival sideshow that offered audiences an exhibition of the astonishing, the outrageous and the taboo. By the

1950s the 'classic' era of exploitation had passed, but new traditions emerged on the back of the rising youth market and a spate of moral panics about delinquency. The independent studio American-International Pictures (AIP) led the way with films such as *Reform School Girl* (dir. Edward Bernds, 1957), *The Cool and the Crazy* (dir. William Witney, 1958) and *Riot on Sunset Strip* (dir. Arthur Dreifuss, 1967). Superficially, these 'youth-sploitation' pictures purported to preach against the 'evils' of reckless adolescence but, beneath this veneer, the films gloried in their spectacle of the daring and the sensational, and much of their box-office pull lay in the way they offered young audiences the vicarious thrills of delinquent rebellion.

The liberalisation of American obscenity laws during the 1960s also allowed for the growth of 'sexploitation' cinema, as independent filmmakers took advantage of new opportunities to tempt audiences with nudity and sex. It was a niche filmmaker Russ Meyer virtually made his own, with a sensationalised mix of sex and violence in films such as *Faster, Pussycat! Kill! Kill!* (1965) and his sleazy take on the machinations of show-business, *Beyond the Valley of the Dolls* (1970). Meyer's oeuvre was a wry mixture of the salacious and the satiric, qualities that appealed to Malcolm McLaren as he sought a director to helm a film vehicle for his punk protégés, the Sex Pistols.[38]

McLaren had an early interest in cinema, producing an unfinished student film, *Oxford Street*, while at art college.[39] And, after the Pistols hit the headlines in late 1976, he quickly secured a £200,000 deal with Warner Brothers and Twentieth Century Fox for a movie featuring the band. Impressed by Meyer's work, McLaren hired him to direct, reputedly wanting something similar to *Beyond the Valley of the Dolls* 'but much stronger'.[40] McLaren already had a draft plot titled 'Anarchy in the UK', which intermixed the Pistols' history with visions of insurrectionary mobs during the 1778 Gordon Riots, and comedy talents Johnny Speight and Graham Chapman were both considered as writers, but rejected. Instead, the Dutch writer-director, Renée Daalder, was recruited to develop McLaren's outline, but was soon ditched. So, too, were most of McLaren's ideas, which Meyer disliked. Instead, Roger Ebert (who had scripted *Beyond the Valley of the Dolls*), was drafted in to produce a screenplay for what was initially titled *Who Killed Bambi?*

As envisioned, the movie saw the Pistols embroiled in an over-the-top sexploitation romp based around the murder of 'M.J.' – a decadent rock star redolent of Mick Jagger. Replete with the sex, violence and outrage that was Meyer's trademark, writer Ebert later recalled that *Who Killed Bambi?* was intended as 'a statement of anarchic revolt against the rock millionaires, and the whole British establishment'.[41] Initial scenes were shot but, from the outset, production was fraught. The fifty-five year-old Meyer never really 'got' punk rock, while his martinet discipline was anathema to the Pistols. Meyer and McLaren quickly fell out and the director was loathed by bassist Sid Vicious and singer Johnny Rotten (irked at being cast as a sex fiend). Financial chaos also reigned supreme, prompting Twentieth Century Fox to freeze funding. As a consequence the film was put on hold and an unpaid Meyer walked out, leaving the idea of a Russ Meyer/Sex Pistols collaboration a tantalising 'what if … ?'

McLaren, however, was wedded to the idea of a movie and new finance was secured from Virgin Films, movie producer Don Boyd and McLaren's own management company. The *Bambi* script was junked and American sexploitation director Jonathan Kaplan was hired as Meyer's replacement. When this fell through, Kaplan was replaced by British horror/sexploitation luminary Pete Walker, but the new recruit's plans came to nothing as the Pistols fragmented. At the beginning of 1978 the Pistols' first American tour collapsed acrimoniously and Johnny Rotten quit the band, subsequently refusing to have any dealings with McLaren or the movie. With no band, the prospect of a Sex Pistols film seemed more remote than ever. But McLaren soldiered on, enlisting Julien Temple as the movie's fourth director.

Temple had been a Pistols confederate from the beginning. As a twenty-three year-old student at the National Film School, he had first seen the band in 1976. Captivated, he quickly began shooting the group with a camera smuggled into gigs because McLaren refused unauthorised filming. Gradually, however, McLaren was won round and assigned Temple to produce two short promotional films for the band. Temple also worked as Russ Meyer's assistant on the aborted *Bambi* project, and was understandably keen when McLaren enlisted him to co-write and direct a freshly conceived Sex Pistols movie, *The Great Rock 'n' Roll Swindle* (1980). The film takes remnants of its previous incarnations (imagery of the Gordon Riots and some completed sequences from *Who Killed Bambi?)* and stitches them together with Temple's early Pistols material, assorted animated segments, TV news footage and a variety of newly filmed scenes to create a comedic quasi-documentary charting the band's rise and fall. McLaren features as 'The Embezzler', a manipulative Svengali, who explains in a series of aphoristic 'lessons' to his diminutive sidekick, Helen (Helen Wellington-Lloyd), how he created the Pistols – and punk in general – as an elaborate scam to reap 'cash from chaos'. Meanwhile, Steve Jones plays a private eye pursuing McLaren through a variety of set pieces in an attempt to get his hands on the purloined money.

Swindle's formal qualities were partly born of necessity. Effectively, they were strategies to construct a narrative around a band that no longer existed. But they were also inspired by Temple's interest in filmmaking traditions such as the *Nouvelle Vague* and Sergei Eisenstein's theories of montage, in which meaning is created through the collision and juxtaposition of images. *Swindle*, however, blends these avant-garde influences with formal techniques rooted in the practices of exploitation filmmaking. Russ Meyer was long gone, but the style of exploitation movies remained prominent, with the film pushing gleefully towards the shocking and the outrageous. One sequence, for example, sees a nude pubescent girl morph into a spectacularly coiffured punk. Another sees Steve Jones and Paul Cook travel to Brazil to recruit new band members in the form of the escaped train robber, Ronnie Biggs, and fugitive Nazi, Martin Bormann. The film's conclusion, meanwhile, sees Jones having sex with British porn star Mary Millington in the stalls of a cinema screening – with a neat touch of self-referential irony – *Who Killed Bambi?*, a sleazy exploitation picture chronicling the Pistols' misdeeds. Indeed, irony is pervasive in *The Great Rock 'n' Roll Swindle*, Temple later recalling how the film 'was meant to be a joke on many levels, to puncture the way people put them [the Pistols] on a pedestal'.[42] But, along with its savour of irony, *Swindle* also boasts the 'carnivalesque' proclivities that distinguish exploitation cinema.

The notion of the carnivalesque is rooted in the ideas of the Russian literary scholar, Mikhail Bakhtin. Writing during the 1920s and 1930s, Bakhtin depicted the carnivals of pre-industrial Europe as spaces where the forbidden and the fantastic suddenly became possible. The carnival, Bakhtin argued, was an explosion of exuberant misrule where prevailing systems of authority were suspended and conventional morality gave way to an eruption of the vulgar, the mocking and the grotesque. While the original moments of carnival are long defunct, Bakhtin's ideas have been embraced by many social theorists in analyses of more recent cultural phenomena.[43] For Schaefer, exploitation films are exemplary. While he sees exploitation pictures as 'politically ambiguous', Schaefer argues they also possess markedly carnivalesque qualities in the way they 'privilege the "lower body stratum", overturn a classical aesthetics based on formal harmony and good taste' and thereby present a 'challenge to the system of orderly presentation of material to well-mannered spectators that was encouraged by Hollywood'.[44] Punk's carnivalesque traits were also pronounced. As Neil Nehring argues, the 'combination of comic parody and angry billingsgate' that characterises the carnival found echoes in punk's relish for the incendiary and the irreverent.[45] And it is these qualities that infuse *The Great Rock 'n' Roll Swindle*. Blending punk's jeering belligerence with exploitation cinema's appetite for outrage, *Swindle* represents a neat piece of 'punksploitation' that unleashes a carnivalesque torrent of mockery and misrule.

The subversive potential of exploitation film also appealed to No Wave pioneer Nick Zedd. The director was a fan of youth-sploitation pictures of the 1950s and 1960s and, as he later recalled, saw their larger-than-life depictions of youth run wild as the basis for a film that could lampoon the febrile responses to punk:

> I really liked these low-budget, quickie juvenile delinquency exploitation movies like *Riot on Sunset Strip* and I wondered why nobody had made a movie satirizing the dominant culture's opinion of punk rock. ... So I thought I would make a low-budget comedy shot in Super 8 that would exaggerate the demonization of punk rockers, and that's when I wrote the screenplay for this feature called *They Eat Scum*.[46]

Premiered at Max's Kansas City in 1979, *They Eat Scum* features Zedd's fellow filmmaker Donna Death as Suzi Putrid, the leader of 'death rock' band, The Mental Deficients. As the band's following grows, Suzi kills off her dysfunctional family and embarks on a spree of sexual depravity and murder. One especially visceral sequence sees Suzi humiliate and torture a punk poseur, forcing a live rat down the young girl's throat, before eviscerating her with a buzzsaw and feeding the remains to her fans. After Suzi is murdered on stage, her twin sister renames herself 'Queen of Death' and announces she has irradiated New York's water supply. Equipped with protective suits, the death rockers are the only survivors, but ultimately meet their match facing a scourge of ferocious disco mutants. Described by Zedd as 'intentionally transgressive and provocative but with humor', *They Eat Scum* is an archetype of carnivalesque punksploitation which – like *Swindle* – uses a combination of jokey parody and outrageous excess to impishly tweak the tail of mainstream tastes and conventions.

A similar sensibility also surfaces in *D.O.A.: A Rite of Passage* (1980), Lech Kowalski's documentary based around the Sex Pistols' disastrous US tour. In the late 1970s Kowalski, a graduate of New York's School of Visual Art, was working in the porn business but nursed more creative aspirations. Enthralled by the developing punk scene, Kowalski secured backing from Tom Forcade – founder of the marijuana magazine, *High Times* – to film the Pistols' ill-fated trek across the American South.[47] Interspersed with footage of other bands (including the Dead Boys, Generation X and Sham 69), *D.O.A.* chronicles the Pistols' chaotic US appearances, culminating in their notorious final gig at San Francisco's Winterland Ballroom. The film is vivid testimony to the band's disarray and despondency on the tour but, in true 'exploitation' style, it also constructs the punk milieu as a spectacle of the wanton and the weird. Footage of fans outside the Pistols' shows is especially outré. One angry Texan recounts how Sid Vicious beat him over the head with a bass guitar; a young girl writhes on the kerb, ripping off her dress; and a curly-haired youth with sticking plaster inexplicably taped in a large 'X' across his face berates the film crew maniacally. Meanwhile, an extended interview with Sid Vicious and his brassy girlfriend, Nancy Spungeon, mesmerises like a slow-motion car-crash. A heroin-addled Vicious struggles to stay awake (let alone coherent) while Spungeon repeatedly tries to rouse him, until the viewer is jarred with a caption showing the dates of their deaths, just a few months later.

Rock 'n' Roll High School was also rooted in exploitation traditions. Executive producer Roger Corman had cranked out low-budget delinquency, horror and sci-fi pictures for AIP (the leading US exploitation studio) since 1954. His trademark was miniscule costs and lightning-fast production sched-ules, but his films were also characterised by dark humour and an edge of social criticism; and movies such as *The Wild Angels* (1966) and *The Trip* (1967) had skilfully tapped into the shifting character of American youth culture. Striking out on his own, Corman set up New World Pictures in 1970 and emulated the AIP approach, producing cheapo exploitation movies that could generate big profits. Following this formula, in 1977 he was planning to cash in on the disco boom with a high school musical called *Disco High* when Allan Arkush, Corman's young assistant, sold him on an alternative. In his teens, Arkush later recalled, he had daydreamed 'about putting on a rock 'n' roll concert in my high school and blowing up the school, and having motorcycle races in the hallways', and he convinced Corman that the fantasy would make for a great movie. Moreover, Arkush assured Corman that 'you can't blow up a school to *disco* music' and persuaded the studio boss to rename the picture *Rock 'n' Roll High School*.[48] The film's plot was lifted from the 1956 rock 'n' roll exploitation movie, *Shake, Rattle & Rock!* (dir. Edward L. Cahn), and first choice for the central band were doughty rockers Cheap Trick – though, when they proved too expensive, punk trailblazers the Ramones were drafted in.

The Ramones may not have been first pick for *Rock 'n' Roll High School*, but the band's aesthetic suited the film perfectly. Their sound was a three-chord tornado that harked back to the 1960s proto-punk of The Stooges and the MC5, but it also drew influence from the bouncy pop of the 1960s and early 1970s; and songs like 'I Wanna Be Your Boyfriend' and 'Rockaway Beach' both lionise and sardonically pastiche the stock stereotypes of US teen mythology. The same sensibility is at the heart of *Rock 'n' Roll High School*. A satirical take on classic high school movies such as *Blackboard Jungle* (dir. Richard Brooks, 1955) and *High School Confidential* (dir. Jack Arnold, 1958), the film simultane-ously celebrates and parodies the junkyard of American teen culture. Indeed, none of the movie's wayward school kids are recognisably 'punk'. Instead, they are a goofy send-up of squeaky-clean, middle-class adolescence. Riff Randell, for example, is a spoof of the adoring teenage fan who fondly imagines her idol

– Joey Ramone – serenading her in a personal bedroom performance. And, strolling into her bathroom in a lovesick daze, she comically stumbles upon the rest of the band. Pulled aside, a shower curtain reveals a sopping wet Dee Dee Ramone playing bass, while a closet door swings open to reveal Marky Ramone beating out a rhythm on his drum kit. Principal Togar, meanwhile, is a hilarious caricature of the uptight disciplinarian. Togar's loathing of rock 'n' roll, for instance, is apparently vindicated by her deranged experiments on lab mice – a pair of 'before' and 'after' photos graphically demonstrating how, after exposure to rock music, a meek white mouse develops an insolent swagger and sports a leather jacket and wrap-round shades. Further experimentation has Togar gauging the impact of rock 'n' roll with a comical 'rock-o-meter'. She pushes the machine's settings through the levels of Kansas and Peter Frampton, all the way up to Ramones intensity, causing a luckless mouse to explode through the sheer sonic power of punk rock. Other rodents, however, clearly break out from Togar's madcap research – as, at the Ramones' finale show, a pair of large, white mice can be seen pogoing wildly.

This jokey, knowing theatricality is redolent of the aesthetic codes and mischievous mentality of camp. In her 1964 landmark essay, 'Notes on Camp', Susan Sontag popularised the notion of camp as a sensibility that revels in irony and playful exaggeration; so that camp 'sees everything in quotation marks. It's not a lamp, but a "lamp"; not a woman, but a "woman"'.[49] As Fabio Cleto notes, however, Sontag can be accused of eliding camp's origins within gay subculture, and of blunting its critical edge, turning camp into 'a simple matter of ironically relishing an indulgence in what is "so-bad-it's good"'.[50] In contrast, Cleto suggests that camp's delight in artifice and vulgar excess can amount to a form of 'queer' cultural sabotage; a stratagem for resistance and questioning that reverses the principles of 'normality' and throws into doubt the 'natural' order. As such, Cleto argues, camp has a clear affinity with the Bakhtinian carnivalesque, both sharing the qualities of 'hierarchy inversion, mocking paradoxicality, sexual punning and innuendoes and – most significantly – a complex and multi-layered power relationship between the dominant and the subordinate (or deviant)'.[51] These qualities were a rich seam running through punksploitation cinema, but they were also a distinctive facet of the punk subculture more generally. Indeed, as Hoberman and Rosenbaum observe, while 'camp's vanguard subculture was the urban homosexual' and punk's 'was the suburban teen', they still shared much in common:

> As a sensibility, punk is closely related to camp. Both ironically reclaim
> the dated styles of the recent past, discovering their fashions and fetishes
> in the thrift shops and old movies. But while camp is largely tied to the

Hollywoodiana of the twenties, thirties, and forties, punk history only begins
with the post-World War II youth culture: television, atomic bombs, E.C.
horror comics, Elvis Presley, and drive-in movies. ... For the aestheticizing,
pseudo-aristocratic camp sensibility, the key element in American pop culture
is its mass-produced glamour. For moralistic, pseudo-lumpen punk, the
corresponding elixir is America's mass produced sleaze. Camp appreciates
the poetic Universal horror flicks of the 1930s; punk prefers Roger Corman,
Herschell Gordon Lewis, and Brian De Palma.[52]

Punk cinema's popular peak

Punk cinema's association with camp and the carnivalesque continued in John
Waters' *Polyester* (1981). Waters' work, in many ways, anticipated punk aes-
thetics through its enthusiasm for the transgressive and the taboo.[53] Waters'
'Trash Trilogy'– *Pink Flamingos* (1972), *Female Trouble* (1974) and *Desperate
Living* (1977) – established his reputation as a maestro of shock cinema, and
Polyester maintained the oeuvre. The only movie ever made in 'Odorama'
(complete with scratch 'n' sniff smell cards), *Polyester* is a camped-up festival
of vulgar excess. It features drag-queen Divine (a regular in Waters' films) as
Francine Fishpaw, a rich suburban housewife whose life spins out of control
when her husband (who runs the local porn cinema) runs off with his blonde
secretary, her son Dexter is exposed as a glue-sniffer with a foot-stomping
fetish and her daughter Lu-Lu is knocked-up by a neighbourhood hoodlum.
Polyester, however, is not simply a bonanza of bad taste. Like all Waters' films,
the shock tactics are underpinned by a radical agenda that challenges the audience's cultural assumptions and raises an insolent middle finger to conservative
prejudices. It was an attitude that made Waters a natural fan of punk rock and in
Polyester he allied himself with punk by including a clutch of Blondie numbers
in the soundtrack and casting Stiv Bators (the Dead Boys' frontman) as Bo-Bo
Belsinger, Lu-Lu Fishpaw's thuggish beau.

   Other punk-related films, however, played things straight. Brian Gibson's
Breaking Glass (1980), for example, was aimed squarely at the mainstream.
With entertainment financier Dodi Al-Fayed (son of the billionaire owner of
Harrods) as its executive producer, the film tapped into classical traditions of
the Hollywood musical, tracking the rise and tragic fall of an aspiring new wave
singer (Hazel O'Connor) as she is cynically manipulated by music business
moguls. *Breaking Glass* is often scorned as a 'diluted' commercial appropriation
of punk sensibilities, Donnelly pronouncing it 'a highly conventional backstage

musical story ... dressed up ... in punk apparel'.[54] But Claire Monk argues the film deserves credit for being the only British punk-related film (apart from *Jubilee*) to centre on a female protagonist. As Monk notes, while punk's liberating impact for women has been widely acknowledged, 'female punk vocalists and musicians are highly visible and audible – yet rarely commented on – in early documentaries such as *Punk in London*, while women were surprisingly marginal or marginalised in *Rude Boy* and *The Swindle*'.[55]

The USA, in contrast, saw a spree of punk-related films featuring female leads. *Times Square* (dir. Allan Moyle, 1980), for instance, was a big budget production that cast two unknowns as the sheltered Pamela (Treini Alvarado) and the feisty Nicky (Robin Johnson), who abscond from a mental clinic to forge a new life on the streets of New York. Linking up with sympathetic disc jockey Johnny LaGuardia (Tim Curry), the girls form an underground punk band, The Sleez Sisters, and become an inspiration for the city's disillusioned teens.[56] Female characters are also central to *Ladies and Gentlemen, The Fabulous Stains* (dir. Lou Adler, 1982). Financed by the major studio Paramount, the movie was scripted by Oscar-winning screenwriter Nancy Dowd, who recruited Caroline Coon (one of the first journalists to chronicle London's punk scene) as a creative consultant. Originally titled *All Washed Up*, the picture sees Corinne 'Third Degree' Burns (Diane Lane) determined to break out of a decaying Midwestern steel town. Tired of selling hamburgers, she is inspired by English punk band The Looters (fronted by actor Ray Winstone and featuring ex-Sex Pistols Steve Jones and Paul Cook, and Paul Simenon of The Clash). Seizing the moment, Corinne forms an all-girl punk group – The Stains – with her sister and cousin, and blags the band a support slot on tour with The Looters and has-been rockers The Metal Corpses. Bursting with gutsy energy, The Stains become an overnight sensation and win an army of ardent girl fans, the self-christened Skunks. But, as The Stains transform into a slickly marketed pop act, their fans desert them and the band ultimately splits.

Behind the scenes, however, Dowd and Coon were disappointed with *The Fabulous Stains*. Both felt the film's proto-feminist agenda had been diminished by director Lou Adler, who skewed the movie towards more orthodox (and more masculine) rock traditions. Indeed, after Dowd disowned the movie, Adler changed its name to foster an association with the classic 'rockumentary', *Ladies and Gentlemen: The Rolling Stones* (dir. Rollin Binzer, 1973). But Paramount was also unhappy with the film and it was brusquely shelved after poor preview screenings. Limited releases came in 1982 and 1984, but the movie attracted little interest. Subsequently, however, *The Fabulous Stains* has won a cult following. The film's sexual politics may have been curbed during production, but enough of the spark survived to enthuse an audience and the movie has often been cited as influence on the Riot Grrrl movement of the 1990s.[57]

The early 1980s boom in independent filmmaking also brought several punk-oriented films centred on young women. For instance, Dennis Hopper, a trailblazer of US independent cinema, produced *Out of the Blue* (1980). A gritty drama set in rural Texas, the film sees young, alienated Cebe (Linda Manz) embrace punk as an avenue of rebellion against her abusive parents. The movie's punk theme was actually a late addition, incorporated only when Hopper became aware of the burgeoning punk scene in Vancouver (where the movie was shot). As a consequence, the 'punk' elements seem superficial and unconvincing, though Laderman recognises elements of compelling social commentary in the film, arguing it (like many punk musicals of the period) engages in 'an ethnographic exploration of how teenagers get into punk, how they "make it matter"'.[58]

Smithereens (dir. Susan Seidelman, 1982) and *Liquid Sky* (dir. Slava Tsukerman, 1982) also cast female protagonists in punk-related narratives. Both focus on women struggling to establish a foothold in the New York punk scene. *Smithereens* sees the ambitious Wren (Susan Berman) seeking a sense of belonging in the helter-skelter clubland of the East Village; while *Liquid Sky* focuses on the androgynous and bisexual Margaret (Ann Carlisle), who seeks success as a new wave fashion model amid a darkly humorous (and utterly bizarre) plot in which sci-fi aliens infiltrate the sex- and drugs-fixated world of the pretentious fashion set. Both movies feature strong, confident female characters but, as Laderman notes, the films' pervasive sense is one of nihilism, with the conclusion of each presenting a 'reiteration of the femme fatale's doomed fate: the freeze-frame of Wren, desolate and abandoned, wandering the highway, poised to become a prostitute; and Margaret's high-tech, sci-fiorgasmic dance of death'.[59]

More generally, several independent filmmakers developed a sustained relationship with punk as a both a theme and a source of creative inspiration. Penelope Spheeris, for instance, began her movie career producing and directing *The Decline of Western Civilization* (1981), a documentary portrait of California's early punk underground. Alongside performances by The Germs, X, Black Flag and The Circle Jerks, the film features interviews with band members, promoters, club owners and fans, capturing the scene's chaos, vitality and wit. Spheeris's approach found imitators in a series of further 'punkumentaries', including *The Slog Movie* (1982), David Markey's raw account of the West Coast punk scene, and *Another State of Mind* (1984), Adam Small and Peter Stuart's account of life on tour with Social Distortion and Youth Brigade.

Spheeris herself maintained an affinity with punk, but shifted into a narrative approach with both *Suburbia* (1983) and *Dudes* (1987).

Set among LA's hardcore squatter community, *Suburbia* was produced by Roger Corman, though the exploitation-meister's trademark sensationalism is played relatively low. Instead, Spheeris's film is a compelling portrayal of young, alienated punks who struggle to get by in a world of cynicism and social decay. *Dudes* is more tongue-in-cheek, with a trio of New York punks (Jon Cryer, Daniel Roebuck and Flea (co-founder of the Red Hot Chili Peppers)) quitting the big city for a trip out West in a battered Volkswagen Beetle; an odyssey cut tragically short when the threesome tangle with a gang of psychotic rednecks. The irony continued in *The Decline of Western Civilization Part II: The Metal Years* (1988), Spheeris's document of the decadence and unabashed immaturity of Hollywood's heavy metal scene, a theme the director turned into mainstream success with her metalhead comedy, *Wayne's World* (1992). But Spheeris returned to her punkumentary roots with *The Decline of Western Civilization Part III* (1998). The film deals with the resurgence of LA hardcore during the late 1990s but, whereas the original *Decline* had largely focused on bands, *Part III* concentrates on fans. Moreover, in contrast to the underlying positivity of the original, *Part III* strikes a distinctly bleaker tone in its depiction of the tragic, self-destructive lives of LA's homeless 'gutter punks'.

Punk influences are also writ large in the career of cult luminary, Alex Cox. *Repo Man* (1984), Cox's directorial debut, sees LA punk Otto (Emilio Estevez) wandering the streets alone and depressed after being fired from his dead-end supermarket job, getting dumped by his girlfriend and learning his parents have donated his college fund to a televangelist. Recruited as an apprentice car repossession agent, he stumbles into a web of wackiness and intrigue as he tracks down a lunatic government scientist driving a 1964 Chevy Malibu with a top secret cargo in the trunk. A critical and commercial hit, *Repo Man* represents a campy, film noir/sci-fi satire of Reaganite America. But it also neatly captures the energy and cynical edge of the early 1980s punk scene, and boasts a soundtrack that showcased some of Southern California's top hardcore bands of the time – Black Flag, Suicidal Tendencies, The Circle Jerks and The Plugz.

On the back of *Repo Man*'s success, Cox went on to his second punk picture, *Sid and Nancy* (1986), a downbeat biopic centred on the ill-starred relationship between Sid Vicious (Gary Oldman) and Nancy Spungeon (Chloe Webb). While the punk cognoscenti gave *Sid and Nancy* a mediocre reception, and Cox himself has expressed reservations about the film, it was another box-office hit and allowed Cox to move on to make *Straight to Hell* (1987), a comic homage to Spaghetti Westerns. Again, punk influences and input were in clear evidence – with cameo appearances from Joe Strummer,

The Pogues and Elvis Costello – but *Straight to Hell* is easily the weakest of Cox's 'punk trilogy'. Messy and disjointed, on its release it was roundly panned by film critics and punk fans alike.

Alongside the endeavours of independent auteurs, the relationship between punk and exploitation cinema also endured. For example, as Chris Barber notes, a stream of sci-fi and horror punksploitation followed the success of George Miller's *Mad Max* (1979) and *Mad Max 2: The Road Warrior* (1981).[60] Miller's dystopic action movies feature Mel Gibson as a leather-jacketed avenger pitched against feral motorcycle gangs in a post-apocalyptic Australian wasteland. Heralding a surge in the Australian film industry, the movies were an international hit, acclaimed for their tightly edited action scenes. But the movies' visual elements also stood out, particularly costume designer Norma Moriceau's mohawked bikers festooned in leather bondage-gear – an image that both plundered from and, in turn, inspired punk style of the early 1980s. After Miller's success, *Mad Max* imitations ensued worldwide. From the Philippines, armies of leather-jacketed mohawks marauded through a post-nuclear wilderness in *W is War* (dir. Willie Milan, 1983) and *Wheels of Fire* (dir. Cirio Santiago, 1985). From Japan, Gakuryu Ishii offered visions of punk-esque motorcycle gangs rampaging through a near-future Tokyo in *Crazy Thunder Road* (1980) and *Burst City* (1982). And, from Mexico, an outrageous circus of punk-themed misfits unleashed a frenzy of carnage in *Intrepidos Punks* (dir. Francisco Guerrero, 1983) and its gleefully excessive sequel, *La Venganza de los Punks* (dir. Damián Acosta Esparza, 1987). But it was Italy that became home to punk-themed dystopic sci-fi. The Spaghetti Westerns of their day, a host of sagas featuring 'post-apocalyptic pasta punks' rolled out of Italian exploitation studios, including *Rats: Night of Terror* (dir. Bruno Mattei, 1983), *Raiders of Atlantis* (dir. Ruggero Deodato, 1983), *Warrior of the Lost World* (dir. David Worth, 1983), Giulliano Carnimeo's *1990: The Bronx Warriors* (1982) and *Exterminators of the Year 3000* (1983), and Enzo Castellari's *The New Barbarians* (1982) and *Escape From the Bronx* (1983).

In the USA mohawked gangs in studded leather also populated a spurt of dystopic punksploitation pictures. The roster included *Future-Kill* (dir. Ronald W. Moore, 1985), *Land of Doom* (dir. Peter Maris, 1986), *Surf Nazis Must Die* (dir. Peter George, 1987) and *Last of the Warriors* (dirs. Michael Mazo and Lloyd A. Simandl, 1989). Other punksploitation movies, however, harked back to the delinquency films of the 1950s, substituting sneering punks for the classic, switchblade-toting greasers. *Savage Streets* (dir. Danny Steinmann, 1984), for instance, pitches a teenage vigilante (Linda Blair) against a scuzzy punk gang who rape her handicapped sister and kill her best friend, while *Punk Vacation* (dir. Stanley Lewis, 1987) sees no-good, big city 'punkers' wreak chaos in a sleepy Californian town. But the sub-genre is defined by Mark L. Lester's *Class of 1984* (1982). Produced in Canada, the film sees idealistic teacher Andy Norris (Perry King) newly appointed to a high school terrorised by vicious, drug-dealing punks led by the gloriously psychotic Peter Stegman (Timothy Van Patten). The villainous gang maintain their reign of violence, rape and murder until a climactic showdown between Norris and Stegman sees the punk psycho plummet to his death from auditorium rafters amid the school orchestra's debut performance.

Class of 1984 evoked the carnivalesque sensationalism of 1950s delinquency films, but other punksploitation pictures were rooted in the tongue-in-cheek traditions of camp. It was a field in which Troma Entertainment excelled. Founded by Lloyd Kaufman and Michael Herz in 1974, Troma made its name in low-budget send-ups of 1950s exploitation movies. With their taste for grotesque zaniness, Troma's films always had something of a punk sensibility, while punk characters regularly cropped up in cameo roles and took centrestage in Troma's punksploitation parody, *Class of Nuke 'Em High* (dirs Richard W. Haines and Lloyd Kaufman, 1986). Spoofing *Class of 1984*, *Nuke 'Em High* sees Tromaville High School menaced by The Cretins – a group of hardworking Honours Students transformed into a gang of malevolent punks through exposure to toxic waste. Decked out in outrageously punk apparel – the usual studded leather and dyed hair accentuated by face-paint, huge nose-rings, a Hitler moustache and a rubber chicken hat – The Cretins delight in tormenting and bumping-off their classmates; and turn the survivors into drooling mutants by peddling dope contaminated with noxious radiation.

A similar aesthetic characterises Dan O'Bannon's *Return of the Living Dead* (1985). A jokey homage to the zombie horror genre, *Return of the Living Dead* sees the rotting corpses of Louisville, Kentucky re-animated when bumbling employees at a medical warehouse accidentally release a deadly gas concocted by the military. To a raucous garage-punk soundtrack (that includes numbers from The Cramps and The Damned), the flesh-eating undead infest the town, forcing a cluster of wastrel punks to hole-up in a mortuary with the blundering warehousemen. Full of dark humour, *Return of the Living Dead* is a cartoon-like, splattery gore-fest. But lurking beneath the visceral slapstick are pronounced elements of political satire. As Barber observes, the film's zombies stand (or shamble along) as a neat metaphor 'for the "old", "parental", reactionary conservative citizens – the establishment of the Nixon era coming back from the grave to kill the young', while the movie's relentless pessimism projects 'complete mistrust and cynicism towards the state power structures that supposedly protect us'. Indeed, despite being produced in association with Fox Films, there is, as Barber puts it, 'an angry, bad-tempered punk attitude running through this film, which runs deeper than the DIY fashion accessories on the body count fodder punk rockers'.[61]

This spate of punksploitation, however, sits somewhat uncomfortably in Stacy Thompson's delineation of 'punk cinema'. Though films like *Class of Nuke 'Em High* and *Return of the Living Dead* were created by nominally independent filmmakers, their processes of finance, production and distribution were still indebted to the mainstream corporate structures that are anathema to Thompson. Moreover, these pictures' avowedly goofy sensibilities hardly equate with the rather earnest 'open, writerly asethetic' that Thompson champions. Nevertheless, punksploitation's impulse for the wry, critical edge of camp gives it a satirical bite that is unmistakable. Sending up media clichés and cocking a defiant snook at filmmaking niceties, punksploitation pictures boast a playful yet rebellious aesthetic that locates them squarely within 'punk' traditions.

The fall and rise of punk cinema

The early to mid-1980s were punk cinema's high-water mark. Of the countless punk-related movies released, many were box-office turkeys, but others enjoyed considerable success. Penelope Spheeris's punk pictures were hits both critically and commercially, while *Repo Man* and *Sid and Nancy* established Alex Cox's reputation as a doyen of cult filmmaking. Several punksploitation pictures were also big successes. *Class of 1984*, *Class of Nuke 'Em High* and *Return of the Living Dead* were all box-office hits, spawned several sequels and maintained enduring fan followings through subsequent VHS and DVD releases. Punk characters and cameo roles, meanwhile, cropped up in everything from *The Woman in Red* (dir. Gene Wilder, 1984) to *Star Trek IV: The Voyage Home* (dir. Leonard Nimoy, 1986), while a specialised casting agency – Janet Cunningham's CASH – did a brisk trade catering to Hollywood's demand for punk-looking actors and extras to feature in myriad films, TV series and advertising campaigns. By comparison, the 1990s were leaner times for punk cinema. As punk's newsworthiness and topicality waned, the big-screen appeal of punk themes and characters also faded.

But, as the original punk generation reached reflective middle-age, a new surge in independent filmmaking brought a fresh burst of punk-related movies. A flurry of biopics, for example, recreated the lives and times of personalities from the punk era – most notably *24 Hour Party People* (dir. Michael Winterbottom, 2002), *Control* (dir. Anton Corbijn, 2007), *What We Do Is Secret* (dir. Rodger Grossman, 2007), *The Runaways* (dir. Floria Sigismondi,

2010) and *Good Vibrations* (dirs Lisa Barros D'Sa and Glenn Leyburn, 2012). A renaissance in documentary filmmaking also brought a spate of retrospective profiles of a variety of punk bands. In Britain, for example, Julien Temple revisited his punk roots with both *The Filth and the Fury* (2000), a frank retelling of the Sex Pistols' career, and *Joe Strummer: The Future Is Unwritten* (2007), a celebration of the life of the Clash's legendary frontman. Similarly, Don Letts returned to his punk past with his history of The Clash, *Westway to the World* (2000), and his expansive subcultural survey, *Punk: Attitude* (2005). In the USA, meanwhile, Jim Fields and Michael Gramaglia delivered the excellent *End of the Century: The Story of the Ramones* (2003), Scott Crary's *Kill Your Idols* (2004) recounted the history of New York's No Wave, and Paul Rachman's *American Hardcore* (2006) related the story of LA punk. And punk filmmaking, itself, was the subject of a documentary retrospective in *Blank City* (2010), Celine Danhier's tribute to the No Wave underground and the Cinema of Transgression.

But recent punk filmmaking is not simply rooted in wistful nostalgia. During the mid-1990s, punk's original do-it-yourself ethos and spirit of innovation inspired the emergence of a 'new punk cinema'. As Nicholas Rombes observes, 'new punk cinema' is less a coherent, unified school of film than a loose set of filmmaking styles and production strategies informed by the sensibilities of punk.[62] Emblematic are the films of Dogma 95, a Danish film movement led by the directors Lars von Trier and Thomas Vinterberg whose work – for example, von Trier's *The Idiots* (1997) and Vinterberg's *The Celebration* (1998) – deliberately effaces glossy production values in favour of an unabashedly amateurish, DIY style redolent of 1970s punk.[63] While Rombes identifies the Dogma 95 group as leading figures in 'new punk cinema', he insists on its global character, citing as examples the filmmaking styles of German director Tom Tyker, American directors Harmony Korine and Darren Aronofsky, and the British directors Danny Boyle, Mike Figgis and Christopher Nolan. Animated by the same do-it-yourself approach that characterised 1970s punk, Rombes argues, these 'new punk' directors share 'an almost romantic notion that anyone can create something that matters, a troubled desire for and yet suspicion of authenticity and the Real, an approach to film-making that foregrounds the medium of film itself, and an interest in simplicity which, ironically, allows for great freedom and experimentation.'[64]

This democratic spur and antipathy to Hollywood orthodoxy has a distinct affinity with Thompson's 'punk cinema' ideals. Yet Rombes also identifies marked facets of self-aware irony in the 'new punk' sensibility. For Rombes, 'new punk' films recall 1970s bands like Blondie and the Ramones in the way they blur the boundaries of sincerity, irony and camp, 'creating worlds that both acknowledge and deconstruct pop-culture narratives'.[65] In this way the various traditions of 'punk cinema' are drawn together; 'new punk' films melding together the experimentalism of avant-garde auteurship with punksploitation's distinctive taste for the carnivalesque, the camp and the mischievously tongue-in-cheek.

Notes

1   R. Sabin, 'Introduction', in R. Sabin (ed.), *Punk Rock: So What?: The Cultural Legacy of Punk* (London: Routledge, 1999), p. 5.
2   *Ibid.*
3   See R. Bestley and A. Ogg, *The Art of Punk* (London: Omnibus Press, 2012); J. Kugelberg and J. Savage (eds), *Punk: An Aesthetic* (New York: Rizzoli, 2012); and M. Sladen and A. Yedgar (eds), *Panic Attack!: Art in the Punk Years* (London: Merrell, 2007).
4   K. Donnelly, 'British Punk Films: Rebellion into Money, Nihilism into Innovation', *Journal of Popular British Cinema*, 1 (1998), 111–12.
5   J. Hoberman and Jonathan Rosenbaum, *Midnight Movies* (New York: Harper & Row, 1983).
6   Z. Carlson and B. Connolly, *Destroy All Movies!!: The Complete Guide to Punks on Film* (Seattle, WA: Fantagraphic, 2010).
7   D. Laderman, *Punk Slash! Musicals: Tracking Slip-Sync on Film* (Austin, TX: University of Texas Press, 2010).
8   J. Sargeant, *Deathtripping: The Cinema of Transgression* (Creation, London, 1999). With Chris Barber, Sargeant also collects a diverse body of writing dealing with punk-related films in *No Focus: Punk on Film* (London: Headpress, 2006).
9   N. Rombes (ed.), *New Punk Cinema* (Edinburgh: Edinburgh University Press, 2005); S. Thompson, 'Punk Cinema', *Cinema Journal*, 43:2 (2004), 47–66; and *Punk Productions: Unfinished Business* (New York: State University of New York Press, 2004); and 'Punk Cinema', in Rombes (ed.), *New Punk Cinema*, pp. 21–38.
10 Thompson, 'Punk Cinema' (2004), 47.
11 Thompson, *Punk Productions*, p. 25.
12 Thompson, 'Punk Cinema' (2004), p. 51.
13 The title was taken from Richard Hell's proto-punk anthem and was graphically represented in the film's credits as *The Generation*).
14 Laderman, *Punk Slash!*, p. 34.
15 According to Letts, the film could not be distributed due to a legal injunction from Malcolm McLaren, the Sex Pistols' manager, who was then preparing his own punk movie, *The Great Rock 'n' Roll Swindle*. See D. Letts (with D. Nobakht), *Culture Clash: Dread Meets Punk Rockers* (London: SAF, 2007), p. 107.
16 *Ibid.*

17 Thompson, 'Punk Cinema' (2004), p. 51.

18 R. Barthes (trans. R. Miller), *S/Z* (New York: Hill and Wang, 1974), p. 4.

19 Thompson, 'Punk Cinema', 51.

20 Letts, *Culture Clash*, p. 105.

21 Donnelly, 'British Punk Films', 105.

22 Alison Pearlman suggests the term was derived from 'New York New Wave', a 1981 exhibition curated by Diego Cortez that featured work by artists such as Keith Haring, Robert Mapplethorpe and Jean Michel Basquiat. See A. Pearlman, *Unpackaging Art of the 1980s* (Chicago: University of Chicago Press, 2003), p. 188.

23 For accounts of the No Wave scene and its subsequent influence, see P. Court, *New York Noise: Art and Music from the New York Underground 1978–88* (London: Soul Jazz, 2007); M. Masters and R. Young, *No Wave* (London: Black Dog, 2007); and T. Moore and B. Coley, *No Wave: Post-punk, Underground, New York, 1976–80* (New York: Abrams Image, 2008).

24 There are some similarities with the agitprop films produced at roughly the same time by Crass, Britain's post-punk, anarchist collective. In short films such as *Autopsy* and *Choosing Death*, Crass filmmaker Mick Duffield used jump-cuts and collage/montage techniques to confront audiences with a view of modern society's barbarism and cruelty.

25 A franchise of six *New Wave Hookers* 'follow-ups' (along with a 'remake') came later – though only *New Wave Hookers 2* was directed by Dark, and (to my eye) the hookers in the sequels do not seem especially 'new wave'.

26 D. Jarman (ed. S. Allen), *Dancing Ledge* (London: Quartet, 1984), p. 176.

27 J. Savage, *England's Dreaming: Sex Pistols and Punk Rock* (London: Faber & Faber, 1991), p. 337.

28 The T-shirt's print was a rambling 'open letter' to Jarman denouncing his picture as 'the most boring and therefore disgusting film I had ever seen'. An example of the shirt (incorrectly dated as 1976) is held in the V&A collections and can be seen online at http://collections.vam.ac.uk/item/O68609/top-mclaren-malcolm/.

29 C. Barber, 'No Future Now: Derek Jarman', in Barber and Sargeant (eds), *No Focus*, p. 52.

30 Büld also directed *Brennende Langeweile* (aka *Bored Teenagers*, 1979) for the West German TV station, ZDF. The semi-narrative film follows two young fans who accompany British punk band The Adverts on a German tour.

31 Savage, *England's Dreaming*, p. 519.

32 P. Kiszely, 'First Wave on Film: Ray Gange, *Rude Boy* and *The Great Rock 'n' Roll Swindle*', *Punk and Post-Punk*, 1:2 (2012), 193.

33 Thompson, 'Punk Cinema', 55.

34 *Ibid.*, 54.

35 The Clash themselves quickly disowned *Rude Boy*. The reasons remain unclear, but explanations suggested include contractual disputes, the band's unhappiness with the film's technical standards and their possible desire to distance themselves from

the overtly 'political' facets of their early career. See M. Gray, *Last Gang in Town: The Story and Myth of The Clash* (London: Fourth Estate, 1995), pp. 342–4.

36   Carlson and Connolly, *Destroy All Movies!!*, p. 326.

37   E. Schaefer, '*Bold! Daring! Shocking! True!*': *A History of Exploitation Films, 1919–59* (Durham, NC: Duke University Press, 1999), p. 5.

38   Accounts of the film's gestation and development can be found in J. McDonough, *Big Bosoms and Square Jaws: The Biography of Russ Meyer* (London: Vintage, 2006), pp. 321–7; and Savage, *England's Dreaming*, pp. 379–80, 523–7.

39   McLaren returned to the theme in *The Ghosts of Oxford Street*, a film he directed for Channel 4 in 1991.

40   Cited in D. McGillivary, 'Twenty-Five Years On: Julien Temple and *The Great Rock 'n' Roll Swindle*', in Barber and Sargeant (eds), *No Focus*, p. 18.

41   Cited in McDonough, *Big Bosoms*, p. 323.

42   Cited in McGillivary, 'Twenty-Five Years On', p. 20.

43   See J. Docker, *Postmodernism and Popular Culture: A Cultural History* (Cambridge: Cambridge University Press, 1994); J. Fiske, *Understanding the Popular* (Boston: Unwin Hyman, 1989); R. Stam, *Subversive Pleasures: Bakhtin, Cultural Criticism, and Film* (Baltimore, MD: Johns Hopkins University Press, 1992).

44   Schaefer, '*Bold! Daring! Shocking! True!*', pp. 122, 134.

45   N. Nehring, *Flowers in the Dustbin: Culture, Anarchy, and Postwar England* (Ann Arbor, MI: University of Michigan Press, 1993), p. 318; and *Popular Music, Gender and Postmodernism: Anger is an Energy* (London: Sage, 1977), p. 175.

46   Cited in Carlson and Connolly, *Destroy All Movies!!*, p. 444.

47   Kowalski continued his filmmaking associations with punk, later directing documentaries based on the lives of Johnny Thunders and Dee Dee Ramone – respectively, *Born to Lose: The Last Rock and Roll Movie* (1999) and *Hey! Is Dee Dee Home?* (2002).

48   Cited in C. Koetting, *Mind Warp!: The Fantastic True Story of Roger Corman's New World Pictures* (Bristol: Hemlock, 2009), p. 164.

49   S. Sontag, 'Notes on "Camp"', in F. Cleto (ed.), *Camp: Queer Aesthetics and the Performing Subject* (Edinburgh: Edinburgh University Press, 1999), p. 59.

50   F. Cleto, 'Introduction: Queering the Camp', in Cleto (ed.), *Camp*, p. 10.

51   *Ibid.*, p. 32.

52   Hoberman and Rosenbaum, *Midnight Movies*, pp. 275–6.

53   The same is also true of the stage and screen productions of Jim Sharman and Richard O'Brien's *The Rocky Horror Picture Show* (1975).

54   Donnelly, 'British Punk Films', 110.

55   C. Monk, '"Now What Are We Going to Call You? Scum! ... Scum! That's Commercial! It's All They Deserve!": *Jubilee*, Punk and British Film in the Late 1970s', in R. Shail (ed.), *Seventies British Cinema* (London: BFI/Palgrave MacMillan, 2008), p. 87.

56   In the audio commentary to the film's DVD release, director Moyle reveals that the film's subtle queer subtext was originally more overt but was downplayed at the

insistence of producer Robert Stigwood (an Australian showbiz mogul and manager of the Bee Gees).

57 See N. Palmer, 'The Disapperarance and Re-Emergence of *Ladies and Gentlemen: The Fabulous Stains*', in Barber and Sargeant (eds), *No Focus*, pp. 217–24.

58 Laderman, *Punk Slash!*, p. 96.

59 *Ibid.*, pp. 102–3.

60 C. Barber, 'Punksploitation', in Barber and Sargeant (eds), *No Focus*, p. 203.

61 Barber, 'Punksploitation', pp. 215–16.

62 N. Rombes, 'Introduction', in Rombes (ed.), *New Punk Cinema*, p. 3.

63 For an account of the Dogma 95 movement and its relationship with 'new punk cinema', see S. Chaudhuri, 'Dogma Brothers: Lars von Trier and Thomas Vinterberg', in Rombes (ed.), *New Punk Cinema*, pp. 153–67.

64 Rombes, 'Introduction', p. 12.

65 N. Rombes, 'Sincerity and Irony', in Rombes (ed.), *New Punk Cinema*, p. 75.

12

'Punk belongs to the punx, not business men!': British DIY punk as a form of cultural resistance

MICHELLE LIPTROT

At the start of the British punk phenomenon, the journalist John Collis wrote 'punk rock is designed simply to make money'.[1] Thirty-six years on there seems to have been some accuracy in Collis's prediction. For example, the construction and commodification that was integral to punk from the beginning can be illustrated by the fact that Malcolm McLaren put together his 'punk project' in the form of the London band, the Sex Pistols.[2] McLaren's commercial intention was realised when the Sex Pistols signed to EMI, shortly after certain members brought punk to the nation's attention by swearing on national television.[3] The Sex Pistols were also central in the construction and commodification of punk style by wearing Vivienne Westwood's clothing designs, which could be purchased at 'Sex', the famous King's Road shop she established with McLaren.[4] The commercial viability of 1970s punk (or, to be precise, its nostalgia market) was more recently demonstrated in 1996 when, eighteen years after they split, the Sex Pistols, reformed for a 'blatant cash grab' tour.[5] Moreover, the celebrity status of the band's front man, John Lydon (otherwise known as 'Johnny Rotten') was made apparent in 2006, when he featured in the reality television show 'I'm a Celebrity, Get Me Out of Here!' and, two years later, when he was the central character in a television advertisement for Country Life butter.

Punk's presence in large-scale, mainstream commerce is, however, only part of the punk story. As Roger Sabin argues, the 'orthodox' way that punk has previously been examined, particularly with the focus on the Sex Pistols and London, is problematic because it leaves a part of punk's history out of the picture; specifically, that 'part of the punk tradition that was never fully co-opted ... and which is still thriving today'.[6] Part of this 'punk tradition' includes contemporary DIY punk, the focus of this chapter.

Contemporary DIY punk, what I prefer to call a subcultural movement, is a relatively autonomous form of punk within the wider, global punk subculture. This subcultural movement has its origins in the Do-it-Yourself (DIY) self-production ethic of 1970s punk, whereby participants followed in the DIY tradition of jazz, skiffle and the sixties counter-culture to produce their own music, visual style and media (in the form of fanzines).[7] Another important aspect of the DIY ethic in punk was that bands were (and remain) audience members, underlining punk's participatory nature and conveying a sense of egalitarianism. This DIY ethic was developed during the 1980s by British anarcho and American hardcore punk, both of which placed greater emphasis on DIY activities and collectivism – as I will show these features have remained to be fundamental and interconnected aspects of contemporary DIY punk. This chapter seeks to understand why participants value the DIY ethic and how this ethic provides DIY punk with 'relative' autonomy from both large- and small-scale punk commerce. I emphasise that DIY punk is 'relatively' autonomous because it is neither entirely void of commerce nor completely autonomous. As David Hesmondhalgh argues: 'commodification and culture [are] entwined. ... Complete autonomy is impossible, but it is a goal towards which many ... aspire'.[8] In line with DIY punk's relatively autonomous status, I aim to explain why DIY activities should be seen as a form of cultural resistance. Although DIY punk exists on a global scale, I will consider only the contemporary subcultural movement in Britain.

Subcultural movement

In describing contemporary DIY punk as a subcultural movement, I follow George McKay, who refers to punk as being part of a tradition of subcultural movements that together form a wider, counter-cultural movement; as he puts it: 'cultures of resistance feed the culture of resistance'.[9] Similar to McKay, I will argue that DIY punk should be viewed as a movement that is connected to a broader DIY cultural movement. Another reason why I refer to DIY punk as a subcultural movement is that my wider research shows that it reflects certain features that are consistent with both a 'subculture' (it has 'distinction', 'consistency', and 'counter-hegemonic resistance') and a new social 'movement'

(NSM) (it also has 'horizontal organisation', 'heterogeneity and unity' and 'cultural resistance').[10]

My argument is partly influenced by classic subcultural theory, originating at the University of Birmingham's Centre for Contemporary Cultural Studies (CCCS). More specifically, I adhere to the CCCS's view that subcultures have 'a clear, coherent identity' and reflect counter-hegemonic resistance to the dominant 'mainstream' culture.[11] While the CCCS's work is generally viewed as having little bearing on the fluid, ephemeral, classless groupings that are seen to characterise late modern society, Paul Hodkinson found that contemporary goth 'was characterised by a set of values and tastes which, although diverse and changeable, were sufficiently distinctive and consistent' to justify the phrase 'goth subculture'.[12] This view, that a subculture can reflect distinctiveness and consistency, is central to my own work, where I found that the DIY ethic, present in 1970s punk, persisted in contemporary DIY punk. Where distinction is concerned, I found that participants see DIY activities as providing the subcultural movement with relative autonomy from both large- and small-scale punk commerce, and more generally from the mainstream. More specifically, I argue these DIY activities should be seen as counter-hegemonic.

Antonio Gramsci's concept of 'counter-hegemonic resistance' was adopted by the CCCS to describe how post-war subcultures resisted dominant cultural values through particular forms of behaviour and spectacular visual styles.[13] Dick Hebdige, for example, draws on the concept of 'bricolage' to explain how punk 'bricoleurs' would adapt existing items to 'generate new meanings'; in this case, a subverted statement of '(un)fashion'.[14] However, the CCCS saw the resistant aspects of subcultures (their style and music) as short-lived because they were eventually 'incorporated' into the dominant 'mainstream' culture.

Jason Toynbee more recently draws on Gramsci's theory of cultural hegemony. In his case, to explain 'mainstreaming' as a hegemonic process whereby music cultures move from a relatively obscure, marginal status to one of global recognition.[15] Toynbee has argued that for mainstreaming [and hegemony] to occur there must be an 'alliance' between a 'low-other' music and the mainstream. He also argues (along the same lines as Gramsci) that where those involved in the 'low-other' music oppose the idea of their music becoming part of the mainstream, it is '*anti*-hegemonic' (original emphasis).[16] As already indicated, in the mid-1970s punk established an alliance with the mainstream market. However, alongside these forms of punk commerce there emerged a relatively autonomous DIY punk commerce that came to use the DIY ethic on principle. Using the DIY ethic in this principled way indicates an oppositional stance to the large-scale, commercial market, evoking what Pierre Bourdieu refers to as an 'economic world reversed ... an upside-down economic world', and thereby resisting the hegemonic process of 'mainstreaming'.[17]

While, like Toynbee, I follow the CCCS commitment to Gramsci's notion of counter-hegemonic practices, I will demonstrate how this 'framework of resistance ... [can] be stretched to encompass new actors and spaces from which counterhegemonic consciousness is expressed'.[18] NSM theory can accommodate the idea that counter-hegemonic consciousness can be expressed culturally through DIY activities (in DIY punk this includes participants themselves being responsible for the production and selling of its music, events, artwork and media), and through the lifestyles of its participants. In other words, DIY culture can be seen to 'challenge the logic of complex systems on cultural grounds' whereby 'resistance or opposition is sewn into the very fabric of daily life'.[19] That is, DIY punk should be seen as a form of 'cultural resistance' in that, through its DIY activities, the subcultural movement reflects an oppositional, counter-hegemonic stance to large-scale commerce.

The anti-capitalist element to this cultural resistance is reflected by the punk slogan 'Punk Belongs to the Punx, Not Businessmen'.[20] Likewise, Stephen Duncombe's description of fanzine producers is pertinent because fanzines (zines) are an integral part of DIY punk: 'defining themselves against a society predicated on consumption, zinesters privilege the ethic of DIY, do-it-yourself: make your own culture and stop consuming that what is made for you. ... Zinesters consider what they do as an alternative to and strike against commercial culture and consumer capitalism'.[21] To reiterate, though, DIY culture 'strikes against consumer capitalism' on a cultural level, whereby a cultural space that is alternative to large-scale mainstream commerce is created.[22] The idea that DIY cultural spaces are oppositional is also suggested by Paul Chatterton and Stuart Hodkinson in their depiction of DIY culture as providing 'places of creativity and experimentation where the colonising, dehumanising and exploitative logic of capitalism is actively resisted by people trying to live and relate to each other as equals'.[23] The latter part of this comment again emphasises the cultural level of this resistance. It also highlights the collective nature of DIY culture. As with an NSM, collectivism in DIY punk is reflected in its non-hierarchal horizontal networks (which in DIY punk include band members, gig organisers, distributors, record label owners, and zine producers).

DIY is an ambiguous concept, which comprises various positions on a spectrum ranging from those committed to non-profit-making to those who aspire to receiving financial reward. Although, as I have argued, DIY punk is consistent with the notion of the 'economic world reversed', the motivations and aspirations of individual performers and organisers confound any neat packaging of DIY as a category and, consequently, any attempt to depict contemporary DIY punk in a rigid manner. This ambiguity is demonstrated by the fact that some DIY punk bands have gone on to achieve success in the commercial mainstream (examples include Green Day and Chumbawamba). The tension, indicated here, between DIY integrity and individual career aspiration is also a feature of the small-scale punk commerce currently known as 'Rebellion' festivals. These festivals (which have been held at the seaside towns of Blackpool and Morecambe in the north-west of England since 1996) were formerly known, respectively, as 'Holidays-in-the-Sun' (HITS) and 'Wasted'. I will use the term 'Wasted' because this is what they were known by when the research was conducted. Although DIY bands perform at these festivals, it is the more commercially-orientated bands that were popular in punk's past (notably during the 1970s and 1980s) that are central. Thus, as Ian Glasper indicates, these festivals meet the punk nostalgia market: 'many of the second wave punk bands have reformed ... as a direct (or at least indirect) result of the Holidays-in-the-Sun festivals, either having been asked to play or encouraged by the new-found interest in their music'.[24]

While organised by participants themselves Wasted festivals generate financial rewards for both organisers and some performers.[25] Further, although these bands do not have the same level of popularity or receive the same financial reward as those that are a part of large-scale commerce, they operate in much the same way (in that they receive financial reward, and often work with more formal management, using roadies), albeit on a much smaller scale. They are also often attached to an independent label which is sometimes (but not always) connected to a major.

Despite the interconnections between DIY and large-scale and small-scale punk commerce, its commerce is distinct because it is typically motivated by personal integrity rather than profit. It is by participants using the DIY ethic to produce their own culture that contemporary DIY punk has maintained relative autonomy from these other forms of punk commerce. As already argued, DIY punk also reflects anti-large-scale commerce sentiments and should, therefore, be viewed as a form of cultural resistance that is fundamentally counter-hegemonic.

My research

My interest in researching DIY punk stems from my lengthy personal involvement with the subcultural movement. My mainly ethnographic research involved the collection of data over a two-and-a-half-year period, from September 2004 to May 2007. During this time, I interviewed forty-three current participants, plus had informal conversations and made observations. Interviewees ranged in age from fifteen to forty-five years, and were mostly (two-thirds) white males. There was also a quantitative element to my research in the form of a questionnaire, which produced 205 responses (47 female and 158 male). Survey respondents ranged in age from fifteen to fifty, but most (45 per cent) were aged thirty to thirty-nine years. I distributed the questionnaire in person, by post, by email, and through a webpage. While I took measures to distribute the questionnaires nationally, it was inevitable that the majority of the returns would come from the north-west, north-east, and the Midlands because this is where I most frequently attended gigs. To examine the diverse yet unified nature of DIY punk, data was collected at a range of DIY and small-scale punk gigs and festivals. This also provided insight into how DIY and small-scale commerce intersect. My original intention to have an equal number of female and male respondents was abandoned due to having a lack of control over the distribution of the survey (for example, some respondents sent the questionnaire on to their own contacts and it was even posted on a DIY punk website without my prior knowledge). To protect the identities of those involved, survey respondents were assigned a numerical code preceded by a capital 'R', and interviewees were provided with a pseudonym.

Laying the foundations of DIY punk: a historical overview

In 1976 punk was a newly emerging music culture that went largely unreported by the mainstream media; in fact, as Jon Savage reports 'at the end of 1976, the mainstream media were closed to punk'.[26] The absence of punk music in the media motivated Mark Perry to produce Britain's first punk fanzine, *Sniffin' Glue*. Perry describes how, by using an old typewriter and a black felt-tip pen, the fanzine had 'the same "back to basics" approach as the music that I was to feature … it put across the punk message perfectly. It celebrated the DIY ethic'.[27] So, although punk's DIY approach did not necessarily stem from choice but necessity, those involved saw this approach to be compatible with punk culture.

David Simonelli explains that the typical 1970s punk fanzine 'emphasised community' and 'enhanced the punk reader's sense that it was "us vs them"', and the constant attack on punk by the mainstream media contributed to this attitude as well'.[28] This 'constant attack', due to the notoriety that became attached to punk music and culture after the Sex Pistols' swearing on television, meant that the majority of British punk bands found it difficult to access the mainstream market. DIY principles, once again, proved to be the solution.

As the DIY ethos in punk escalated, hundreds of punk bands went forth to produce their music themselves or turned to one of the independent labels that mushroomed in the wake of punk.[29] As David Hesmondhalgh explains, independent record companies 'challenge[d] previously existing structures of musical production and distribution [in that they were] independent of the "major", vertically integrated corporations'.[30] The less formal, non-hierarchal way that independent labels conducted their business, meant they were considered as being egalitarian compared to what might have been seen as the exploitative methods of the corporate labels. Thus the principles by which the independent label operated were more in keeping with the sense of creative freedom that was integral to the DIY ethic; therefore a degree of integrity could be retained by those punk bands to whom it mattered.[31]

1978 is often seen as marking the demise of punk both in the commercial mainstream and in the independent sector.[32] However, punks throughout Britain had been engaging in such DIY activities as music-making, organising gigs, producing fanzines, making their own clothing and, importantly, forming a sense of shared identity. Thus a whole subcultural DIY movement began to mobilise around punk music.

From the participants who would take punk forward there emerged a 'new', or second, wave of punk.[33] Existing as an alternative to the fashion-centred punk led by the Sex Pistols, second-wave punk later split into what became recognised as 'street punk' and a more politicised 'anarcho-punk', instigated by the band and collective, Crass. While both styles of second-wave punk were important to helping maintain the interest of some existing participants and in attracting a new generation of young people to punk, it was Crass and anarcho-punk that, by building on the remnants of DIY punk, would lay the foundations for the contemporary DIY punk subcultural movement in Britain.

Crass's DIY activities included self-produced pamphlets, artwork, film, poetry and music.[34] As with earlier punk bands, it was necessity that motivated Crass to establish their own record label, Crass Records (later changed to Corpus Christi). In Crass's case, this followed a disagreement with the independent label, Small Wonder, who refused to include their blasphemous track 'Reality Asylum'.[35] Crass went on to release the music of like-minded, anarchist-orientated bands such as Conflict, Flux of Pink Indians and Poison Girls. The DIY methods of Crass's self-releases were evident in their simple stencilling techniques, used on record covers, and the fact that record covers themselves were constructed from folded, A3 pieces of paper. In refusing to accept what they saw as exploitative methods employed by large-scale music companies, many of Crass's releases stated 'pay no more than' followed by a recommended price. Their introduction of this 'pay no more than' ethos to punk was important because it communicated in a simplistic way that records could be produced and sold for much less than the prices charged at high street record shops. Other punk bands followed Crass's example and the 'pay no more than' slogan and ethos became common practice of DIY and independent punk releases.[36]

Crass's emphasis on self-production and collectivism was also a feature of early American hardcore punk, which emerged in San Francisco in the late 1970s. Anarcho and hardcore punk were (and remain) connected by their similar anarchist stance. Like Crass, some hardcore bands set up their own labels (the three most recognised are The Dead Kennedys' Alternative Tentacles, Black Flag's SST, and Ian McKaye's (of Minor Threat) Dischord); moreover, in keeping with the DIY ethos, their products were and, on the whole, remain absent of barcodes; they were also often anti-copyright and distributed via local networks of independent shops and individual distributions. Importantly, 'the members of the networks worked hard, not with financial motivations but with a common belief in the integrity of the networks and a common opposition to the mainstream industry'.[37]

Aside from independent record shops, the networks also involved DIY distributors (who would 'trade' goods such as music and fanzines with each other), and bands themselves who, in exchange for a blank cassette and a 'stamped addressed envelope', would make a copy of their music at no additional cost. From this idea a global punk cassette-trading culture emerged, whereby participants would exchange punk music recorded onto cassettes (in fact, it became standard practice to have a listing of the records and cassettes available for copying). This practice was an important part of DIY punk culture because not only did it contribute to the dissemination of DIY punk music globally but it also helped nurture a sense of collectivism and of a global DIY punk subcultural movement that has continued to this day.

Contemporary DIY punk: cultural resistance through lifestyle, music and media

Those involved in the contemporary DIY punk subcultural movement place much value on the DIY ethos because they see it as providing the subcultural movement, and those who participate in it, with a sense of autonomy. This was something expressed by a survey respondent: 'The DIY underground is a place where you can make your ideas a reality, and where you can take some control back of your life' (R173, male, age 39). Similarly, another survey respondent said: 'DIY sums up my attitude to life – we shouldn't let some distant authority figure run our lives when normal people can organise to run their own lives non-hierarchically so much better' (R104, female, age 29). These comments reflect the self-empowering aspect of DIY punk. In addition, the second comment draws attention to the non-hierarchal way that the subcultural movement is seen by participants to operate. This is not to say that DIY punk is entirely void of hierarchy. On the contrary, hierarchy exists in various ways including age, length of participation, and gender.[38]

The DIY aspect of punk was seen to be the 'essence' (R103, male, age 29) of the subcultural movement because it gave punk its sense of autonomy and resistance to the mainstream and more commercial forms of punk. As this participant explained: 'I have always seen DIY as an essential part of punk' (R131, female, age 38). This view was shared by another, Mick, saying that DIY was one of

> the main things to come out of punk … and that continues to this day …
> anyone can still form a band, anyone can start a website, anyone can put
> on shows, anyone can use the internet to get in touch on a worldwide scale
> outside the entertainment industries' idea of what we should listen to or what
> we should watch and this still really thrills me and still really inspires me.
> (Male, age 40+, email communication)

This comment points to how the participatory nature of 1970s punk has persisted in contemporary DIY punk and still continues to demonstrate how rather than simply consuming goods, those involved in the subcultural movement are active in its production. A major part of the DIY ethos, then, is that participants have the opportunity to be directly involved in producing the culture, which, in turn, gives them a sense of being part of a collective. This was a particularly important aspect for Rob: 'There is a generous, caring thing going on. The whole process of releasing music, producing fanzines and so on involves the creation of relationships and friendships. I do it because it's caring, ethical' (Male, age 40). This comment again emphasises that there is 'a sense of co-operation rather than competition' (R149, male, age 37) between participants and reiterates the view of Chatterton and Hodkinson, mentioned previously, of DIY culture involving 'people trying to live and relate to each other as equals'.[39]

Rob's comment above shows how the musical and social aspects of punk intersect in its underlying philosophy. In other words, for its participants punk is 'a way of thinking' (R81, male, age 38) that affects their daily lives. This was also true of much younger participants. Thus, an eighteen year-old male gig organiser, who had been involved in punk for two years, talked passionately about 'bands that I feel need to be heard that I want to help' (R1). His ability to organise gigs at such an age points to the accessibility of DIY punk, which, as a male participant recognised is integral to the DIY ethic: 'Our culture is more accessible to those who want to contribute/get involved (The *True* punk ethic!)' (R149, age 37, respondent's emphasis). This accessibility, in turn, derives from DIY punk's democratic nature, which also explains the fact that its participants are its performers, organisers, distributors and advisers too.

Participants saw DIY music-making as autonomous because the artists have full creative control; they, rather than a record company, decide if and when to release a recording: 'we don't have to deal with capitalist scum for bands to make music – no parasite managers, or major blood sucking, control-ling bastards' (R149, male, age 37). This comment reiterates that participants see DIY punk commerce as being distinct from both large-scale and small-scale punk commerce. DIY punk bands see themselves as self-reliant in the sense that they manage and promote themselves as well as relying on word-of-mouth and zine reviews. However, there is a contradiction here in that DIY punk bands also receive promotion through various mainstream social networks, such as Facebook, or even, as was the case of a DIY punk gig promoter in Manchester, through an advertisement in mainstream rock magazine *Kerrang*.

In keeping with the DIY ethic, entry to DIY punk gigs is inexpensive (sometimes free), thus making DIY punk an especially accessible form of music. In addition to seeing bands perform and meeting up with other punks, live music events were also considered important places for the buying and selling (or, as is sometimes the case, the trading or even bartering) of recorded music and related merchandise (such as band T-shirts and so on), or for ob-taining and distributing political and music-related information. The collective aspect of the DIY ethic is reflected in how DIY distributors, bands and zine producers come together in the selling and trading of goods at gigs. This col-lectivism is also demonstrated by the fact that consuming DIY-produced goods was seen as more than simply buying material items; it was also seen as a way of supporting DIY producers and, in turn, as contributing to the continuity of the subcultural movement.

As indicated previously, DIY punk is not devoid of commercialism, but rather its commerce is distinct from more commercially orientated forms; notably because it is typically motivated by personal integrity rather than profit. During my fieldwork I observed various examples where 'bricolage', indicated earlier as a long-standing practice in punk, was used in DIY punk commerce. For example, I met Steph (male, age 37) selling T-shirts and patches at a 'stall' at a DIY punk festival. Steph explained that he worked at a printing company and that at the end of the day, when the ink was scraped from the printing screen, instead of throwing it in the bin he collected and reused the ink to print his own designs on T-shirts and patches. As he said: 'T-shirts are art, you know, you can own it and make a couple of quid'. As this example suggests, then, those involved in DIY punk are not necessarily against the idea of making a small profit as long as the reasoning behind it is not what participants see as exploitative.

A second example occurred at an 'all-dayer' in a Cumbrian town, which had been organised by 40 year-old Karl. There was a vegetarian barbecue and Karl had volunteered to cook. During a quiet moment he explained that the food was not free but was being sold at a reasonable price (as I recall, it was £1 for a burger), which was necessary to generate 'money to pay the bands … playing tonight. … . We don't make any money. We're non-profit making and all the money we make goes straight back to the bands or repairing the equipment'. A similar story came from Rob, already mentioned, who had run a DIY record label for fourteen years. He explained: 'I haven't made any [profit] so far. I've made losses. I made a £1,000 loss on [a spoken word] event and a loss on the summer festival. Any money I may have left over from my personal income is ploughed back into events I organise' (Male, age 40).

Rob's comment about money being 'ploughed back' into the project reiterates the point made by Karl above, that DIY punk is motivated by something other than profit. However, Rob adding he has not made profit 'so far' suggests that, similar to Steph above, he is not opposed to his DIY activities generating personal profit. The tension between DIY integrity and the commercial goals of individual participants is highlighted in this comment by a survey respondent:

> What I don't agree with is so called DIY shows where promoters bang on about bands playing for free etc and then going off down the road with the night's takings … If you're going to promote the DIY side of things, do it right and for the right reasons. (R82, male, 38 years)

This example, demonstrating that some participants are motivated by individualistic rather than collective goals, points to the inconsistent way that DIY principles are used in DIY punk. It also illustrates that DIY punk is not entirely free from entrepreneurism.

Despite there being inconsistencies in the motivations and goals of some participants, I see them as involved in 'restricted production, in which producers provide for other producers and the field of large-scale production … is symbolically excluded and discredited'.[40] Punks use a variety of methods to 'symbolically exclude and discredit' large-scale media and commerce including slogans on clothing and language and artwork in zines. However, participants saw DIY activities as extending beyond symbolism in that they 'stop big money companies cashing in on the scene' (R62, female, age 33), avoiding 'corrupt[ion] by money grabbing capitalists' (Ade, male, age 39).

Rob also saw DIY activities as being about creating an 'alternative cultural experience' that, in turn, reflects the type of 'cultural politics' reflected by NSMs.[41] Rob explained it in terms of

> the human aspect of achieving things autonomously. I review [CDs] in the fanzine, I also give [them] away to people free of charge. In doing this I'm helping to create an alternative space, an alternative way of living ... The whole thing about what is involved in living by the punk ethic, zines etc, many punks wouldn't regard as political but it is. (Male, age 40)

This comment suggests that some participants recognise the DIY ethic as providing the basis for cultural resistance. It also shows that DIY punk achieves this through 'submerged networks' (including zines, bands, reviewers, and the practice of trading and giving away items for free) and its non-hierarchal 'horizontal organisation.'[42]

It is perhaps due to the subcultural movement's horizontal organisation (illustrated by its participatory nature and anti-hierarchal stance) that 'the scene is full of bands that make no money, have no agents, and make music for the hell of it rather than with dreams of fame and fortune' (R174, male, age 32). It is because of this that punk bands with commercial aspirations are frequently received with suspicion.

During the 1990s two former DIY punk bands made the transition to large-scale mainstream commerce. Both the American band Green Day and the English band Chumbawamba were criticised by some participants because they had seemingly abandoned their DIY punk integrity. However, such criticism was not consistently made, in that there was a hint of respect for Green Day, whereas Chumbawamba received little but disapproval. For example, although Steph recognised that '[Green Day's] rebellion is a product like form, like Coca Cola', he also said: 'I think it's cool if Green Day, giving up their jobs, their position. I'm quite happy for them. But they kinda released Pandora's box ... They make it ok to be punk. You know all these kids out on the streets ... And I'm a grumpy old man' [laughs] (male, age 37).

Chumbawamba, in contrast, were seen more simply to have sold out.[43] In 1997 the band signed to corporate EMI and had chart success with 'Tubthumping' (1997).[44] There is some irony here, in that this was a band that, in the late 1980s, had been involved in a compilation album entitled *Fuck EMI*.[45] It is unsurprising, then, that some participants perceived them as having lost their integrity and betrayed DIY punk. In response to Chumbawamba's decision to become commercial, a compilation of DIY punk bands was released entitled *Bare Faced Hypocrisy Sells Records*.[46] The following year staunch anarcho-punk band Oi Polloi released the song 'Sell Out' through DIY channels, the reasons for which they explained: 'One minute it's "D.I.Y., D.I.Y.", attacking big businesses in their excellent booklet "Dirty Fingers in Dirty Pies" and Danbert appearing on an LP entitled "Fuck EMI", the next someone waves a cheque book and Hey Presto! – they're actually on EMI!'.[47]

Despite these general criticisms directed at Chumbawamba, one long-standing participant pointed to the fact that the band's success in the mainstream had provided the members with the opportunity to financially assist anarchist projects, such as the setting-up of a rehearsal/recording studio at Bradford's anarchist cooperative '1 in 12 club'.[48] It appears, though, that participants generally choose to discount positive contributions made by bands that have 'sold out'. This is a point highlighted in Chumbawamba's self-produced documentary 'Well Done. Now Sod Off', in which a member of the band reads aloud letters of condemnation from punks who see the band as having sold out on their DIY credentials.[49] The band responds to what is indicated as the rigidity of DIY punk, by explaining their move to the mainstream as providing them with an opportunity to introduce left-wing, anarchist politics to the mainstream; a feat that would have been unachievable had they remained within the insular confines of DIY punk.[50]

Participants also distinguished DIY punk from the small-scale punk festivals known as Wasted. For example, a finding from my survey shows the Wasted festival was considered acceptable 'if it's treated as a weekend out nostalgia thing but it ain't the true face of punk rock by a long shot' (R3, male, age 21). Another individual said that such festivals are 'great fun though not in the true spirit of punk' (R79, male, age 33). These comments show that younger and older individuals shared the opinion that such events were entertaining, but far from being authentic to punk. One reason why this type of punk was not seen as authentic was due to it being centred on reformed bands that performed songs that were popular in the past. In contrast, DIY punk was seen by participants as a progressive and 'evolving' (Andy, male, age 30+) form of punk. Another reason was that festivals like Wasted 'defeat the object of punk as they are based on profit' (R15, female, age 30). Some considered such festivals expensive, and were particularly critical of organisers and well-known bands who, they believed, received huge cash rewards. Karl, mentioned previously as an organiser of DIY gigs, frequents Wasted but feels that 'it shouldn't be for commercial profit … for your own pocket, they should be doing it for the scene only' (male, age 40). Another participant regarded the festivals as 'nothing different to the music biz we're often so critical of' (R8, male, age 37). Sharing this view, another said: 'I don't see it as being any different to [the large-scale festivals of] Donington or Reading' (R104, female, age 29). Even while some recognised that, compared to large-scale festivals, Wasted and similar festivals were 'pretty good value' (R124, female, age 33), they still wanted to distance themselves from the values represented; as this same individual put it, 'they're not for me – punk loses its ethic in a stadium setting'.

I suggested to one of the organisers of Wasted that although the festivals were not on the same economic level as larger, commercial festivals, Wasted was, nevertheless, a commercial venture. I therefore asked about its position in relation to large-scale and DIY punk commerce. She replied: 'I guess we fall somewhere in the middle. There is just [my partner] and myself booking it all, promoting it, sending the flyers, replying to emails from bands, punters and everyone else who emails so we are pretty DIY – we just do it on a bigger scale. We get a little sponsorship along the way which all helps but it's a pretty small affair really' (Anon., age unknown).

Some individuals expressed opposition to this small-scale punk commerce by organising DIY alternatives. In 2002, Leeds punks' picnic was aptly named 'Holidays-in-the-Slums'. The weekend-long event was held at a pub (with the picnic in a park), and focused on performances by DIY bands. Further, money raised was donated to Women's Aid and Rape Crisis.

Taking DIY punk's participatory nature into account, it is unsurprising that participants generally avoid the term 'fan' to describe themselves. As Ant, the producer of an established DIY hardcore punk zine pointed out, it is on the same grounds that fanzines are simply referred to as 'zines': 'the reason 'fan' was dropped from punk zines, is because it implied fan clubs etc and bands being separate or better than fans, and that the word fan implied someone who was simply a fan of a band and nothing else, which goes against the ideals of the diy punk band, where a band is no better or not separate to the audience/ punter' (Male, age 40). Thus, the use of this neologism can itself be seen as a form of cultural resistance.

Despite the presence of e-zines and social networking sites such as Facebook and more specific punk websites (e.g. *Punk and Oi!, Punk77),* the traditional paper zine seems to remain important as an authentic form of punk media. Paper zines are cheap to buy (typically no more than £1) and pro-ducers keep costs low by using DIY principles at various levels. For example, black-and-white print rather than colour, using a photocopier or cheap printer (the ethical dimension of some zine producers, including Ant, is illustrated by them paying for the services of a co-operative printer). Text can be typed or handwritten, or be a combination. Importantly (like DIY music) DIY zines are not subject to censorship laws, thus allowing those who produce them to have full creative power.

Bricolage features in the 'rebellious language' of punk zines, which typically involves 'well-known imagery appropriated from the popular media [being] subverted and assigned new meanings that are understood readily by the readers'.[51] Frequently, these new meanings make fun of or denigrate both individuals and groups, such as royalty (as Triggs notes), the police, government figures and celebrities; in turn, then, DIY punk zines continue in the 1970s punk tradition of reinforcing a sense of 'us vs them' (as mentioned earlier by Simonelli).[52]

Even though the subcultural movement sees itself as being relatively autonomous of the mainstream, when it comes to using mainstream technology punks generally embrace rather than object to it. This leads me to suggest that the most likely reason why a producer would write a zine by hand is to try to create a sense of authenticity (i.e. the emphasis is placed on it being self-produced). For instance, *Attitude Problem*, a DIY hardcore punk zine, is entirely handwritten but its producer is contactable via email.[53] In addition to DIY principles being at the fore of production methods, DIY zines typically emphasise DIY values in their content. For example, *Anarchoi* zine, from Scotland, emphasises its authenticity by stating on its front cover, '100% D.I.Y. Punk Rock'.[54] A similar statement of authenticity is made by the producer of *Hell and Damnation*, which announces in capital letters: 'PUNK BELONGS TO THE PUNK'S [*sic*], NOT THE BUSINESSMEN', before continuing: 'And fuck 'barcodes'! … I only cater for honest non-profit DIY labels, bands and activities … DIY or get fucked off! No compromise!!'.[55]

DIY culture stands as an attractive and potentially profitable niche for the industries that have attempted (and sometimes succeeded) in drawing in (via 'mainstreaming') DIY producers, though this is not to suggest that the producers themselves have no part in this. Having already explored attitudes towards bands that are seen to have sold out, I will now turn to consider how punks (amongst others) resist the 'mainstreaming' of zines.

Stephen Duncombe explains that in 1993, Chris Boarts, editor of American hardcore punk zine *Slug & Lettuce*, reported that she had been contacted by *Elle* magazine who had expressed their interest in receiving a copy of *Slug & Lettuce* to help with an article on fanzines.[56] Boarts is an active participant in US DIY hardcore punk and *Slug & Lettuce* is well known in punk circles internationally. Although the practice of zine production had existed for decades, it suddenly became a potential story to be sold to a large, global readership. Duncombe describes Boarts' confusion at being contacted by *Elle*: 'Like other zinesters, she uses her zine to represent herself and her interests as "other," against the mainstream. Why would a world she's not interested in have any interest in her?'[57]

Duncombe argues that the answer lies in the mainstream consumer industry and that, at the time, the DIY feminist movement 'Riot Grrrl' had reached overground popularity in the USA. This illustrates another example of 'mainstreaming' of what began as a small DIY movement. Although there is no mention of Boarts taking up the request, examining her ideological stance in the wider context of Duncombe's evaluation, it can only be assumed that she declined. However, had Boarts gone ahead with *Elle's* request, it would be highly likely that she would have lost respect from her fellow participants and be condemned for selling out. Boarts' assumed refusal to take part in large-scale commerce is illustrative of how DIY cultures preserve their position in the autonomous field of cultural production and resist the 'mainstreaming' process. It also underlines how zine production is seen as political action, thus reinforcing Duncombe's statement: 'the politics of culture never announce themselves as political … the politics expressed within and through culture become part of us, get under our skin, and become part of our "common sense"'.[58] This is what gives the politics of culture their power.

Conclusion

I have shown that the DIY ethic, present in 1970s punk, is vital in how those involved in contemporary DIY punk authenticate this subcultural movement. These principles are used both on a collective level and individually through lifestyle and in creative expression, which, in turn, results in participants gaining a sense of empowerment and relative autonomy. I have also shown that while continuity is vital to this subcultural movement, those involved view DIY punk as a progressive form of punk that has evolved over thirty-six years. Participants, therefore, distinguish DIY punk from the nostalgia-centred punk commerce, known as Wasted. Although looked on as entertaining, this form of punk commerce is considered irrelevant to punk as an evolving cultural form. Participants were also critical of the entrepreneurism that is attached to Wasted; as shown, however, DIY punk is not absent from entrepreneurism. This contradiction between DIY integrity and the personal aspirations of individual participants is a long-standing one in punk. Despite this contradiction, though, participants not only see DIY practices as central in distinguishing DIY punk from more commercial forms of punk, but also in defining DIY punk as a form of cultural resistance that is fundamentally counter-hegemonic to large-scale mainstream commerce.

Notes

1 J. Collis, 'Media Manipulated', *Time Out* (17 December 1976), p. 13.
2 D. Simonelli, 'Anarchy, Pop and Violence: Punk Rock Subculture and the Rhetoric of Class, 1976–78', *Contemporary British History*, 16:2 (2002), 131.
3 J. Savage, *England's Dreaming: Sex Pistols and Punk Rock* (London: Faber & Faber, 1991), p. 264.
4 This is highlighted in Savage's detailed examination of the Sex Pistols and punk.
5 A. Greene, 'Flashback: Sex Pistols Reunite for "Filthy Lucre" Tour in 1996', *Rolling Stone* (31 January 2013), www.rollingstone.com/music/videos/flashback-sex-pistols-reunite-for-filthy-lucre-tour-in-1996-20130131, accessed May 2013.
6 R. Sabin (ed.), *Punk Rock: So What? The Cultural Legacy of Punk* (London: Routledge, 1999), p. 4.
7 The presence of the DIY ethic in earlier music cultures is discussed by G. McKay, *Senseless Acts of Beauty: Cultures of Resistance Since the Sixties* (London: Verso, 1996); and *Circular Breathing: The Cultural Politics of Jazz in Britain* (Durham, NC: Duke University Press, 2005); J. Street, *Rebel Rock: The Politics of Popular Music* (Oxford: Basil Blackwell, 1986).
8 D. Hesmondhalgh, *The Cultural Industries* (London: Sage, 2013 edn), pp. 410 and 414.
9 McKay, *Senseless Acts of Beauty*, p. 6.
10 M. Liptrot, 'Beyond the Lifespan of a Scab: the Longevity of the DIY Punk Subcultural Movement in Britain', unpublished Ph.D. thesis, University of Bolton, 2012.
11 J. Clarke, S. Hall, T. Jefferson and B. Roberts, 'Subcultures, Cultures and Class', in Stuart Hall and Tony Jefferson (eds), *Resistance through Rituals: Youth Subcultures in Post-War Britain* (London: Hutchinson, 1976), p. 14.
12 P. Hodkinson, *Goth: Identity, Style and Subculture* (Oxford: Berg, 2002), p. 195.
13 A. Gramsci, *Selections from the Prison Notebooks* (New York: International Publishers, 1971); Clarke *et al.*, 'Subcultures, Cultures and Class'; P. E. Willis, *Learning to Labour: How Working-Class Kids Get Working-Class Jobs* (Aldershot: Saxon House, 1977).
14 D. Hebdige, *Subculture: The Meaning of Style* (London: Routledge, 1979), pp. 103 and 107.
15 J. Toynbee 'Mainstreaming, from Hegemonic Centre to Global Networks', in D. Hesmondhalgh and K. Negus (eds), *Popular Music Studies* (London: Arnold, 2002), pp. 149–63.
16 Toynbee, 'Mainstreaming, from Hegemonic Centre to Global Networks', p. 156.
17 P. Bourdieu, *The Field of Cultural Production* (Cambridge: Polity Press, 1993), pp. 39–40. Previous researchers who have also used Bourdieu's notion of an autonomous field of cultural production to explain the cultural space that punk occupies include R. Moore, 'Friends Don't Let Friends Listen to Corporate Rock: Punk as a Field of Cultural Production', *Journal of Contemporary Ethnography*, 36:4 (2007), 438–74; A. O'Connor, *Punk Records and the Struggle for Autonomy* (Plymouth: Lexington Books, 2008).

18 J. H. Mittleman and C. B. N. Chin, 'Conceptualizing Resistance to Globalization', in L. Amoore (ed.), *The Global Resistance Reader* (London: Routledge, 2005), p. 20.

19 A. Melucci, *Nomads of the Present: Social Movements and Individual Needs in Contemporary Society* (London: Hutchinson Radius, 1989), pp. 23 and 71.

20 The slogan originates from the lyrics of the song 'Take Heed' by anarcho-punk band Flux of Pink Indians (Overground, 1997). Although it began as an anarcho-punk slogan, it has been embraced more generally by those involved in DIY punk.

21 S. Duncombe, *Notes from the Underground: Zines and the Politics of Alternative Culture* (London: Verso, 1997), pp. 2–3.

22 See A. Spencer, *DIY: The Rise of Lo-Fi Culture* (London: Marion Boyars, 2008), p. 11.

23 P. Chatterton and S. Hodkinson, 'Why we Need Autonomous Spaces in the Fight Against Capitalism', in The Trapese Collective (eds), *Do It Yourself: A Handbook for Changing Our World* (London: Pluto, 2007), p. 201.

24 I. Glasper, *Burning Britain: The History of UK Punk 1980–84* (London: Cherry Red, 2004), p. 396.

25 Several members of DIY punk bands informed me that although they did not receive cash payment in return for performing at Wasted, they did receive free entry to the event.

26 Savage, *England's Dreaming*, p. 279.

27 M. Perry, cited in T. Rawlings (ed.), *Sniffin' Glue: The Essential Punk Accessory* (London: Sanctuary, 2000), pp. 15–16.

28 Simonelli, 'Anarchy, Pop and Violence', 137.

29 The two most notable examples of DIY punk music releases from the late 1970s are *Spiral Scratch* (1977) by Buzzcocks and the Desperate Bicycles' single, *Smokescreen* (1977). These releases are recognised as being particularly inspirational because, not only did these bands finance their recordings themselves, but they also released the singles on their own labels (Buzzcocks on their New Hormones label; the Desperate Bicycles on their Refill label). For a discussion on 1970s independent punk record labels see D. Laing, *One Chord Wonders: Power and Meaning in Punk Rock* (Milton Keynes: Open University Press, 1985).

30 D. Hesmondhalgh, 'Post-Punk's Attempt to Democratise the Music Industry: The Success and Failure of Rough Trade', *Popular Music*, 16:3 (1998), 256.

31 See R. Young, *Rough Trade* (London: Black Dog Publishing, 2006).

32 The 'death' of British punk is discussed by S. Reynolds, *Rip it up and Start Again: Post-punk 1978–84* (London: Faber & Faber, 2006), p. xvii; the decline of punk independents during the late 1970s is indicated in Young's examination of Rough Trade.

33 Savage, *England's Dreaming*, p. 583.

34 See G. Berger, *The Story of Crass* (Oakland, CA: PM Press, 2009); I. Glasper, *The Day the Country Died: A History of Anarcho Punk 1980–1984* (London: Cherry Red, 2006); G. McKay, *Senseless Acts of Beauty*.

35 P. Rimbaud, *Shibboleth: My Revolting Life* (Edinburgh: AK Press, 1998).

36 For example, the independent label 'No Future' declare on the record sleeve of the compilation album, *A Country Fit for Heroes* (1981): 'The material is a good cross selection of what new Punk & Skin bands are doing up and down the country ... O.K. some of them may not be the greatest, but ... hopefully it will give encouragement to those of you that have recently started a band. Finally if you have paid more that £2.25 for this 12" E.P., take it back to the place where you bought it from, get your money back and tell them to stuff it. Post £2.25 to us at the address below and we'll send you one.'

37 T. Gosling, '"Not for Sale": the Underground Network of Anarcho-Punk', in A. Bennett and R. A. Peterson (eds), *Music Scenes: Local, Translocal and Virtual* (Nashville, TN: Vanderbilt University Press, 2004), p. 172.

38 I discovered this in my own research – see Liptrot, 'Beyond the Lifespan of a Scab'.

39 Chatterton and Hodkinson, 'Why we Need Autonomous Spaces in the Fight Against Capitalism', p. 201.

40 Bourdieu, *The Field of Cultural Production*, p. 39.

41 G. Martin, 'Conceptualizing Cultural Politics in Subcultural and Social Movement Studies', *Social Movement Studies*, 1:1 (2002), 73–88.

42 Melucci, *Nomads of the Present*, p. 44.

43 See also Glasper, *The Day the Country Died*.

44 Chumbawamba, 'Tubthumping' (EMI, 1997).

45 Various Artists, *Fuck EMI* (Rugger Bugger, 1989).

46 Various Artists, *Bare Faced Hypocrisy Sells Records* (Ruptured Ambitions, 1998).

47 Oi Polloi, 'Sell Out', on *Fuaim Catha* (Skuld Records, 1999).

48 Personal conversation with a member of the 1 in 12 club (2004).

49 Chumbawamba, *Well Done. Now Sod Off* (Chumbawamba, 2000).

50 This point is demonstrated by footage of Chumbawamba's performance on the David Letterman show, where the lyrics of a song are changed to chant 'Free Mumia Abu-Jamal'. At the time Mumia Abu-Jamal, a political activist, was on death row for allegedly shooting and killing a police officer, but in 2012 ambiguities surrounding evidence led to his sentence being changed to life imprisonment. During my fieldwork, leaflets highlighting the campaign to 'Free Mumia' (see Free Mumia, www.freemumia.com) were distributed at some DIY punk gigs I frequented. While the distribution of such material at gigs is undoubtedly important in raising awareness among punks, Chumbawamba's mainstream status enabled them to reach a much broader range of individuals, globally.

51 T. Triggs, 'Alphabet Soup: Reading British Fanzines', *Visible Language*, 29:1 (1995), 72–87, 85.

52 Triggs, 'Alphabet Soup', 84; Simonelli, 'Anarchy, Pop and Violence', 137.

53 *Attitude Problem* (Leeds, 2003/04), p. 34.

54 *Anarchoi*, 11 (Ayrshire, 2004).

55 C. Astro, 'Editorial', *Hell and Damnation split issue with Ripping Thrash*, 12 (Sheffield: People for Print, 2009).

56 Duncombe, *Notes from the Underground*, p. 131.

57   *Ibid.*
58   *Ibid.,* p. 175.

13

Normality kills: discourses of normality and denormalisation in German punk lyrics

MELANI SCHRÖTER

Punk and normality seem mutually exclusive; whoever is normal cannot be a punk, and whoever is a punk cannot be normal. Debates regarding the demarcation between 'real' and 'fake' punk(s) can be boiled down to a question of true deviation (essentially not normal) versus mere imitation (disguised as not normal). Because punk defies normality, being a punk is not easy. Firstly, denormalisation involves risk, e.g. psychological disintegration, marginalisation, social isolation, detention. Secondly, punks do not live in a normal world in which you can put trust in the calculability of what is to come; punks more likely live in anticipation of catastrophe. Thirdly, punks must fear widening margins of normality and increasing tolerance of deviation/'individuality', both of which pose a threat to punk's identity as 'not normal' and suspicion of normality.

What has so far been descriptively claimed will be empirically validated with an analysis of a corpus of 1,100 punk song lyrics written by twenty-six German punk bands (an average of forty-three lyrics per band) between 1979 and 2012.[1] Punk's lyrical concern with normality will then be discussed in relation to the 'history of the idea of normality' as developed by Jürgen Link.[2] On the one hand, this provides a useful background to the contextualisation of punk's relationship with normality, especially the extent to which the shift away from a rigid protonormalist paradigm with high pressure to conform towards a flexible normalist paradigm with greater tolerance for deviation makes it difficult for punks to escape the suffocating embrace of normality. On the other hand, it helps to argue that punk's defiance and subversion of normality is an important counter-discursive move against the pervasiveness of the idea and desirability of normality. Last but not least, it helps identify and underpin the main threads or topoi of dealing with normality in punk song lyrics: that is, pressure towards normalisation coming from 'normal people', visions of denormalisation, and the notion of '(un)normal' progression.

Some punk band names openly display a concern with normality. Bands such as Alarmsignal and Abwärts ('downhill') suggest catastrophic or negative development pertaining to 'unnormal' progression, whereas the name Chaos Z alludes to the absence of categorisation according to which developmental progression may be measured and against which progression may be mapped. Fehlfarben, meanwhile, refers to norms in the (industrial) production process – a development linked to normalisation – and presents the band (members) as faulty products that fail to conform to the norm: Fehlfarben denotes prints that have not come out in the desired colour. Other band names, like Die Toten Hosen, suggest flat progression – the German colloquial idiomatic expression 'tote Hose' (dead trousers) means that nothing is going on. There is also an ironic play with normality in the band name Normahl. The mis-spelling, with a superfluous 'h', suggests lengthening the 'a' sound into something resembling a yawn and thereby indicating the boredom of normality.

Even though the texts are German, this chapter does not set out to make claims specific to German punk. Rather, the author believes that such concern with normality may be traced as a generic feature of punk discourse; an essential ingredient rather than a national flavour, even if it may be 'cooked' in slightly different ways. The examples happen to be German not because the concern with normality is specific to German punk, but because the author happens to be a Germanist and therefore more competent in this area than in others.

The chapter is based on Critical Discourse Analysis (CDA), 'a problem-oriented interdisciplinary research movement, subsuming a variety of approaches' with 'a shared interest in the semiotic dimensions of power, injustice, abuse, and political-economic or cultural change in society.'[3] In terms of academic disciplines, CDA is pursued mostly by linguists and sociologists. One purpose of this article is to promote the study of language use/discourses in relation to subcultures/punk, but also to trigger the interest of critical discourse analysts in the study of subcultural texts and discourse because of their potential to undermine hegemonic discourse.

A critical discourse analysis view on punk

In the last few decades, linguistic interest in the relationship between language and the social world has increasingly come to realise that when we use language, we not only transmit information via symbolic interaction, but we do so under certain social conditions and thereby develop, define and maintain relationships with others. This interest has extended far beyond accounting for grammatical relations within artificial sentences isolated from any context towards empirical research of often very large amounts of linguistic data. Sociolinguistics and, more recently, discourse analysis now look at how broader social factors – power relations, social hierarchies, symbolic capital (national/ethnic/group) identity – determine our uses of and attitudes toward language. Researchers critical of the social circumstances that determine our ways of speaking in various genres have thus developed what is known as Critical Discourse Analysis.[4]

Though not always explicitly drawing on Foucault – if to some degree influenced by his thinking about discourse and 'knowledge' – CDA understands discourse to both constitute and reinforce social reality via symbolic interaction in social contexts.[5] The way we speak is influenced by the discourse around us, especially at a macro level such as media discourse which is likely to determine socially shared 'knowledge' about a particular issue. The ways in which social phenomena are referred to influences perceptions of 'problems in society'. For example, 'illegal immigrants' problematises the conduct of individuals who act in a way that negatively affects 'us'. Counter strategies to hegemonic perspectives can be developed. By referring to 'illegalised immigrants', the grammatical set-up of a single word shifts the focus of problematising away from people towards the law which frames them as 'a problem'. Hegemonic discourse is pervasive, but not almighty. In speaking in certain ways, we also contribute to these discourses at a micro level and either maintain or perhaps even challenge its presuppositions. CDA, therefore, 'oscillates … between a focus on structures (especially the intermediate level of the structuring of social practices) and a focus on the strategies of social agents'.[6] Bourdieu's notion of 'symbolic power' acknowledged that certain styles of speech are protected by elites and the education system as proper and legible, whereas others get devalued and marginalised – amply demarcating class/ethnicity and cultural hegemony.[7] Power is at the core of understanding how discourse defines the boundaries of the sayable and the way in which we talk about certain issues such as immigration.[8] 'Gramsci's observation that the maintenance of contemporary power rests not only on coercive force but also on "hegemony" (winning the consent of the majority) has been particularly influential in CDA', especially as it encouraged a focus 'on how the structures and practices of ordinary life routinely normalize capitalist social relations.'[9]

Somewhat surprisingly, subversive or defiant discourses remain rather neglected in the broad variety of CDA-based empirical studies, despite the fact that one of its aims is to promote critical language awareness.[10] Critical language awareness can be fostered not only by critically analysing texts that represent hegemonic discourse, but also by looking at practices that challenge or undermine hegemonic discourse, changing perspectives and drawing attention to what remains absent from (hegemonic) discourse.[11] The majority of CDA-inspired studies look at top-down hegemonic discourses and how these may determine majority opinions rather than at bottom-up attempts at discursive defiance. Nor do they pay attention to subcultures.[12]

Punk, in several ways, attempts to undermine or deny the presumptions of hegemonic discourse. It makes deliberate use of dis-preferred, provocative and exaggerated styles of expression; it avoids suitability for easy consumption.[13] Punk can be seen as a (more or less temporarily) lived anti-statement against established forms of musical and stylistic expression; an alternative to mainstream popular music and its discourse about leisure, fun, romantic love and success; an opposition to the elite cultures of the educated middle classes and the rich (whatever the latter may be in detail as they tend to be more secluded);[14] and deliberately ignorant of what institutionalised education deems worth knowing about.[15] This is what makes the study of punk (and other subcultures) interesting for CDA, revealing the potential for subversion, counter-discursive intervention or discursive defiance; an at least partial or temporary avoidance of the golden path of normality; an element of doubt in the received wisdom about what we need to make an effort for to succeed in/with life.

Studies of subcultures/punk tend to focus on documentation[16] and social/historical context, as well as on style in the widest sense.[17] I would like here, therefore, to argue in favour of integrating a discourse perspective and attention to concrete subcultural text production with existing research in subcultures/punk.[18]

Normality as modern discourse dispositive

Jürgen Link's essential study of 'normalism' examines the history of the idea of normality from the second half of the eighteenth century, focusing on the discursive production and (re-)construction of normality.[19] It is very much in line with Foucault's approach to investigating the history of ideas and ideologies, in which normality already features – if less explicitly – as one of the most pervasive discourse dispositives of modern times.[20] According to Link, normalities are produced by specialist discourses with sectorial (e.g. psychology, medicine, sociology) validity. These permeate into interdiscourses (e.g. public sphere, media) and amalgamate with broader cultural ideas of normality; that is, a cross-sectoral imagination of normality becomes a point of orientation and a way to position the self in the social world. Individuals constantly reassure or adjust themselves with regard to whether or not what they think or do is normal.[21] The term 'dispositive' captures a relatively stable historical constellation in which interdiscourse and power relations combine and appear to mutually support one another. But these power relations also rely on non-discursive practices, especially in institutions, that are set 'alongside a polarity of disposing and disposed subjectivity: as regards normalism, for example, doctor–patient, psychiatrist–neurotic, pedagogue–disciple, generally expert–lay.'[22]

Normality must be seen as a historically determined and dynamic construct; i.e. the boundaries of what is considered and tolerated as normal continue to shift.[23] Thus, Link differentiates between modern normality as a discursively established social-ideological construct and related notions such as 'norm' (which comes with possible sanctions) and 'norms' in industrial production.[24] He points out that in fields of normality (imaginations of) social reality is constructed, represented and reproduced at the same time. In its essential complexity, social reality defies representation, thus representation means simplification and fields of normality represent social reality in – simplified – graded continuums: for example, intelligence, health, achievement, standards of living, population (growth), social stratification, etc. Fields of normality require homogenisation (i.e. there must be one dimension which makes entities comparable, e.g. level of income), continuation (with regard to the dimension of comparability, there can be no gaps between classes of entities; it applies to all entities, only more or less), and graduation (ideally, each entity can be positioned between two neighbouring entities and under dynamic conditions; it can shift to/with neighbouring positions). Establishing fields of normality requires data collection, probability calculation and statistics. But Link shows that since fields of normality have now been internalised, they can be more or less dependent on quantification. For example, Link discusses how the Kinsey reports introduced the idea of sexual satisfaction as an achievement in quantified terms.[25] Equally, graded continuums indicating normality and extremes can be constructed as continuums that are not based on measurability or quantification, such as the political left, right and centre.[26]

For most of us, confrontation with established fields of normality may be understood in the form of omnipresent mediatised curves. Progression curves have a horizontal (time span) and vertical (dynamic growth) dimension; steep progression curves signal crisis or un-normal, unsustained growth. Bell curves represent distribution horizontally, the big belly in the middle indicating 'normal' distribution, flattening towards the extremes at the margins: to the left low and, to the right, a high quantity of the quality in question.[27] Link goes so far as to suggest that individuals have internalised these ideological, normality-indicating curves, which then help steer their imagined ego-vehicles through an imagined landscape of curves, positioning them as more or less normal in nearly all aspects of their existence and calculating the risk of denormalisation. That we are encouraged to imagine ourselves in this way does not mean we are completely discouraged from being not entirely normal. However, there is no 'outside' of normality; we can only be at the extreme end on the continuum. Always being at the centre with no deviation would be too boring, so we may steer our ego-vehicles towards the extreme ends for some time and in some respects. For how long, in how many aspects and how far depends on our inclination to risk, while the threat of uncontrolled – i.e. not self-managed – denormalisation is more often experienced as crisis and may induce angst.

Punk and normality

Template people

Many of the punk lyrics included in the current corpus take issue with 'normal', or 'template', people whose existence is reduced to their being a subject of administration – an otherwise imperceptible element of the mass. As such, they are seen to have no authentic quality of life, no dreams, feelings or critical, enquiring mind (Chaos Z, 'Moderne Krüppel'). Such existence is reduced to automatic physical functioning, with those happy to exist in this way seeking to destroy any sparks of life around them with the boredom of their own everyday lives (Vorkriegsjugend, 'Wir sind die Ratten'). Die Goldenen Zitronen suggest that 'normal ("honest") people' are similar to robots: the result of mass production, reproducing at the assembly line so that the colour of their skin matches that of their cars. In other words, the norms of living are linked to the norms of industrial production ('Diese Menschen sind halbwegs ehrlich'). Similarly, Abwärts maintain that 'normal people' all do the same thing, live the same lives, and look so similar as to resemble eggs ('Die Zeit').

A number of lyrics deal with the contempt shown by 'template people' towards punk. Some appear little more than whiny complaints about 'normal people's' intolerance of deviation. Knochenfabrik's 'Grüne Haare', for example, laments the majority's judging punks because they are different and cannot be fooled. Similarly, Fahnenflucht wonder whether asking questions and not accepting everything is really so outrageous ('Minderheit'). Others, however, emphasise punk's own contempt for 'template people': 'You laugh about me because I'm different, but I laugh about you because you are all the same' (Alarmsignal, 'Sklaven der Langeweile').[28]

Punk's defiance of the normal serves to affirm its difference from the mass; it reasserts a willingness to fight rather than adhere to their norms (But Alive, 'Wir werden'). On 'Mein Girl is höchstgradig kriminell', Die Goldenen Zitronen construct a lyrical dialogue between two guys boasting about their respective partners, a pleasant left-liberal middle-class girl and a notorious criminal. The singer-persona positions himself against the progressive yet acceptable left-liberal consensus to insist on the attraction of being radical and opting out of the bell-curve belly described by Link: 'My girl is extremely criminal, she builds bombs and swallows piles of drugs, yeah my girl knows exactly what she wants, to never ever be like your girl at all'.[29] The band Toxoplasma seem especially obsessed with 'template people' in their lyrics. 'Aktenzeichen', for example, states: 'You are just a file code … you are administered, sedated and forced into line … you are only a number, one of many not alone in this world who is only supposed to shut up … registered, filed, X-rayed and seen through, conform to the norm, born into shape, at ease with yourself'.[30]

Toxoplasma's lyrics also describe 'normal people's' hatred of those at the flatter ends of the bell curve, where the punks position themselves ('Asozial'). In two of their lyrics, they interpret such intolerance of anyone different from their norm as latent fascism. In 'Pass dich an', old men are quoted as saying punks should be put into concentration camps; in 'Alle Irren', the band allude to some people's appreciation of the Nazi period. If 'normal' people do not want to be disturbed by displays of un-normality, then allusions to the Third Reich suggest a protonormalist paradigm, i.e. wherein normality is conceptualised more strictly and rigidly, and where sanctions for not being normal are severe.[31] However, post-war Western democracies have in fact shown a shift towards flexible normalism, wherein the spectrum of what can be considered normal has broadened to suggest more freedom for the individual and more tolerance for deviation. Even then, such a shift only encourages the internalisation of normality control and coerces people into the more flexible field of normality under the pretence of support and the 'healing process'. This is observed in Knochenfabrik's 'Zurück an Land', in which well-meaning 'normal people' offer a helping hand to an apparently crisis-ridden punk without even asking for gratitude.

Such critique is echoed by Fahnenflucht's 'Kontrollierte Freiheit', in which the band argue that the increased freedom for individuals to (temporarily, or to a certain degree) display deviant behaviour is in fact a controlled freedom that serves to discourage true deviation. In other words, an illusion of freedom is available to those who roam within the widening boundaries of tolerance, an illusion that discourages any attempt to move beyond the limits of the acceptable. Not dissimilarly, the band But Alive dismissed the more moderate view that appreciated the freedoms granted within the flexible paradigm of normality: even when you can determine the colour of the walls around you, they suggest, that does not mean the walls disappear ('Nennt es wie ihr wollt'). If the flexible paradigm allows and accommodates choice in favour of deviation to some degree, then normality as a 'normative' premise is still there.

If the majority's contempt helps define punk's deviation, then it becomes more difficult for punks to position themselves outside of normality when normality extends to accommodate punk (or a shallow imagination of it) within a (post-)modern flexible paradigm. Seen in this light, the above-quoted complaints about the 'template people's' normalist rigidity and discrimination seem rather futile – it is their embrace that poses a threat to punk identity. A number of lyrics deal with this ambivalence, examining in different ways punk's becoming itself a victim of normality.

Firstly, if a bell curve is drawn for 'real' punk, then those not within its big belly become marginalised. The band Alarmsignal rejected the idea of punk being defined and punk 'laws' being applied in favour of individualism ('Keine Marionette'). Wohlstandskinder, meanwhile, observed that to escape from the field of normality seemed impossible, suggesting that those who tend to extremes are still orientated towards the norm ('Mehr sag ich nicht'). Whether you come under the big belly of normality or move to the flat ends of extremity at its margins, you are always playing within the field: extremism depends on conceptualisations of normality.

Secondly, punk's embrace within the flexible paradigm of normality comes with commercialisation; a tolerance of punk, an appreciation of its style and acceptance of its deviant gesture leads to the purchase of punk imagery. Just as Die Goldenen Zitronen sing of 'souvenirs and icons of past revolts, instantly upon purchase bereft of their healing power' in their 'Auf dem Platz der leeren Versprechungen', so Alarmsignal's 'Aufruf zur Revolte' imagines Che Guevara (an 'icon of past revolts') stepping down from his shop-window display to bomb his way across a Germany where ideals are for sale and punk rock is dying.[32] Vorkriegsjugend, too, describe punk as a closing-down sale in their

'Punkrock Ausverkauf'. People calculate the risks of denormalisation and are hardly willing to give up their normality for the sake of a marginalised existence. But the centre of normality would, in all respects, be so boring that they may steer their ego vehicles towards the margins. Indulging in a second-hand, commercialised punk experience provides a good way to stay normal; to adopt punk styles and gestures serves as a risk-free experience of non-conformity.

Visions of denormalisation

Punks do not live in a normal world. Their world is one of ruins (Fehlfarben, 'Paul ist tot'; Normahl, 'Trümmertango'); the city they live in emerges from bad dreams (Abwärts, 'Dies ist die Stadt'); their social environment is hostile (Fahnenflucht, 'Ich bin dein Feind, mein Freund'); a state of emergency is the set condition (Fehlfarben, 'Apokalypse'). Punk lyrics deal with catastrophes: fire (Hans-A-Plast, 'Es brennt'; Zaunpfahl, 'Es brennt'), bombs, war and terror (Toxoplasma, 'S.O.S.'; Atemnot, 'Kollaps'; Fahnenflucht, 'Ich sehe Tod'). Below the thin ice of normality, denormalisation looms and nothing is as it seems (Chaos Z, 'In Gefahr'; Wohlstandskinder, '2 Jahre noch 4 Tage'). Chaos and suicide are pending (Fahnenflucht, 'K.O. System'; Zaunpfahl, 'Was lange währt'; But Alive, 'Ohnmacht'; Knochenfabrik, 'Der nackte Golfer'; Zaunpfahl, 'Erwin'); anticipation of the end is such that landing on a hard surface becomes the final wish for the suicidal lyrical 'I' (Abwärts, 'Hoffentlich ist es Beton').

Punk appears to indulge in visions of denormalisation in an attempt not to submit to the angst of denormalisation. With its explicit denormalisation paranoia, punk addresses the issue head-on – whatever happens will make things worse. Another reaction to denormalisation angst would be to suppress it; to avoid denormalisation by being 'normal' and behaving as 'normally' as possible. Punks already live in a state of denormalisation: the world around them is not normal, as they themselves are not. A number of lyrics therefore deal with physical or psychological disintegration, be it as a result of drugs or the wrong medication (Zaunpfahl, 'Das Ende'; Abwärts, 'Küss mich'; Vorkriegsjugend, 'Tilt'; Toxoplasma, 'Amok'). On 'Kleine Sünderlein', ZK's singer-persona speaks from behind the bars of a mental asylum, observing how people outside live in asylums they have created themselves. No existence is normal, neither one that is declared mad nor one that 'madly' submits to self-coercion.

More often than not, psychological disintegration is causally linked with a maddening state of the world. Chaos Z describe the psychological disintegration of a deprived individual, with violence giving way to a madness depicted in visions of dictatorship and uniforms ('Gewalt' and 'Ignoranz').

Not dissimilarly, madness is triggered by the stupefying effects of normality (Fahnenflucht, 'Ziviler Ungehorsam') or booze-induced disintegration fuelled by looming global catastrophe (Vorkriegsjugend, 'Schöne neue Welt'; Knochenfabrik, 'Filmriss').

Politics are de-normalised in punk lyrics, they are stripped bare of democratic procedure. Fascists and multinationals rule the country, while the colours of the German flag represent a black sky, a red earth, and the golden hands of the rich (Slime, 'Deutschland'). With the world and nation-state in the midst of catastrophe, its elites are murderous (Slime, 'Computerstaat'; Fehlfarben, 'Stop! (Genug ist genug)'; Alarmsignal, 'Panzer für die neue Welt'). The law is based on violence; the police protect the fascists; those who carry the flag will go down with it (But Alive, 'Perverse Zeiten'; Atemnot, 'Deutsche Polizisten'; Slime, 'Gewalt'; Toxoplasma, 'An der Wand lang'). In the political world of punk, no hope is given to 'normalised' democratic legitimacy, accountability or transparency, to fairness or justice. There is no trust in the quantified normalist paradigms of measured consensus and majority – rule is illegitimate and based on violence, greed and exploitation. It should be noted, however, that the genre of lyrics lends itself to poignant, condensed statements and expressions of states of mind. The impression created in punk lyrics is not incisive of the real world grassroots political activism and agitation also typical for punk.[33] Even if distanced or in opposition to 'corrupt' elite politics, such activism does not suggest disengagement to the degree expressed in punk's lyrics.

Progression, regression, stagnation, circularity

The most extreme expression of the absence of progression among 'normal people' is in lyrics that present them as zombies, as born dead, or as already-dead-yet-still-alive (Alarmsignal, 'Willkommen in Celle'; But Alive, 'Perverse Zeiten'; Toxoplasma, 'Aktenzeichen'; Canalterror, 'Tot geboren'; Wohlstandskinder, 'Vorstadt'). The 'normal people's' existence is here presented as purely mechanical, resembling death more than life because of its lack of depth of experience or sensational authenticity – perhaps the ultimate form of stagnation and pure routine.

But even those in search of experience or authenticity have problems finding it, instead ending up 'at the centre of the raging standstill', on 'Empty Promises Square', where people 'are searching for the party in eternal anticipation, the party that does not take place right now' (Die Goldenen Zitronen, 'Auf dem Platz der leeren Versprechungen').[34] Even distraction from the routine becomes a routine exercise in itself, when every Friday the lyrical 'I' is out in the pub getting drunk while waiting for something to happen (but

which never does) (Hans-A-Plast, 'Rock 'n' Roll Freitag'). For Daily Terror
('Leerkopf'), life is a permanent state of waiting for something that does not
happen; for Die Toten Hosen, apparently in allusion to The Godfather's song
'Birth, School, Work, Death', life's progression peaks at the point of finding of
work, after which it stagnates and remains flat in prelude to a death that will
end the (time)line ('Wir sind das Volk'). Other punk lyrics suggest regression;
every day is the same and, where it's not, then it will only get worse (Atemnot,
'Armut und Leid'). Toxoplasma and Slime both released songs in 1994 entitled
Stillstand (standstill).

As this suggests, punk lyrics show a deep scepticism towards the 'normal'
progression curves assumed in hegemonic discourse, in which putting in effort
or resources will lead to growth or gain over time. The above-quoted 'raging
standstill' is symptomatic of this scepticism. There is movement, of either time
or subjects, but it is futile and without development. People just spend their
lives living day-by-day in work camps and the world offers nothing to them.
They have no time for introspection, reflection and authenticity (Chaos Z, '45
Jahre'). Some lyrics suggest that time itself – or the world in which subjects
live – moves too fast; and even though it does move, it does not mean anything; it does not add any quality to life so far as the rather immovable subject
is concerned. There is no development; just the mechanical and unstoppable
passing of time; an automatic process bearing no inherent chance for progression of any quality.

> Everything stands as it was ... but time didn't wait, ticked away secretly, tick
> tack, second after second until the curtain drops, you miss every opportunity
> because standstill doesn't count in the face of time, because the world keeps
> on turning while you remain in the same spot or in the past because then
> standstill is the future.[35]

Similarly, those subjects who themselves move (too fast) do not advance.
Rather, they move in circles, either for fear of freedom (denormalisation angst)
– 'I run like a rat in a pet's exercise wheel ... no standstill, standstill would mean
to leave the given path, standstill would mean to stop running the danger that
I cannot deal with freedom, so I run and go on running'[36] (Razzia, *Laufrad*
2004) – or because life has sucked the subject into an unproductive dynamic
too difficult to resist. Life is presented as a great round dance – or a wheel of
fortune – that will provide you with a privileged window seat and/or make
you an outcast (Daily Terror, 'Heile Welt').

But while the above-quoted lyrics lay out a pretty gloomy idea of life,
and thereby undermine the hegemonic/normalist 'landscape of curves' of
progression over time, there are some punk songs that suggest a way out based

on dismissing the idea of a timeline. Instead, they care only for the moment and not about what was before or what will come after (Alarmsignal, 'Leben is mehr'). Fehlfarben's 'Hier und Jetzt', for example, dismisses the shadow of the past and the future as difficult. Only the here and now, they conclude, is worth its while.

Conclusion

An analysis of a substantial corpus of German punk song lyrics shows that normality hardly seems to exist within the genre. Denormalisation is either obvious or lurking beneath the surface of normality. The world is inherently not normal (politics, the state); or it is on the brink of denormalisation (catastrophe, crisis). Individuals, too, exist on the edge of psychological disintegration, chaos and suicide. Where normality is supposed to exist, its boredom and normative force is destructive. 'Normal people' appear denormalised (robots, zombies), while the prospect of normalisation provides a threat to punk itself. By underpinning an analysis of punk's lyrical topos with Link's discussion of normality-as-ideology, it is possible to see punk's critique of normality as a counter-discursive move integral to the punk identity.

According to Link, the idea and ideology of normality accounts for how people in modern societies organise the social world, construct social reality, and position themselves on a continuum that locates extremity at the margins (thrill/risk) and normality at the centre (boredom/security). Punk questions the desirability of normality, emphasising the boredom that exists in tandem with it and suggesting that the security it brings comes at the cost of 'real life' (resulting in a zombie-like existence). Link also maintains that modern individuals have got used to ranking themselves in scales relating to specific characteristics; a pervasive example being the psychological tests published in magazines that reveal how ambitious, jealous, vain, melancholic, alcoholic, anxious, flirting we are (un-normally little, normally average, un-normally extreme). By undermining the desirability to be normal and appreciating individual uniqueness, punk seeks to release the pressure of positioning oneself in these graded continuums and rankings. Finally, Link describes how modern ideas on development are informed by the notion of 'normal progression'. Punk undermines this by maintaining that (a life's) progression curve may well remain flat; that despite putting in effort or resources, the curve may just go downhill.

To examine punk's response to the ideology of normality is to trace both its discursive defiance and its attempt to undermine one of the most pervasive premises of hegemonic discourse; i.e. that normality exists, that it can be measured (objectively), is given rather than constructed, applies to everyone and everything, and is desirable. It also further demonstrates that subcultures do not exist in context-free zones, but that they react to discourses that they find themselves exposed to. Song lyrics and subcultures have not so far received much attention from (critical) discourse analysts. But punk's potential for discursive defiance should make the study of punk/subcultural discourse dear to CDA.

Notes

1 For practical reasons (to accrue a large corpus of punk lyrics for a range of analyses), the lyrics were downloaded from free user-fed song lyric internet forums golyr.de and lyrix.at. This does mean that there are occasional errors in the lyrics (mostly spelling), but spot checks were carried out to ascertain accuracy. Where spot checks were made, in no case were the lyrics incomplete or the effect of errors such that they would cause a distortion of meaning. However, this procedure also means that only bands with a certain level of popularity could be included. The current corpus consists of West German punk bands, but a previous study based on a smaller corpus of song lyrics by East German punk bands showed similar concerns with normality. See M. Schröter and S. Pappert, 'Der Punk-Diskurs in der DDR', in B. Bock, U. Fix and S. Pappert (eds), *Politische Wechsel – sprachliche Umbrüche*. (Berlin: Frank & Timme, 2011), pp. 171–93 (though the chapter does not focus on normality). All the quotations were translated from German into English by the author; the German originals are provided in the notes. Band names and song titles (in italics) remain in the original form.

2 J. Link, *Versuch über den Normalismus. Wie Normalität produziert wird* (Göttingen, Germany: Vandenhoek & Ruprecht, 3rd edn, 2006).

3 N. Fairclough, J. Mulderring and R. Wodak, 'Critical Discourse Analysis', in T. A. van Dijk (ed.), *Discourse Studies: A Multidisciplinary Introduction* (London: Sage, 2011), p. 357.

4 See, for example, J. Blommaert, *Discourse: A Critical Introduction* (Cambridge: Cambridge University Press, 2005); A. Jaworski and N. Coupland (eds), *The Discourse Reader* (London, New York: Routledge, 2006 edn); R. Wodak and M. Meyer (eds), *Methods of Critical Discourse Analysis* (London: Sage, 2009).

5 S. Jäger and F. Maier, 'Theoretical and Methodological Aspects of Foucauldian Critical Discourse Analysis and Dispositive Analysis', in Wodak and Meyer (eds), *Methods of Critical Discourse Analysis*, p. 37.

6 N. Fairclough, 'A Dialectical-relational Approach to Critical Discourse Analysis in Social Research', in Wodak and Meyer (eds), *Methods of Critical Discourse Analysis*, p. 165.

7　P. Bourdieu, *Language and Symbolic Power* (Cambridge: Polity, 1991).

8　For example, N. Fairclough, *Language and Power* (London: Longman, 1989); T. A. van Dijk, *Discourse and Power* (Basingstoke: Palgrave Macmillan, 2008).

9　Fairclough, Mulderring and Wodak, 'Critical Discourse Analysis', p. 360.

10　N. Fairclough, *Critical Discourse Analysis: The Critical Study of Language* (Harlow: Pearson Education, 1995).

11　See Blommaert's critique of CDA for the latter two points, in Blommaert, *Discourse*, p. 31ff.

12　There have been recent attempts to counter-balance this tendency by promoting 'Positive Discourse Analysis', looking at alternative, non-hegemonic discourse practices. The gist of these, however, is to look at 'healing' discourses that 'make the world 'a better place'. See T. Bartlett, *Hybrid Voices and Collaborative Change: Contextualising Positive Discourse Analysis* (London: Routledge, 2012); J. R. Martin, 'Positive Discourse Analysis: Solidarity and Change', *Revista Canaria de Estudios Ingleses*, 49 (2010), 179–200. There is reason to doubt that punk could be seen, or that punks would like to be seen, in these terms.

13　D. Laing, *One Chord Wonders: Power and Meaning in Punk Rock* (Milton Keynes: Open University Press, 1985) p. 81.

14　For example, C. Thurlow and A. Jaworski, 'Silence is Golden: The "Anti-communicational" Linguascaping of Super-elite Mobility', in A. Jaworski and C. Thurlow (eds), *Semiotic Landscapes: Language, Image, Space* (London, New York: Continuum 2010), pp. 187–218.

15　This chapter is based on a notion of punk as a bundle of observable characteristics rather than a 'proper' definition. It embraces an ethnographic approach based on the participants' categorisations: if a band considers itself punk, and if there is evidence that (a part of) their audience and/or others outside of the band do so as well, then I treat the texts it produces as part of the punk discourse.

16　For West German punk, see I. G. Dreck auf Papier (ed.), *Keine Zukunft war gestern. Punk in Deutschland* (Berlin: Archiv der Jugendkulturen, 2008). For East German punk, see M. Boehlke and H. Gericke (eds), *Too Much Future. Punk in der DDR* (Berlin: Verbrecher Verlag, 2007 edn); G. Furian and N. Becker, *Auch im Osten trägt man Westen. Punks in der DDR – und was aus ihnen geworden ist* (Berlin, Archiv der Jugendkulturen, 2008 edition); R. Galenza and H. Havemeister (eds), *Wir wollen immer artig sein. Punk, New Wave, Hiphop und Independent-Szene in der DDR von 1980 bis 1990* (Berlin: Schwarzkopf & Schwarzkopf, 2005 edn).

17　K. Gelder and S. Thornton (eds), *The Subcultures Reader* (London: Routledge 1997). For a substantial study on subcultural discourse practice, see S. Widdicombe and R. Wooffitt, *The Language of Youth Subcultures: Social Identity in Action* (New York: Harvester Wheatsheaf, 1995). This is based on specifically conducted interviews (i.e. not genuine subcultural text production) with a sociological/sociolinguistic interest in language as a means of establishing and maintaining (subcultural) group identity (e.g. by accepting or rejecting labelling/categorisation).

UNIVERSITY OF WINCHESTER
LIBRARY

18 There have also been moves in CDA to look beyond textual semiotic spheres to Multimodal Discourse Analyses, which would provide scope for broader semiotic analyses of punk than demonstrated in this chapter. See G. Kress and T. van Leeuwen, *Multimodal Discourse: The Modes and Media of Contemporary Communication* (London: Arnold, 2001).

19 Link's book was first published in 1998. A third, revised edition was published in 2006 (see note 2). Unfortunately, this important study has not yet been translated into English.

20 M. Foucault, *Madness and Civilisation: A History of Insanity in the Age of Reason* (London: Tavistock, 1971); and *The Birth of the Clinic: An Archaeology of Medical Perception* (London: Routledge, 1989); and *History of Sexuality. Vol. 1: The Will to Knowledge* (Harmondsworth: Penguin, 1990).

21 Link, *Versuch über den Normalismus*, p. 20.

22 [' ... längs einer Polarität von disponierender und disponierter Subjektivität: am Beispiel des Normalismus etwa Arzt-Patient, Psychiater-Neurotikerin, Pädagog-Zögling, allgemein Experte-Laie. ' Translated by the author from *ibid.*, p. 43.

23 *Ibid.*, pp. 39 and 279ff.

24 *Ibid.*, pp. 271ff and 330ff.

25 *Ibid.*, p. 419ff.

26 *Ibid.*, p. 342ff.

27 The term 'bell curve' describes the shape of the curve, but it is also known as a Gauss curve after the German mathematician who developed the idea of normal distribution in the early nineteenth century. The curve's characteristic shape indicates the proportions for the centre and margins of the curve; for our purposes, the majority/normal are at the centre, with rare extremes at the flat ends. For a good example of a 'bell curve' as applied to human intelligence, see the graph at www.hoogbegaafdvlaanderen.be/01_Hoogbegaafd/hoeveel.html, accessed 31 March 2014.

28 'Ihr lacht über mich weil ich anders bin, aber ich lache über euch, denn ihr seid alle gleich'. Written by Alarmsignal, with lyrics used by kind permission of Alarmsignal. This does not seem to be a conscious translation of a lyric by Korn's Jonathan Davis (Korn), which makes a similar statement.

29 'Mein Girl ist höchstgradig kriminell, sie baut Bomben und schluckt Drogen massenhaft, yeah mein Girl weiß genau was sie will, auf keinen Fall so werden wie dein Girl'. Lyrics, used used with kind permission, by Ted Gaier.

30 'Du bist nur ein Aktenzeichen ... du wirst verwaltet, ruhiggestellt und gleichgeschaltet ... du bist nur eine Nummer, eine Zahl, einer unter vielen, nicht alleine auf der Welt, von dem man nur erwartet, dass er die Fresse hält ... eingetragen, abgeheftet, durchgeleuchtet und durchschaut, normkonform zurechtgeboren selbstzufrieden'. Lyrics, used with kind permission, by Wally Walldorf.

31 Link, *Versuch über den Normalismus*, p. 51ff.

32 'Souvenirs und Ikonen vergangener Revolten, augenblicklich beim Kauf ihrer Heilkraft beraubt'. Lyrics, used with kind permission, by Ted Gaier.

33 See, for example, G. McKay, *Senseless Acts of Beauty: Cultures of Resistance Since the Sixties* (London, New York: Verso, 1996), pp. 73–101; M. Worley, 'One Nation Under the Bomb: The Cold War and British Punk to 1984', *Journal for the Study of Radicalism* 5:2 (2011), 65–83.

34 '… im Zentrum des rasenden Stillstands' … 'auf dem Platz der leeren Versprechungen'. Lyrics, used with kind permission, by Ted Gaier.

35 Toxoplasma, *Stillstand* (1994). 'Alles steht genauso da, doch die Zeit hat nicht gewartet, hat sich schnell und heimlich davongetickt – TickTack, Sekunde um Sekunde, bis dann der Vorhang fällt, verpaßt man jede Gelegenheit, weil der Stillstand für die Zeit nicht zählt, weil die Welt sich weiter dreht, während man auf der Stelle steht, oder in der Vergangenheit verharrt, weil der Stillstand dann die Zukunft ist'. Lyrics, used with kind permission, by Wally Walldorf.

36 'Ich laufe wie die Ratte im Laufrad … kein Stillstand, Stillstand hieße auszuscheren, Stillstand hieße aufzuhören, auf die Gefahr hin, dass ich dann, mit der Freiheit nix anfangen kann, darum laufe und laufe ich weiter'. Lyrics, used with kind permission, by Andreas Siegler.

14

'Militant entertainment'? 'Crisis music' and political ephemera in the emergent 'structure of feeling', 1976–83

HERBERT PIMLOTT

Images of riots, demonstrations and strikes from across the world in the aftermath of the 2008–09 global economic 'meltdown' and subsequent factory closures, bankruptcies and job losses, provoke a strong sense of déjà vu. Some thirty-odd years ago, during the first major economic downturn of the post-war era, job prospects dimmed and social unrest grew as a generation of working-class school leavers, facing the worst unemployment rate since the 1930s, were marked: 'No Future' (memorialised in the Sex Pistols' 1977 classic 'God Save the Queen').[1] Suddenly, radical working-class youth had a slogan and a soundtrack.

As memories fade, a dominant track plays the now conventional historical narrative of the successful, hegemonic project of 'Thatcherism' with its (white) skilled worker-cum-entrepreneur who bought *his* council flat and voted Tory. The lived experiences of radical working-class youth have become lost and, with them, our ability to fully comprehend the past.[2] The left contributed to this dominant narrative via two debates; one, which emphasised the 'crisis of the left', was initiated in 1978 by Eric Hobsbawm's 'The Forward March of Labour Halted?' and identified the political consequences of the fracturing of the traditional working class; the other was initiated by Stuart Hall's analysis of Thatcherism in 1979, which emphasised the 'rise of the right'.[3]

While a number of accounts of punk raise criticisms of racism and sexism, other stories of this period remain unacknowledged or neglected, particularly the experience of political punks and radical youth.[4] For some, the 'lived experience' of the 'structure of feeling' still finds greater resonance with 'crisis music' and radical political ephemera of the late 1970s and early 1980s than with the available academic and anecdotal accounts. This is not to take away from the analysis presented or the lived experiences of others, but to recognise that amongst the range of experiences, some are represented less or not at all. Therefore, to rescue something of the 'lived experience' of the 'No Future' generation of politicised, working-class youth from the condescension of 'History', I draw upon Raymond Williams's concepts of 'structure of feeling', 'emergent culture' and 'experience' as 'practical consciousness' to highlight his (largely neglected) contributions to understanding how people, particularly subordinate classes, experienced and understood an historical epoch as they lived through it.

This chapter, therefore, seeks to accomplish three things. First, it outlines Williams's 'structure of feeling' and related concepts and extends the range of cultural practices to be taken into consideration. Second, it reclaims those products of subcultural production as resources for reconstructing the 'emergent' (e.g. alternative, resistant) 'structure of feeling' as revealed through the typeface, layout, words, phrases, symbols and sounds of the music and political ephemera: 'affective elements of consciousness and relationships ... thought as felt and feeling as thought'.[5] Finally, this chapter demonstrates the importance of recovering the 'lived experiences' of a subaltern social class or subculture as a means to gaining a fuller understanding of the past.

'Structure of feeling'

'Structure of feeling' was a concept that Raymond Williams developed over a period of nearly forty years, from its inception in the 1954 *Preface to Film* (co-authored with Michael Orrom), through his ground-breaking *Culture and Society* and *The Long Revolution*, before its most theoretical explication in his 1977 book, *Marxism and Literature*. The concept continued to inform his last works, published in the 1980s, such as *Culture* and *Towards 2000*. Williams's concept offers an approach to understand a period, as only those who experienced it knew it: 'culture as lived'. This is different to the documentary record of an era, and even more so to the selective tradition.[6] The barriers to the structure of feeling include the concepts being used for analysis because they have been part of a 'produced past', which can 'block lines of argument and explanation'.[7] Williams consistently argued for the centrality of 'practical consciousness' or 'culture as lived' as not being 'past' and therefore 'fixed', but as being constantly in flux, a process or processes that shape the structure of feeling during the time it is being experienced.

Separating the 'culture as lived' from set or fixed terms and concepts is important because 'practical consciousness' is almost always different from 'official consciousness'; it 'is what is actually being lived and not only what it is thought is being lived' and it is 'a kind of feeling and thinking which is indeed social and material, but each in an embryonic phase before it can become fully articulate'.[8] Practical consciousness is a process in flux and against which the corresponding 'social character' (class ideology) helps to shape the structure of feeling.[9] It is an ambitious attempt to capture the intangible, to understand how it can structure our lives as we experience them and our experiences as we live them. This is why, Williams says, the phrase structure of feeling is 'contradictory': 'it is as firm and definite as "structure" suggests, yet it operates in the most delicate and least tangible parts of our activity'.[10] For example, Williams points to the 1840s, where there were clear differences between 'the official consciousness of an epoch – codified in its doctrines and legislation', the 'formal ideology of the early Victorian middle class', and the 'whole process of actually living its consequences' as explored in the literature 'its writers produced'.[11] You could sense this 'operating in one work after another which weren't otherwise connected' but it was a sense of 'feeling much more than of thought – a pattern of impulses, restraints, tones, for which the best evidence was often the actual conventions of literary or dramatic writing'.[12]

It is important to recognise that structure of feeling is an attempt to grasp 'human cultural activity' as it is 'in process', still 'forming', rather than as some 'relationship, institution or formation' that is already fixed and set, already 'past'.[13] Since analysis is always 'centred on relations between these produced institutions, formations and experiences', it means that only 'fixed explicit forms exist, and living presence is always, by definition, receding'.[14] Williams critiqued the way that 'conscious history' converted 'relationships, institutions and formations in which we are still actively involved' into 'formed wholes rather than understood as formative and forming processes'.[15] As a result, those relationships and formations still in process are often dismissed as 'personal' and 'subjective'.

The production of culture, Williams points out, is 'never itself in the past tense'; it is 'always a formative process, within a specific present'.[16] Consciousness, experience and feeling are set against 'thought' and fixed forms, set in the past, while the process in which you live, feel, think in the present is never fixed. These processes, Williams suggests, are often asserted as forms themselves, in contention with other known forms: 'the subjective as distinct from the objective; experience from belief; feeling from thought; the immediate from the general; the personal from the social'.[17]

While social forms are frequently understood in fixed past senses, they 'become social consciousness only when they are lived, actively, in real relationships, and moreover in relationships which are more than systematic exchanges between fixed units'.[18] The focus on analysis between fixed practices takes place in terms of 'institutions, formations and experiences' and is responsible for the separation of the social from the 'inalienably physical' and personal, that which is known by those who live through the period: 'this, here, now, alive, active, "subjective"'.[19] Williams even contrasts the notion of 'thought', which is described 'in the same habitual past tense', against 'more active, more flexible, less singular terms – consciousness, experience, feeling'.[20]

We can see the responses of those 'who were there', in the various personal accounts of punk, which should be read not just as the outpourings of an older generation nostalgic for their youth, but as attempts to recapture that sense of what it was like to live through that period: the structure of feeling. The 'authoritativeness of autobiographical authenticity', the proclamation that 'I was there', is hard to refute; the reaction of those who have lived through a period to attempts by others to represent it will often be quite visceral and personal.[21] Yet, we know that any form of representation involves a process of selection, by which some things are excluded and others included. For this author, the writing and representation of the 'History' of this period is seldom effective at capturing its structure of feeling except through certain types of music and political ephemera which captures the 'this, here, now, alive, active, "subjective"' of the sense of an alternative future, the potential at that particular moment, lost as history took a different path than the alternative one that it might have taken had the 'pre-emergent' culture supplanted the dominant.[22]

Since culture as lived can and does contradict or challenge dominant ideological beliefs, values and attitudes, it cannot be explained simply by pointing to the role of ideas as fixed and produced via dominant institutions. It is this practical consciousness which, Williams says, is critical in recognising an emergent culture, whether or not it is able eventually to supplant the dominant culture. 'At times the emergence of a new structure of feeling is best related to the rise of a new class … at other times to contradiction, fracture, or mutation within [a] class … when a formation appears to break away from its class norms, though it retains its substantial affiliation, and the tension is at once lived and articulated in radically new semantic figures'.[23] When it cannot be articulated by a subaltern class, they will seek it out in the cultural output from others of another class. For example, Williams identified how middle-class writers of

1840s fiction, such as Elizabeth Gaskell, were sought out by working-class readers because of their ability to represent their structure of feeling.

The structure of feeling therefore plays an integral role in identifying an 'emergent culture' which requires 'not only distinct kinds of immediate cultural practice', but also and crucially 'new forms or adaptations of forms'. This is especially evident at those 'historically definable moments when every new work produces a sudden shock of *recognition*' (original emphasis): 'on these occasions [it] is that an experience, which is really very wide, suddenly finds a semantic figure which articulates it ... [the] *pre-emergent*' (added emphasis).[24] An 'emergent culture' for Williams, therefore, is where 'new meanings and values, practices, relationships and kinds of relationship, which are substantially alternative or oppositional to the dominant culture', are manifest.[25]

However, Williams makes the mistake of assuming that working-class expressions of the structure of feeling are missing from the period that he studied, which was in part a result of an emphasis on his formal education in dramatic and literary forms of the selective tradition. E. P. Thompson offers a corrective via his 1963 work, *The Making of the English Working Class*, where he writes about the development of a consciousness of a class *in* itself, *for* itself, most notably by drawing on not only examples of 'official consciousness', such as legislation, statistics, parliamentary debates and newspaper reports, but also examples of practical consciousness, such as ballads, broadsides, personal correspondence, the radical press, diaries and (auto)biographies.[26]

Thompson identifies the development of a consciousness of a new class in formation (the title's emphasis on *Making*), which is brought about via political and cultural ephemera that constitute the structure of feeling, 1780–1832. Thompson's emphasis on the prosaic and personal (re)sources of a 'class in the making' also informed his correction of Williams's view of culture as 'a way of *life*' to 'a way of *struggle*'.[27] Since the 'complex relation of differentiated structures of feeling to differentiated classes' cannot be simply reduced to their respective ideologies, it is therefore not about identifying nor critiquing the dominant ideology; structure of feeling is about attempting to understand a period as it was experienced by those who lived it.[28]

In the second part of this chapter, I draw upon Williams's approach to investigate the 'structure of feeling' of a subaltern social formation in the conjuncture of 1976–83. Since a new structure of feeling is related to the fracturing within or transformation of a class, we will first identify some of the general social-economic and political developments of this period. To highlight the tension that arises within a social formation when it 'appears to break away from its class norms',[29] we examine the output of a range of alternative and oppositional cultural production, such as music and political ephemera, which provide the means to access the practical consciousness and culture as lived by subaltern social formations. Working against the dominant narrative, these forms of music and political ephemera, from badges to zines, help to identify the intangible elements that make up a subaltern structure of feeling and construct an alternative or oppositional counter-narrative to the dominant one.

These new cultural practices and forms are integral to an emergent culture in which the 'sudden shock of recognition' is palpable. Thus, in trying to reconstruct the subaltern structure of feeling of 1976–83, we attempt to capture the intangible: 'human cultural activity' as it is 'in process', and that means being attuned to practices and artefacts that can be dismissed as 'personal' and 'subjective'. This practical consciousness or lived experience is being lost to 'History', which I seek to (re)capture as part of the '(pre)emergent culture' of a social class in a process of recomposition: one in which there was a general anti-authoritarian feeling and yet was not necessarily or explicitly 'anarchist'. This 'ineffable presence' is captured in Don Letts's documentary, *Punk Attitude*, across a range of musical genres and eras; yet, it is only in the conjuncture of the 1970s that it finds its 'semantic figure' in a 'sudden shock of recognition'.[30]

The conjuncture of the 1970s, 'crisis' and structures of feeling

A pervasive sense of 'crisis' permeated the structure of feeling from the early 1970s through to the mid-1980s. The post-war 'golden era' of capitalism in the West hit a wall in the 1972–73 oil crisis, 'a moment which decisively ended the era of postwar affluence'.[31] In the UK, this translated into rolling power cuts (the 'three-day week'), petrol rationing and wildcat strikes, alongside a rising tide of racism and growing unemployment, which surpassed one million in 1977. Faced with the new and unprecedented economic situation of 'stagflation', a stagnant economy and high inflation, the Labour government of 'Sunny Jim' Callaghan became the first government of a developed country to be subjected to the strictures of an International Monetary Fund (IMF) 'bailout' package, which required public spending cuts worth three billion pounds.

Elite groups playing up this sense of crisis for their own benefit were aided by UK and US media coverage of IMF talks with Labour in the autumn of 1976.[32] 'After Harold Wilson was returned to power in a minority [Labour] government in March 1974, the language of crisis was primarily evoked by those on the political right, on both sides of the Atlantic, who were worried about Britain's supposed descent into state socialism'.[33] The 'authoritarian populism' (aka 'Thatcherism') articulated via the Conservative Party and right-wing think tanks and business interests united social conservatives and economic (neo)liberals for a 'strong state and free market'.[34] This alliance contributed to the sense of crisis during negotiations over the IMF loan in 1976 and with the 'Winter of Discontent' in 1978–79.[35]

As leader of the Conservative Party, Margaret Thatcher won the first of three general election victories on 3 May 1979 and, for over a decade, oversaw a neoliberal agenda of de-regulation, de-industrialisation, privatisation and anti-union legislation. The combination of policies and legislation helped to undermine a powerful trade union movement that had reached its historical peak density at 55 per cent of the workforce by 1979. By 1981, unemployment had nearly tripled to over three million and by 1983 nearly one-in-three manufacturing jobs, including tens of thousands of unionised jobs, had been eliminated.[36]

Although unemployment was used as a weapon against unions, it was the youth who bore the initial brunt of mass unemployment. Faced with fewer job prospects than their parents' generation, they were more likely to be unemployed. With estimates of up to 25 per cent of working-class school-leavers moving straight onto the dole, the 'No Future' generation was born. It was in the cultural realm that such youth found their 'semantic recognition' in music that expressed their everyday experiences or practical consciousness: 'dole queue rock'.[37] This music was soon re-labelled 'punk'. However, it was not only in punk music that this semantic recognition could be found; therefore, I suggest that 'crisis music' is a more appropriate label for the pre-emergent culture as experienced by radical, working-class youth at the time.

The impact of unemployment was just the most visceral and visible part of the process of the recomposition of the working class, to which the upsurge in industrial unrest, 1968–74, was a response. Such unrest alongside the influence of new social movements and 1960s popular culture helped to shape 'crisis music' and its themes of the 'revolt against work' and authority, alienation and unemployment. The process of re-composition was brought about with the shift from permanent, skilled, full-time jobs to the growth of temporary, part-time and service-sector jobs. Thirty years later, we can see that the working class was undergoing a process of mutation, fracturing and reformation via de-skilling, down-sizing, out-sourcing and off-shoring, which has undermined the influence of the working class and its institutions, especially trade unions.

DIY for the working class

Before we can fully appreciate how the structure of feeling was manifested via the various means of cultural production of subaltern social formations, it is important to recognise an important shift that took place during the 1960s and 1970s. Although commercially produced popular culture expanded rapidly, there was also an expansion of cheap communication technologies for consumers of all classes. For example, the rapid spread of '[t]ape-recorders, typewriters, duplicating machines, photocopiers and ... relatively cheap offset litho printing' provided the working class with the means to produce their own culture.[38] In fact, punk represented the first attempt by 'a predominantly working-class youth culture, to provide an alternative critical space ... to counteract the hostile or ... ideologically inflected [media] coverage'.[39]

We can contrast similar forms of popular culture produced for and by the working class, such as the infamous 'youth-sploitation' novels about skinheads and punks, produced by publishing firms, such as the New English Library, and the literature, poetry (auto)biographies and oral histories produced by groups of working-class writers, such as Stepney Words or Basement Writers.[40] Organisations, like the Federation of Worker Writers and Community Publishers (FWWCP), founded in 1976, represented a countervailing trend of cultural innovation and development that enabled the self-expression of the working class, and were not easily co-opted or commodified.[41] By organising access and educational support, the FWWCP enabled the working class to produce its own writers and poets and it did so in a manner that has challenged to some extent at least the dominant elite's hold on 'Literature' and 'Culture'.[42]

By creating such spaces for the working class, the FWWCP's groups 'politicised and democratised the whole process of writing and publishing as one element in a wider radical vision of remaking social relations'.[43] Although the FWWCP groups were committed to producing 'primarily for a working-class readership', their narrow definition of class 'gradually widened with the recognition of a growing diversity of experiences as well as the influx of new constituencies', such as women and ethnic minorities.[44] Although the FWWCP was no match for the capitalist cultural industries, it demonstrated a similar potential to that of punk and Rock Against Racism (RAR) in articulating a pre-emergent culture that would also, ultimately, fail to supplant the dominant. Most importantly, however, it demonstrated the potential for an emergent culture that widespread access to the means of cultural production can mean for the working class.[45]

Practical consciousness and cultural production

For some radical working-class youth, 'practical consciousness' expressed an inseparable aesthetic and political sensibility through the material production of (un)popular cultural artefacts (e.g. badges, leaflets, fly-posters, 45s), events (gigs, rallies, benefits) and practices (do-it-yourself musical and political expression: e.g. forming bands, recording music, producing zines). Subjected to conditions imposed by the government and IMF, working-class youth expressed defiance to all kinds of authority (including an existential anger at one's lot in life), via the sound, images and messages of crisis music and political ephemera.

Before we can consider crisis music and political ephemera, it is important to recognise the music press for their contribution to the structure of feeling. The mainstream media's hostility towards punk ensured an important – and expanded – role for the music press: *Sounds*, *New Musical Express* (*NME*), *Melody Maker* and *Record Mirror*.[46] At the same time, these music papers were 'becoming increasingly radicalised'; both *NME* and *Sounds* 'came under the influence of a generation of journalists and editors who were keen to explore the political ramifications of a music scene that had been profoundly affected by the arrival of punk rock'.[47] They encouraged their readers 'to see music as political and musicians as politicians'.[48]

Reading *NME* felt like getting the latest instalment of *What is to be Done?*, where what musicians in bands like The Clash were saying about an issue or music became important for fans.[49] *NME*'s appeal to a growing segment of youth increased its circulation to between 200,000 and 270,000 copies sold per issue, 1978–81, with a readership 'three or four times that size': *NME* became the leading music paper.[50] Thus, crisis music reached a much greater audience than it might otherwise have if it had been built only around working-class youth subcultures.

Alongside the music papers, the radical press had been growing steadily since the 1960s and provided oppositional news and views. Although political organisations of both the far left and far right were generally unable to recruit punk musicians and fans *en masse*, punk articulated no clear political ideology beyond a commitment to anti-racism and anti-fascism.[51] For many working-class youths, the left felt as old and staid as the Establishment.

Political ephemera

Print ephemera or 'disposable literature' have had a greater influence at different times in history than is generally acknowledged, at least outside of those periods when they were a primary means of communication (e.g. England in the 1600s). For example, the circulation of Communist Party pamphlets in 1935–45 was far greater than its newspaper, *The Daily Worker*, and potentially more influential with the broader left on several issues.[52] With the spread of cheap, accessible technologies during the 1960s and 1970s (typewriters, photocopiers), ordinary people could produce and distribute disposable literature, expressing alternative and oppositional ideas. Political ephemera in this period, however, includes more than disposable literature; it includes a range of media, from graffiti long since painted over ('Eat the Rich'; 'Kill the Poor'; 'The lemmings were pushed') to faded fly-posters and poorly photocopied zines, which retain the structure of feeling in typeface, layout, words, phrases and symbols. The music and lyrics played a role in politicising working-class youth and were linked intertextually with struggles expressed via leaflets, fanzines and pamphlets, which were produced, for example, by welfare claimants in north London and by an anonymous collective offering a radical interpretation of the Brixton riots of April 1981.[53]

The National Front's increasing presence on the streets was made evident by its distribution of five million leaflets per year by the mid-1970s, not to mention the ubiquitous graffiti in inner cities of its symbol, 'NF'.[54] Against this mass distribution, RAR and the Anti-Nazi League (ANL), together distributed more than nine million leaflets and 750,000 badges between 1977 and 1979.[55] During its 'Militant Entertainment' tour in the month before the 1979 election, RAR distributed more than 100,000 leaflets, 30,000 posters and 10,000 copies of its paper, *Temporary Hoarding*.[56] In addition to the mass cultural production of leaflets and badges for RAR and ANL (in an 'agit-punk' style), there were thousands of individuals and groups producing their own badges, leaflets and fanzines, and fly-postering and spray-painting graffiti.

The DIY culture of punk included fans producing zines, which can be seen as 'ideological magazines' creating 'ideological musical communities', which were important in the politicisation of youth subcultures.[57] Zines were irregular publications where contacts and information could be shared, independent outlets for bands, publications and merchandise could be advertised, and of course where radical, critical political and social views could be expressed. 'These small, photocopied, stapled, pamphlet-length zines ... alongside montages of clippings and cutouts from other print media were frequently sold or distributed free at gigs and demonstrations and through postal and personal networks'.[58] The first punk zine was Mark Perry's *Sniffin' Glue*; but it was followed by hundreds, possibly thousands, more, such as *Kill Your Pet Puppy* or *Scum*. As Hebdige and others have pointed out, the language used by punks in these zines 'was determinedly "working class"' with crude words 'and typing errors and grammatical mistakes, misspellings and jumbled pagination', all of which contributed to the sense of 'urgency and immediacy ... of memos from the front line'.[59] The cut-and-paste style of punk zines provided inspiration for RAR's *Temporary Hoardings* and even the Trotskyist SWP's weekly newspaper, *Socialist Worker*, was influenced by 'punk' style for a short period of time.[60]

From 'dole queue rock' to 'crisis music'

A critical approach to understanding the structure of feeling is to seek a broader understanding of the music that terms such as 'punk' serve to limit. In particular, I would argue that the term 'crisis music' and, in its earlier incarnation, 'dole queue rock' act to express the musical forms as they then existed, which helps to identify the situation of the social class in the pre-emergent culture to which many radical youth belonged. I draw the term from the editorial in the first issue of *Temporary Hoardings*: 'We want Rebel music, street music. Music that breaks down people's fear of one another. Crisis music. Now music. Music that knows who the real enemy is. Rock against Racism. Love Music Hate Racism.'[61]

Crisis music expressed the practical consciousness of the period, which articulated resistance to authority and hierarchy, the world of work, bourgeois values and the state. It became part of the most explicit political alliance of the era, RAR, which was represented most publicly at the carnivals. However, crisis music was also experienced at the local level: various forms of political activities, such as demonstrations, rallies and pickets, and even attending gigs (which felt *politically* important at the time). Against the soundtrack of crisis music, youths leafleted, put up posters and graffittied walls to give voice to their anger and to announce their presence.

'Crisis music' encompasses a range of musical genres, including punk, reggae, ska, two-tone and dub poetry.[62] This name is apt because of the ways in which, contrary to the 'crisis' which elite discourses promoted, the 'No Future' generation of working-class youth were experiencing a 'crisis' of work, identity and ideology in their everyday lives. Crisis music was one of the adaptations of cultural forms that expressed the practical consciousness of an oppositional, pre-emergent culture.

When punk music first erupted in 1976, it was the antithesis to 'stadium rock'; rock stars complained about unions and taxes, but lacked any connection to their fans' lived experiences, unlike 'dole queue rock', which signified the 'No Future' generation's prospects and spoke directly to and about many fans' everyday lives. The economic situation of many working-class youths was clearly articulated in song lyrics during this period, which revealed a defiance of authority, whether at work or on the street, and a resistance to both the dominant culture and fascists and racists.[63]

While Dick Hebdige suggested that all working-class youth subcultures could be understood as 'a phantom history of race relations since the war', Paul Gilroy argued that 'race' was a signifier for broader issues of social relations generally.[64] In *Policing the Crisis*, Stuart Hall and four graduate students identified how the American term 'mugging' came to signify more than just the criminal act it denoted and thereby played a role in the 'law and order' agenda of the emerging 'authoritarian populism' named as 'Thatcherism'.[65] In many ways, punk music and other forms of crisis music were responding to the lived experience of Thatcherism's 'heavy manners' in the streets and neighbourhoods of the inner cities. Covers of reggae songs, inflected by the intense energy of punk, such as The Clash's version of the Junior Murvin song 'Police and Thieves', and Stiff Little Fingers' version of Bob Marley's 'Johnny Was', not only conveyed the sense of being 'under siege' by the forces of the state, but also enabled white youth to identify more closely with black youth, who were frequently targetted by police under 'stop and search' (aka 'SUS') laws.[66]

The appeal of reggae, ska and two-tone music for white punks who attended various RAR gigs should not be overlooked. Lloyd Bradley, who wrote the 'encyclopaedic history of reggae', claims that reggae music's commercial success in the UK during this period was possible only because 'RAR and punk rock' helped to create 'an explosion of interest in reggae amongst white youth'.[67] The 'first major success story' of UK reggae, for example, was Steel Pulse, nicknamed 'Jah Punk', who played numerous RAR events and produced a song explicitly expressing their and RAR's stand against racism and fascism: 'Jah-Pickney-RAR'.[68]

This interest should not be a surprise since, as Don Letts put it, 'you could hear the influence of reggae on the early punk bands – in the heavy basslines, in the rebellious lyrics, and in the idea of songs as musical reportage'.[69] We hear this in the song lyrics about unemployment, alienation and work, politics and war, love and loneliness. There is arguably a homology, therefore, to extend between the musical 'miscegenation' of some punk bands, such as The Clash, which was not accidental but part of the semantic figure indicative of a broader political-economic crisis, and the social and cultural 'miscegenation' of the working class, which had become the 'Other', as black and Asian British became part of the working class in transformation.

Out of this 'explosion of interest', some working-class punks sought out the dub poetry of artists like Linton Kwesi Johnson, aka 'LKJ', whose 'songs' expressed the practical consciousness of race and class. While his work also included love songs, LKJ articulated narratives of defiance and resistance at times critical of the rebels, and at times focusing on capitalism, government or police. His dub poetry was 'the first draft of history', articulating the 'structure of feeling' of black and white working-class youth, who were 'Mekkin Istri'. LKJ's dub-poetic 'reportage' in particular becomes crucial to providing alternative voices and understandings of these struggles, including 'Di Great Insohreckshun', an account of the April 1981 Brixton riots in response to a large police presence in the community (aka 'Swamp '81').[70]

Indeed, most encounters with racists and fascists on the streets were not part of the larger picture of mainstream media representations of occasional clashes, such as the August 1977 'Battle of Lewisham', which at least was represented more favourably by the radical left press. However, it was the everyday experience of 'being chased by the National Front' in the 'Concrete Jungle' (The Specials), or being attacked 'Down in a Tube Station at Midnight' (The Jam) by thugs 'who smelled of Wormwood Scrubs and too many right-wing meetings', which resonated with fans. Mark Steel's account of being a teenager with a small ANL branch leafleting at a suburban shopping centre and being rescued from NF skinheads by a stranger, was an incident that 'amounted to just another Saturday morning in 1979' for 'tens of thousands'.[71]

In many ways, the frenetic sounds of crisis music remained as an instant 'adrenaline rush' and complete inversion to the enforced boredom of everyday life on council estates, in dole queues, schools and dead-end jobs. These were made via sounds and lyrics that constructed an homologous relationship between the social relations of work/dole and home/self in the increasingly fractious and polarised state of living in 'Krisis Time 1977' in 'Labour Party Capitalist Britain'.[72] Crisis music conveyed the 'specifically affective elements of consciousness and relationships' that make up the structure of feeling via the 'characteristic elements of impulse, restraint, and tone' in the sounds of the music:[73] the discordant clashes between off-beat rhythms, cacophonous guitars, ear-shattering bass, out-of-tune instruments. The frenetic guitar chords of The Clash, the basslines of LKJ's dub poetry or the Gang of Four's 'taut geometrical paroxysm of the guitar, bass and drums', conveyed this sense of desperation, alienation and anger of the 'No Future' generation.[74]

Providing a voice to the everyday experiences of work or the lack of it was a primary concern affecting working-class youth. For example, the band UB40, named after the ubiquitous form required for signing on for unemployment benefits, made *Top Of The Pops* with their 1981 single about unemployment, '1-in–10', while The Specials rejected the 'Rat Race' and The Clash slammed 'Career Opportunities' for working-class youth. The Clash made it 'alright to be angry', especially in resisting the expectation 'to be grateful' which was conveyed by the latter song's lyrics in the lines, as noted by Mark Steel: 'Career opportunities, the ones that never knock/ The only job they offer you's to keep you out the dock'. At the end of which, he adds: 'So, it wasn't just me'.[75] This is 'thought as felt' and 'feeling as thought': the 'practical consciousness of a present kind, in a living and inter-relating continuity'.[76]

It was not only in the lyrics but also in the accents, where working-class identity was affirmed and even promoted: musicians and fans alike emphasised or mimicked working-class accents and manners of speech. If working-class people had been made to feel inadequate for their speech ('branded by your tongue'), punks and skinheads turned this on its head and defiantly asserted their 'working-classness' via speech as well as clothes and behaviour. Other linguistic markers of difference, such as West Indian accents and Jamaican patois, were also asserted by reggae, ska and dub musicians as a matter of both pride and resistance. For example, LKJ's 'black British vernacular' combined London and Jamaican accents at times to reveal linguistically in the immediate, everyday sense, the tensions on the streets and, over the longer term, the recomposition of the working class.[77] This black British vernacular provided a counter-narrative to the then dominant discourse about the global crisis and offered the listener hope in asking, 'Wat about di Workin Claas?', as resistance spread 'fram Inglan to Poelan/ evry step acraas di oweshan', and 'di rulin claases', of both capitalist West and communist East, found themselves 'in a mes' as 'di yout dem rebelin evrywhey'.[78]

Conclusion

The global economic 'meltdown' of 2008–09 has brought back public discussion of the working class and economic inequality. For most of the last thirty years, the working class has been absent except when defined negatively. 'Class, which was once principally defined by gender and occupation, is now largely defined by lack of employment, social marginalisation and even criminalisation'.[79] This has been the consequence of the 'cultural' impact of the processes of neoliberalism and the fragmentation of an identity that had been built around work over generations via the defeat of working-class political, economic and cultural organisations (e.g. 'Old Labour'; Communist Party; trade unions; FWWCP).

While this chapter makes no claims that the lived experiences of radical or politicised working-class youth were what most experienced, histories of class resistance and rebellion, no matter how transitory, offer a way of understanding subaltern structures of feeling. As the means to reconstruct the structure of feeling of radical working-class youth, 1976–83, cultural practices provide us with a means to understand how groups within subaltern social formations can constitute an emergent culture associated with either a new social class in formation or an older one in transformation.

At a time when forms of 'authoritarian populism' were gaining ground as 'common sense' in the UK, USA and Canada, RAR was perhaps the best example of a pre-emergent culture forming in a process but limited in its objectives to combating racism and fascism. Some innovations in cultural form can be seen in two-tone and punk music, dub poetry, zines and the graphic design of 'agit-punk'.

These examples of cultural production deserve to be recorded and recognised for their contribution to a pre-emergent, anti-authoritarian culture which challenged Thatcherism prior to the incorporation of punk and two-tone music into the mainstream music industry.[80] Thatcherism's 'inevitability' was due in part to the failure of the pre-emergent culture of crisis music to become fully 'emergent' and supplant the dominant culture. Instead, aspects of crisis music were incorporated into the commercial, 'classless' youth culture produced by corporations. For example, it was not just the failure of independent record labels or the music industry's takeover of punk music that were to blame; by the mid-1980s, youth culture magazines (e.g. *The Face, i-D*) had recuperated and incorporated the 'punk attitude' of working-class cultural production into their aesthetics and rhetoric, while increasingly distancing class and politics from consumerism and 'fun'. There was even an attempt to incorporate these aesthetics into the official 'zines' of global music stars: the full incorporation of the pre-emergent into the dominant culture.[81]

In this chapter, I have argued that to gain a sense of culture as lived, 1976–83, it is useful to draw upon Williams's concepts of structure of feeling, practical consciousness and (pre)emergent culture. Following Thompson's example, I have suggested that by drawing upon the DIY subcultural production of music and political ephemera, we can see how this oppositional structure of feeling reveals the practical consciousness of a social formation in the process of (re)composition, in their tone, affect, typeface, layout, sound, lyrics, gestures: 'thought as felt and feeling as thought'.[82] The genre of punk music at the level of cultural form at least encapsulated the lived experiences and practical consciousness of radical youth at a time of crisis when their future was uncertain as 'career opportunities' disappeared. Their practices and products were 'those genuinely new meanings and values, practices, relationships and kinds of relationship, which are substantially alternative or oppositional to the dominant culture'.[83] The later incorporation of punk music into the 'youth culture' industry undermined the former's subversiveness as the appeal of anti-statist, libertarian rhetoric of the 'free marketeers' and the seemingly 'democratic' promise of consumerism replaced the anti-authoritarian rhetoric and 'punk attitude' of crisis music in the 1980s.

That crisis music survived to some extent is a testimony to the power of cultural form. However, it is that shock of recognition when cultural form reflects the structure of feeling of a social class during a conjuncture or crisis that highlights a pre-emergent culture. The cultural formation of crisis music, formed around different musical genres and youth subcultures, was partially incorporated into the dominant culture but it still offered possibilities for a working class to challenge, not just the dominant ideology, but also the very cultural forms that made it dominant.

Acknowledgements

The author gratefully acknowledges the financial support provided to present an earlier version of this chapter at the Subcultures Network Conference (2011). These funds were received from a grant partly funded by Wilfrid Laurier University Operating Funds, and partly by the SSHRC Institutional Grant awarded to Laurier. I also wish to thank the organisers of the Conference, Matt Worley, and the two anonymous reviewers.

Notes

1 Sex Pistols, 'God Save the Queen' (Virgin Records, 1977). The record was released one week before the Queen's Jubilee celebrations; its original title was 'No Future'.
2 E. Hobsbawm, *The Politics of a Rational Left* (London: Verso, 1989); O. Jones, *Chavs: The Demonization of the Working Class* (London: Verso, 2011), pp. 39–52.
3 S. Hall, 'The Great Moving Right Show', *Marxism Today*, 23: 1 (January 1979), pp. 14–20; H. Pimlott, *'Wars of Position': Marxism Today, Cultural Politics and the Remaking of the Left Press, 1979–90* (forthcoming), Chapter 2.
4 See, for example, R. Sabin, 'I Won't Let That Dago By: Rethinking Punk and Racism', in Sabin (ed.), *Punk Rock: So What? The Cultural Legacy of Punk* (London: Routledge,

1999), pp. 199–218; I. Goodyer, *Crisis Music: The Cultural Politics of Rock Against Racism* (Manchester: Manchester University Press, 2009), pp. 28–32.

5   R. Williams, *Marxism and Literature* (Oxford: Oxford University Press, 1977), p. 132.

6   R. Williams, *The Long Revolution* (Harmondsworth: Penguin, 1961), p. 66.

7   Williams, *Marxism*, p. 128.

8   *Ibid.*, p. 130–1.

9   Williams, *Long Revolution*, p. 80.

10 *Ibid.*, p. 64.

11 R. Williams, *Politics and Letters* (London: NLB, 1979), p. 159.

12 *Ibid.*

13 Williams, *Marxism*, p. 128.

14 *Ibid.*

15 *Ibid.*, p. 132.

16 *Ibid.*, p. 129.

17 *Ibid.*

18 *Ibid.*, p. 130.

19 *Ibid.*, p. 128.

20 *Ibid.*

21 A. Medhurst, 'What Did I Get? Punk, Memory and Autobiography', in Sabin (ed.), *Punk Rock: So What?*, p. 219.

22 Williams, *Marxism*, p. 128.

23 *Ibid.*, pp. 134–5.

24 Williams, *Politics*, p. 164.

25 Williams, *Marxism*, p. 123.

26 E. P. Thompson, *The Making of the English Working Class* (Harmondsworth: Penguin, 1963).

27 D. Dworkin, *Cultural Marxism in Postwar Britain* (Durham, NC: Duke University Press, 1997), p. 102 (emphasis added).

28 Williams, *Marxism*, p. 134.

29 *Ibid.*, pp. 134–5.

30 Don Letts, *Punk Attitude* (2009).

31 J. Moran, '"Stand Up and Be Counted": Hughie Green, the 1970s and Popular Memory', *History Workshop Journal*, 70:1 (2012), 176.

32 *Ibid.*

33 *Ibid.*

34 S. Hall, C. Critchley, T. Jefferson, J. Clarke and B. Roberts, *Policing the Crisis: 'Mugging', the State and Law and Order* (London: Hutchinson, 1978).

35 More recent accounts challenge both the reality *and* discursive construction of the 'Winter of Discontent': C. Hay, 'Chronicles of a Death Foretold: The "Winter of Discontent" and the Construction of the Crisis of British Keynesianism', *Parliamentary Affairs*, 63:3 (2010), 446–70; J. Thomas, '"Bound in by History": The

Winter of Discontent in British Politics, 1979–2004', *Media, Culture & Society*, 29:2 (2007), 263–83.

36   Jones, *Chavs*, p. 52.

37   See note 4 in M. Worley, 'Oi! Oi! Oi! Class, locality and British punk', Chapter 2 in this collection.

38   Cited in T. Harcup, 'An Insurrection in Words: East End Voices in the 1970s', *Race & Class*, 51:2 (2009), 5.

39   D. Hebdige, *Subculture: The Meaning of Style* (London: Methuen, 1979), p. 111.

40   B. Osgerby, '"Bovver" Books of the 1970s: Subcultures, Crisis and "Youth-Sploitation" novels', *Contemporary British History*, 26:3 (2012), 299–332.

41   E.g. T. Woodin, 'Muddying the Waters: Changes in Class and Identity in a Working-Class Cultural Organisation', *Sociology*, 39:5 (2005), 1001–18.

42   *Ibid*. The FWWCP was dissolved in 2007.

43   T. Woodin, '"Chuck out the Teacher": Radical Pedagogy in the Community', *International Journal of Lifelong Learning*, 26:1 (2007), 89.

44   Woodin, 'Muddying the Waters', 1014.

45   The Greater London Council supported such cultural production until abolition in 1986 (see Pimlott, 'Wars of Position', Chapter 6).

46   S. Reynolds, *Rip It Up and Start Again: Postpunk 1978–84* (London: Penguin, 2006), p. 9.

47   Goodyer, *Crisis Music*, p. 28.

48   J. Street, Seth Hague and Heather Savigny quoted in *ibid*.

49   E.g. T. Parsons, 'The Clash: Thinking Man's Yobs', *New Musical Express* (2 April 1977).

50   Reynolds, *Rip It Up*, p. 9.

51   M. Worley, 'Shot by Both Sides: Punk, Politics and the End of "Consenus"', *Contemporary British History*, 26:3 (2012), 333–54.

52   H. Pimlott, '"Eternal Ephemera" or the Durability of "Disposable Literature"', *Media, Culture & Society*, 33:4 (2011), 526.

53   Campaign for Real Life, *Unwaged Fightback* (London, 1987); Riot Not to Work Collective (RNWC), *We Want to Riot, Not to Work* (London: RNWC, 1982).

54   D. Renton, *When We Touched the Sky: The Anti-Nazi League, 1977–81* (Cheltenham: New Clarion, 2006), p. 175; D. Widgery, *'Beating Time': Riot 'n' Race 'n' Rock 'n' Roll* (London: Chatto and Windus, 1986), p. 39.

55   Renton, *Touched the Sky*, p. 175; Widgery, *Beating Time*, p. 39.

56   D. Widgery, 'The Rise of Radical Rock', *New Socialist* (November/December 1981), p. 38.

57   C. Atton, 'Popular Music Fanzines: Genre, Aesthetics, and the "Democratic Conversation"', *Popular Music and Society*, 33:4 (2010), 520.

58   Pimlott, 'Eternal Ephemera', p. 526.

59   Hebdige, *Subculture*, p. 111. See also T. Triggs, 'Alphabet Soup: Reading British Fanzines', *Visible Language*, 29:1 (1995), 82–3.

60   P. Allen, '*Socialist Worker*: Paper With a Purpose', *Media, Culture and Society*, 7:2 (1985), 205–32.

61   Cited in Widgery, *Beating Time*, p. 60.

62   RAR also included other musical forms but these were not always well promoted or received by fans and organisers.

63   See D. Hebdige, *Cut 'N' Mix: Culture, Identity and Caribbean Music* (London: Comedia/Routledge, 1987).

64   Hebdige, *Subculture*, 1979, p. 45; P. Gilroy, *There Ain't No Black in the Union Jack* (London: Routledge, 1987), p. 129.

65   Hall *et al.*, *Policing the Crisis*; Hall, 'The Great Moving Right Show', pp. 14–20.

66   E.g. LKJ, 'Sonny's Lettah (Anti-Sus Poem)', *Forces of Victory* (Island Records, 1979).

67   Goodyer, *Crisis Music*, pp. 38–9.

68   The song was released on their second album in 1979. K. Walker, *Dubwise* (Toronto: Insomniac Press, 2005), p. 189.

69   Quoted in Goodyer, *Crisis Music*, p. 39.

70   RNWC, *Riot*.

71   M. Steel, *Reasons to be Cheerful* (London: Scribner, 2001), p. 37.

72   Cited in Gilroy, *There Ain't No Black*, p. 129.

73   Williams, *Marxism*, p. 132.

74   Reynolds, *Rip It Up*, p. 9.

75   Steel, *Reasons*, pp. 12–13.

76   Williams, *Marxism*, p. 132.

77   A. Dawson, 'Linton Kwesi Johnson's Dub Poetry and the Political Aesthetics of Carnival in Britain', *Small Axe*, 21 (2006), 55.

78   LKJ, 'Wat about di Workin Claas?', *Making History* (Island Records, 1983).

79   Ken Worpole cited in Woodin, 'Muddying the Waters', 1013.

80   D. Simonelli, 'Anarchy, Pop and Violence: Punk Rock Subculture and the Rhetoric of Class, 1976–78', *Contemporary British History*, 16:2 (2002), 121–44.

81   Triggs, 'Alphabet Soup', 82–3.

82   Williams, *Marxism*, p. 132.

83   *Ibid.*, p. 123.

15

Punk zines: 'symbols of defiance' from the print to the digital age

MATT GRIMES AND TIM WALL

In this chapter we examine the development of punk fanzines from the late 1970s to the present, exploring the role of these music fan-produced publications in giving meaning to the experience of a music community. This discussion of the punk fanzine's longitudinal existence allows us to investigate the variety of ways that the fanzines and webzines make sense of punk as music, a set of political ideas and as a subcultural scene. In particular we want to trace the way that fanzines have operated as a medium of communication for punk fans and activists, as part of the visual bricolage of punk's semiosis, and as a sign of authenticity amongst online punk culture in the twenty-first century.

We argue that fanzines became one of punk's many 'symbols of defiance', not just in the way that they visually and verbally represented punk's DIY ethos and activism, but also in the way they embodied the labour of 'fan-eds' as organic intellectuals[1] undertaking ideological work in which discourses of defiance and opposition are constructed, signified and reinforced. While other studies have often pointed to the importance of the communicative or symbolic functions of fanzines, and the role of editor/activists is occasionally alluded to, there has been too little emphasis on the way that the zine authors take on leadership roles.

Additionally, we are interested in the way that fanzines, and the symbolic value of the fanzine, have changed over time. We start with a discussion about the way that punk zines have been understood in broader analyses of punk culture in the last forty years. However, we also want to focus on two particular instances of the punk zine; two moments in which the specific meanings of specific fanzines can be explored in a little greater detail than those offered in the grander narratives of the punk fanzine.

In the first moment, a case study of one early 1980s anarcho-punk fanzine enables us to examine the way that such publications operated at the inter-section of political activism and DIY music criticism, constructing idealised notions of music, politics and community against which the actual activity within local punk scenes were judged. Anarcho-punk, as a sub-genre and a scene, provides a particularly useful way to think through the role of fanzines because it has a pivotal place within punk politics and music culture. Self-proclaiming themselves as the true and original voice of punk, a range of artists allied themselves to more self-consciously political positions associated with different strands of anarchist thought, and pursued a DIY music ethos and a commitment to different forms of direct action.[2] We suggest that through the 1980s anarcho-punk fanzines established a sort of evolving 'guide' or mani-festo to the cultural and political ideologies that were emerging within the developing British anarcho-punk subcultural scene. It is likely that, for many, those fanzines ordered the way in which readers (or even contributors) moved from an enthusiasm for punk as a music to a more politically and ideologically motivated participation, inspired and informed by the lyrical content of punk records. Triggs, for instance, sees this as inevitable.[3]

The second moment that we examine is thirty years later when the idea of the punk zine is used in websites with a focus on punk from the 1970s or 1980s, or music or artists that continue its ethos and/or sound. Given the strong emphasis within literature on the internet, its potential as a democratic space, and the role of websites and blogs as exemplars of DIY communications culture, it would be easy to assume that the practices and associations of the printed fanzine have more recently simply migrated online. By evaluating the continuities and discontinuities between the two moments of fanzine pro-duction, and the degree to which they articulate the ideology and identities of anarcho-punks, we argue that more often it is the symbolism and visual rhetoric of earlier print fanzines that predominates. While many internet advocates saw the early world-wide-web as a space for the sort of decentred political and cultural activism that had characterised 1980s anarcho-punk, there is little evidence that online fanzines continue to organise and order an engaged music culture.

In what follows, then, we move through three key areas of analysis. Firstly, we interrogate some of the principal studies of punk fanzines in order to try and contextualise their role and importance within punk music culture, especially in the late 1970s. Secondly, we focus on one example of a British regional anarcho-punk fanzine and the way that it constructed anarcho-punk as music, politics and, most importantly, as a community and movement. Specifically we seek to understand how the zine author produced a publication, a sense of regional activity and a discourse of anarcho-punk authenticity. Finally, we look to more recent online uses of the idea of a punk webzine, and evaluate the degree to which the visual, verbal and editorial practices of earlier print fanzines are reproduced in internet publishing. This raises interesting questions about the globalisation and commodification of the ideas and symbols of punk that were originally made in British regional culture.

Fanzines in punk music culture

Fanzines have long been seen as representing the underground or independent sector, or to provide an alternative to mainstream publishing, as the communities that develop around fanzines both produced and consumed this vernacular journalism. The term had its origins in realms outside music, most notably in science fiction fandom where fan-produced magazines were used to communicate between enthusiasts from the early twentieth century.[4] Fanzines are ascribed a key place in punk culture. It is widely assumed that when punk emerged, fanzines soon became one of the main means through which the new subculture represented and constructed punk musical style and ethos, and they embodied the developing cultural practices of the new DIY culture in the way that they were produced and distributed. *Sniffin' Glue* (SG) is widely seen as the first punk zine in 1976.[5] It took its title from the lyrics of a Ramones song that inspired its creator's enthusiasm, reproducing the lyrics in *SG* 1. The full title of this first issue – *Sniffin' Glue: and Other Rock 'n' Roll Habits* – indicated the intentionally anti-social stance of the editorial content, but also the place of the journal in a moment of celebrating rock's earlier, rawer, approach to music-making. The titles of the fanzines that followed in its wake – *Bombsite, Burnt Offering, Chainsaw, Communication Blur, Jamming, Love and Molotov Cocktails, Ripped & Torn, To Hell With Poverty* and *Vague* – signal clearly the way they positioned themselves in the emerging oppositional punk culture.

For Hebdige, the fanzines represented an 'alternative critical space', were 'immediately and cheaply produced from the limited resources at hand', and characterised by swear words, typing errors and misspellings: 'a paper produced in indecent haste, of memos from the frontline'.[6] *Sniffin' Glue* 1 shouted its intended readership, 'FOR PUNKS', while *Sideburns* 1 represented its commitment to DIY music culture in its now famous declaration 'Here's one chord, here's two more, now form your own band'.[7] Laing suggests there were more than fifty British punk fanzines being produced in 1977–78[8] and so strong was the link between the fanzines and the emerging music culture that looking back from the mid-1980s the editor of US fanzine *Hippycore* declared 'Zines are Punk'.[9]

There is certainly an emphasis in existing literature on the way that fanzines have operated as a medium of communication and propagation, and an interest in the way that such publications blur the line between producers, fans and activists. For Conway and Crowther, 'what really distinguishes fanzines from magazines is that much of the content is submitted by amateur writers amongst the fanzine readership, with readers' letters and discussion columns providing a crucial mechanism for interaction between readers'.[10] For O'Hara punk fanzines remained the primary form of communication amongst punks into the twenty-first century, propagating the ideas which define 'punk culture and philosophy': anarchy, sex-related issues, environmental philosophies, and the politics of punk business.[11] Likewise, in her exploration of fanzine visual design, Teal Triggs has asserted that fanzines 'provided a focal point and unifying vehicle for establishing and reinforcing shared values, philosophy and opinions'.[12] In a later publication she declares that 'as independent self-published publications, fanzines became vehicles of subcultural communication and played a fundamental role in the construction of punk identity and a political community'.[13]

Most interestingly, though, most analyses of punk zines pay particular attention to the visual language of these publications and the way this symbolised punk. As we have noted, in Hebdige this is seen in terms of the same bricolage that characterised punk dress and music. Such studies usually point to the fact that earlier punk fanzines were characterised by their use of cut-and-paste, hand-written and roughly typed narrative content, combined with a mixture of music and political ideology.[14] Triggs goes as far as suggesting *Sniffin' Glue* represents a 'graphic language of resistance' and analyses in detail covers from *SG*, *Chainsaw* and *Ripped & Torn*, placing their aesthetics in the wider context of modernist art and design theory.[15] Hebdige connects the visual design of *SG*, and the wider deployment of graffiti and ransom note iconography, explicitly to the visual imagery of the Sex Pistols' 'God Save the Queen' record sleeve, T-shirts and posters, but without reference to the controversy surrounding the major record company that produced it.

There is a tendency in the literature to produce an overly determining and fundamentally structuralist reading of punk, and in fanzines (as with other activities) visual design is seen as the primary language, culture an anthropological activity of display, and class as the primary definer of social agency.

This template was set by Hebdige's 1979 analytical emphasis on 'the meaning of style', together with the broader subcultural approach from which it emerged. Triggs's art college incorporation follows this line when she states that 'punk arguably represented the politics of the working-class experience', but she marshals only the citation of Hebdige and other antecedent subcultural studies as support, before drawing consistently on examples of appropriations of earlier design practices that do not obviously have any connection to working-class experience.[16]

By contrast, Dave Laing's broader reading of punk as discursive practice has been less often used as the basis for thinking through punk fanzines, even though it arguably offers a much wider context.[17] Placing the history of punk fanzines in a longer history of music politics and emphasising productive activity as much as symbolism he opens up a way of understanding the role of such publications at different points in time. In particular, Laing notes the productive power of the very idea of 'punk', the DIY culture it utilised and celebrated, as well as those attempts by agents of the state to crudely control emergent punk practices. In discussing punk fanzines, Laing locates them in a longer history and wider set of practices of DIY culture which he connects to the early sci-fi fanzines, the tradition of economic independence from the music industry, xerox record labels, and the idea of punk as a vernacular music.[18]

Likewise, for George McKay punk and its fanzines are less a rebirth of alternative values and more one of a number of stopping-off places in a longer history of 'cultures of resistance since the sixties'.[19] Many of his interests in music as cultural politics, in community music and DIY culture, expressed in other publications, are distilled in this cultural history.[20] In McKay's history, unlike more traditional popular music histories, punk does not become completely incorporated into the mainstream of the popular music industry, but the importance of the punk critique is sustained through the more self-conscious politics of the anarcho-punk movement. British anarcho-punk emerged as a subcultural DIY musical scene during the late 1970s, picking up on some of the earlier punk rhetoric of anti-authority, anarchism and DIY culture and making them a central tenet of its perspective. Activists encouraged people in the scene from all areas of Britain to directly link the vibrant music to an attempt to collectively construct a politicised culture that encompassed ideologies and philosophies of anarchist/pacifist politics, personal freedom, anti-capitalism and animal rights amongst many others. These positions were presented as a direct challenge to the politics of a 'mass society', the political economy of the record industry and the commodification of 'mainstream' punk. At the centre of this challenge was the commitment to the emergence of a 'DIY' music culture. Such ideologies were promoted by anarcho-punk bands such as Crass, Poison Girls, Flux of Pink Indians and Conflict, to name but a few.[21]

For their readers, anarcho-punk fanzines played a central role in disseminating and reinforcing these ideological positions, and in offering alternatives to the popular media's representations of punk. Taking our approach from Laing's more nuanced poststructuralist position, we argue that it is the low-tech cut-and-paste techniques of fanzines production, the effort involved in such production, and the clearly articulated positions of their editors, which constitute the central characteristics of punk fanzines. In doing so, we seek to move beyond the simpler notion that fanzines were simply channels of communication and their designs symbols of punk, to the idea that fanzines represent cultural work, and that their 'fan-eds' were key agents in defining what punk was or should be. It is, we contend, through this cultural work that the editors stake a claim for the necessary passion and commitment to warrant their status as an arbiter of taste, the authority amongst readers to assert specific ideological positions, and the subcultural capital to allocate classifications of authenticity.

Our analytical approach to examining fanzines, therefore, emphasises the discursive practices of the 'fan-eds' just as much as the textual meanings and repertoires of visual design and political philosophy they encoded. To grapple with this we have applied Norman Fairclough's approach to deal with both the single moments of representation but also the broader orders of discourse.[22] In the former Fairclough suggests attention is paid to texts as representational forms which generate identities and relationships as well as to the conventions and production practices of the creators, while in the latter he focuses on discursive practices of the community in which the single text is produced. Such a systematic approach can be demonstrated most clearly in two examples: firstly in 1980s anarcho-punk print fanzines; and secondly with 2010s punk webzines.

Anarcho-punk fanzines as practices of cultural work

It is useful to take the example of a single publication to see how this cultural work is realised and how particular discursive constructions are articulated. The punk to anarcho-punk fanzine *Acts of Defiance*, published in the north-east of England during the early 1980s, demonstrates this particularly well.

Acts of Defiance certainly used the same 'low-value production techniques' that Triggs identifies as characteristic of the earlier fanzines: 'photocopying and Letraset, employing the graphic elements including ransom note cut-outs, handwritten, stencilled, scrawled or typewritten texts, or collage images'. In terms of its design, then, the example of *Acts of Defiance* seems to support Triggs's contention that these design characteristics 'went some way to establish a set of commonly used principles and a way of creating a distinctive graphic language'. However, we would be more cautious about her claim that this language 'ultimately mirrored the particular aesthetic of punk music'. Rather than symbolising punk, or representing a wider punk aesthetic, we would contend that it was the very activities of punk zine producers which produced 'punk'.[23]

This may seem like a small shift in emphasis, but it has important implications. Triggs's argument seeks to privilege the history of design and modernist aesthetics above the important processes which were at work in fanzine production. In particular, using the example of *Acts of Defiance* we take issue with Triggs's argument that this was a 'language of graphic resistance steeped in the first instance in the ideology of punk and its anarchical spirit and in the second instance, that which emerged from their position in a continuous timeline of self-conscious Dadaist and Situationist International "art" practices'.[24] We do not want to suggest that there was not an emerging 'ideology of punk' with an associated 'anarchical spirit', nor that there are not obvious connections to Dadaism or Situationism, but that an analysis which moves from 'how it looks' to 'what it means' and then to 'what caused it to mean that', is mistaken. Instead, we need to examine what the editors were doing, with what practical and discursive resources, with what purposes. In this context the verbal language of the fanzines was as important as the visual language, and that both of these are discursive practices which produced important senses of what it was to be 'a punk', what role music, symbolism and scene had in this construction, and what role a 'fan-ed' had in such an activity. What is interesting about the later fanzines like *Acts of Defiance*, is that these very issues are central to the discourse of the editorial content itself.

There is a strong and consistent ideological and philosophical discourse apparent across the issues of *Acts of Defiance* which is anchored by the very title of the publication and its allusion to a form of activism and opposition which verges on political nihilism. It is also notable that *Acts of Defiance*, as a regional publication, represents the localisation of punk within Britain in the late 1970s, at the very moment that the music was attracting a global audience and the politics of punk was connecting different internationalist trajectories of thought together. *Acts of Defiance* was one of many anarcho-punk fanzines that carried on the cut-and-paste aesthetic of the early fanzines but used them for a much more systematic articulation of a political position. In fact for one of the authors of this chapter (Grimes), at least, it was these editorial arguments that had a critical influence on his own political/ideological development, and engaged him as an active participant in the early British anarcho-punk scene. The editorial content defined what it was to be a member of a scene that increasingly constructed a discourse of defiance, anarchism and anti-authoritarianism. These personal responses are also clearly articulated in the editorials of *Acts of Defiance*, which are centred around the idea that the fanzine is a site for identity-creation, ideological engagement, and action. In this study, therefore we wanted to view the editorial content as the inscription of certain forms of cultural work. As we have already suggested, we want to argue that it was not the iconography of punk zines which carried their meaning, but the low-tech cut-and-paste techniques of production. By that we mean their style was a product of the way they were made just as much as an attempt to draw on existing ideas of DIY communication (the typewriter), anonymity (the cut-and-paste ransom note), and the highly personal response (handwriting and annotation). Far from being immediate, there was substantial effort in-volved in making a punk zine, which no doubt accounted for the short life of most of them. They both required and exhibited substantial commitment and insider knowledge, and the editorial content was often peppered with clearly articulated justifications for this cultural labour.

So, for instance, in seeking to understand the way three single editorials in issues 5, 6 and 7 of *Acts of Defiance* (*AOD*) function we need to examine the relationship constructed between the 'fan-ed' and 'fan-reader', and the relation-ship the text defined for the participants.

AOD editorial issue 5 [spelling and punctuation as in the original]:

> Here it is then 1983, and things are as bad as they ever were same old boredm and apathy that's all ways been around. Punk I thought was supposed to be about energy, life, originality (remember them?) ... Even some of the so called anarcho-punks can't find anything to do but sit around and moan about it, these (you) are the people who should be going out and doing things (other than getting pissed). Its much easier to say that its all the fault of the system – well maybe it is but you can still do a few things ... Its all very well to moan and do nothing if things are boring then its up to you to get out and change them.

AOD editorial issue 6 [spelling and punctuation as in the original]:

> Its funny isn't it, how many people who have got anarchy signs all over themselves and claim to know what its all about – peace and love and all that isn't it? And yet despite this how many act as if they actually meant it – not bloody many ... People who claim to believe in anarchy but let us

down on the most basic thing – trust … they say that anarchy begins with
the individual but its still right, you always complain that your mistreated by
'society' but unless you fulfil peoples trust in you your going to remain isolated
and unless you can learn to trust fully then we are going nowhere.

AOD editorial issue 7 [spelling and punctuation as in the original]:

Now its time to become more involved, to really get down to things seriously.
So all you 'punks' out there who thought that you were helping the revolution
by buying records on Crass label and spraying anarchy signs all over think
again. There are loads of things really worth doing … you can always start with
yourself (I said this in the last issue and probably the one before and I'll keep
saying it until someone listens). If you are going to go around calling yourself
an anarchist then at least try and act like you mean it.

What comes through in the discourses of the editorial in the three printed
fanzines is how strong and forcibly the identity of being a 'punk' is articulated.
In particular, a distinction is made between those who use the signs of being
a punk – critique of the status quo; sporting anarchy signs; 'buying records
on Crass label' – and those who take personal responsibility to act. These
statements are part of an ongoing critique of the local scene and the perceived
apathy that is characteristic of its activities. Here the editors, through their
seeming frustration and anger, are using the editorial to remind and reinforce
what they think anarcho-punk is about and how it is down to individual responsibility to make it work as an ideological practice. The editors highlight/
reinforce what they believe defines and constitutes anarcho-punk and anarcho-
punk identity through the discourses of DIY ethics, anarchism and individual
responsibility.

By issue 7, though, there is a discernible shift in the discourse of *Acts of
Defiance*. There is a continuing variance between two strikingly different discourses. The first relates to professional practices of production and market
success, while the second relates to the primary ideological function of an
anarcho-punk fanzine. So, interestingly, the editorial talks about both improve-
ments and success in increasing circulation in the past two issues. However,
they also state their decision to cut down on the amount of music/gig/band
reviews to include what they consider to be more important issues. There is
certainly some uneasiness about the editors' right to lead on ideological questions, to interpret the state of the scene, and maybe even to make editorial
decisions. These conflicting discourses are, though, made more coherent by
reference to an idealised anarcho-punk community [spelling and punctuation
as in the original]:

Right then as you must have noticed this issue is a much improved version of AOD, we've also increased the circulation to 1,000 due to the success of the last couple of issues so we hope this issue is up to standard.

Since we first started doing this zine we've slowly cut down the number of bands we've interviewed and generally cut down on the music side of the zine, this is not due to the fact we don't like music or the bands but we feel that there are plenty of other fanzines, magazines etc that cover music and hardly any that contain interesting, informative articles which we feel are far more important than pages and pades of the same band interviews and handouts. We've been accused, recently, of just preaching all the time, but a lot of the things we write about and say are important issues to us and we feel we must speak about them, so there!

The transition of *Acts of Defiance*'s construct can be seen emerging on page 4 of issue 3. Previous editions had mostly focused on gig and music reviews, but by issue 3 the writers had started to investigate and debate the ideologies of anarcho-punk with a whole page dedicated to anarchism (the only page that carried any specific political ideology in that issue). By issue 5 more than half (thirteen pages) of the fanzine content is given over to political/punk ideology covering animal rights, feminism, nuclear threat, police brutality and a critical view of state education.

These editorials are themselves a critique of Triggs's notion that there is a useful 'language of graphic resistance' at the heart of punk, offering instead that such symbols allowed some participants to act as if they were punks without them taking the necessary ideological and activist positions that the editors assert are at the centre of being a 'true' punk. The authority of the editors to be able to define what is and isn't punk, what the role of music and the scene is within punk, and how symbols should (and should not) operate, comes from their willingness to undertake the demanding work of producing the fanzine in the first place. Although in the late 1970s and early 1980s most of the benefits of the desk top publishing revolution had not yet arrived, it was possible to produce quite convincing facsimiles of professionally designed publications. In fact our own experiences of producing publications would suggest that there was greater work involved in creating publications which looked and read like these punk fanzines. While aspiring professional designers may have utilised the look of such publications and connected their aesthetic to the shock tactics of Dadaism and Situationism, for most regionally based punk zine editors it was the act of cultural and political work in the verbal language which was centrally important.

Looking through other British anarcho-punk fanzines of that era – and we would include *Mucilage, Necrology, Harsh Reality, Allied Propaganda* and *Guilty of What* as exemplars – similar constructs appear in the editorials of them all. Although we would not go as far as saying that there is a homogenous construction of the British anarcho-punk fanzine – there are different degrees of importance placed on some discourses in different fanzines – the issues of symbolism, identity and action are consistent.

It is through this editorial content, rather than the design, that the (shared) values, ideologies and philosophy of the British anarcho-punk movement are disseminated amongst the fanzine readership. And it is through this activity that the fanzine is constructed as a site for defining identity, ideology, defiance and opposition.

Online fanzines

Commentators and academics alike have often pointed to the potential of the internet to offer a communication and cultural space that greatly expands the sorts of 'alternative critical space', provide a 'crucial mechanism for interaction between readers', and serve as a 'unifying vehicle for establishing and reinforcing shared values, philosophy and opinions' – all of which may also be seen to characterise punk fanzines.[25] Given these arguments, it is not fanciful to suggest that we could see the punk fanzines of the 1970s and 1980s as prototypes for the cultural interactions that would take place in virtual space. Given this, and the continued vitality of a live and recorded punk scene, it would be easy to assume that the practices and meanings associated with the earlier printed fanzine have simply migrated online. However, as we will show, while there is evidence of an obvious attempt to reproduce the iconography of the print punk zines in online sites, this is most often a superficial act of iconic signification, and there is a more diverse and complex range of practices and products than found in earlier print incarnations of the fanzine phenomenon.

Looking broadly at web sites and blogs that are listed in a Google search for punk fanzines, we can see a pattern emerging. Firstly, there is a considerable amount of heritage activity around earlier print punk and anarcho-punk zines from the 1970s and 1980s. For instance, it is possible to examine scans of most, if not all, of the issues of all the fanzines cited in this chapter online, along with a whole host of other regional fanzines not mentioned. This, we suggest, is indicative of the reverence towards such music culture products held by many, and recognition of the importance of specific fanzines amongst many punk fans. Secondly, the term fanzine and fanzine iconography is widely used in, or associated with, websites or blogs that do not have the same production practices or cultural role as the earlier print fanzines. Most often this deployment of the term fanzine, or the use of fanzine iconography, is part of a mainly marketing or commercial aim. In some cases the web presence is there to support and sell as print-based fanzine, but more often it is used to market other forms of product associated with punk. These include recordings and other forms of merchandising. Finally, we should note that there is a considerable amount of online activity which was formally hosted within the printed pages of punk zines, but which is less often listed against an online search for punk fanzines. This would include the editorial enthusiasm for certain bands, participant reviews or exchanges about a shared musical interest, or editorial positions on a whole range of which are explicitly linked to anarcho-punk philosophy. We would suggest that it is this activity which most closely matches the cultural practices and products of punk zines, but it usually takes place without any reference to terms like fanzines or webzines, and without the deployment of any of the iconography of the 1970s and 1980s print fanzines. It is also worth noting, that our observations are only built upon web platforms that most closely reproduce the idea of a fanzine publication: the web site or blog. There are, at first sight, even more Facebook pages linked to the term 'punk fanzine', and other social media platforms like Twitter contain an even greater range of fan activity around the contemporary punk and anarcho-punk music scenes.

To explore contemporary online activity associated with punk fanzines in a little more detail we examined three exemplar sites or blogs. We chose these in part because, on the basis of Google algorithms at least, they represent popular destinations for online users interested in punk and anarcho-punk fanzines, and in part because they show remarkably different approaches to continuing the traditions of the print fanzine. The sites we selected are also instructive in thinking through the themes of fanzine iconography and cultural practice we raised in the earlier discussions of first- and second-wave print punk zines.

Lights Go Out is a blog built around a print fanzine and includes details about past issues of the publication (which at the time of writing had reached issue 19), an ecommerce backend to sell issues of the fanzine and associated merchandise, and some news and link pages. *No Front Teeth* is the web site for a record label of the same name which issues LP and 7-inch vinyl records broadly within the punk genre. At the time of our initial research in late 2011, *Taped* was a blog connected with the Taped DIY label where free downloads to musical releases are available, though its name – and much of the top-level terminology – is drawn from the cassette-sharing culture associated with punk in the 1970s and 1980s. By the time we came to study the site most of the recent posts were explanations for its declining activity, and proposals for a site redesign. By the time we came to finalise this chapter for publication the site was no longer online.

All three web sites made some reference to the iconography of the late 1970s and early 1980s print fanzine we have discussed so far. *Lights Go Out* and *Taped* used banners which seemed to reference graffiti writing, while *No Front Teeth* clearly referenced 'ransom note' stylisation, used montage techniques and typewriter or stencil-styled typefaces. *Taped* used a type that resembles a dot-matrix printer, which did replace typewriters to generate copy in fanzines from the mid-1980s. All three, but especially *Lights Go Out*, used the layout structures and design elements of website and blog templates.

The 'landing page' for *Lights Go Out* (www.lightsgoout.co.uk) has a selection of drop down menus including sections on news, reviews and interviews. One click through the news section reproduces press releases and lists bands and artists' tour dates. The reviews and interviews sections list the contents of the printed issues where the reviews and interviews appear, and an opportunity to purchase the printed issues (though the drop down link to the shop shows a not found error). There is also an online exclusives section that has interviews and reviews that are not available in the printed version of *Lights Go Out*. The about section reveals that there is an editor, though no editorial, and has the profiles of regular contributors to the fanzine. On closer inspection of the content of the printed fanzine issues, it seems to be a general music fanzine broadly about indie rock music with some emphasis on punk and pop-punk bands.

No Front Teeth (www.nofrontteeth.co.uk) was also identified when using 'punk webzine' on Google search. On its landing page header it refers to itself as 'Punk Rock Records, Mailorder and Zine for Spastics'. It employs some of the graphic style of earlier punk fanzines, however this 'webzine' appears to be a shop front for a punk rock record label as there is no 'zine' content such as reviews, interviews or editorial. Its 'news' section is predominantly about forthcoming releases on their record label or other labels featuring members of No Front Teeth. This would suggest that they are also a punk band, however their Facebook profile points to the fact that No Front Teeth are a DIY punk rock record label where the people who run the label play in punk rock bands. The 'label' link on their landing page links to a shop where records/CDs can be purchased via PayPal. Its Radio link and MySpace link are both inactive and the contact link hyperlinks to Outlook Express email. The *No Front Teeth* 'friends' link leads to a set of hyperlinked banners for skateboarding, footwear and fashion companies.

UNIVERSITY OF WINCHESTER
LIBRARY

Taped (www.taped.org.uk) was also listed when we set 'punk webzine' and 'punk fanzine' in our Google search. Under further investigation, they are perhaps the closest of the three to what we might associate with the editorial structure of earlier print punk fanzines. Here the homepage acts as a type of editorial as it describes the author's account of where he is regarding the lack of recent content posted in the previous fifteen months and the restructuring of the site. Other pages on the site contain interviews, reviews and forthcoming gigs. There is also access to the Taped DIY label where free downloads to musical releases are available. Much of the content appears to be based around focused discussions about the local Dorset and south-west England music scene, though this is not restricted only to punk. This would suggest that the author of the fanzine lives in that area of the UK.

It should be clear that Lights Go Out and No Front Teeth did not replicate any of the practices and constructs that appear in the print fanzines we analysed earlier in this chapter. In particular, there did not seem to be any clear sense of a 'fan-ed', although they were often written in a style that suggested such an agent at work. In addition, there were none of the wider contributions from readers that characterised the earlier print publications. One could speculate that they made significant use of the term fanzine and iconic reference to the print 'zine' status as a promotional tool. There were certainly none of the discursive repertoires of punk identity, ideology, defiance and opposition that were prominent in print publications. Even though Lights Go Out presented itself as a UK fanzine about music, the focus was more broadly on a range of high-energy forms of indie music rather than any clear punk scenes. Given that the reviews and interviews that made up the print fanzines were international in scope, it was hard to see what function the national tagline had. There are certainly echoes here of Chris Atton's suggestion that the majority of e-zines are primarily interested in 'product' and the promotion of that product.[26] The content of Taped, however, seemed to draw close comparisons to some of the other discursive practices found in the print fanzines. There were interviews/reviews and discussions around a local scene. However, the explicit emphasis on identity, defiance and opposition found in Acts of Defiance and similar fanzines was wholly absent.

Fanzine culture, 1976–2013

In this chapter we have aimed to consider and analyse the fanzine as a discursive practice. In doing so we have sought to encompass the usual emphasis on fanzines as channels of communication and symbols of wider punk practices, but to ensure we recognise that it was the fanzine which was one of the key ways in which punk and anarcho-punk was made meaningful. We would argue, then, that simply focusing on the characteristic visual design of the print fanzine limits our understanding of its cultural role and the position of its 'fan-ed' cultural agents. This important point also allows us to understand the extent to which webzines replicate the discursive practices of the print fanzine. Overall, while many web sites or blogs may include visual references to fanzines, and may even use the term in their titles or primary banners, they do not include the sorts of editorial organisation, the cultural practices or the discursive constructions of identity and opposition which characterised print fanzines. It is notable that many of these cultural practices and discursive constructions are immediately apparent in other online activity around punk, and around political activism associated with anarcho-punk. For this reason, the disjuncture between print and web zines cannot be seen as a clash between contemporary punk rock as a music product and 1970s to 1980s ideological punk.

That is not to ignore the obvious cultural caché that the terms fanzine and zine, and the visual references, have for the owners of websites and blogs who want to attract audiences, especially if they want to engage with potential customers for punk records, print fanzines or merchandise. Nor do we make this point to undermine the clear heritage value that the older print fanzines have in representing and telling the story of punk's history for all those who carefully archive scans of these publications. However, we should recognise that in both these cases, online activity tries to align recent cultural or commercial work with the subcultural capital of 'fan-eds' and the oppositional ideologies that have been historically associated with fanzines in popular culture.

More importantly, perhaps, we need to understand that it is not in their iconography and symbolism that the print fanzines were relevant and meaningful. Their visual design was an epiphenomenon of the discursive practices of the 'fan editors' who produced the fanzines in a manner which indexed their DIY nature and the investment of effort of the editors as agents. It is the low-tech cut-and-paste production of fanzines, the passion and effort involved in producing fanzines, which gave them their essence of authenticity. In particular this DIY practice is central to the ethos of anarcho-punk. The print publications needed further effort in the physical act of selling and distributing fanzines at punk gigs, the face-to-face interaction that holds cultural value amongst punk's subcultural groups.

One could speculate that perhaps there is a resistance amongst anarcho-punk and punk zine producers to use the web as an alternative to the traditional physical form of the fanzine, perhaps because the cultural work involved does not provide the same sort of construction of authenticity.

However, the issues are more complex than this. Firstly, as Liptrot has argued, many of the practices of the 1980s British anarcho-punk scene have over the last twenty years been absorbed into wider contemporary DIY punk and hard-core punk scenes across the world. In these scenes the anarcho-punk DIY ethic is still prominent and the print fanzine remains one of the key means of ideological communication within the subculture.[27] Secondly, even a cursory investigation shows that the issues of identity, ideology, defiance and opposition are widespread on online message boards, blogs and in social media. Taking just two examples which explicitly link their current activity with the earlier history of punk, the anarcho-punk blog oldpunksneverdie.com and anarchopunk.net both demonstrate some of the language and format of the print fanzines associated with punk/anarcho-punk. Neither uses visual design or has a major emphasis on using terms like fanzine or zine. The internet presents a wholly different set of potential communicative and practices, the cultural work it demands is very different, and it does not demand that its DIY status is signalled so strongly in its visual form.

Notes

1 We derive this term from Antonio Gramsci as intellectual leaders who emerge from a group, although we take it in terms wider than those discussed by Gramsci himself in Q. Hoare and G. N. Smith (eds), *Selections from the Prison Notebooks of Antonio Gramsci* (New York: International Publishers, 1971).

2 For authors who articulate or explore this idea see G. Berger, *The Story of Crass* (London: Omnibus Press, 2006); I. Glasper, *The Day the Country Died: A History of Anarcho-Punk, 1980–84* (London: Cherry Red, 2006); G. McKay, *Senseless Acts of Beauty: Cultures of Resistance Since the Sixties* (London: Verso, 1996); C. O'Hara, *The Philosophy of Punk: More Than Noise* (Edinburgh: AK Press, 1999).

3 T. Triggs, 'Scissors and Glue: Punk Fanzines and the Creation of a DIY Aesthetic', *Journal of Design History*, 19:1 (2006), 70.

4 S. Moskowitz, 'The Origins of Science Fiction Fandom: A Reconstruction', *Foundation*, 48 (1990), 5–25.

5 D. Hebdige, *Subculture: The Meaning of Style* (London: Routledge, 1979), p. 111; D. Laing, *One Chord Wonders: Power and Meaning in Punk Rock* (Milton Keynes: Open University Press, 1985), p. 15.

6 Hebdige, *Subculture*, p. 111.

7 *Sideburns*, 1 (1977), 2.

8 Laing, *One Chord Wonders*, p. 14.

9 Quoted in P. Rutherford, *Fanzine Culture* (Oldham: Springhead Books, 1995), p. 3.

10 S. Conway and D. Crowther, 'Virtual Networking Pre- and Post-Cyberspace: An Assessment of the Implications for Social Cohesion', *Journal of Management Research*, 1:1 (2002), 1–12.

11 O'Hara, *The Philosophy of Punk*, p. 62–9.

12 T. Triggs, 'Generation Terrorists: Fanzines and Communication', in T. Triggs (ed), *Communicating Design : Essays in Visual Communication* (London: B.T. Batsford, 1995), p. 34.

13 Triggs, 'Scissors and Glue', 70.

14 See, for instance, P. Stoneman, *Fanzines: Their Production, Culture and Future* (University of Stirling: M.Phil. thesis, 2001); Triggs, 'Scissors and Glue', 69–83.

15 Triggs, 'Scissors and Glue', 72.

16 *Ibid.*, 73.

17 Laing, One Chord Wonders.

18 *Ibid.*, pp. 15–16.

19 McKay, *Senseless Acts of Beauty*.

20 See, for instance, G. McKay, 'DIY Culture: Notes Towards an Intro.', in G. McKay, *DIY Culture: Party and Protest in Nineties Britain* (London: Verso, 1998); P. Moser and G. McKay, *Community Music: A Handbook* (Lyme Regis: Russell House, 2005).

21 Glasper, *The Day the Country Died*.

22 N. Fairclough, *Media Discourse* (London: Arnold, 1995).

23 All quotes are from Triggs, 'Scissors and Glue', 76.

24 *Ibid.*, 74.

25 Hebdige, *Subculture*; Conway and Crowther, 'Virtual Networking Pre- and Post-Cyberspace'; Triggs, 'Scissors and Glue' respectively.

26 C. Atton, *Alternative Media* (London: Sage, 2002), p. 70.

27 M. Liptrot, 'Beyond the Lifespan of a Scab: The Longevity of DIY Punk in Britain, unpublished Ph.D. thesis, University of Bolton, 2012).

Afterword
The cultural impact of punk:
an interview with Jon Savage

MATTHEW WORLEY

Among the numerous accounts of punk's origins and early development that now exist, Jon Savage's *England's Dreaming* (1991) is peerless. Combining sharp critical analysis with participatory insight, it locates British punk squarely within its socio-economic, cultural and political context. Indeed, Savage's reading of punk may be traced back to his 1976-produced fanzine *London's Outrage*, which interspersed media clippings and pop cultural references with an essay forewarning Britain's descent into fascism. Thereafter, he chartered punk's course through the pages of *Sounds* and *Melody Maker*, championing those – such as Linder, Joy Division, Wire, Subway Sect, X-Ray Spex, Devo, Pere Ubu, Throbbing Gristle and Cabaret Voltaire – whom he felt best chronicled their time and complemented punk's initial urge to question and experiment. Though Savage's writing and broadcasting work has since led him to explore far wider vistas of popular culture, he remains a foremost commentator on punk's history and continuing relevance. The interview below, therefore, sought to ascertain Savage's thoughts on the core themes of this book; that is, on punk's import beyond the music and in terms of identity, space and communication.

> MW: One of the premises of the book is that punk was/is more than simply rock 'n' roll. How far, if at all, do you think we can disentangle punk from punk rock?

JS: Well, at that time, music was the prime youth cultural focus. You know, it's thirty-seven years ago and before many things. It's pre the internet; it's pre the great expansion in the mass media and the youth media. It's pre social media; it's pre mobile phones etc. etc. So with music then the focus of youth culture, punk rock was very important because rock 'n' roll was the hook and the focus for punk in the early stages: you can't disentangle the two of them.

But then I always thought that pop music – and that includes rock 'n' roll – was more than just music. I'm one of a generation that got a lot of artistic, political and even philosophical input from popular music in the way that people did in these islands. You know, they don't in France because they have a proper political and philosophical dialogue; but in the UK we don't. And so pop music was the focus for an enormous amount of dissident energy; a kind of gnostic text. So disentangling the two didn't make much sense then because it's quite possible to be in a pop group or in the pop arena and be about more than music anyway. The music in the early days was a very accurate representation of the attitude and music is obviously a performance – it's audio visual, an overwhelming experience. So you'd go and see the Sex Pistols and you'd see the clothes and you'd hear the noise: and it was a noise. The noise was very important because it was harsh and distorted and there was a lot of feedback and it was all a representation of chaos, which is exactly what punk rock was trying to promote in the early days.

MW: I spoke to Fred Vermorel recently and he suggested that Malcolm McLaren was more interested in the space that rock 'n' roll occupied rather than the rock 'n' roll itself.

JS: I don't think McLaren was very interested in music. His taste was pretty basic. You know, the Juke Box in *Sex* is a pretty good example. It contained rock 'n' roll classics and a smattering of garage punk. I think it even had 'We Sell Soul' by The Spades on there, which was Roky Erickson's first group and a particularly demented garage punker.[1] A lot of the hardcore music fans, like myself, who became involved with punk rock were huge garage punk fans. There was a cult around the *Nuggets* album, which was an incredibly important record; going back to basics, two or three chords, middle finger extended etc.[2]

MW: There also seemed to be something of a contested relationship between punk and rock 'n' roll. Was punk trying to save it, kill it or move beyond it?

JS: Well, initially, punk began in many things. I mean the music began in a sort of fan-activist culture and if you've got the fan-activist culture then you're going to have Glen Matlock liking The Small Faces and wanting to bring some of that energy back. Which is a perfectly valid thing to do because The Small Faces were great, you know. So there's a side of early punk that's very much taking from the past. In the UK, it was very much taken from that hard-edged mod pop that had got completely lost in the mid-70s. Punk was much more involved with the past than it pretended to be. And the Sex Pistols were basically a sort of Faces or Small Faces with a demented wild-card lead singer who pushed it into something else. When I first saw The Clash in late 1976, they reminded me of a sped-up version of The Who and The Kinks so, in that respect, The Clash were quite easily understandable. And obviously, by the middle of 1977, you started to get a whole load of bad punk rock groups speeding up and dyeing their hair. I mean there was one group in particular, The Maniacs, who you just looked at and thought, 'oh dear, it's all going wrong'. And, you know, you got The Jam, who in the early stages were pretty bad and doing a sort of refried mod; you got The Stranglers cutting off as much as they could of their prog past (though it still comes up in their tunes). Punk became a template and so you start to get the 'anti' – the anti-rock 'n' roll discourse that was very much promoted by Subway Sect in 'We Oppose all Rock and Roll'/'Rock and Roll Even'. Certainly, by 1978 when I interviewed Vic Godard, he was assiduously promoting this line: 'we don't want any Americanisms in our songs. We don't want to use the word "baby", no Chuck Berry', all that kind of stuff. By the end of 1977, the Sex Pistols looked very traditional … things were moving so quickly.

MW: A key theme to the book is that of 'identity'. Early on, at least, punk seemed incredibly diverse in terms of gender, class, age etc.

JS: Well, you also had a lot of gay people which was terribly important. I always thought that punk was, sort of, the freaks and the outcasts in the early days; and, obviously, I felt like an outcast being gay. It's well documented that there were, you know, teenage prostitutes and all sorts of people that didn't fit in involved at the beginning. And that was what I thought pop music – and rock music in particular as it developed – should be about. It's for the outcasts; it's for the weirdos. The normal kids went off and played sport. It wasn't kind of, 'hey, we're here', but more kind of desperation really. If you feel alienated when you're young then it's actually quite hard, but to find a whole bunch of people who also feel alienated and then come together is an incredibly powerful thing. And that's really what I see punk as. You look at a lot of the people involved in punk in the early days and it's an incredibly different mixture of teenage prostitutes, bright dead end working-class kids like Jah Wobble and, you know, an older hard core of sixties lefties or squatters. So, yes, a big mix.

MW: With such a mix of disaffected types, I guess you also have the seeds of the later divisions – or tensions – within punk. Now, when people talk about punk in the round, they'll tend to pick out a particular class angle or they'll look at the evolution into riot grrrl later on, or queer core, whatever.

JS: Which is great … I mean I had an upper middle-class education; I'm suburban, but I had an upper middle-class education and after eight years of that I was completely bored of it and I didn't like those people in the main. So I found the class mix you got in early punk very interesting and exciting because, you know, pop music was one of the places where the classes could mix on reasonably equal terms – which has now gone of course. But that was interesting; it was fascinating to talk with people like Pete Shelley, Steve Walsh and the different people you met in that period. It was a great time to meet people; I met some extraordinary characters at that point.

MW: I'm very keen on the idea of punk attracting the disaffected, as if coming together into a cultural space.

JS: It's true, that was the whole point, I thought.

MW: This makes it all the more interesting once it comes out the other end – when it's defined and the differences within punk are designated, especially by the media.

JS: Punk was obsessed with the media. Punk was actually the first proper media-age, postmodern pop culture. It was postmodern in that it employed bricolage, taking from the past, but was also very involved with and concerned with a kind of ritual dance with the media. And so you had a lot of groups calling themselves Magazine, The Adverts etc. You had the Sex Pistols' song 'I Wanna Be Me', talking about being a magazine and constant references to the *NME* (the enemy). And, of course, all that was sealed by what happened with the Grundy interview in 1976.[3] Punk then became something else; punk actually became a media spectacle with the Sex Pistols at the heart of that spectacle. They did fantastically well to keep it going and keep it interesting for about six or seven months.

MW: It became something of a battle I suppose, between those doing it and those defining it from the outside.

JS: Well, the music press was very important. The much-maligned music press was also incredibly vigorous at that time. Something like *Sounds* sold about 150,000 copies a week; the *NME* sold 250,000. And there was *Record Mirror* and *Melody Maker*, all of which were featuring a lot of articles about punk. So you had four weekly magazines being pumped out at the youth market, with each being read by up to six or seven people. So *Sounds* was probably read by close to a million kids a week. I still get people coming up and saying, 'oh I used to read you in *Sounds* da-de-da-de-da'.

MW: Another issue that relates to the theme of 'identity' is that of supposed authenticity, but also self-realisation and self-reinvention. What are your thoughts on punk and the notion of authenticity?

JS: Well, I'm incredibly suspicious of notions of authenticity in pop music. There's Bruce Springsteen, you know, who's a classic example of a heavily constructed artist who presents as authentic, which drives me nuts. Another example is Mumford and Sons, who really are the most dreadful faux-authentic band; it's just a tragedy, a complete fucking tragedy. I think you want some kind of emotional or existential authenticity. In other words, you want to feel that, you know, we 'mean it, man'.[4] But otherwise it's pop music and I love the fact that the Sex Pistols were so heavily constructed. I love the fact that the Sex Pistols were sort of jammed together by Malcolm McLaren as clothes pegs for the shop. I think that's a fabulous story; the way McLaren actually saw them as the anti-Bay City Rollers. He said to me once that he was so out of his head that he didn't know what he was doing. He created this thing that took on a life of its own.

MW: I've always thought motive and intent were more important than any notion of authenticity.

JS: Yes. On the surface, I thought punk was highly inauthentic – but that was just a mask in a way. You know, the punk records I still play I do so because the still resonate emotionally or, like the first Saints album or some of the Sex Pistols or Buzzcocks or even some of The Clash or The Adverts, there's some kind of truth in them. That's really what you want from pop music – a kind of existential authenticity; that you feel the musicians in that moment are actively engaged with what they are saying and are really committed to what they are trying to say. So, and obviously when you've got gay people involved, then the idea of authenticity goes out the window. And there were gay people involved in early punk, which is another fascinating story that's been written out. I mean, I really disagree with somebody like Joe Carducci in America, who's very involved with the idea of authenticity and machismo.[5] It's like 'fuck off'. You know, really. I hate that reading of punk because it has nothing to do with what I like in pop music in general and it has nothing to do with my experience of punk in the first place. Nor of American punk either. I went to LA in 1978 and I loved the LA punk scene. I spent a lot of time with The Screamers and The Avengers. There were a lot of gay people involved and they had to hide being gay. And really gay people are always written out – it's one of my hobby horses – always written out of pop music history.

You know, I really do dislike punk fundamentalism. It's totally understandable because things do solidify … but I don't like it. That doesn't mean I think any punk after 1976 or 1977 is shit, because it isn't. It still continues to give inspiration to people. I did a lecture at Cornell University recently, and this guy from Costa Rica piped-up and said, you know, there'd been a benefit and a whole load of punk groups got together so that he could go to Cornell and study Law and come back to Costa Rica and get involved in local activism. I thought, 'well, there you are, that's punk rock'. It's self-starting and with an alternative viewpoint. People getting together to try to make something better; that's what I like about punk rock and it's still very vital.

MW: And gender?

JS: Well, I was fascinated by the fact that punk had a different gender agenda to that which pop music had had hitherto. You had very strong women, which was fabulous. I mean, seeing Siouxsie, The Slits and Poly Styrene was amazing. No women had made those noises before; no women had made music like that before. And, at the same time, you had these rather hopeless, helpless boys like Subway Sect, which was riveting as well. You know, I do think Subway Sect were just brilliant; they were about introversion really, they weren't presenting any machismo at all and they were very rigorous about it. I talked to Rob Symmons and he told me that he wouldn't hold his guitar down low because that was a macho pose: it had to be up high.

MW: Much of the early rhetoric, particularly in the fanzines, focused on youth. Yet there were a range of ages involved in early punk. Nowadays, too, there is much academic work geared towards ageing within a subculture – not to mention virtually every old punk band reformed in some way or another. Can punk apply to all ages? Can punk age?

JS: Well my attitude, and I'm now 60, is that it's very much bad faith to completely junk the ideals of your adolescence because they actually do form you. It's an incredibly important time in identity formation. And so to turn your back on it I think is weird. I mean, I still very much identify with how I was in 1976, when I totally despised mainstream popular culture. I was very angry about it and I was angry about a number of other things. I can easily access all that, but I'm certainly not going to go around, you know, wearing leather. It just doesn't work.

So just because I don't particularly look like a punk doesn't mean I still don't retain [it] and, of course, I will always be marked by punk in the media. And people have a certain amount of expectation of you if they think you are marked by punk. They either resent it because so many people would have liked to have been involved at the time and weren't. Or they're a bit intimidated or decide that as soon as punk is mentioned you're going to have some kind of argument. So it comes with a whole load of associations as far as I'm concerned.

I do remember, when I was touring *England's Dreaming* around Germany, my German publisher pointed to some Mohicans on the steps of Cologne Cathedral and said, 'these are your children'. And I said, 'no they're not'. That's like how teddy boys were when punk was happening.

MW: That leads quite neatly into the second theme in the book, which is the transmission of punk; how it went from London, New York, Cleveland and into Manchester and then more provincial places. Why do you think punk resonated in the provinces of Britain, America, Europe and elsewhere?

JS: It was easy to do; it was easy to assimilate. It tapped into a kind of classic teenage obnoxiousness and angst. It was a very good vehicle to express discontent and was a self-starter culture initially. When you look back to London and Britain in 1976, it's amazing how little there was. Despite what's going on politically now, Britain is so much wealthier than it was in the late 1970s. Everybody forgets what it was like in the late '70s: it was awful. Britain in general was violent; it was run down; it was, in many ways, quite desperate and so people were forced – as has been said a lot but is true – to do things for themselves, which is a very powerful impulse that translated obviously into the whole DIY aesthetic as propagated by Buzzcocks and the Desperate Bicycles in the first half of 1977. That, of course is an incredibly important part of punk's legacy, one that has gone right across the board into black American music and then all around the world really. It's like, 'don't wait for record companies, don't wait for people to pick up on you, just do it. See what happens, throw it against the wall and see what happens'. And the thing about punk was that the distance between having an idea and executing it was minimal; that's what was great about it. You wanted to write? Do a fucking fanzine – do it. It doesn't matter if it's shit, just do it.

MW: You mentioned visiting LA and finding a starting point or a new scene. Were there any other places that fascinated you?

JS: I was fascinated by the Cleveland scene and I wrote very early about Pere Ubu. David Thomas now hates punk rock. And, you know, he has a valid point. I don't actually agree with it, but he has a valid point. But back in the day we were all very enthusiastic and I got involved with Ubu and helped to get the first Electric Eels single put out, which is of course a complete masterpiece.[6] But that's a big question and there are so many. I cannot believe the way in which punk has proliferated; it's extraordinary to me. I mean, I knew it was significant at the time and I remember being in The

Roxy thinking, 'wow this is really "it"'. I'd always wanted to be where 'it' – whatever 'it' was – was happening. And it certainly was. We'd all grown up with the 1960s and how fabulous that was, but by the time you were old enough to get involved in popular culture it was all over. You just had 'Adge' Cutler and the fucking Wurzels; terrible records by Abba and Brotherhood of Man, Kiki Dee and Elton John. It was a nightmare. The mainstream pop music of 1976 just made me want to throw up.

MW: Absolutely, there's a lot of revisionism at the moment – giving kitsch value to bland pop.

JS: It was awful. Punk wasn't against prog rock – prog rock wasn't really an issue. It was against dreadful pop music. You know, you just wanted to kill somebody when you heard those records.

MW: Indeed, a feeling that, again, translates to other places across Europe and beyond?

JS: Yeah, it's classic teenage stuff – it's boredom – when you're that age and you come out into the world and see very clearly what's wrong with it. And if you've got any spirit about you, then you want to do something about it. You know, it's terribly simple and happens in all sorts of ways and all sorts of cultures. It's the basic impulse of the young person to do something about the world which she or he didn't create and in which they find themselves. What are you going to do about it? Are you just going to sit back and let everything wash over you, take and eat shit? Or are you going to try and do something about it?

MW: I've read you referring before to that impulse and how it manifested itself in different parts of the world …

JS: Well, everybody thinks that I'm an English punk snob and, you know, partly I am but partly I'm not. At the Cornell event I mentioned, the guy from Bad Religion, Greg Graffin, got a bit snarky about me being an English punk journalist and I said, 'oi', you know, 'I have my own experience of punk, and you have an experience of punk – fine'. I blame here the overwhelming trend in music writing over the last fifteen years to elevate experience (thank you Nick Hornby: fuck off). You know, autobiography above everything else. It's so boring.

MW: Yes, subjective experience presented as universalism – it's the bane of my life whenever I talk about researching punk and youth cultures … As a historian, you try to bring together a number of different experiences in order to explain and analyse, to which you get people saying, 'well I didn't feel like that so it can't be true' or 'that can't have happened to me so it never happened at all'.

JS: Well, that's why I did all those interviews for *England's Dreaming*.[7] But everybody's so obsessed with personal experience, which is so trite. It all becomes, just, 'my scene's better than yours', you know? And I don't feel like that. I think if you're actually doing a history of punk rock, then you really need to put your own experience in a box. You've got to stand outside your experience and stand outside your prejudices as much as you can. Of course, we're all imperfect creatures so it's not always possible. I still get slagged off for disliking The Stranglers but, you know, I've been watching the re-runs of *Top of the Pops* from of 1976, '77 and '78 and I've been thinking, 'right, you're going to examine your prejudices'. So on comes Sham 69 to 'If the Kids are United', and I used to hate Sham 69 but I think, 'you know what, this is a bit of a tune'. And The Jam come on and do '"A" Bomb in Wardour Street' and I think, 'I used to hate The Jam but you know what, this is actually a great song'. I was very impressed. But then on come The Stranglers with 'No More Heroes' and I thought, 'yeah good riff'. And then there was a fucking prog bit and I thought, 'you just couldn't give it up could you?' I thought, 'you know what, you're shit. You look shit and the music's shit'.

MW: Talking of which, punk's transmission contained many negative components, be it the misogyny (as levelled against the Stranglers), its dalliance with the swastika etc.

JS: I didn't see The Stranglers as punk, I thought they were old information and I thought they were bullies and bullying is one of my trigger points. It's just one of those things that gets me really, really angry. And yes, there are two really good books to be written about punk rock and it would need books to do them because it's actually a complicated subject. The first would be gay punk book; somebody really should do that.

   The other book would be on the dark side of punk. Because let's just go back to the word itself. What does 'punk' mean? The word means the young guy in prison who takes the wang up the bung. I said this on American radio recently and they got really upset with me. But it's true! You've got a movement based on a word that describes a younger guy in prison taking a dick up the arse. It really is as basic as that. Once you get to that, a lot of punk rock just becomes really stupid. So any machismo in punk rock is immediately superfluous; it's just pathetic to even think about punk in terms of machismo. It could never be about that with a name like 'punk'. The other meaning of the name is for *Happy Days*, you know, 'you're a dirty punk'; a received kind of 1950s name – 'you're a bad ass and you're probably not very successful'.[8] So it's a bit like being a hopeless criminal who gets sodomised in jail. Well, you're setting yourself up for quite a few

problems if you call yourself a punk rocker … The whole idea that success
is a failure and failure is a success; the whole deliberate exploration of the
dark side, which became very, very trite and difficult and dangerous, as with
Throbbing Gristle and the industrial thing. I listen now to 'Glad To See You
Go' by The Ramones, where they sing about getting the glory like Charles
Manson and I'm thinking, 'not a good idea Dee Dee'. I never liked all that
and I was always alarmed at the use of swastikas. It was taking from Iggy,
the Velvet Underground, you know, it was that dark side of rock music. But
it was also very self-destructive: bad drugs and that kind of stuff.

MW: I always thought the Cambridge Rapist mask that SEX put out was
particularly nasty …

JS: Well, Malcolm and Vivienne were really amoral in that respect, and they
were deliberately pushing every single button they could find. And that,
to me, is a stain on the whole thing. I mean, the whole thing about punk is
that it's ambiguous. When I first saw the Sex Pistols it wasn't, 'oh yeah, this
is a band I've been waiting for all my life'. It was, 'this is absolutely fucking
amazing, but also I'm not quite sure; there's something I'm not quite sure
about'. So both attraction and repulsion. The Clash were much easier to
deal with, because you saw them and thought, 'yeah, they're great – they're
like The Who and The Kinks and they're now and … ' But the Sex Pistols
were much more complicated and that's what made them more interesting.
Where The Clash, who I liked a lot, were reasonably well presented as
a kind of streamlined liberal left rock band, the Sex Pistols were sort of
lumpy and contradictory. You're never going to get 'Holidays in the Sun'
or 'Bodies' on an advert. So, yes, Malcolm and Vivienne – particularly
Malcolm – were just amoral; he just didn't give a shit. So they sold Nazi
memorabilia in the shop and they had, you know, the naked boy T-shirt
that was actually from commercially produced paedophile imagery – really
fucking dodgy. So for that dark part of punk in the UK you have to go back
to Malcolm and Vivienne and to Malcolm's own issues and what kind of
person he was. I mean, I really liked Malcolm but I was under no illusion
about him. He could be wonderful; he was very charming, incredibly
funny, a very good raconteur and very engaging as a person. You wanted
to be around him and he attracted people – not sexually, but just a person
who is very dynamic. He had fabulous ideas and was a wonderful talker,
but he also had this dark side that became imprinted onto punk rock at
the beginning. It's a total can of worms and was really what I wrote my first
fanzine [*London's Outrage*] about, because I was actually really shocked and
didn't like it and thought it was fucking stupid. I still think punk could have

gone that way and there were a few months where it was sort of teetering on the edge of going that way.

MW: Well, right-wing politics continue to get into punk scenes – Russia is a good example.

JS: Obviously, when you looked at The Clash, you knew they weren't like that. But one of the seminal events was Johnny Rotten giving an interview to *Temporary Hoarding*.[9] Although I really disliked Rock Against Racism (RAR) in many ways, I disliked the aesthetic, it was a completely necessary political intervention.

MW: Yes, I find the politically contested nature of punk very interesting. When you talk to people involved in Crass, they remember consciously trying to find a way beyond the left-wing and right-wing – that is, to realise anarchy as more than a slogan.

JS: I thought Crass were brilliant. I met them back in the day and I still have enormous respect for them. In many ways I think they're the most qualitative and long-lasting thing to come out of British punk apart from the DIY independence idea. I went to see them at Dial House in early 1979 and I was just super impressed and still am. It's a total art work, with the posters and the clothes. Everything was considered and thought through; it was a complete presentation. And, you know, they're incredibly talented visual artists, especially Gee Vaucher. Crass are now regarded as one of the best and most inspiring group of artists to come out of that period. The fascinating thing is, too, that you read Penny Rimbaud's autobiography and it ties in with the 1970s pre-punk festival freak scene – and that's the way it should have been. You know, all this going on about hippies drives me nuts, it's so boring. It's a thirty-seven year-old polemic, you know, that got boring thirty-five years ago. A lot of punks were hippies, you know, Lydon was.

MW: It became a throwaway term, maybe a reaction to what hippie had become rather than what it was?

JS: Well, I was just at the top end of the age-range for British punk; I turned twenty-three in the Autumn of 1976 so was a year younger than Joe Strummer. So I was at the upper end of the people who got it – and I lost all my friends, because they just couldn't understand why I was getting involved in this stuff. And, you know, we had wanted to be hippies, but then we realised how fucking horrible hippies were or could be. Particularly by the time Lydon or myself – we're only about eighteen months apart – would have started going to hippy gigs (so probably early 1970s, 1971 or '72), hippies were pretty fucking snotty by then. It wasn't the original 1965–66 San Francisco or London crowd. It was a bunch of Johnny-come-latelies being super snotty and arrogant: horrible. But a lot of punks had been hippies. Strummer had been a hippy. There was nothing wrong with it, because hippies were the antinomian culture at the time. So why shouldn't there be a link between punks and hippies? I liked that in Crass; I liked the fact that there was an obvious continuation and that Penny was a strong enough character that he wasn't about to sell out on what he'd been through in the 1970s. He was interested in taking it forward. I loved 'Do They Owe Us A Living', just so good. And I loved all the hoaxes. 'How Does it Feel to be the Mother of a Thousand Dead' – it's just great. So, yes, they took anarchy seriously and were very involved with CND and all that kind of stuff.

MW: You've alluded to this before, but the whole do-it-yourself thing seems to be punk's most lasting legacy; a process of action and communication that people can still relate to, respond to and engage with.

JS: I was very much promoting that when I worked at *Sounds*, doing the singles reviews. I used to bomb down to Rough Trade, pick up a whole load of independent singles and American stuff, then fill my reviews with independents, because that was what I thought was interesting. Also, the major labels didn't do punk very well. They got the kind of cash-in groups and so there was a real vigour to the independent sector. There was a real point to it. If you look at the records from that period, I think the best ones from late 1978 onwards, they're all on independent record labels.

MW: Thinking more broadly, do you think punk's spirit remains today – in Pussy Riot and elsewhere?

JS: Yes, it's a historical template isn't it? It's like dada or something. It's more than dada, though, because there's a lot of documentation of punk rock, while there's very little documentation of the Cabaret Voltaire in 1916. But despite all the documentation, there remains a lot of work still to be done. I'm amazed at how poor the discourse around punk rock is. Like I say, I've been waiting for the book about gay punk; I've been waiting for the book about the dark side of punk. Punk was dangerous; it was supposed to be dangerous, but BBC4 programmes like *Punk Britannia* never discuss it. Any proper account of punk needs to include that and avoid all the rose-tinted nostalgia and personal experience. It must get beyond personal experience.

The other thing, of course, is what I call the anti-canon of pop music, which is also very tedious. That is, writers who think that everything has been done. This is propagated by aspects of BBC4 when they do those 'here's the secret story of the 1960s – it's Mrs Mills. She was really big in the '60s'.[10] Well, actually, she wasn't: her biggest record only just about made the top twenty. Never mind the Beatles and the Stones and all that, you've got all these people banging on about light entertainment and stuff that

– back in the day – was shit. I remember seeing that stuff as a child and it was as if a chasm of boredom opened up and I'd just want to die.

MW: It's in the Dominic Sandbrook histories too; teleology as revisionist history.

JS: Yes, Dominic Sandbrook is very much a part of this. His thesis reflects his right-wing politics. There's a whole lot of people who want to downplay and rewrite the historical importance of popular culture. Because actually it was very vigorous and it was progressive and it was liberating. You can always find something interesting to say about it. You should go and do your research, not just reproduce lazy bullshit.

Notes

1   Roky Erickson is best known for his 1960s garage band, Thirteenth Floor Elevators.
2   *Nuggets* was a compilation of 1960s garage groups compiled by Lenny Kaye (later in the Patti Smith Group) and Jac Holzman. It was released on Elektra in 1972.
3   The Grundy interview refers to the Sex Pistols' appearance on Thames Television's *Today* programme on 1 December 1976. The band was interviewed live by Bill Grundy and included swearing that caused a furore in the national media the following day. It also led to the bulk of the band's subsequent 'Anarchy' tour being cancelled.
4   This is a reference to Johnny Rotten's lyric in 'Anarchy in the UK'.
5   See Joe Carducci, *Rock and the Pop Narcotic* (Los Angeles: 2.13.61, 1995 edition).
6   Electric Eels, 'Agitated' b/w 'Cyclotron' (Rough Trade, 1978).
7   Jon Savage, *The England's Dreaming Tapes* (London: Faber & Faber, 2009).
8   *Happy Days* was an American comedy that ran from 1974 to 1984. It was set in the 1950s to 1960s.
9   *Temporary Hoarding* was the newspaper/fanzine of Rock Against Racism, a campaign set up in response to racist remarks made by Eric Clapton at a concert in 1976 and references to fascism by David Bowie in the same year. See, for a recent overview, I. Goodyer, *Crisis Music: The Cultural Politics of Rock Against Racism* (Manchester: Manchester University Press, 2009).
10 Mrs Mills was Gladys Mills, who released a series of sing-along, light entertainment records over the 1960s and into the 1970s.

Index

UNIVERSITY OF WINCHESTER
LIBRARY